LOVE and HEART

KAIDO

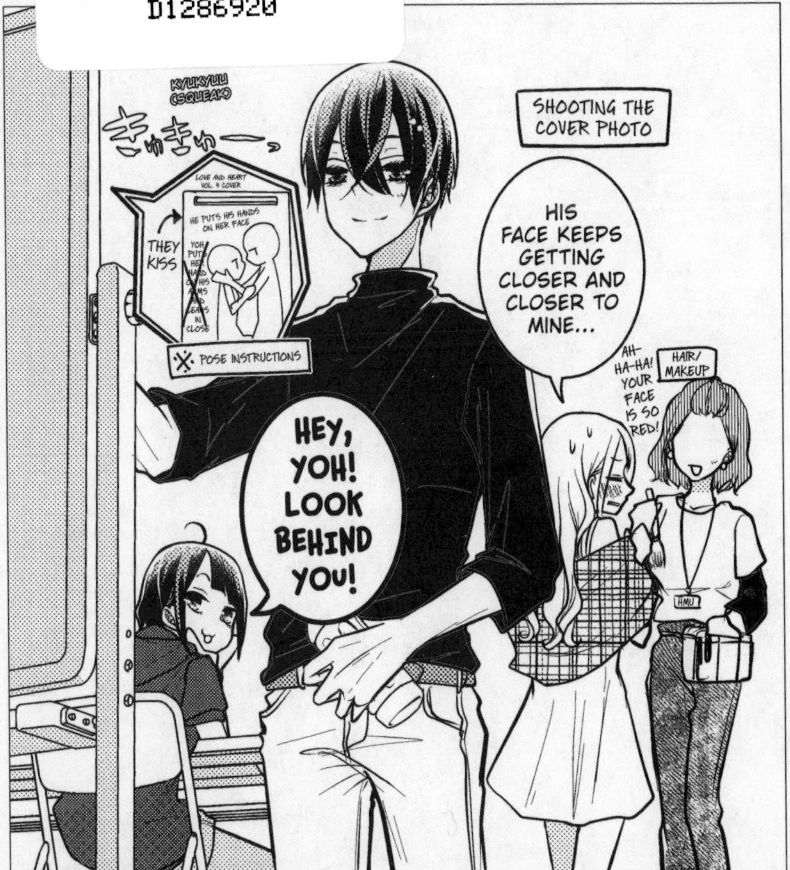
SHOOTING THE COVER PHOTO
HIS FACE KEEPS GETTING CLOSER AND CLOSER TO MINE...
HAIR/ MAKEUP
AH-HA-HA! YOUR FACE IS SO RED!
HMU
KYUKYUU (SQUEAK)
LOVE AND HEART VOL. 4 COVER
HE PUTS HIS HANDS ON HER FACE
THEY KISS
※ POSE INSTRUCTIONS
HEY, YOH! LOOK BEHIND YOU!

CONTENTS

LOVE AND HEART

#50

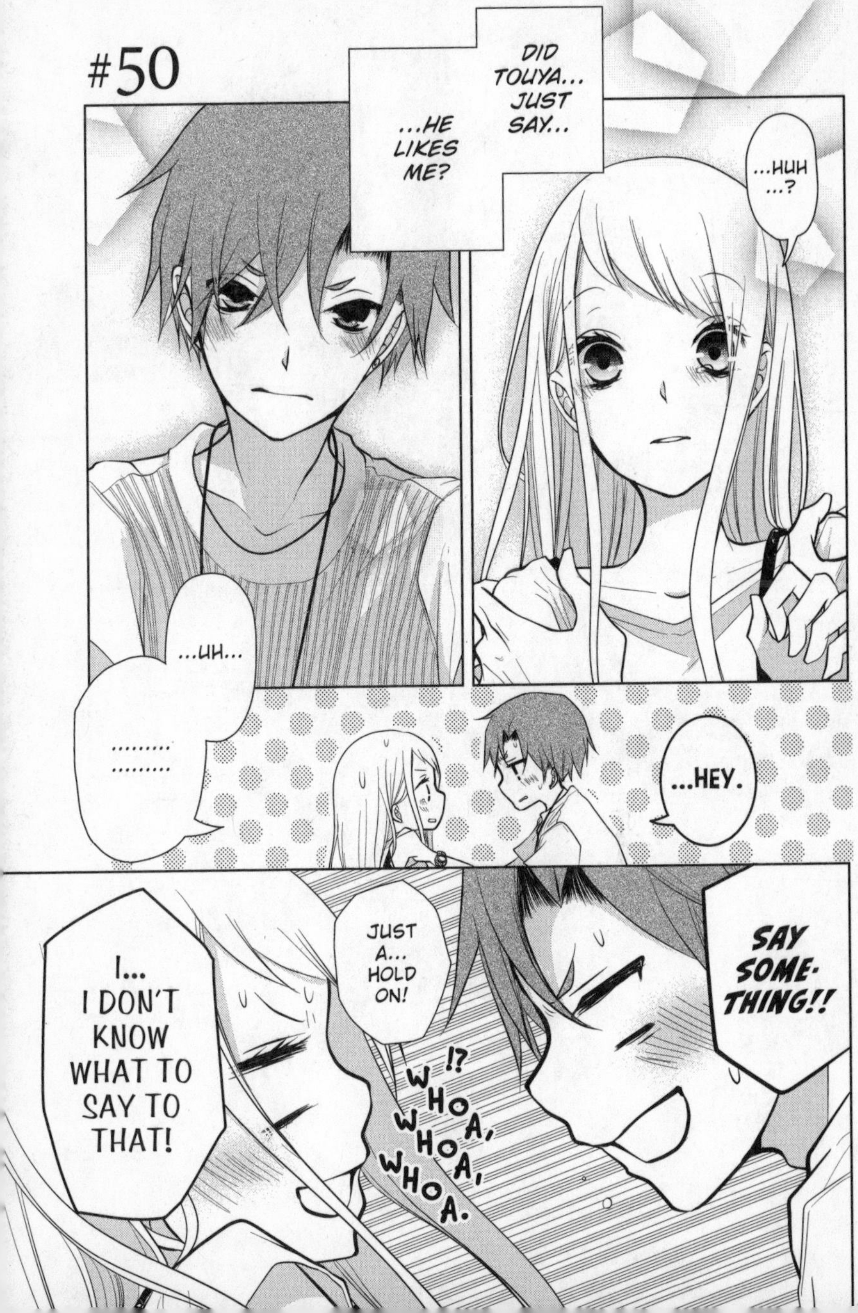
DID TOUYA... JUST SAY...
...HE LIKES ME?
...HUH...?
...UH...
...HEY.
....
....
SAY SOME-THING!!
JUST A... HOLD ON!
!?
WHOA, WHOA, WHOA, WHOA.
I... I DON'T KNOW WHAT TO SAY TO THAT!

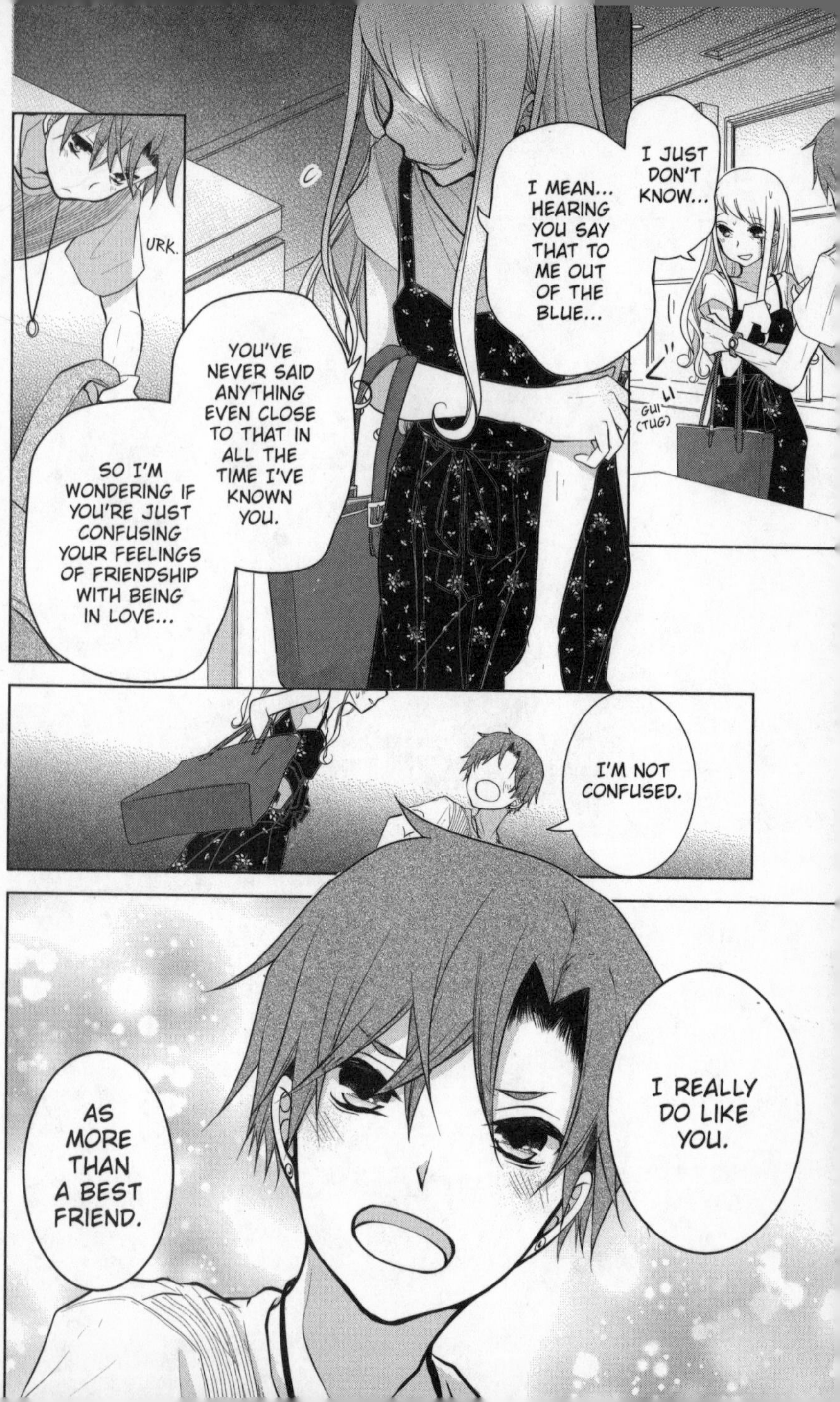
I JUST DON'T KNOW...
I MEAN... HEARING YOU SAY THAT TO ME OUT OF THE BLUE...
GUI (TUG)
YOU'VE NEVER SAID ANYTHING EVEN CLOSE TO THAT IN ALL THE TIME I'VE KNOWN YOU.
SO I'M WONDERING IF YOU'RE JUST CONFUSING YOUR FEELINGS OF FRIENDSHIP WITH BEING IN LOVE...
URK.
I'M NOT CONFUSED.
I REALLY DO LIKE YOU.
AS MORE THAN A BEST FRIEND.

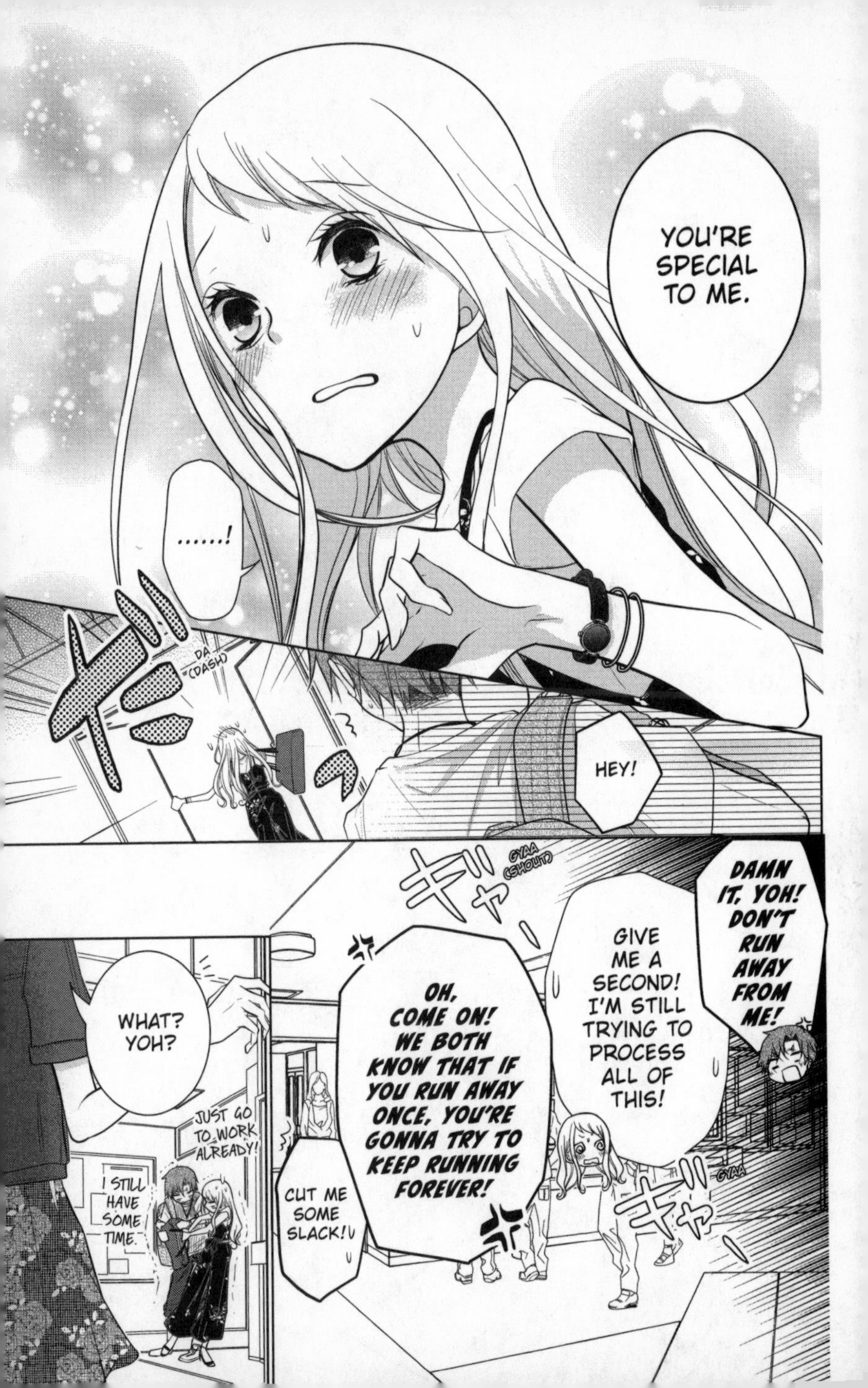
YOU'RE SPECIAL TO ME.
......!
DA (DASH)
HEY!
GYAA (SHOUT)
DAMN IT, YOH! DON'T RUN AWAY FROM ME!
GIVE ME A SECOND! I'M STILL TRYING TO PROCESS ALL OF THIS!
OH, COME ON! WE BOTH KNOW THAT IF YOU RUN AWAY ONCE, YOU'RE GONNA TRY TO KEEP RUNNING FOREVER!
GYAA
CUT ME SOME SLACK!
WHAT? YOH?
JUST GO TO WORK ALREADY!
I STILL HAVE SOME TIME.

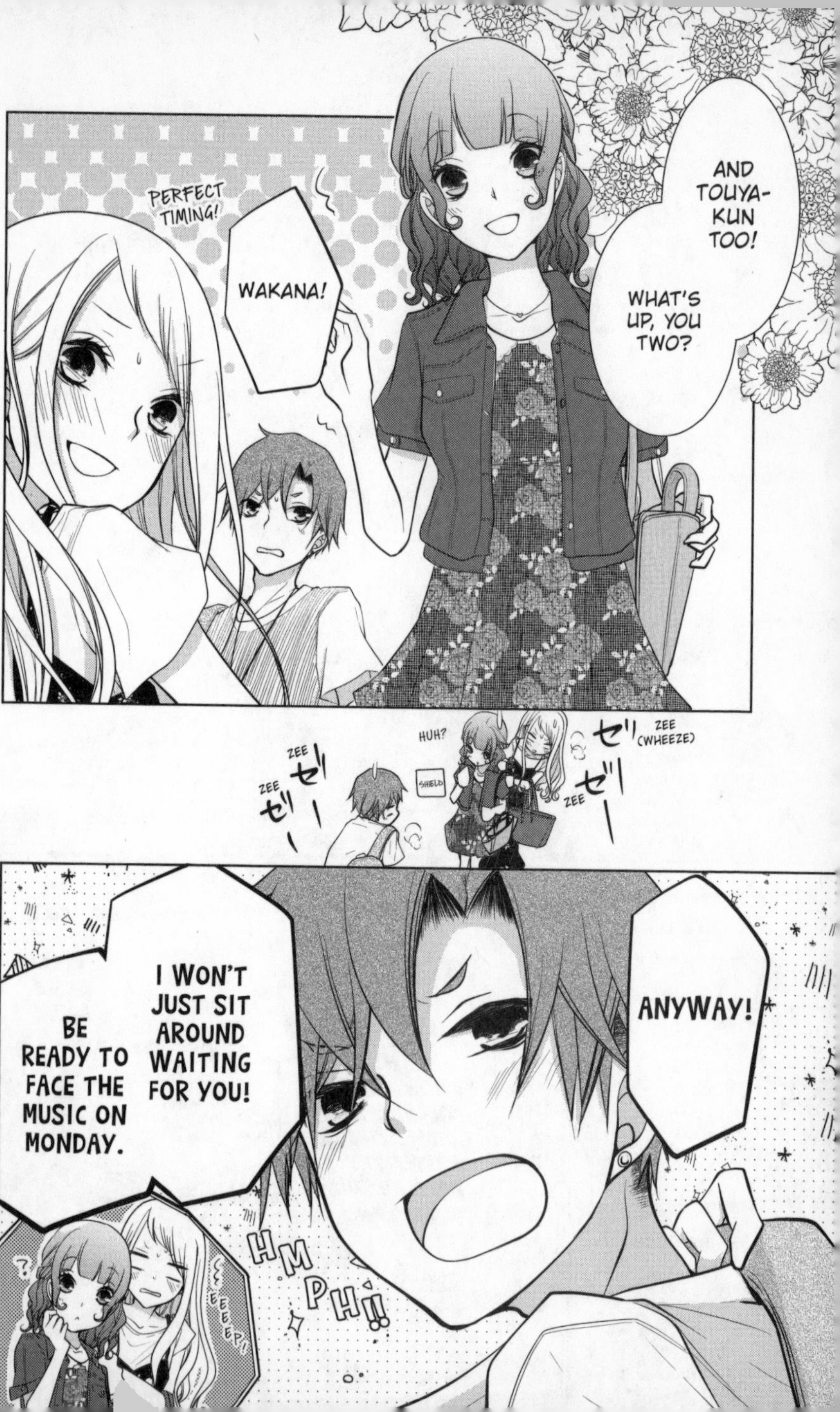
AND TOUYA-KUN TOO!
WHAT'S UP, YOU TWO?
WAKANA!
PERFECT TIMING!
ゼ ZEE (WHEEZE)
ゼ ZEE
HUH?
SHIELD
ゼ ZEE
ゼ ZEE
ANYWAY!
I WON'T JUST SIT AROUND WAITING FOR YOU!
BE READY TO FACE THE MUSIC ON MONDAY.
HMPH!!
EEEEEP!
?

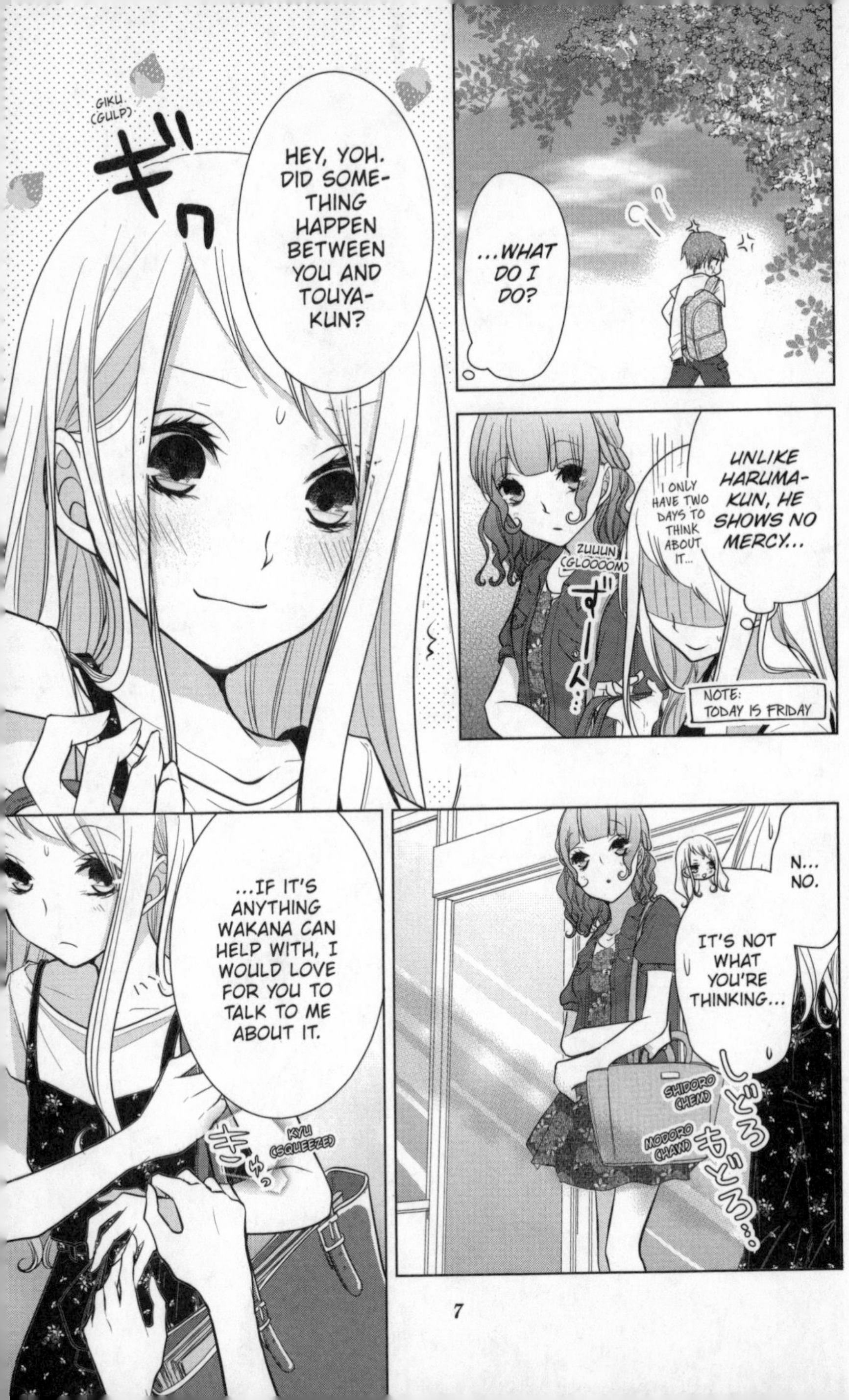
...WHAT DO I DO?
UNLIKE HARUMA-KUN, HE SHOWS NO MERCY...
I ONLY HAVE TWO DAYS TO THINK ABOUT IT...
ZUUUN (GLOOOOM)
NOTE: TODAY IS FRIDAY
HEY, YOH. DID SOME-THING HAPPEN BETWEEN YOU AND TOUYA-KUN?
GIKU (GULP)
N... NO.
IT'S NOT WHAT YOU'RE THINKING...
SHIDORO (HEM)
MODORO (HAW)
...IF IT'S ANYTHING WAKANA CAN HELP WITH, I WOULD LOVE FOR YOU TO TALK TO ME ABOUT IT.
KYU (SQUEEZE)

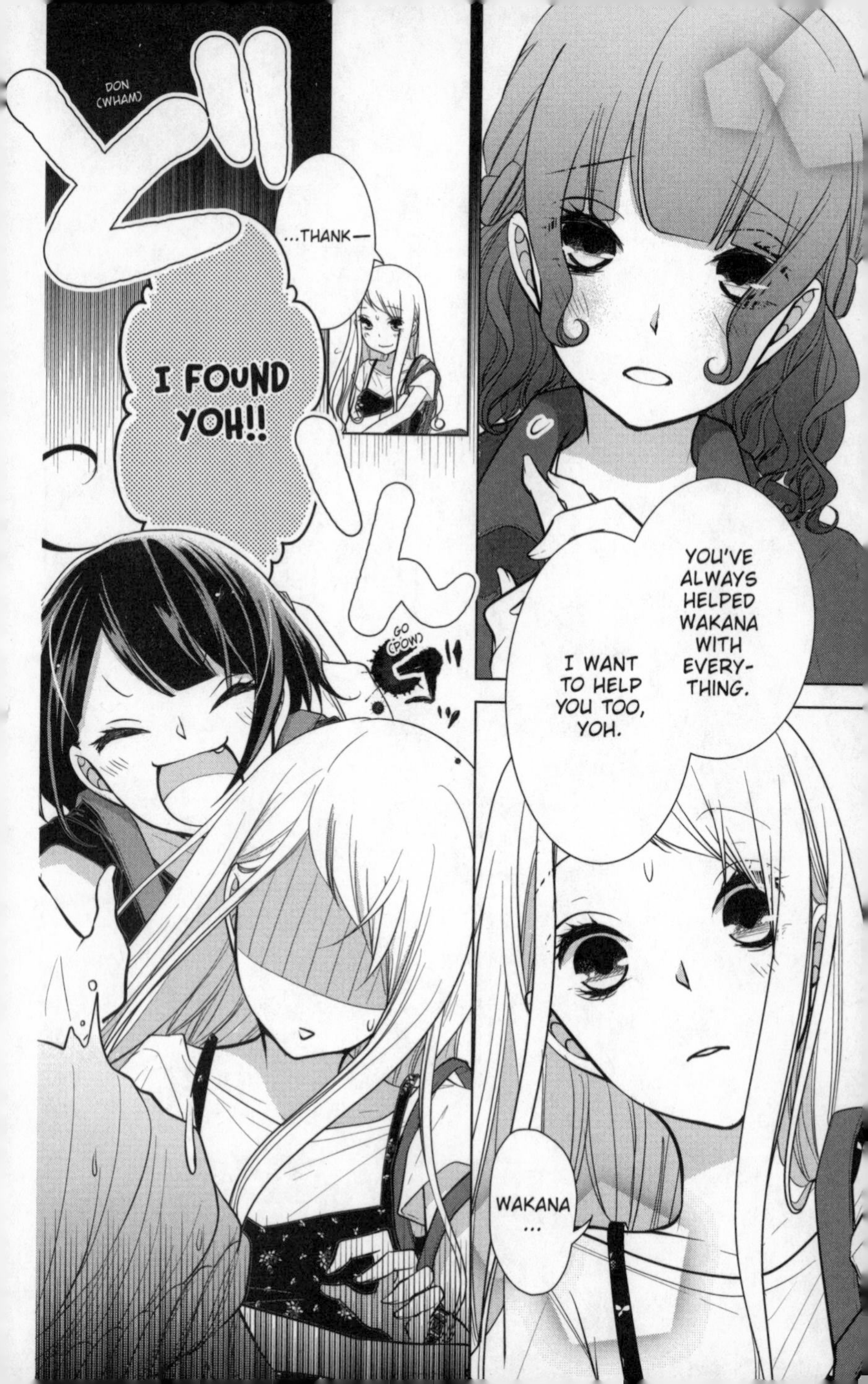
YOU'VE ALWAYS HELPED WAKANA WITH EVERY-THING.
I WANT TO HELP YOU TOO, YOH.
WAKANA ...
...THANK—
DON (WHAM)
I FOUND YOH!!
GO (POW)

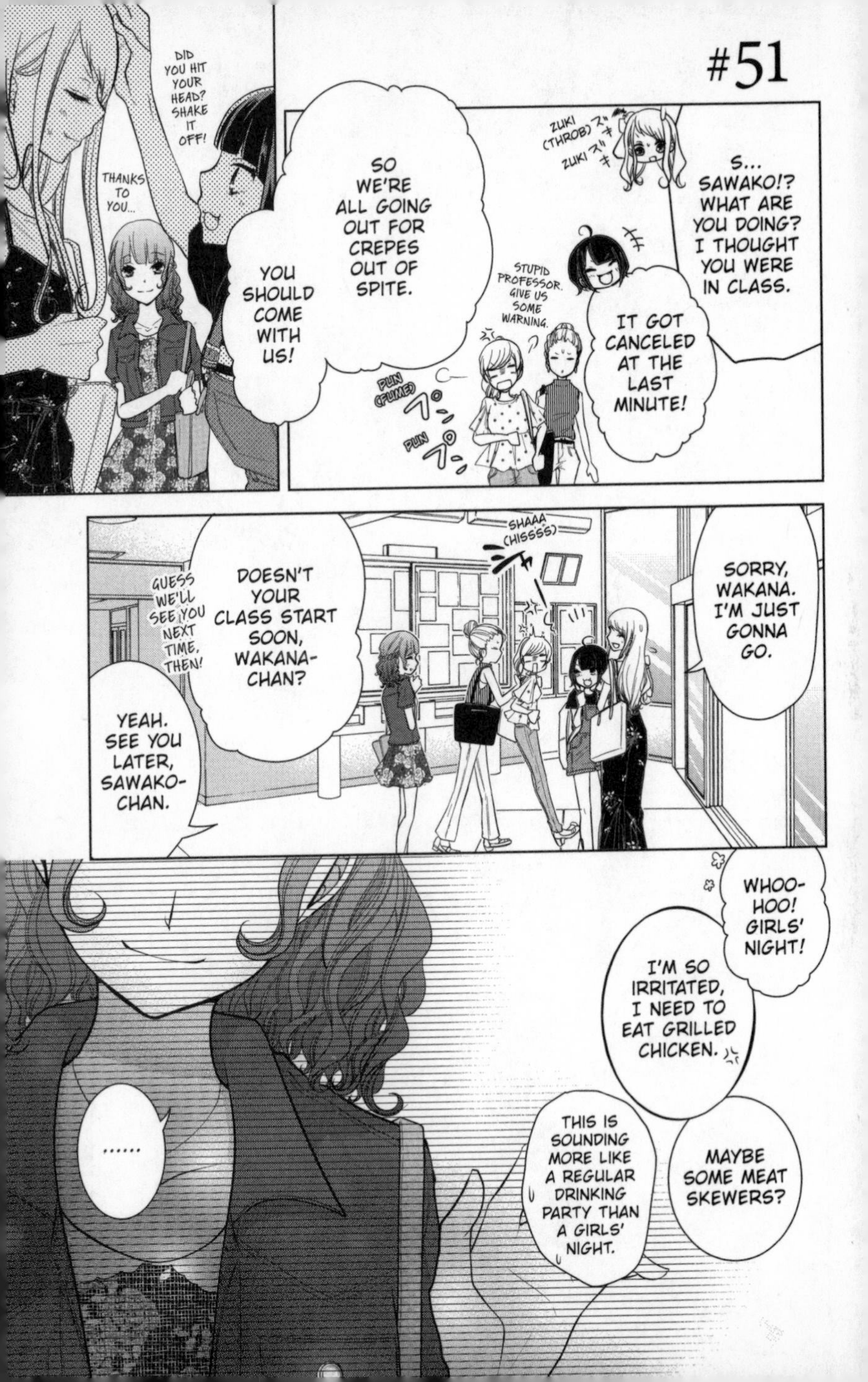
#51
S... SAWAKO!? WHAT ARE YOU DOING? I THOUGHT YOU WERE IN CLASS.
ZUKI (THROB) ZUKI
IT GOT CANCELED AT THE LAST MINUTE!
STUPID PROFESSOR. GIVE US SOME WARNING.
SO WE'RE ALL GOING OUT FOR CREPES OUT OF SPITE.
PUN (FUME) PUN
YOU SHOULD COME WITH US!
DID YOU HIT YOUR HEAD? SHAKE IT OFF!
THANKS TO YOU...
SORRY, WAKANA. I'M JUST GONNA GO.
SHAAA (CHISSSS)
DOESN'T YOUR CLASS START SOON, WAKANA-CHAN?
GUESS WE'LL SEE YOU NEXT TIME, THEN!
YEAH. SEE YOU LATER, SAWAKO-CHAN.
WHOO-HOO! GIRLS' NIGHT!
I'M SO IRRITATED, I NEED TO EAT GRILLED CHICKEN.
MAYBE SOME MEAT SKEWERS?
THIS IS SOUNDING MORE LIKE A REGULAR DRINKING PARTY THAN A GIRLS' NIGHT.
......

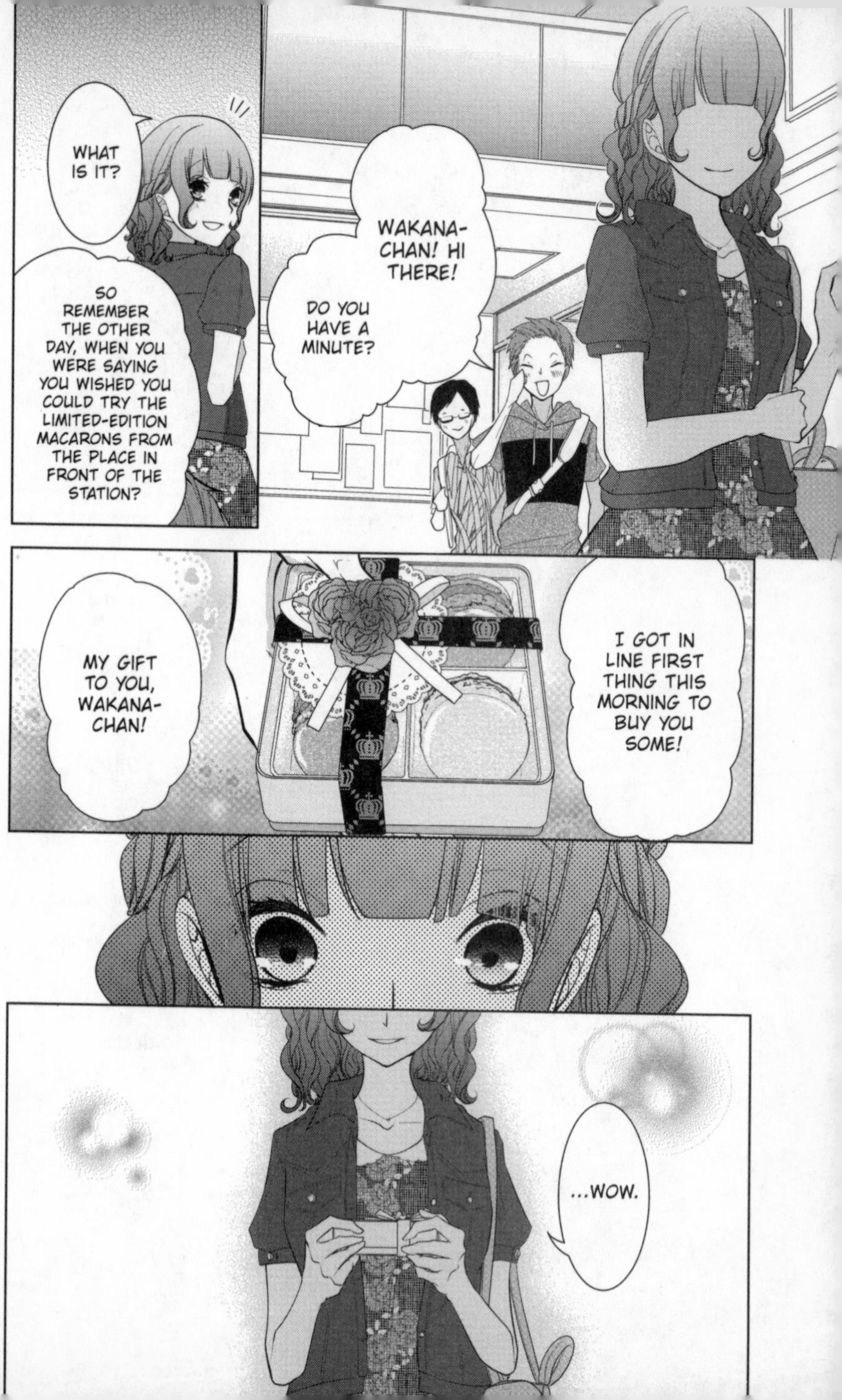
WAKANA-CHAN! HI THERE!
DO YOU HAVE A MINUTE?
WHAT IS IT?
SO REMEMBER THE OTHER DAY, WHEN YOU WERE SAYING YOU WISHED YOU COULD TRY THE LIMITED-EDITION MACARONS FROM THE PLACE IN FRONT OF THE STATION?
I GOT IN LINE FIRST THING THIS MORNING TO BUY YOU SOME!
MY GIFT TO YOU, WAKANA-CHAN!
...WOW.

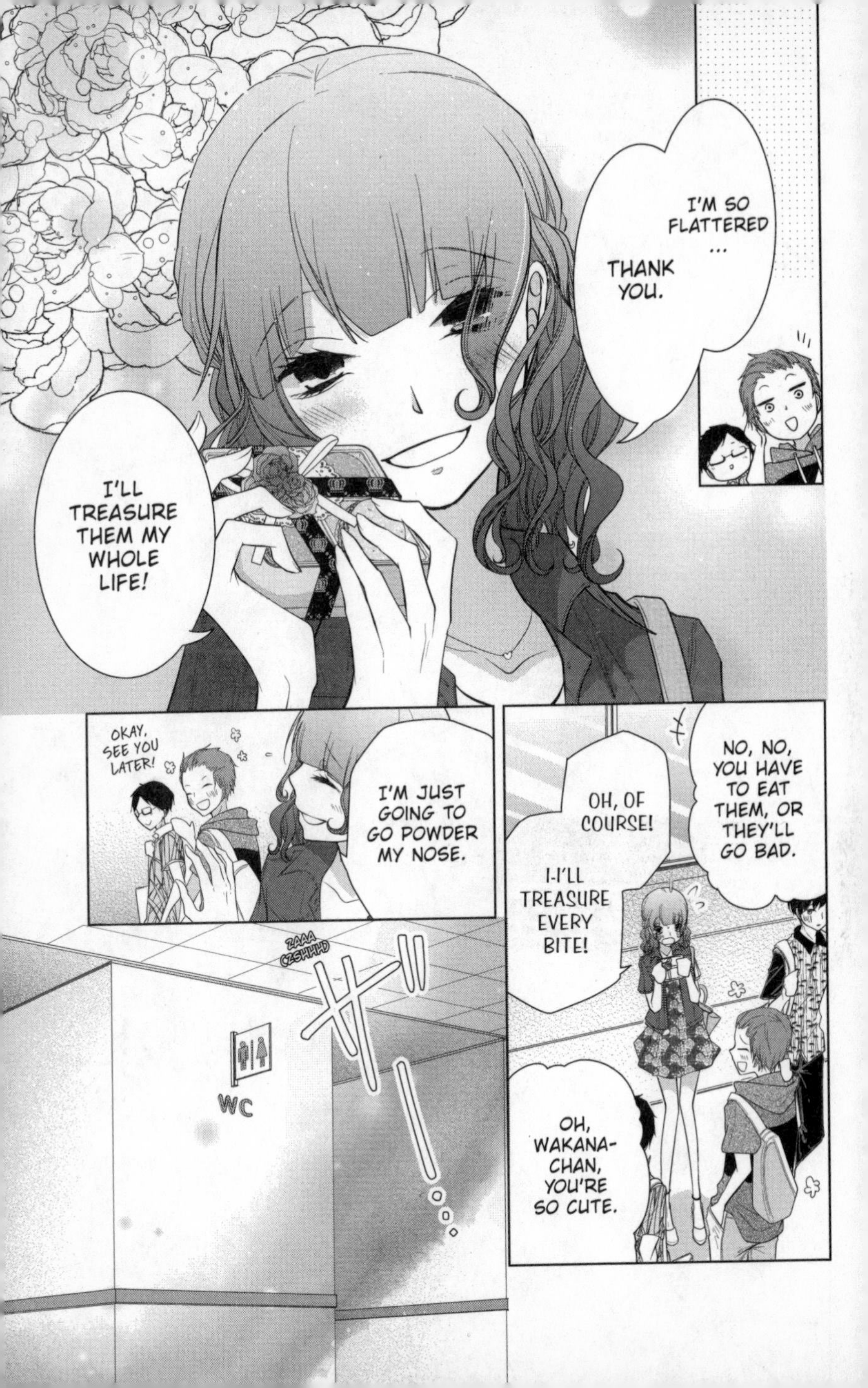
I'M SO FLATTERED ...
THANK YOU.
I'LL TREASURE THEM MY WHOLE LIFE!
NO, NO, YOU HAVE TO EAT THEM, OR THEY'LL GO BAD.
OH, OF COURSE!
I-I'LL TREASURE EVERY BITE!
OH, WAKANA-CHAN, YOU'RE SO CUTE.
I'M JUST GOING TO GO POWDER MY NOSE.
OKAY, SEE YOU LATER!
ZAAA (ZSHHH)
WC

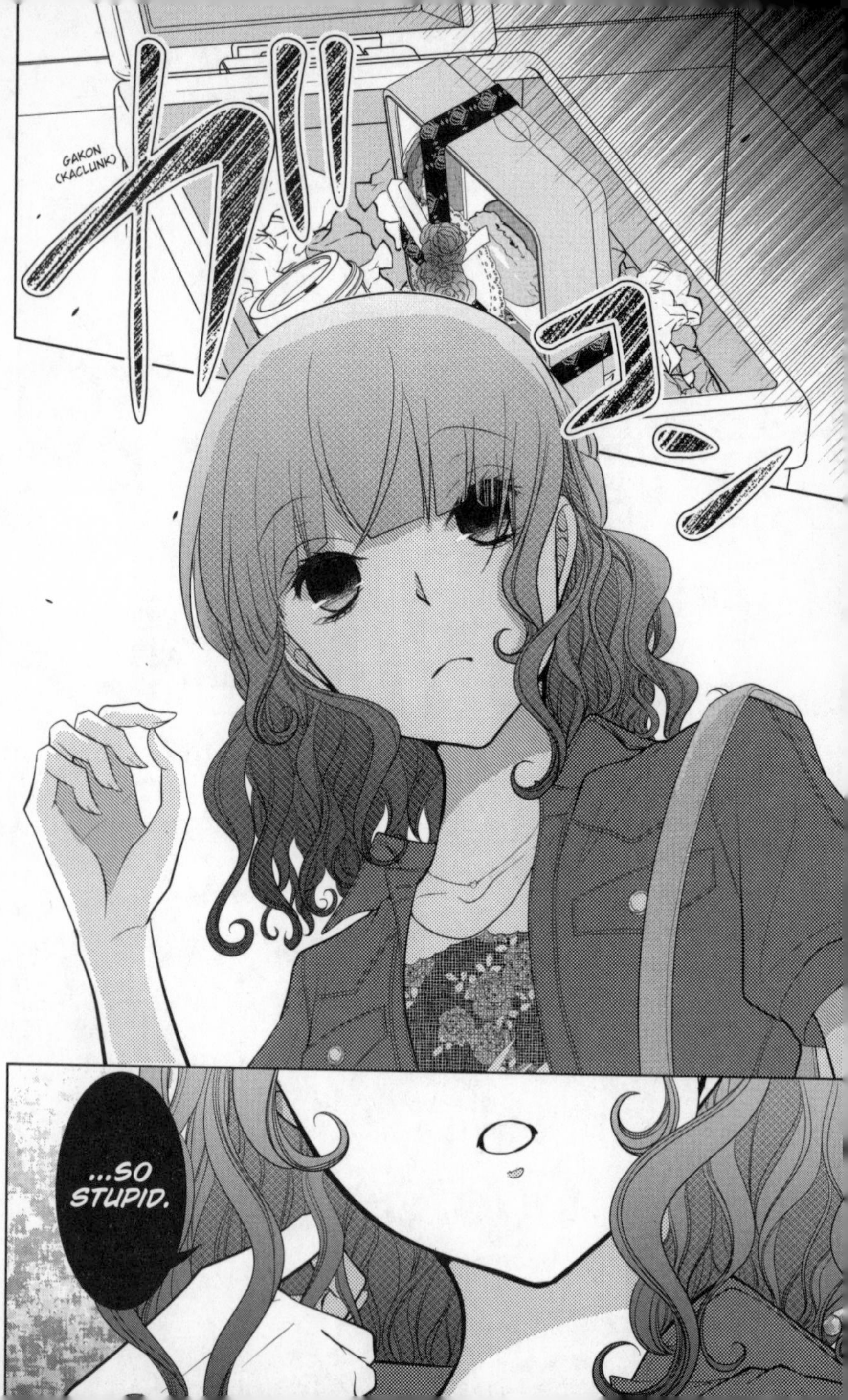
GAKON (KACLUNK)
...SO STUPID.

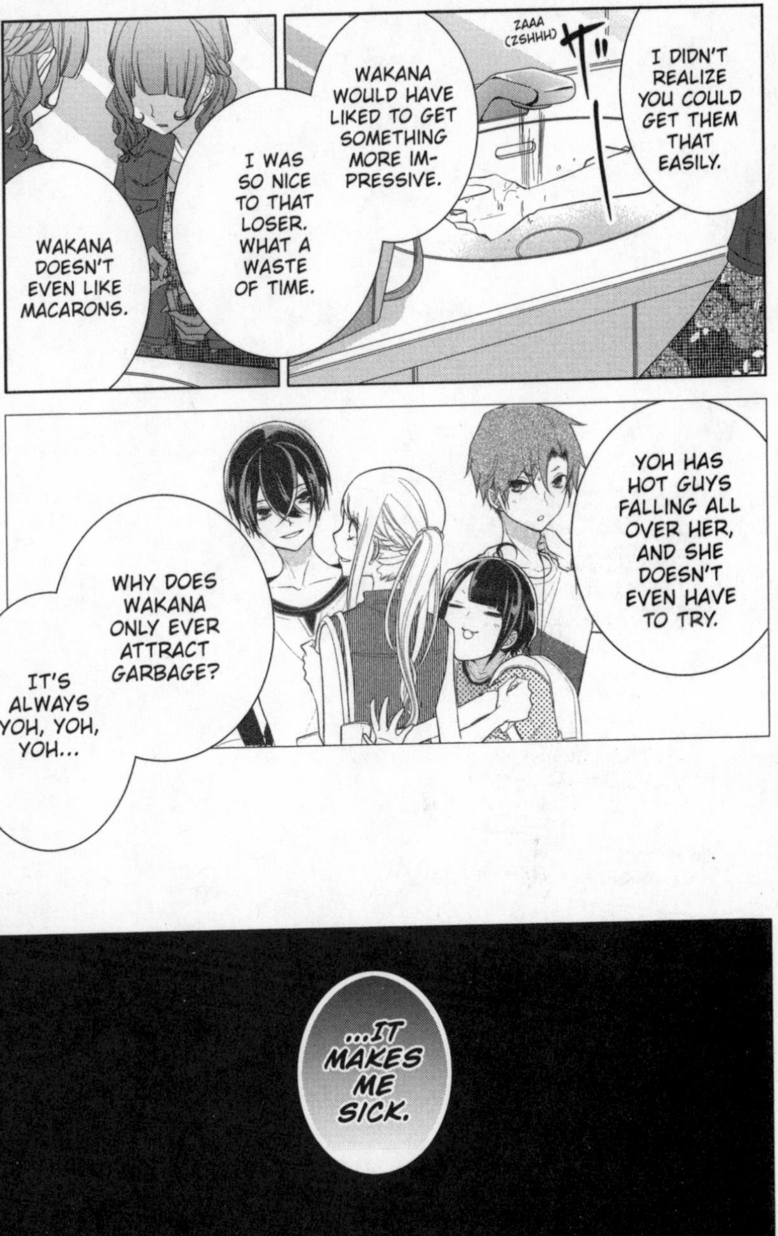
ZAAA (ZSHHH)
I DIDN'T REALIZE YOU COULD GET THEM THAT EASILY.
WAKANA WOULD HAVE LIKED TO GET SOMETHING MORE IM-PRESSIVE.
I WAS SO NICE TO THAT LOSER. WHAT A WASTE OF TIME.
WAKANA DOESN'T EVEN LIKE MACARONS.
YOH HAS HOT GUYS FALLING ALL OVER HER, AND SHE DOESN'T EVEN HAVE TO TRY.
WHY DOES WAKANA ONLY EVER ATTRACT GARBAGE?
IT'S ALWAYS YOH, YOH, YOH...
...IT MAKES ME SICK.

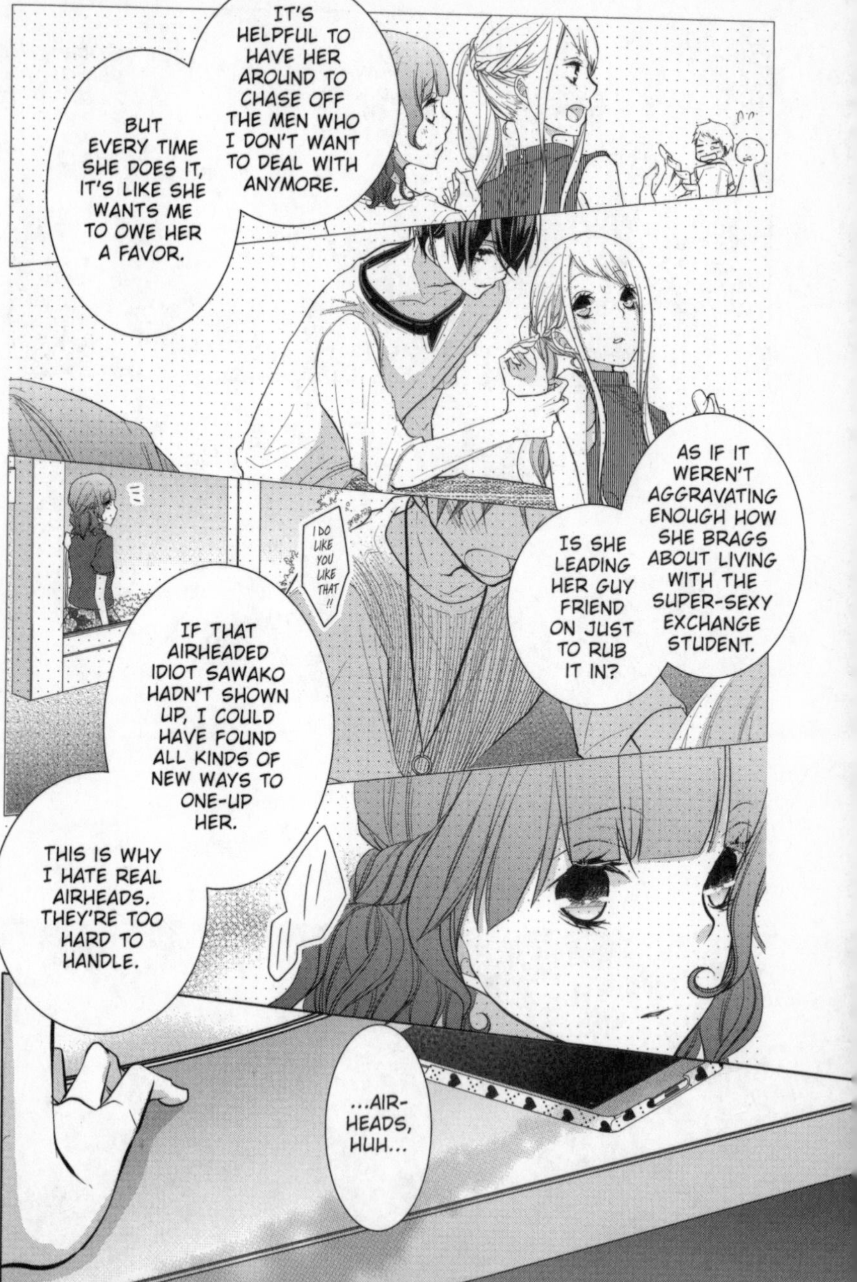
IT'S HELPFUL TO HAVE HER AROUND TO CHASE OFF THE MEN WHO I DON'T WANT TO DEAL WITH ANYMORE.
BUT EVERY TIME SHE DOES IT, IT'S LIKE SHE WANTS ME TO OWE HER A FAVOR.
AS IF IT WEREN'T AGGRAVATING ENOUGH HOW SHE BRAGS ABOUT LIVING WITH THE SUPER-SEXY EXCHANGE STUDENT.
IS SHE LEADING HER GUY FRIEND ON JUST TO RUB IT IN?
I DO LIKE YOU LIKE THAT!!
IF THAT AIRHEADED IDIOT SAWAKO HADN'T SHOWN UP, I COULD HAVE FOUND ALL KINDS OF NEW WAYS TO ONE-UP HER.
THIS IS WHY I HATE REAL AIRHEADS. THEY'RE TOO HARD TO HANDLE.
...AIR-HEADS, HUH...

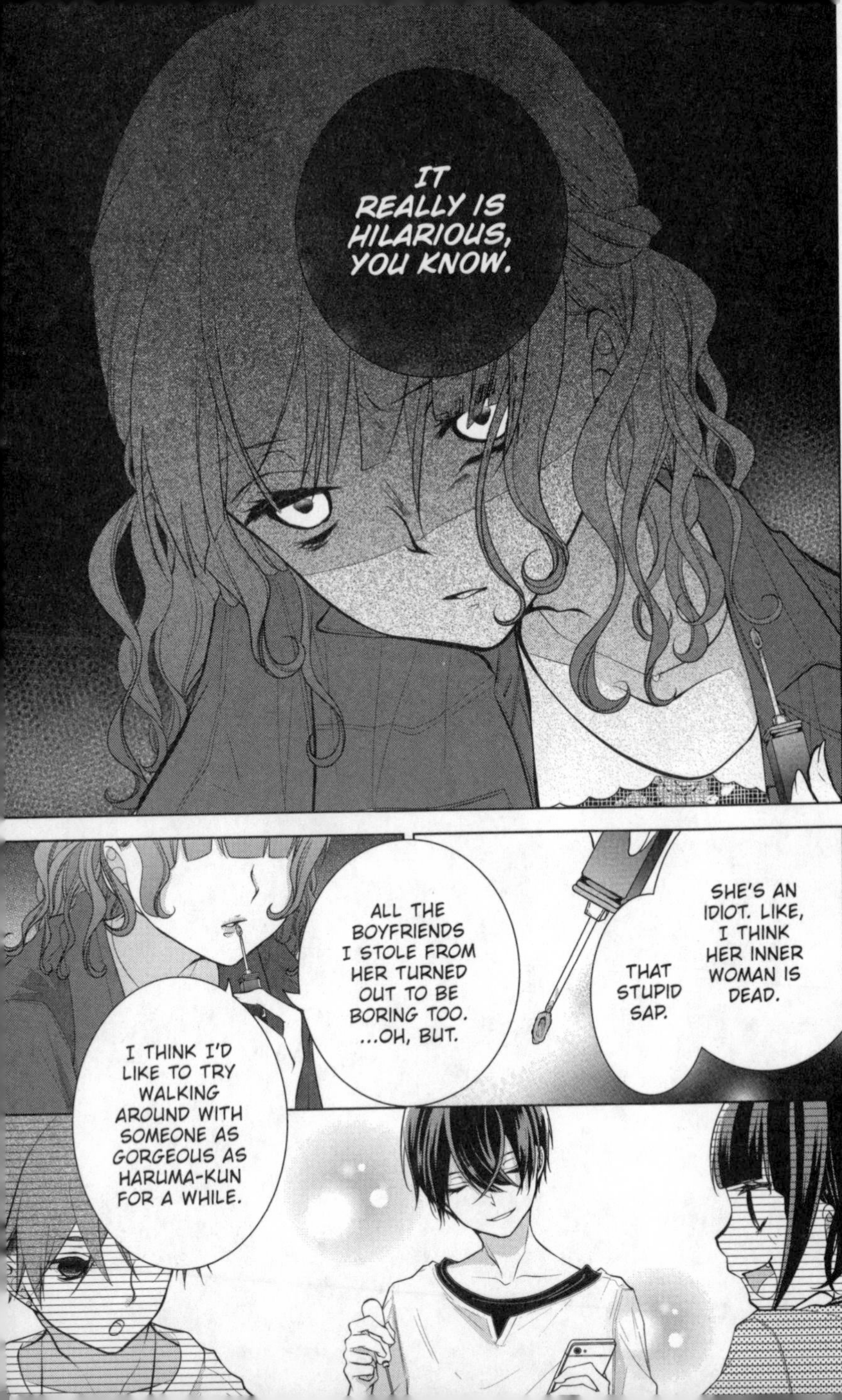
IT REALLY IS HILARIOUS, YOU KNOW.
SHE'S AN IDIOT. LIKE, I THINK HER INNER WOMAN IS DEAD.
THAT STUPID SAP.
ALL THE BOYFRIENDS I STOLE FROM HER TURNED OUT TO BE BORING TOO. ...OH, BUT.
I THINK I'D LIKE TO TRY WALKING AROUND WITH SOMEONE AS GORGEOUS AS HARUMA-KUN FOR A WHILE.

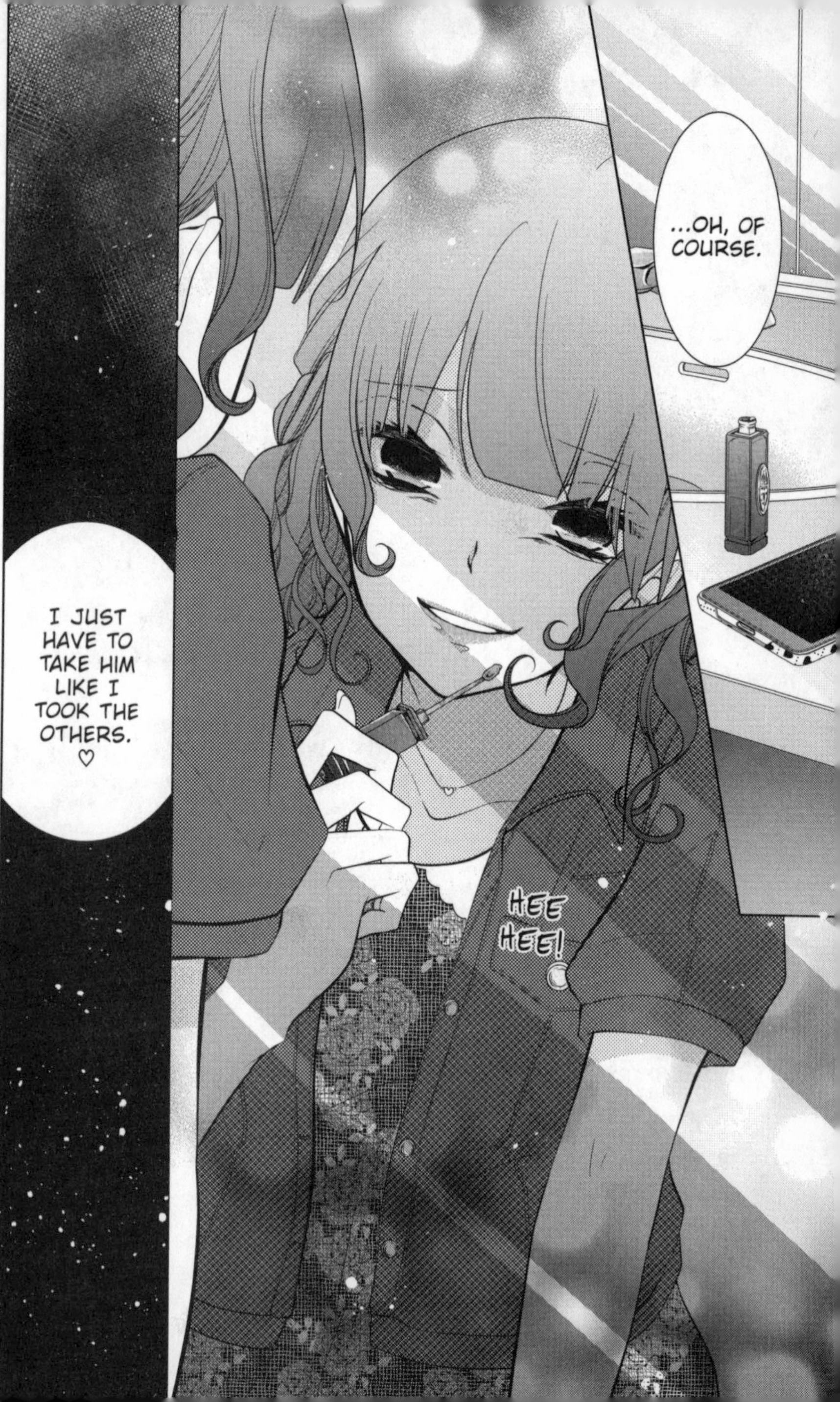
...OH, OF COURSE.
HEE HEE!
I JUST HAVE TO TAKE HIM LIKE I TOOK THE OTHERS. ♡

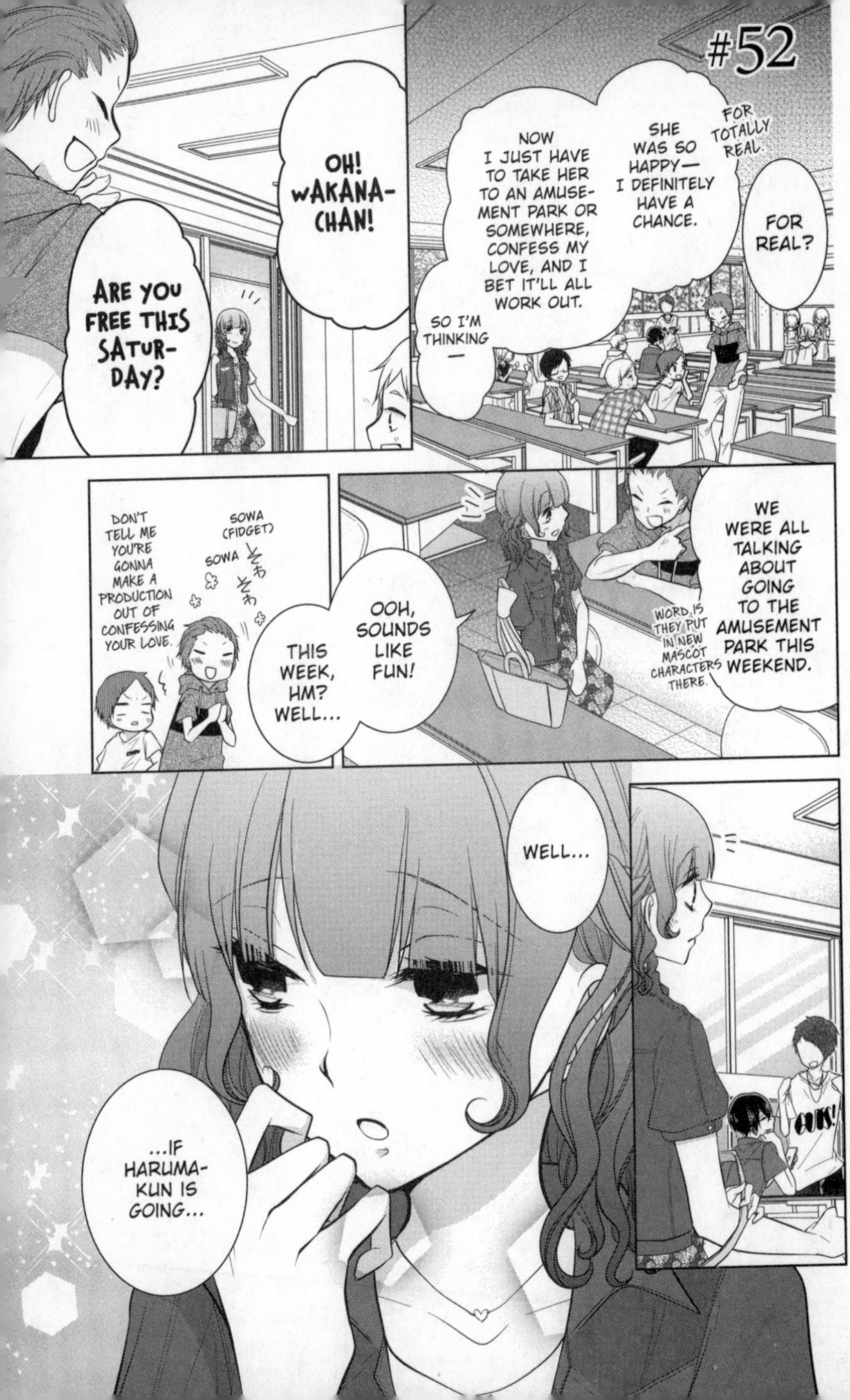
#52
FOR REAL?
FOR TOTALLY REAL.
SHE WAS SO HAPPY— I DEFINITELY HAVE A CHANCE.
NOW I JUST HAVE TO TAKE HER TO AN AMUSEMENT PARK OR SOMEWHERE, CONFESS MY LOVE, AND I BET IT'LL ALL WORK OUT.
SO I'M THINKING—
OH! WAKANA-CHAN!
ARE YOU FREE THIS SATURDAY?
WE WERE ALL TALKING ABOUT GOING TO THE AMUSEMENT PARK THIS WEEKEND.
WORD IS THEY PUT IN NEW MASCOT CHARACTERS THERE.
OOH, SOUNDS LIKE FUN!
THIS WEEK, HM? WELL...
SOWA SOWA (FIDGET)
DON'T TELL ME YOU'RE GONNA MAKE A PRODUCTION OUT OF CONFESSING YOUR LOVE.
WELL...
...IF HARUMA-KUN IS GOING...

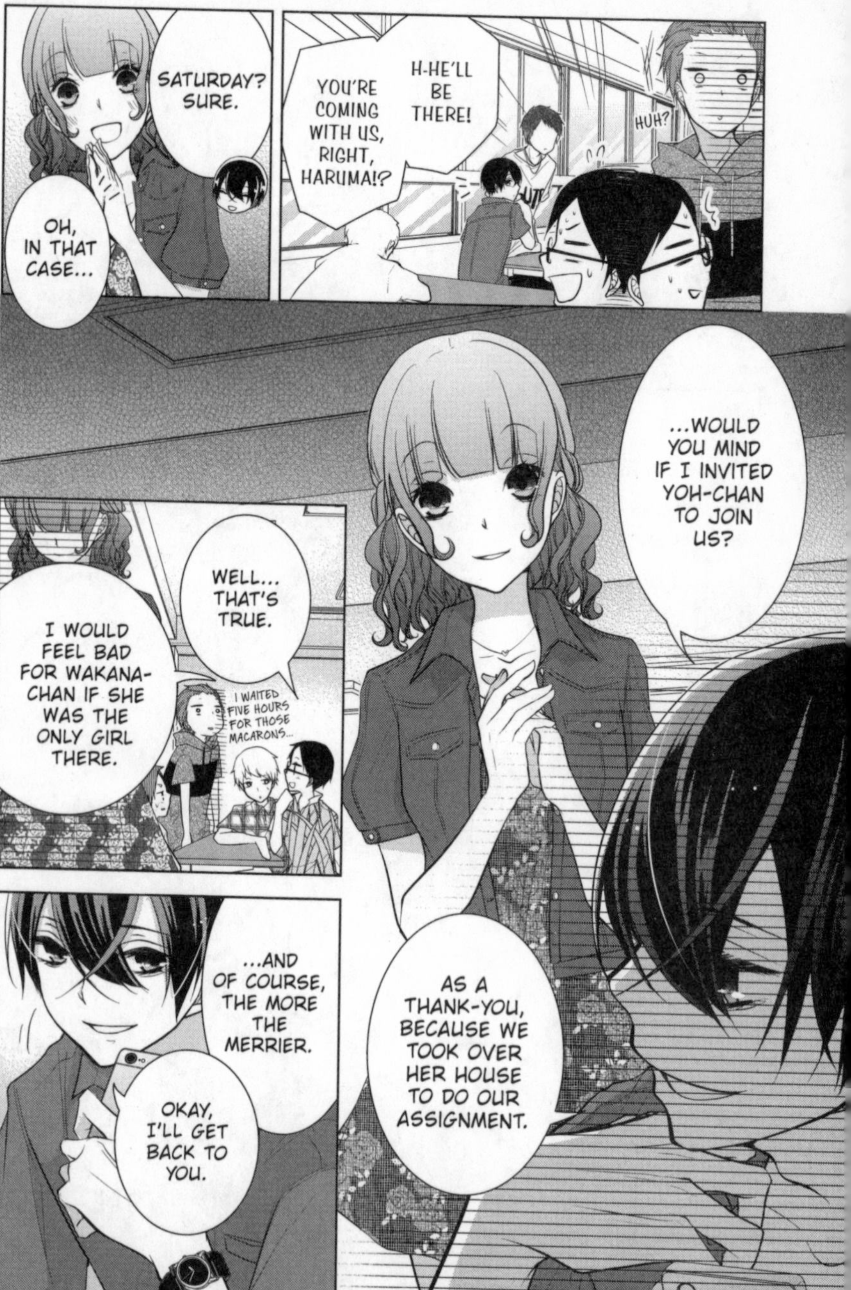
H-HE'LL BE THERE!
YOU'RE COMING WITH US, RIGHT, HARUMA!?
HUH?
SATURDAY? SURE.
OH, IN THAT CASE...
...WOULD YOU MIND IF I INVITED YOH-CHAN TO JOIN US?
AS A THANK-YOU, BECAUSE WE TOOK OVER HER HOUSE TO DO OUR ASSIGNMENT.
WELL... THAT'S TRUE.
I WOULD FEEL BAD FOR WAKANA-CHAN IF SHE WAS THE ONLY GIRL THERE.
I WAITED FIVE HOURS FOR THOSE MACARONS...
...AND OF COURSE, THE MORE THE MERRIER.
OKAY, I'LL GET BACK TO YOU.

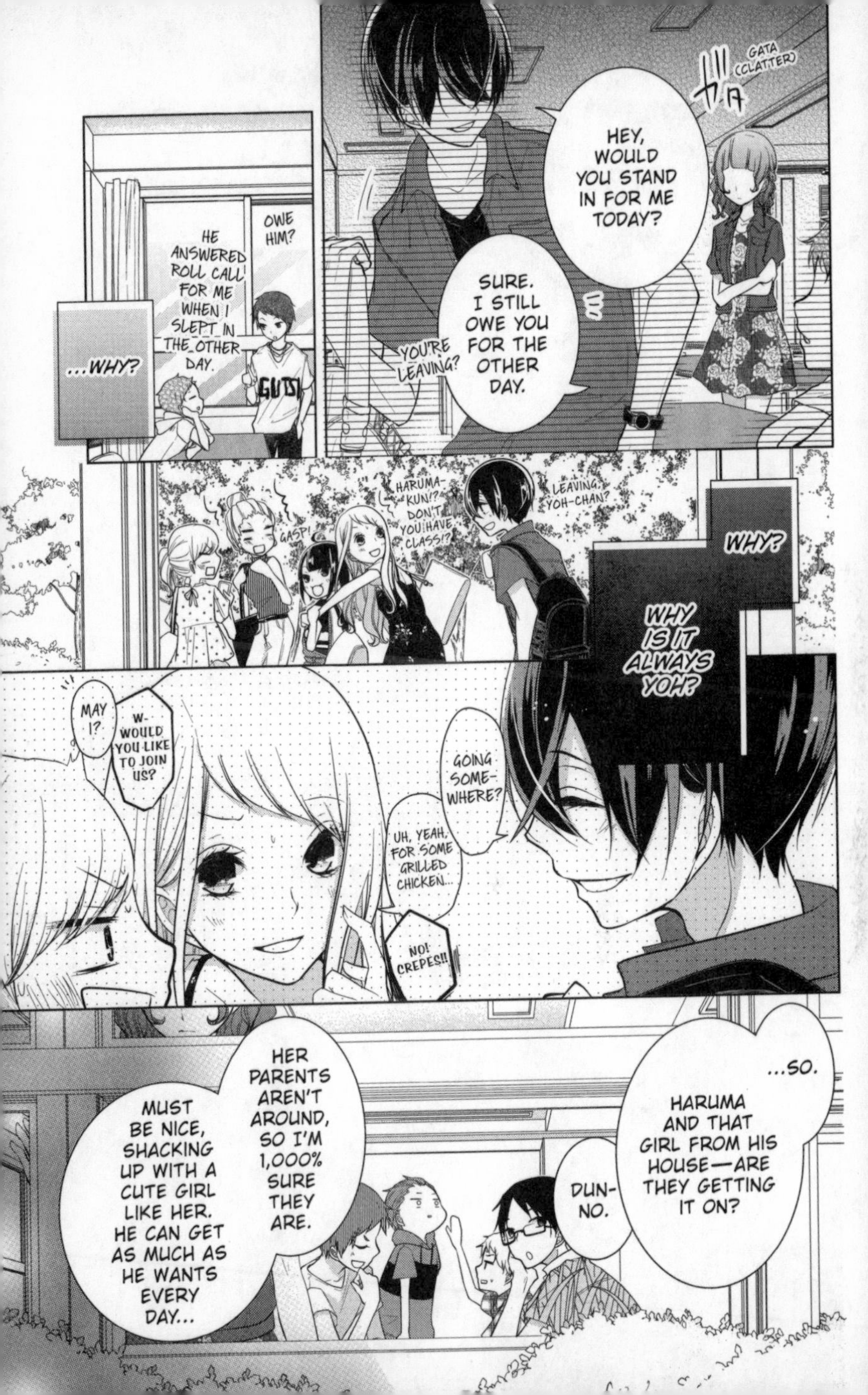
GATA (CLATTER)
HEY, WOULD YOU STAND IN FOR ME TODAY?
SURE. I STILL OWE YOU FOR THE OTHER DAY.
YOU'RE LEAVING?
OWE HIM?
HE ANSWERED ROLL CALL FOR ME WHEN I SLEPT IN THE OTHER DAY.
GUTS
...WHY?
WHY?
WHY IS IT ALWAYS YOH?
LEAVING, YOH-CHAN?
HARUMA-KUN!? DON'T YOU HAVE CLASS!?
GASP!
GOING SOME-WHERE?
UH, YEAH, FOR SOME GRILLED CHICKEN...
NO! CREPES!!
W-WOULD YOU LIKE TO JOIN US?
MAY I?
...SO.
HARUMA AND THAT GIRL FROM HIS HOUSE—ARE THEY GETTING IT ON?
DUN-NO.
HER PARENTS AREN'T AROUND, SO I'M 1,000% SURE THEY ARE.
MUST BE NICE, SHACKING UP WITH A CUTE GIRL LIKE HER. HE CAN GET AS MUCH AS HE WANTS EVERY DAY...

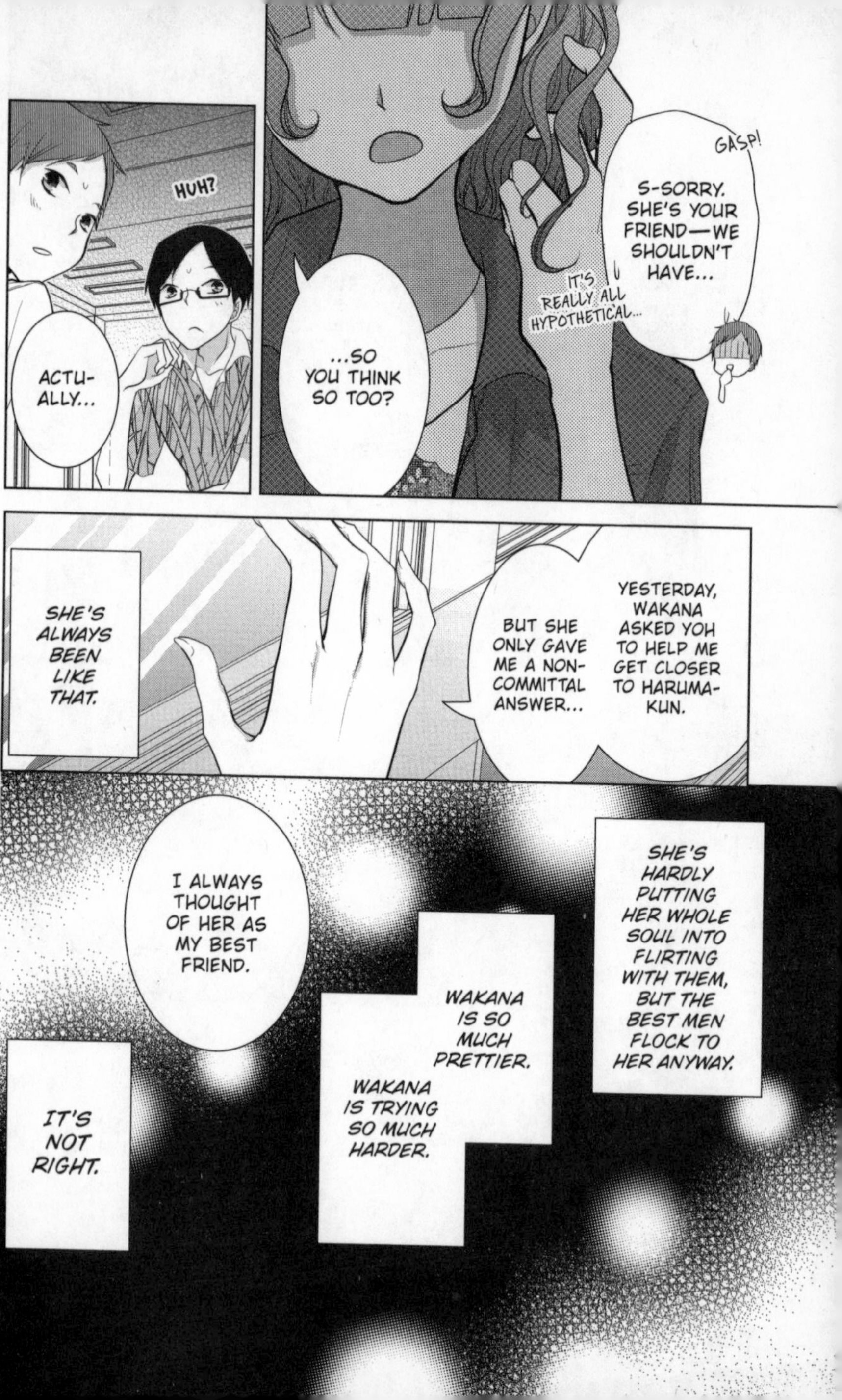
GASP!
S-SORRY. SHE'S YOUR FRIEND—WE SHOULDN'T HAVE...
IT'S REALLY ALL HYPOTHETICAL...
...SO YOU THINK SO TOO?
HUH?
ACTU-ALLY...
YESTERDAY, WAKANA ASKED YOH TO HELP ME GET CLOSER TO HARUMA-KUN.
BUT SHE ONLY GAVE ME A NON-COMMITTAL ANSWER...
SHE'S ALWAYS BEEN LIKE THAT.
SHE'S HARDLY PUTTING HER WHOLE SOUL INTO FLIRTING WITH THEM, BUT THE BEST MEN FLOCK TO HER ANYWAY.
I ALWAYS THOUGHT OF HER AS MY BEST FRIEND.
WAKANA IS SO MUCH PRETTIER.
WAKANA IS TRYING SO MUCH HARDER.
IT'S NOT RIGHT.

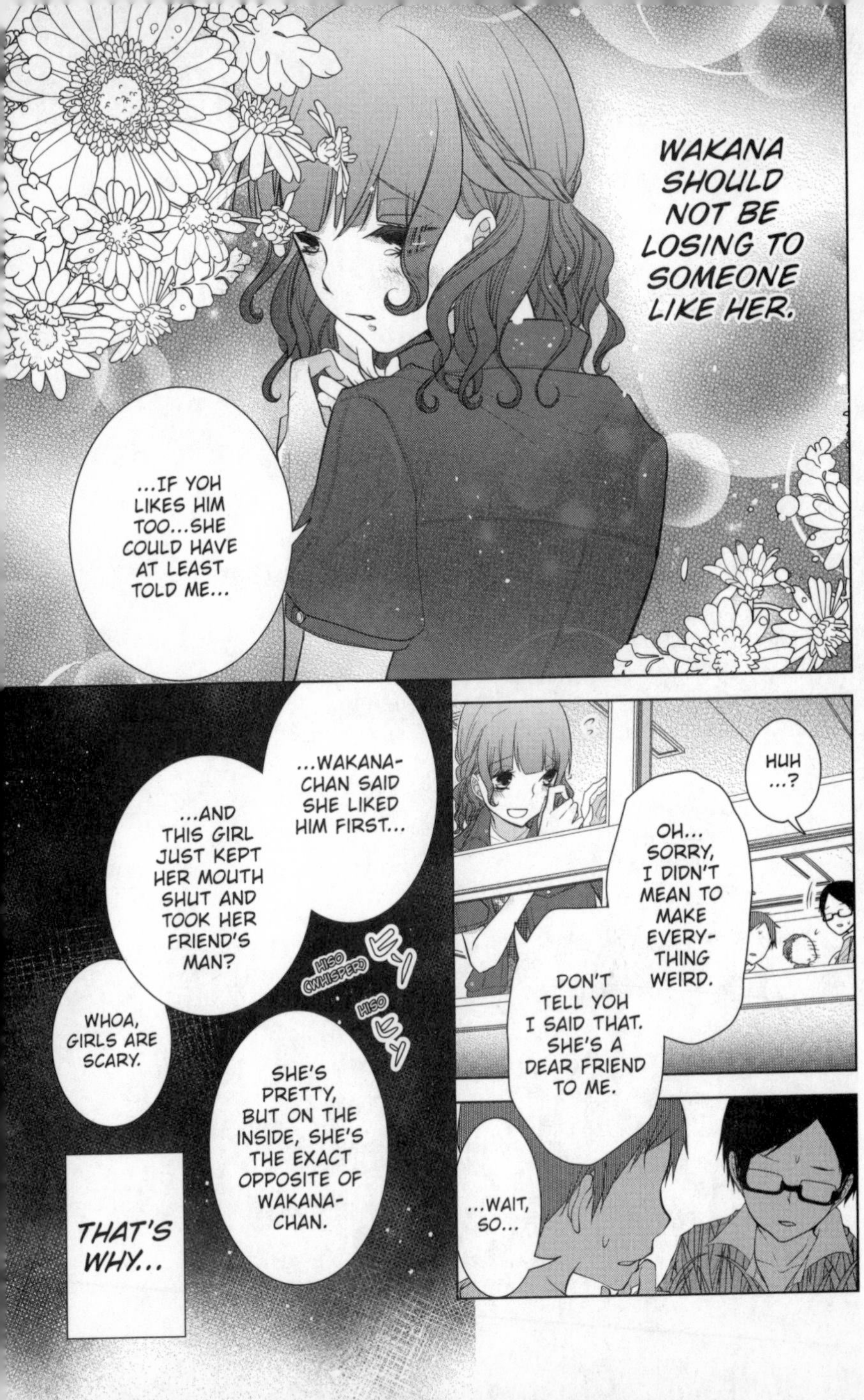
WAKANA SHOULD NOT BE LOSING TO SOMEONE LIKE HER.
...IF YOH LIKES HIM TOO...SHE COULD HAVE AT LEAST TOLD ME...
HUH ...?
OH... SORRY, I DIDN'T MEAN TO MAKE EVERY-THING WEIRD.
DON'T TELL YOH I SAID THAT. SHE'S A DEAR FRIEND TO ME.
...WAIT, SO...
...WAKANA-CHAN SAID SHE LIKED HIM FIRST...
...AND THIS GIRL JUST KEPT HER MOUTH SHUT AND TOOK HER FRIEND'S MAN?
HISO (WHISPER)
HISO
SHE'S PRETTY, BUT ON THE INSIDE, SHE'S THE EXACT OPPOSITE OF WAKANA-CHAN.
WHOA, GIRLS ARE SCARY.
THAT'S WHY...

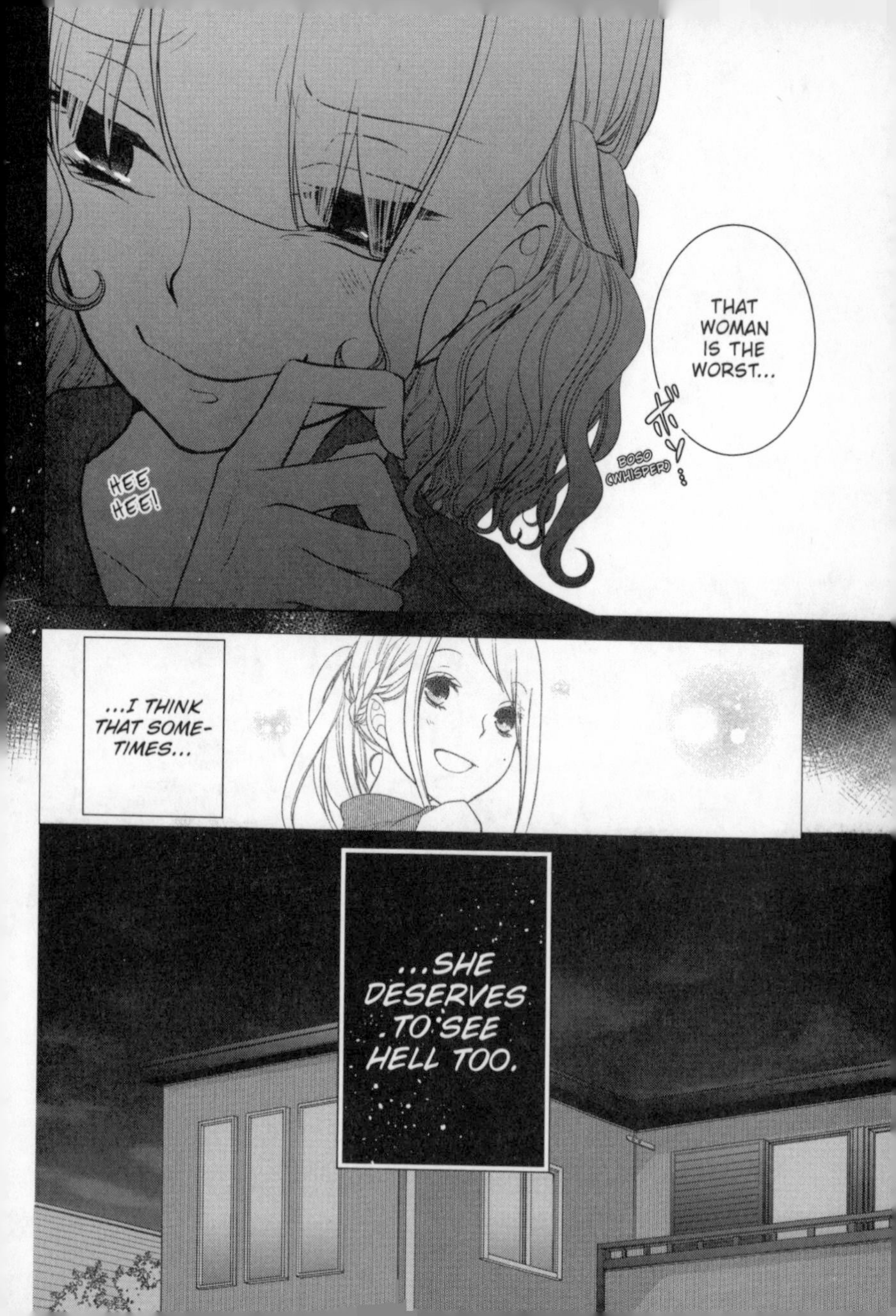
THAT WOMAN IS THE WORST...
BOSO (WHISPER)
HEE HEE!
...I THINK THAT SOME-TIMES...
...SHE DESERVES TO SEE HELL TOO.

#53

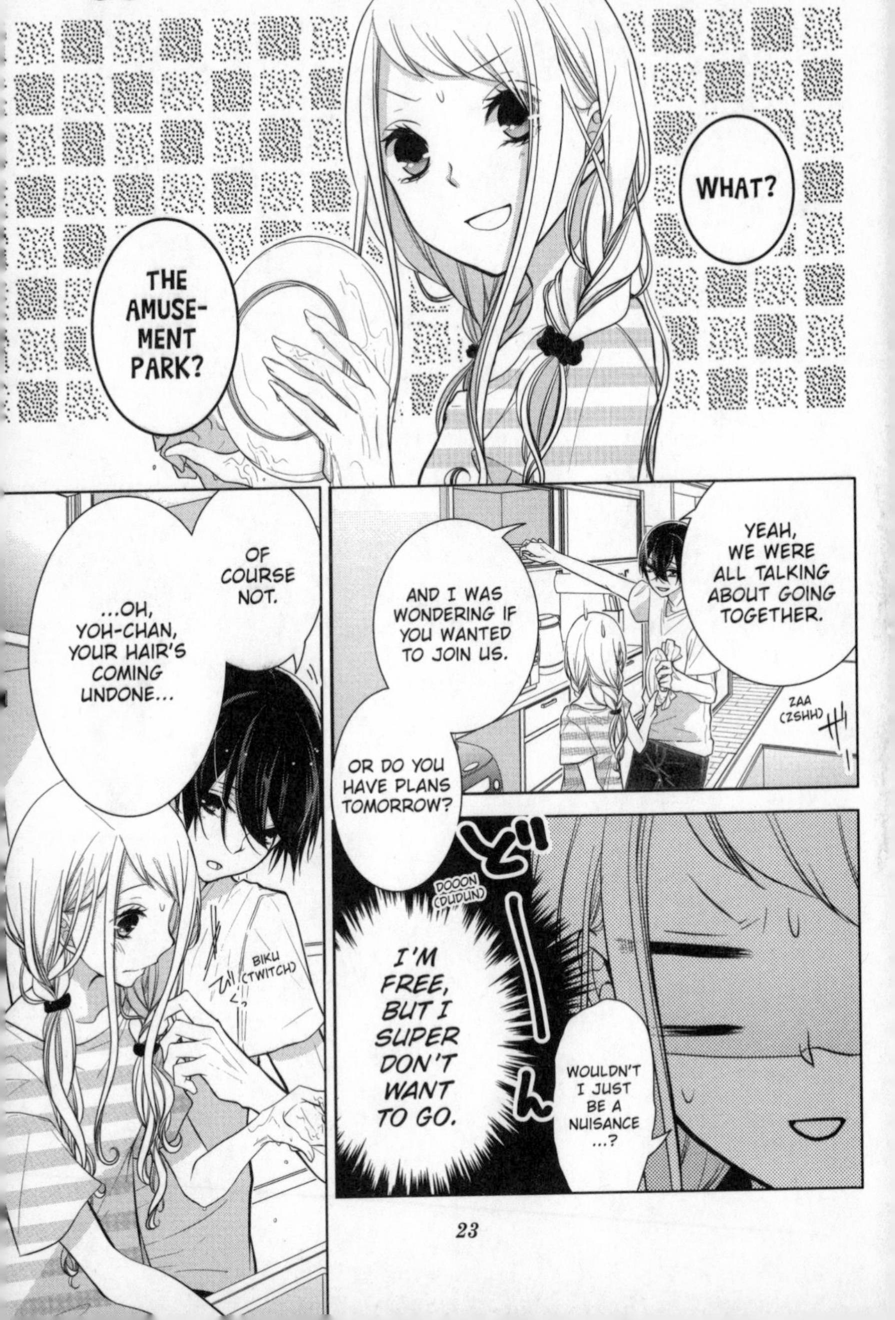
WHAT?
THE AMUSEMENT-MENT PARK?
YEAH, WE WERE ALL TALKING ABOUT GOING TOGETHER.
ZAA (ZSHH)
AND I WAS WONDERING IF YOU WANTED TO JOIN US.
OR DO YOU HAVE PLANS TOMORROW?
DOOON (DUDUN)
I'M FREE, BUT I SUPER DON'T WANT TO GO.
WOULDN'T I JUST BE A NUISANCE ...?
OF COURSE NOT.
...OH, YOH-CHAN, YOUR HAIR'S COMING UNDONE...
BIKU (TWITCH)

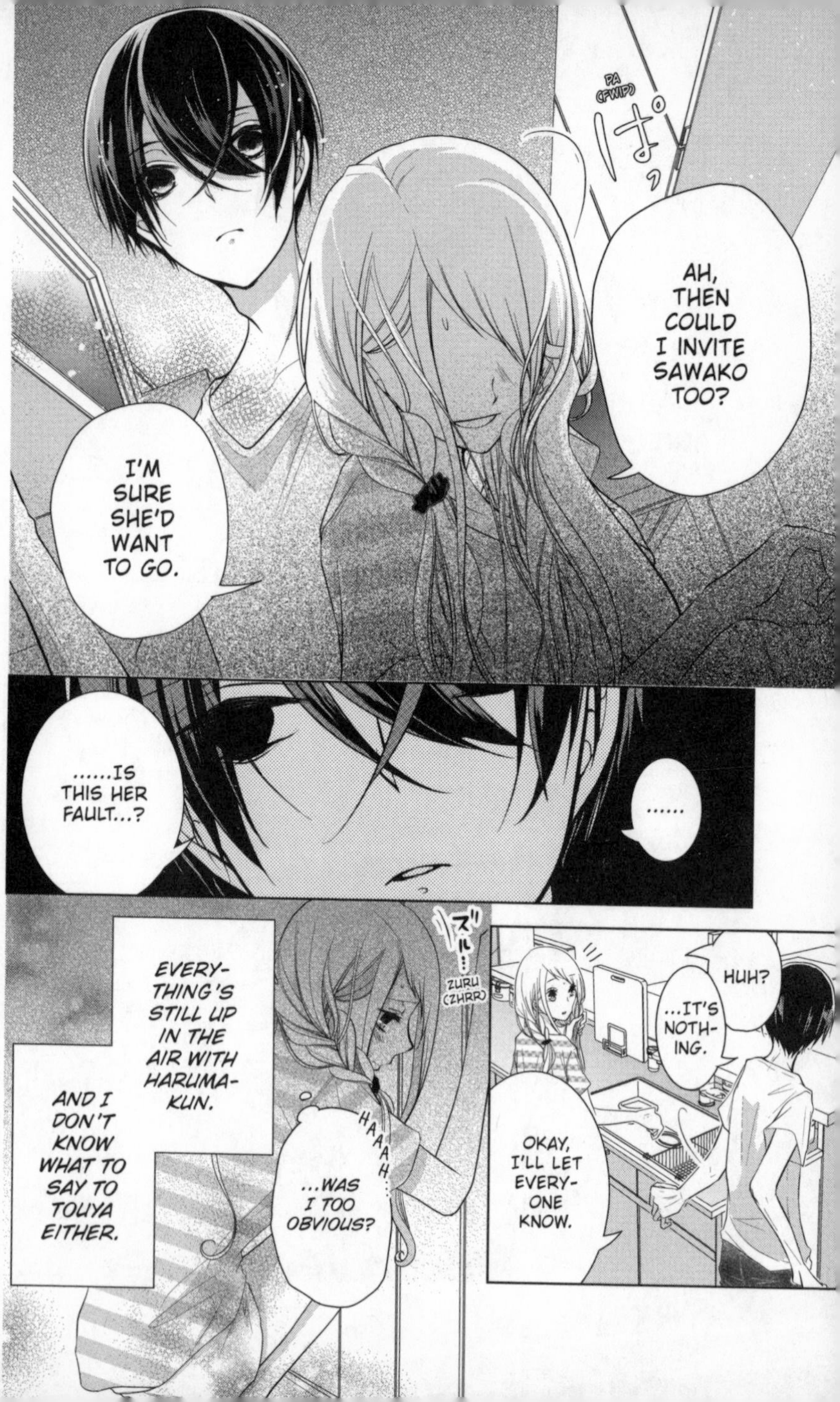
PA (FWIP)
ぱっ
AH, THEN COULD I INVITE SAWAKO TOO?
I'M SURE SHE'D WANT TO GO.
......
......IS THIS HER FAULT...?
HUH?
...IT'S NOTHING.
OKAY, I'LL LET EVERYONE KNOW.
ZURU (ZHRR)
EVERYTHING'S STILL UP IN THE AIR WITH HARUMA-KUN.
AND I DON'T KNOW WHAT TO SAY TO TOUYA EITHER.
HAAAAH...
...WAS I TOO OBVIOUS?

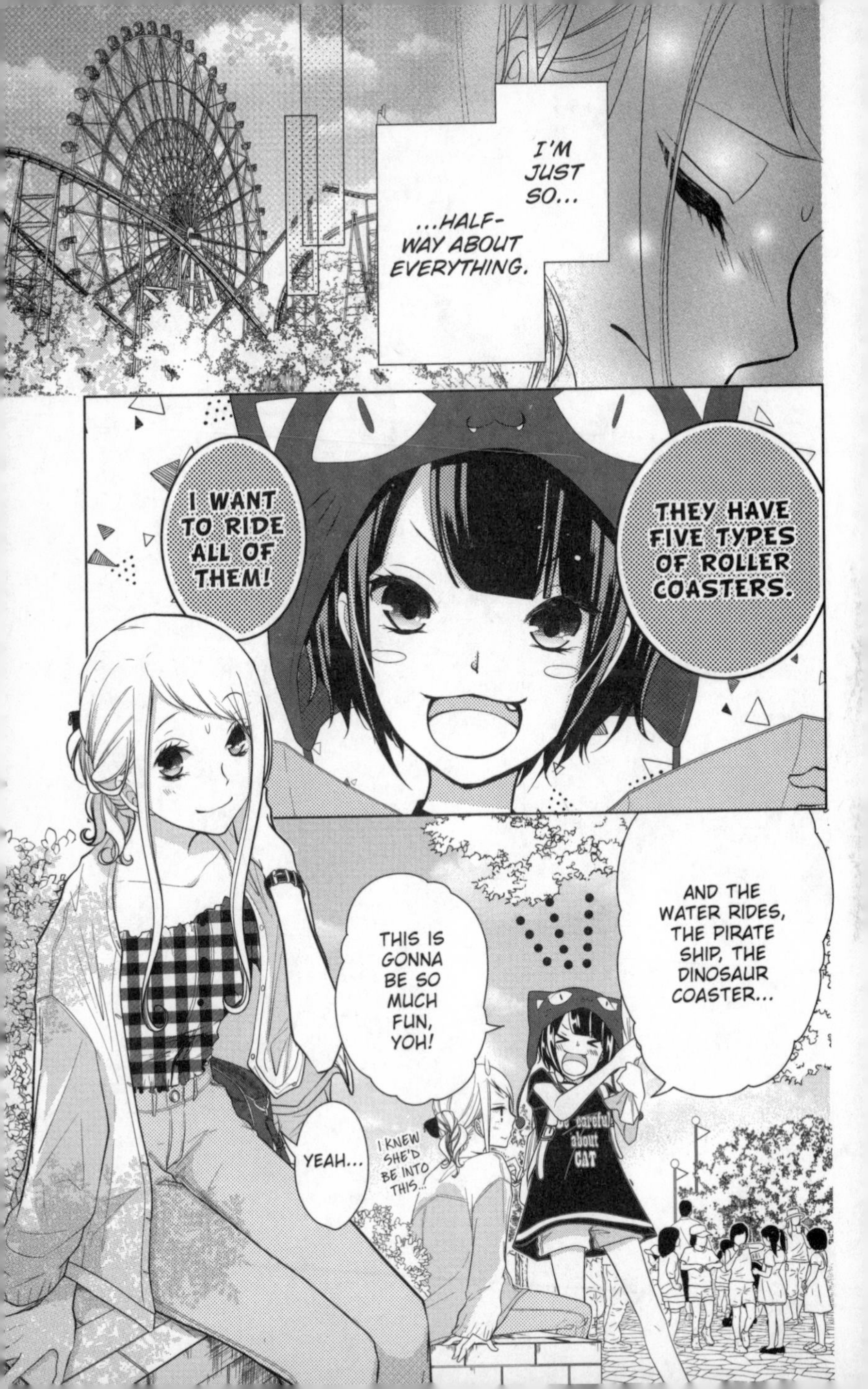
I'M JUST SO...
...HALF-WAY ABOUT EVERYTHING.
THEY HAVE FIVE TYPES OF ROLLER COASTERS.
I WANT TO RIDE ALL OF THEM!
AND THE WATER RIDES, THE PIRATE SHIP, THE DINOSAUR COASTER...
THIS IS GONNA BE SO MUCH FUN, YOH!
I KNEW SHE'D BE INTO THIS...
YEAH...

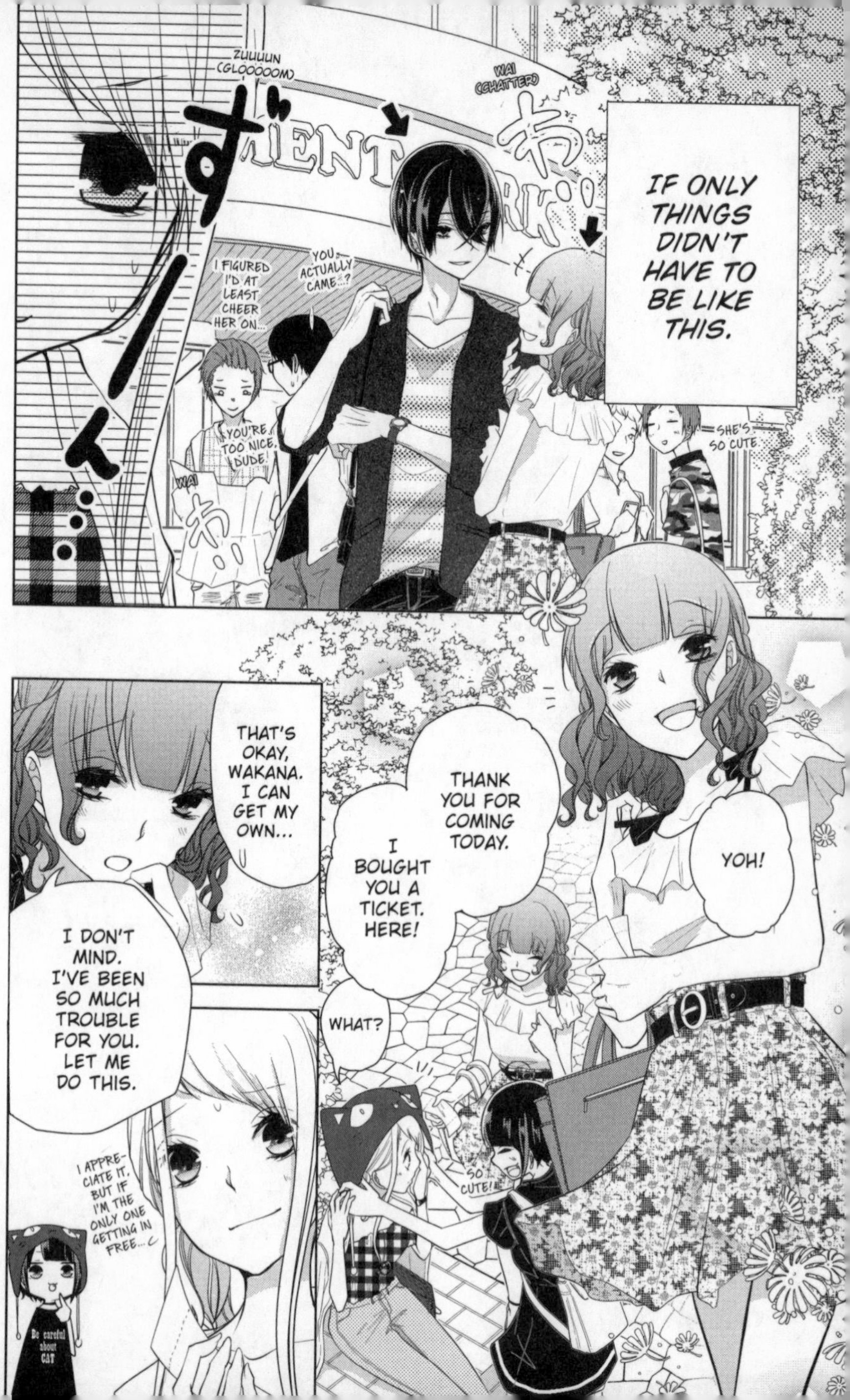
IF ONLY THINGS DIDN'T HAVE TO BE LIKE THIS.
WAI (CHATTER)
ZUUUUN (GLOOOOOM)
YOU ACTUALLY CAME...?
I FIGURED I'D AT LEAST CHEER HER ON...
SHE'S SO CUTE
YOU'RE TOO NICE, DUDE!
WAI
YOH!
THANK YOU FOR COMING TODAY.
I BOUGHT YOU A TICKET. HERE!
WHAT?
SO CUTE!
THAT'S OKAY, WAKANA. I CAN GET MY OWN...
I DON'T MIND. I'VE BEEN SO MUCH TROUBLE FOR YOU. LET ME DO THIS.
I APPRECIATE IT, BUT IF I'M THE ONLY ONE GETTING IN FREE...
Be careful about CAT

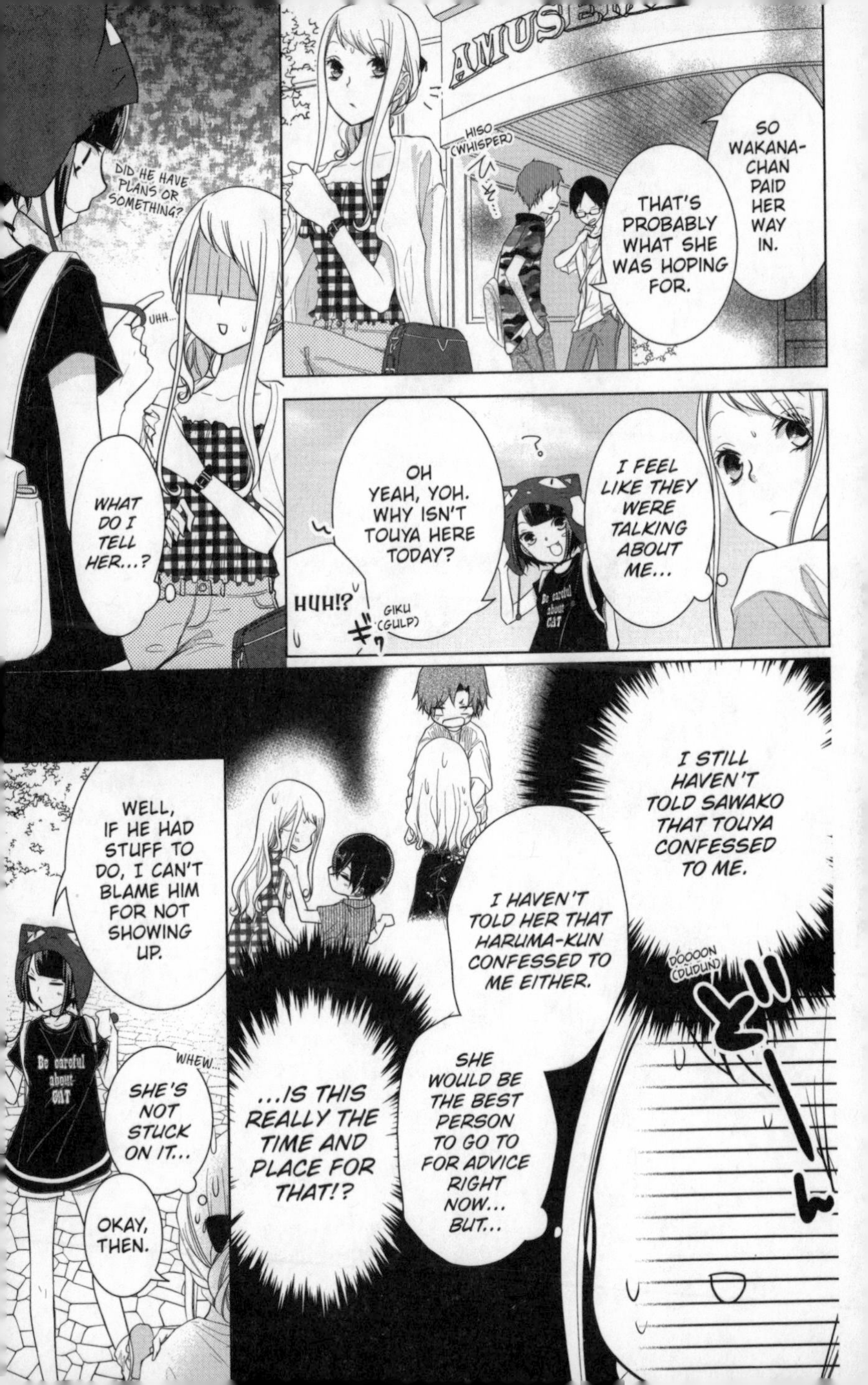

SO WAKANA-CHAN PAID HER WAY IN.
HISO (WHISPER)
THAT'S PROBABLY WHAT SHE WAS HOPING FOR.
I FEEL LIKE THEY WERE TALKING ABOUT ME...
OH YEAH, YOH. WHY ISN'T TOUYA HERE TODAY?
GIKU (GULP)
HUH!?
DID HE HAVE PLANS OR SOMETHING?
UHH...
WHAT DO I TELL HER...?
I STILL HAVEN'T TOLD SAWAKO THAT TOUYA CONFESSED TO ME.
DOOOON (DUDUN)
I HAVEN'T TOLD HER THAT HARUMA-KUN CONFESSED TO ME EITHER.
SHE WOULD BE THE BEST PERSON TO GO TO FOR ADVICE RIGHT NOW... BUT...
...IS THIS REALLY THE TIME AND PLACE FOR THAT!?
WELL, IF HE HAD STUFF TO DO, I CAN'T BLAME HIM FOR NOT SHOWING UP.
WHEW...
SHE'S NOT STUCK ON IT...
OKAY, THEN.

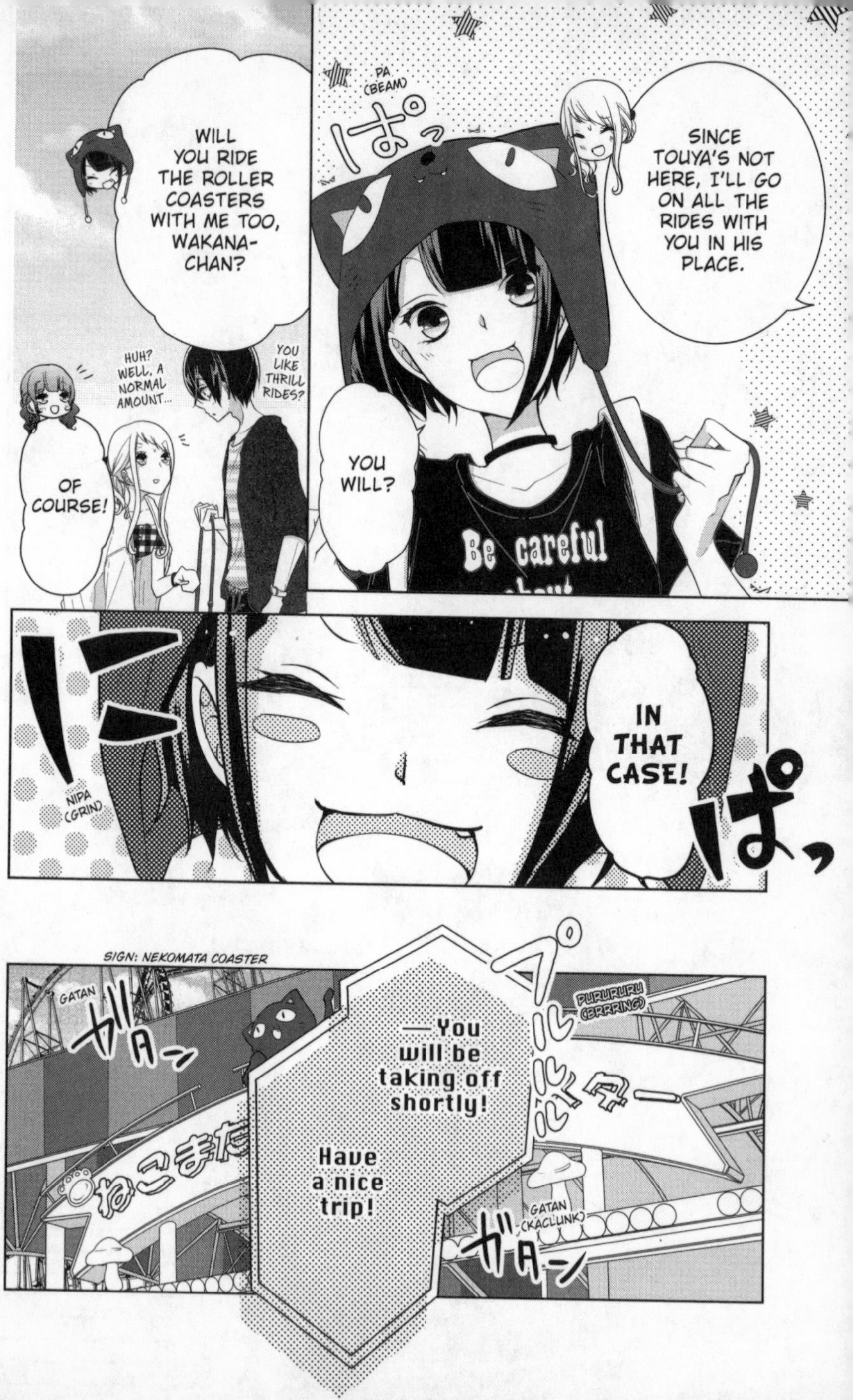
PA (BEAM)
SINCE TOUYA'S NOT HERE, I'LL GO ON ALL THE RIDES WITH YOU IN HIS PLACE.
YOU WILL?
WILL YOU RIDE THE ROLLER COASTERS WITH ME TOO, WAKANA-CHAN?
YOU LIKE THRILL RIDES?
HUH? WELL, A NORMAL AMOUNT...
OF COURSE!
IN THAT CASE!
NIPA (GRIN)
SIGN: NEKOMATA COASTER
PURURURU (BRRRING)
—You will be taking off shortly!
Have a nice trip!
GATAN (KACLUNK)
GATAN

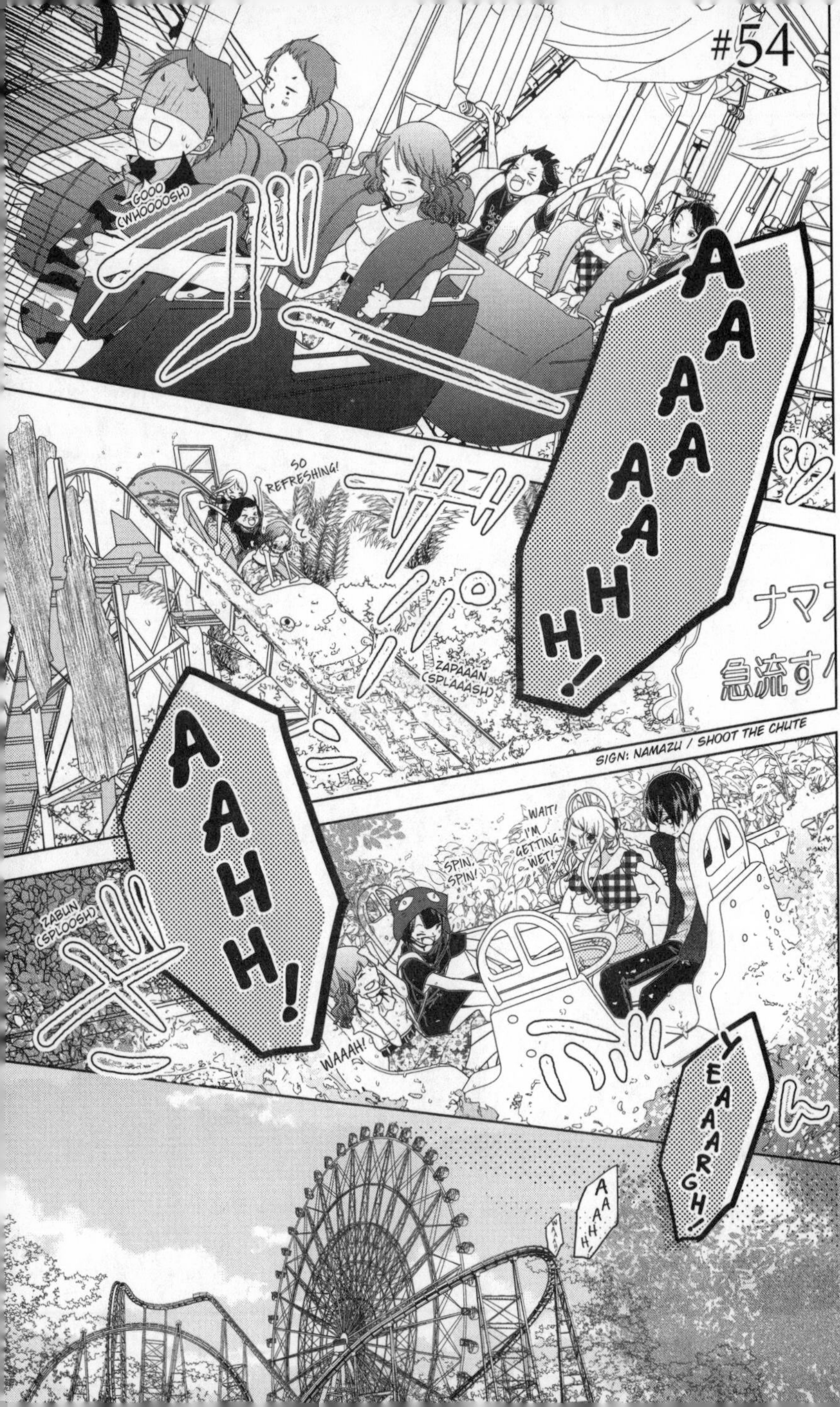
#54
GOOO (WHOOOOSH)
AAAAAAH!
SO REFRESHING!
ZAPAAAN (SPLAAASH)
ナマ
急流す
SIGN: NAMAZU / SHOOT THE CHUTE
WAIT! I'M GETTING WET!
SPIN, SPIN!
YEAAARGH!
WAAAH!
AAHH!
ZABUN (SPLOOSH)
AAAHH!
WAAAH

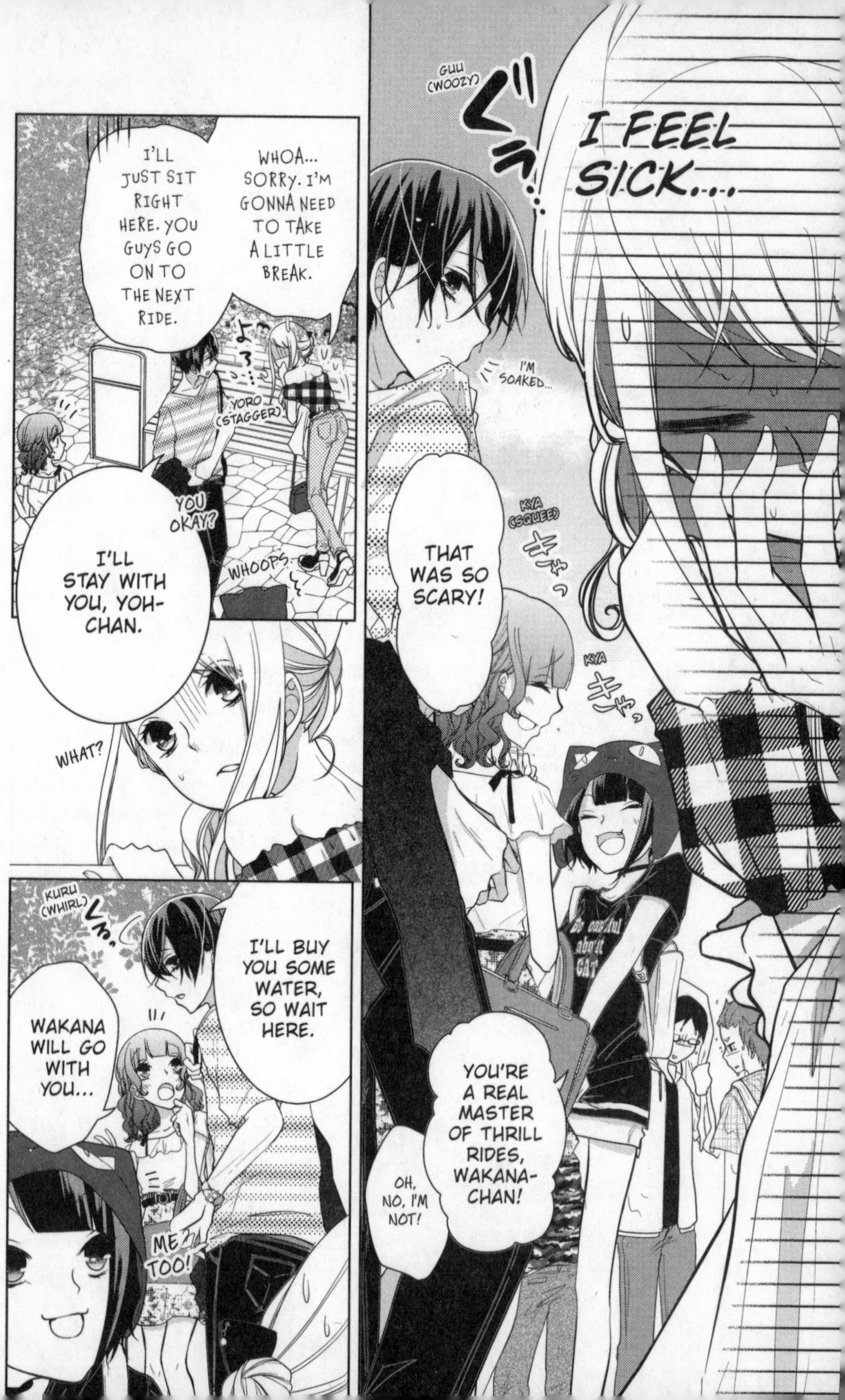
GUU (WOOZY)
I FEEL SICK....
I'M SOAKED...
KYA (SQUEE)
THAT WAS SO SCARY!
KYA
YOU'RE A REAL MASTER OF THRILL RIDES, WAKANA-CHAN!
OH, NO, I'M NOT!
WHOA... SORRY. I'M GONNA NEED TO TAKE A LITTLE BREAK.
I'LL JUST SIT RIGHT HERE. YOU GUYS GO ON TO THE NEXT RIDE.
YORO (STAGGER)
YOU OKAY?
WHOOPS
I'LL STAY WITH YOU, YOH-CHAN.
WHAT?
KURU (WHIRL)
I'LL BUY YOU SOME WATER, SO WAIT HERE.
WAKANA WILL GO WITH YOU...
ME TOO!

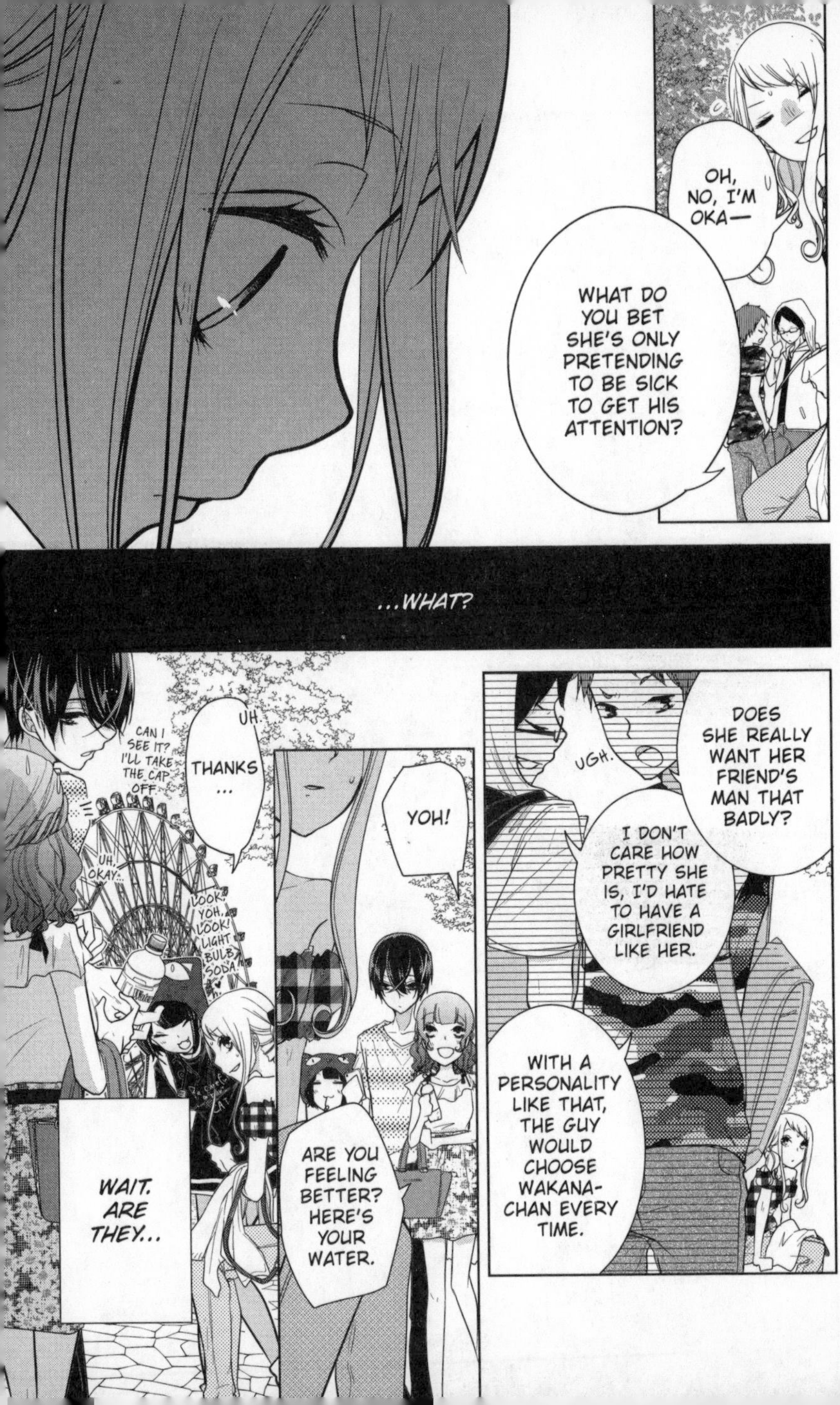
OH, NO, I'M OKA—
WHAT DO YOU BET SHE'S ONLY PRETENDING TO BE SICK TO GET HIS ATTENTION?
...WHAT?
DOES SHE REALLY WANT HER FRIEND'S MAN THAT BADLY?
UGH.
I DON'T CARE HOW PRETTY SHE IS, I'D HATE TO HAVE A GIRLFRIEND LIKE HER.
WITH A PERSONALITY LIKE THAT, THE GUY WOULD CHOOSE WAKANA-CHAN EVERY TIME.
YOH!
ARE YOU FEELING BETTER? HERE'S YOUR WATER.
UH. THANKS...
CAN I SEE IT? I'LL TAKE THE CAP OFF
UH, OKAY..
LOOK, YOH, LOOK! LIGHT BULB SODA!
WAIT. ARE THEY...

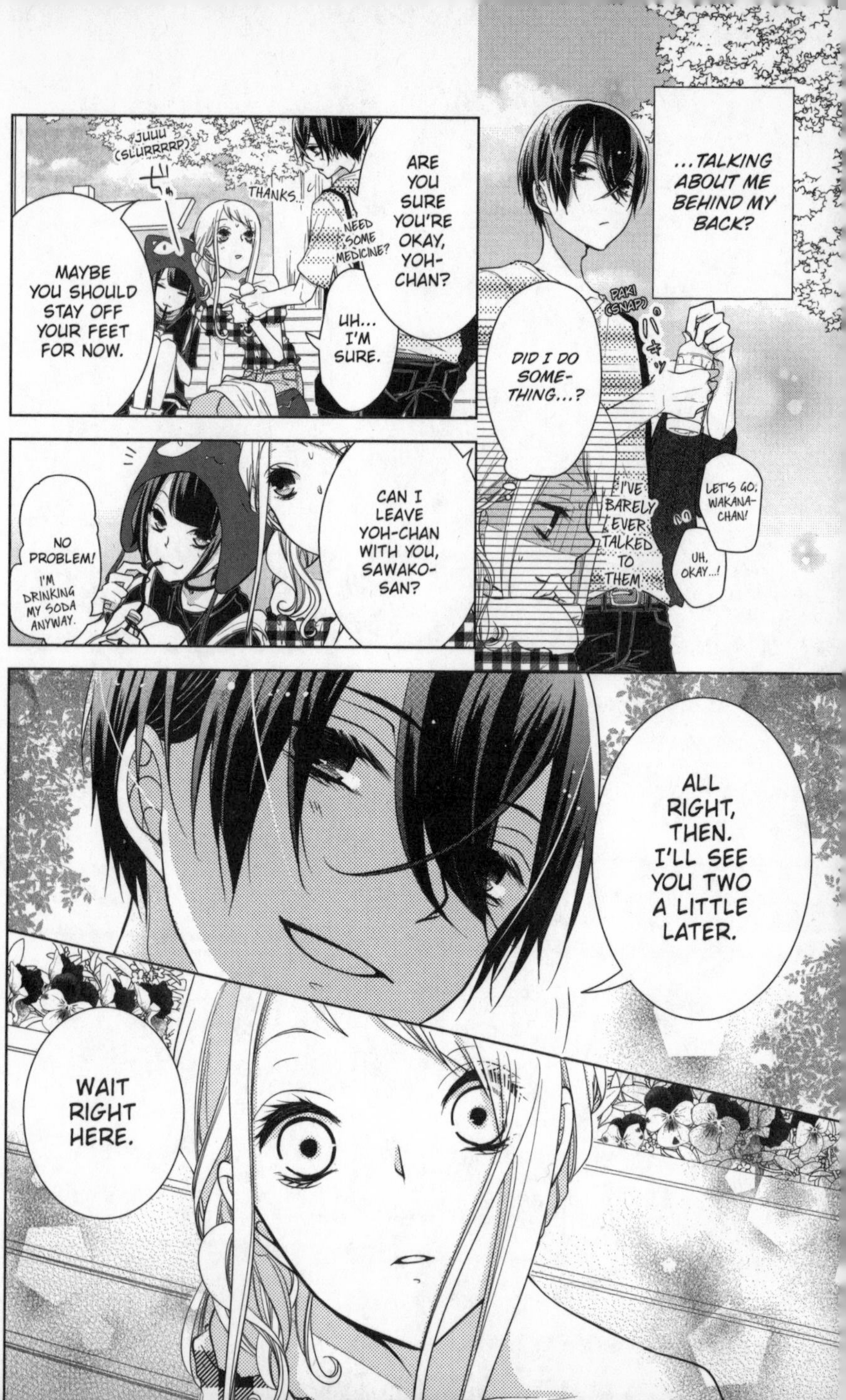

...TALKING ABOUT ME BEHIND MY BACK?
PAKI (SNAP)
DID I DO SOME-THING...?
I'VE BARELY EVER TALKED TO THEM!
LET'S GO, WAKANA-CHAN!
UH, OKAY...!
ARE YOU SURE YOU'RE OKAY, YOH-CHAN?
NEED SOME MEDICINE?
UH... I'M SURE.
THANKS...
JUUU (SLURRRRP)
MAYBE YOU SHOULD STAY OFF YOUR FEET FOR NOW.
CAN I LEAVE YOH-CHAN WITH YOU, SAWAKO-SAN?
NO PROBLEM!
I'M DRINKING MY SODA ANYWAY.
ALL RIGHT, THEN. I'LL SEE YOU TWO A LITTLE LATER.
WAIT RIGHT HERE.

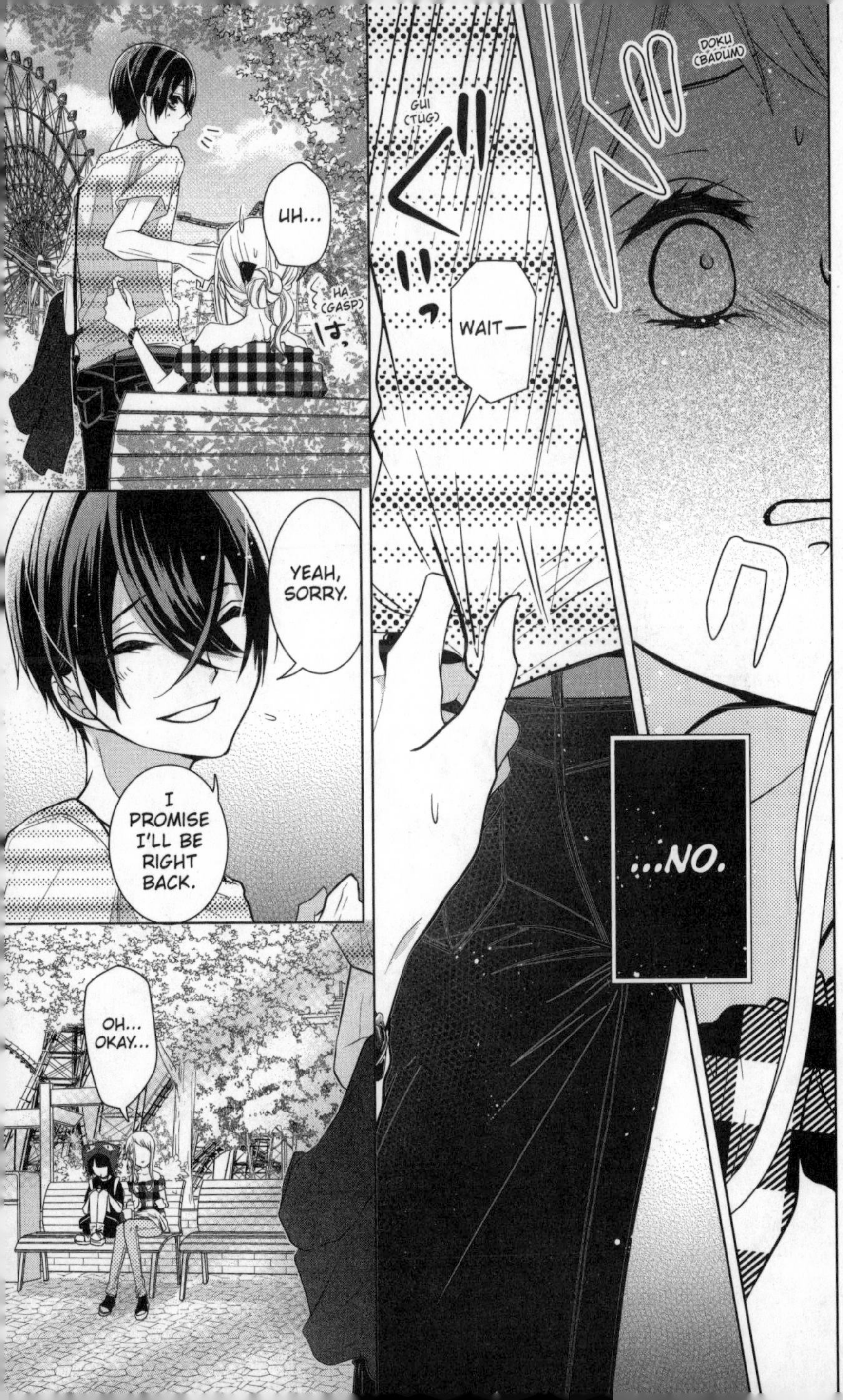
DOKU (BADUM)
GUI (TUG)
WAIT—
...NO.
UH...
HA (GASP)
YEAH, SORRY.
I PROMISE I'LL BE RIGHT BACK.
OH... OKAY...

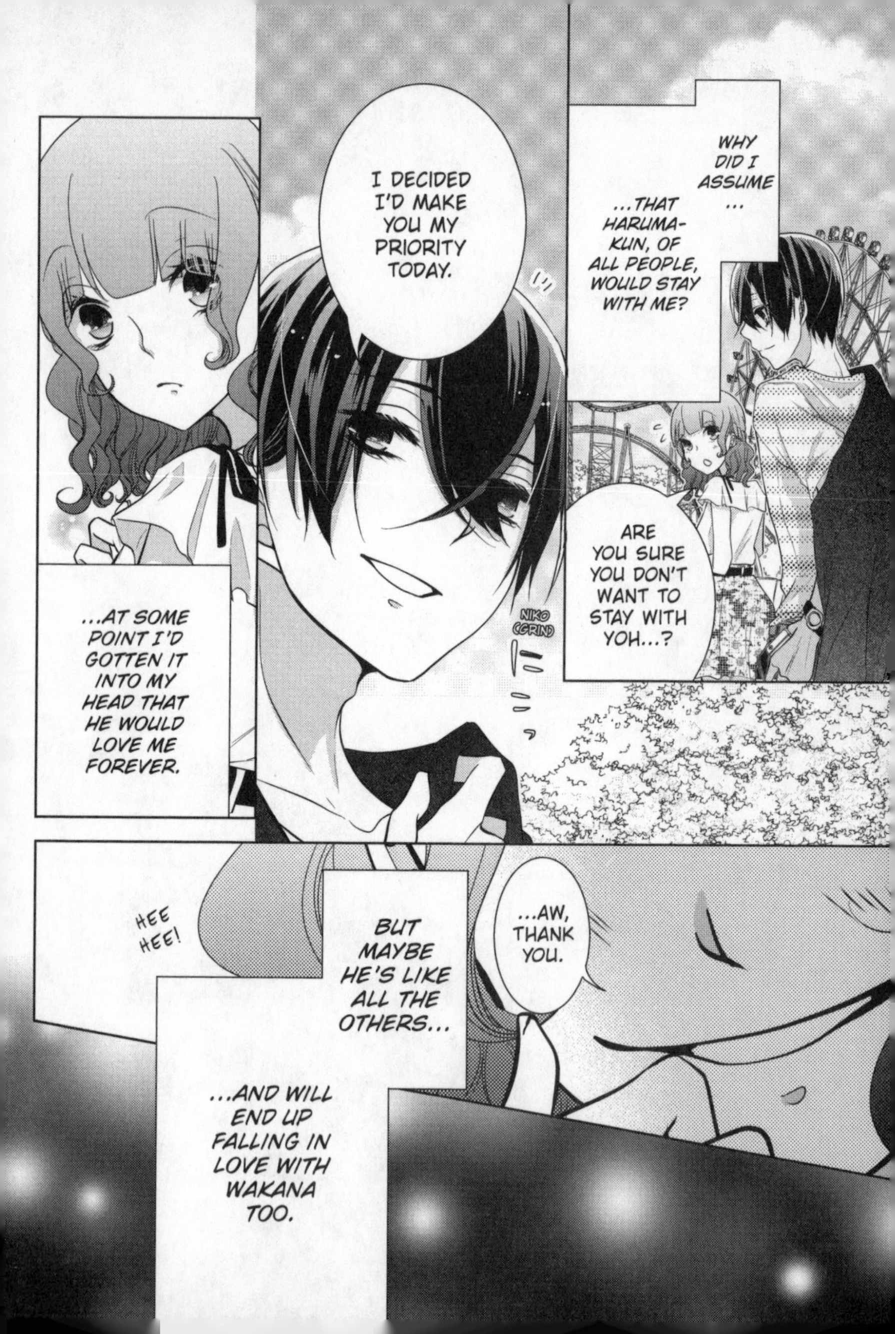
WHY DID I ASSUME...
...THAT HARUMA-KUN, OF ALL PEOPLE, WOULD STAY WITH ME?
ARE YOU SURE YOU DON'T WANT TO STAY WITH YOH...?
I DECIDED I'D MAKE YOU MY PRIORITY TODAY.
NIKO (GRIND)
...AT SOME POINT I'D GOTTEN IT INTO MY HEAD THAT HE WOULD LOVE ME FOREVER.
...AW, THANK YOU.
BUT MAYBE HE'S LIKE ALL THE OTHERS...
HEE HEE!
...AND WILL END UP FALLING IN LOVE WITH WAKANA TOO.

#55

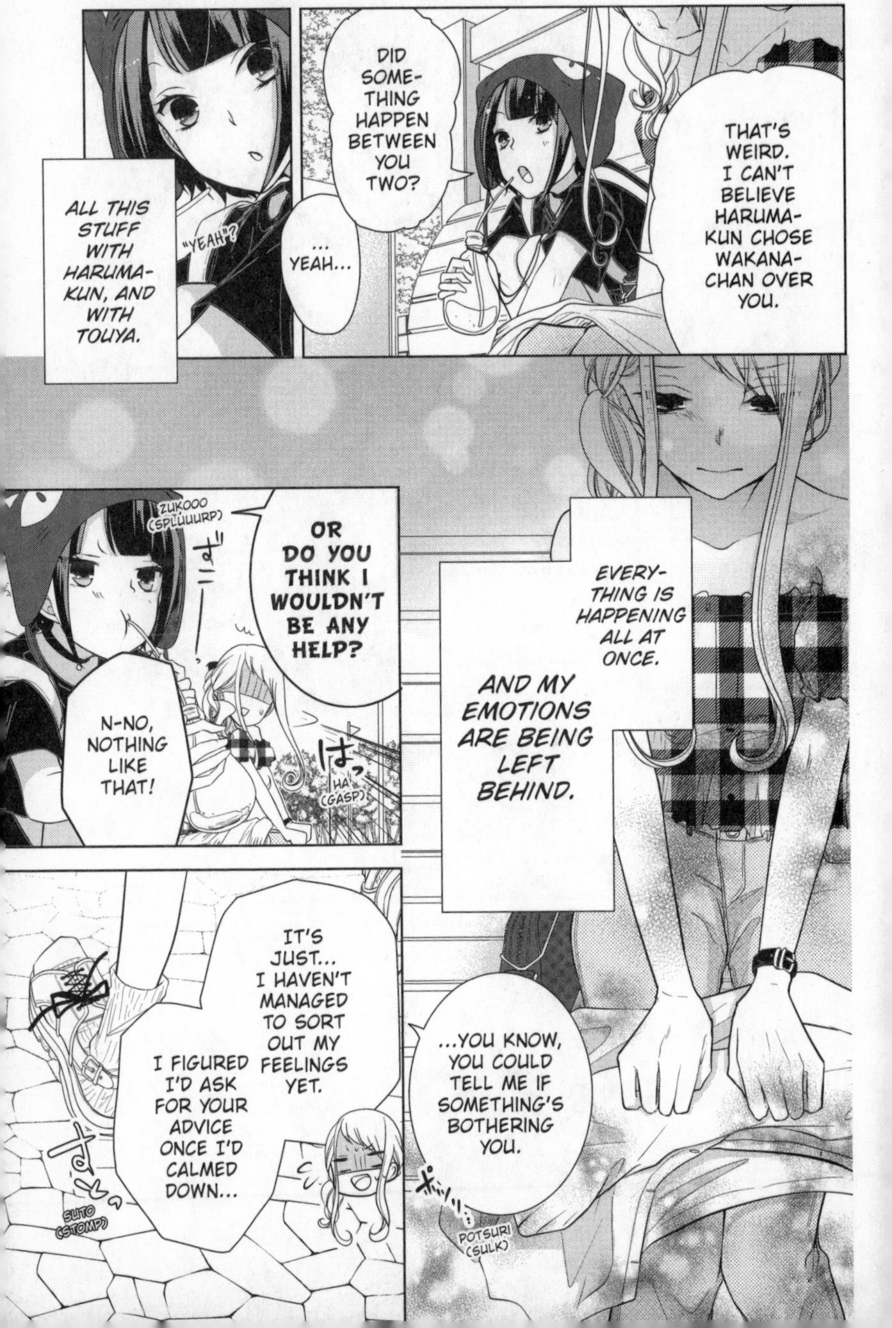

THAT'S WEIRD. I CAN'T BELIEVE HARUMA-KUN CHOSE WAKANA-CHAN OVER YOU.
DID SOME-THING HAPPEN BETWEEN YOU TWO?
... YEAH...
"YEAH"?
ALL THIS STUFF WITH HARUMA-KUN, AND WITH TOUYA.
EVERY-THING IS HAPPENING ALL AT ONCE.
AND MY EMOTIONS ARE BEING LEFT BEHIND.
...YOU KNOW, YOU COULD TELL ME IF SOMETHING'S BOTHERING YOU.
POTSURI (SULK)
OR DO YOU THINK I WOULDN'T BE ANY HELP?
ZUKOOO (SPLUUURP)
N-NO, NOTHING LIKE THAT!
HA (GASP)
IT'S JUST... I HAVEN'T MANAGED TO SORT OUT MY FEELINGS YET.
I FIGURED I'D ASK FOR YOUR ADVICE ONCE I'D CALMED DOWN...
SUTO (STOMP)

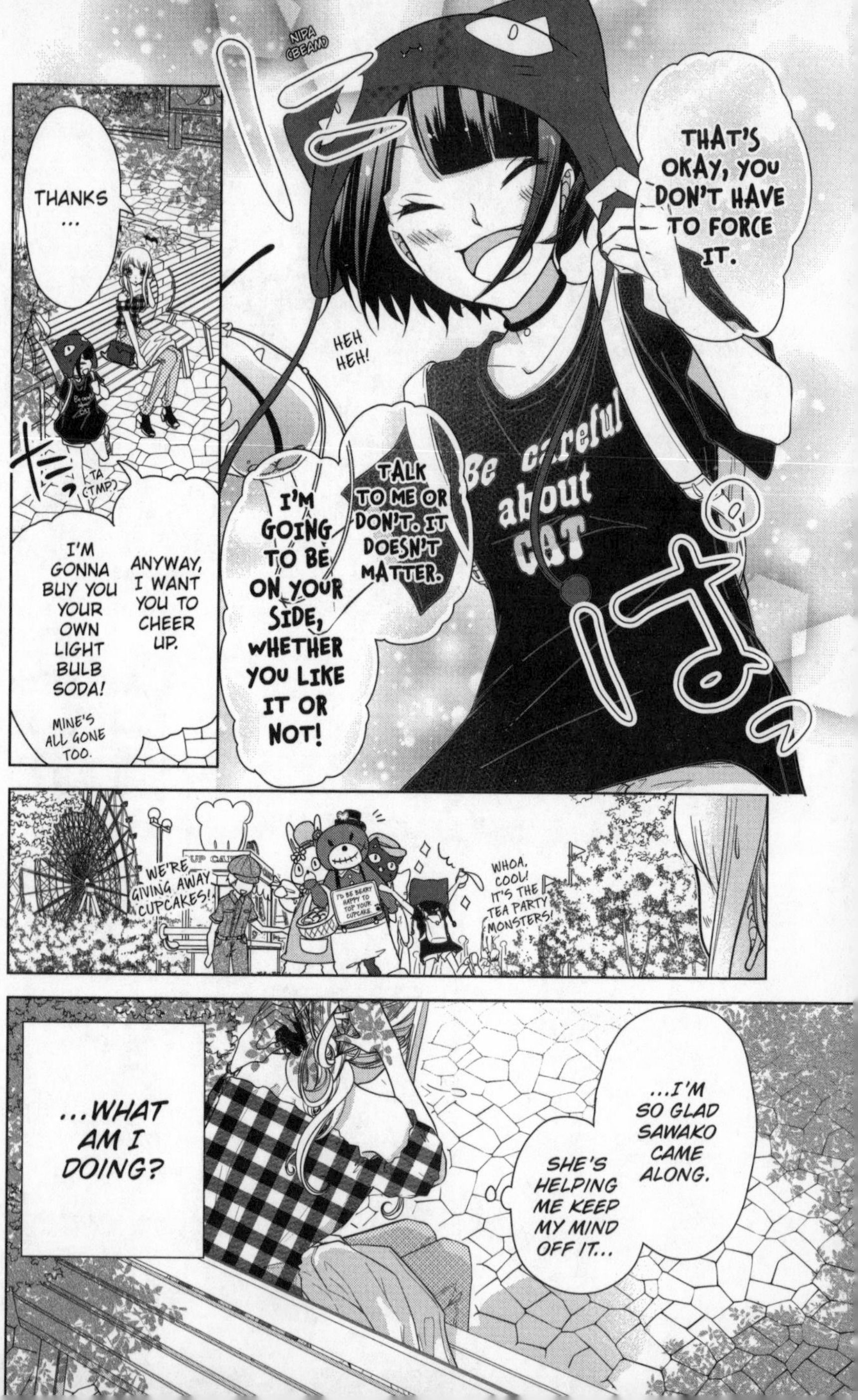
NIPA (BEAM)
THAT'S OKAY, YOU DON'T HAVE TO FORCE IT.
HEH HEH!
Be careful about CAT
TALK TO ME OR DON'T. IT DOESN'T MATTER.
I'M GOING TO BE ON YOUR SIDE, WHETHER YOU LIKE IT OR NOT!
THANKS ...
TA (TMP)
ANYWAY, I WANT YOU TO CHEER UP.
I'M GONNA BUY YOU YOUR OWN LIGHT BULB SODA!
MINE'S ALL GONE TOO.
WHOA, COOL! IT'S THE TEA PARTY MONSTERS!
I'D BE BEARY HAPPY TO TOP YOUR CUPCAKE
WE'RE GIVING AWAY CUPCAKES!
...I'M SO GLAD SAWAKO CAME ALONG.
SHE'S HELPING ME KEEP MY MIND OFF IT...
...WHAT AM I DOING?

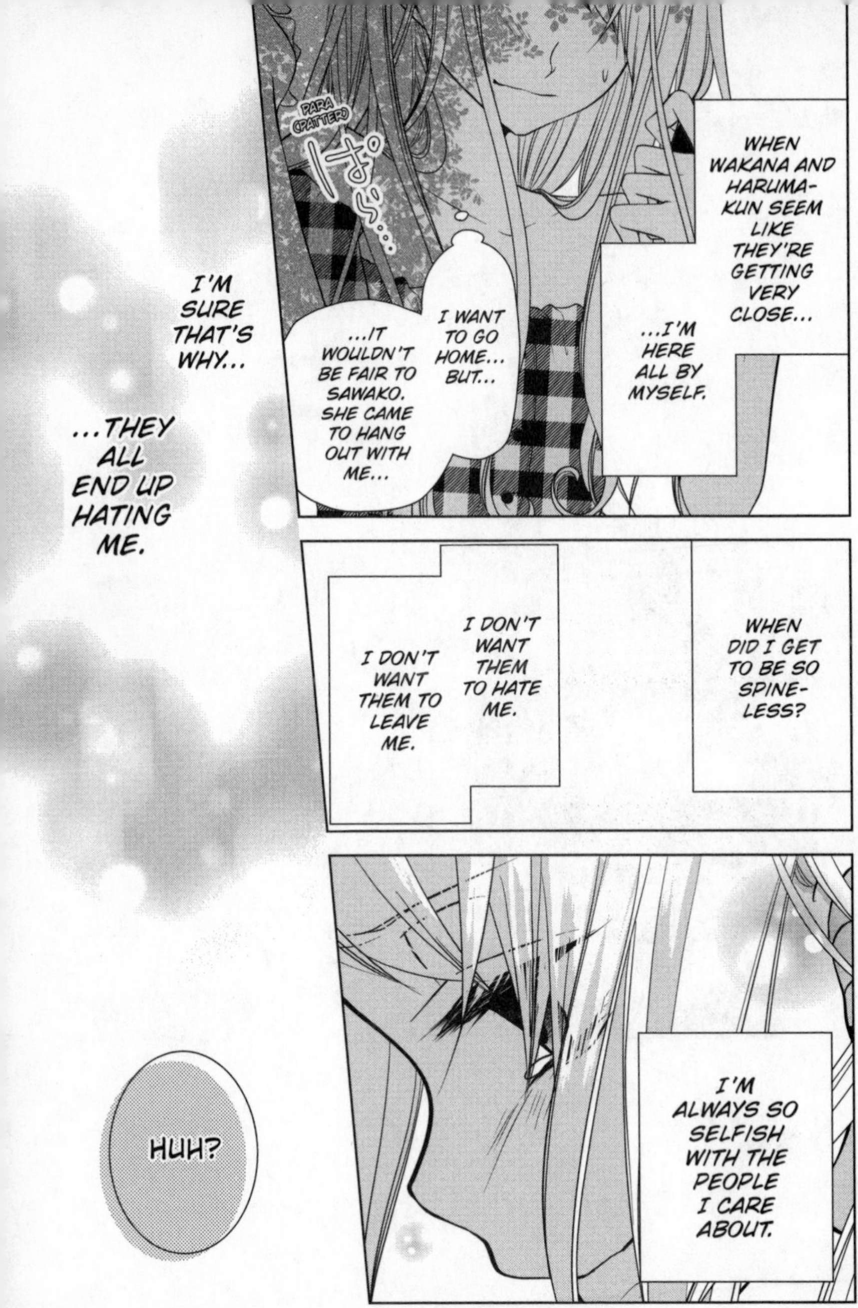
WHEN WAKANA AND HARUMA-KUN SEEM LIKE THEY'RE GETTING VERY CLOSE...
...I'M HERE ALL BY MYSELF.
PARA (PATTER)
I WANT TO GO HOME... BUT...
...IT WOULDN'T BE FAIR TO SAWAKO. SHE CAME TO HANG OUT WITH ME...
I'M SURE THAT'S WHY...
...THEY ALL END UP HATING ME.
WHEN DID I GET TO BE SO SPINELESS?
I DON'T WANT THEM TO HATE ME.
I DON'T WANT THEM TO LEAVE ME.
I'M ALWAYS SO SELFISH WITH THE PEOPLE I CARE ABOUT.
HUH?

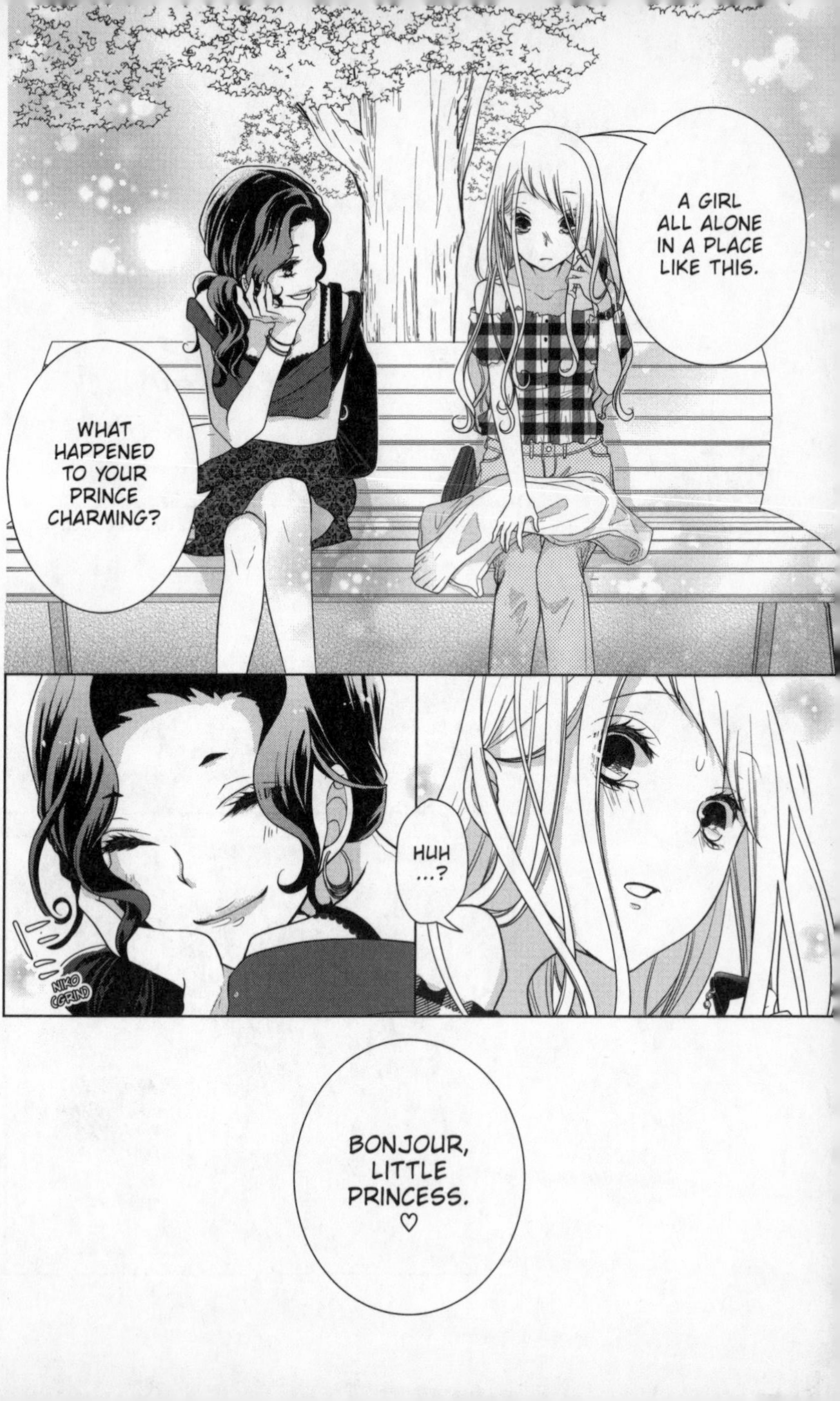
A GIRL ALL ALONE IN A PLACE LIKE THIS.
WHAT HAPPENED TO YOUR PRINCE CHARMING?
HUH ...?
NIKO (GRIN)
BONJOUR, LITTLE PRINCESS. ♡

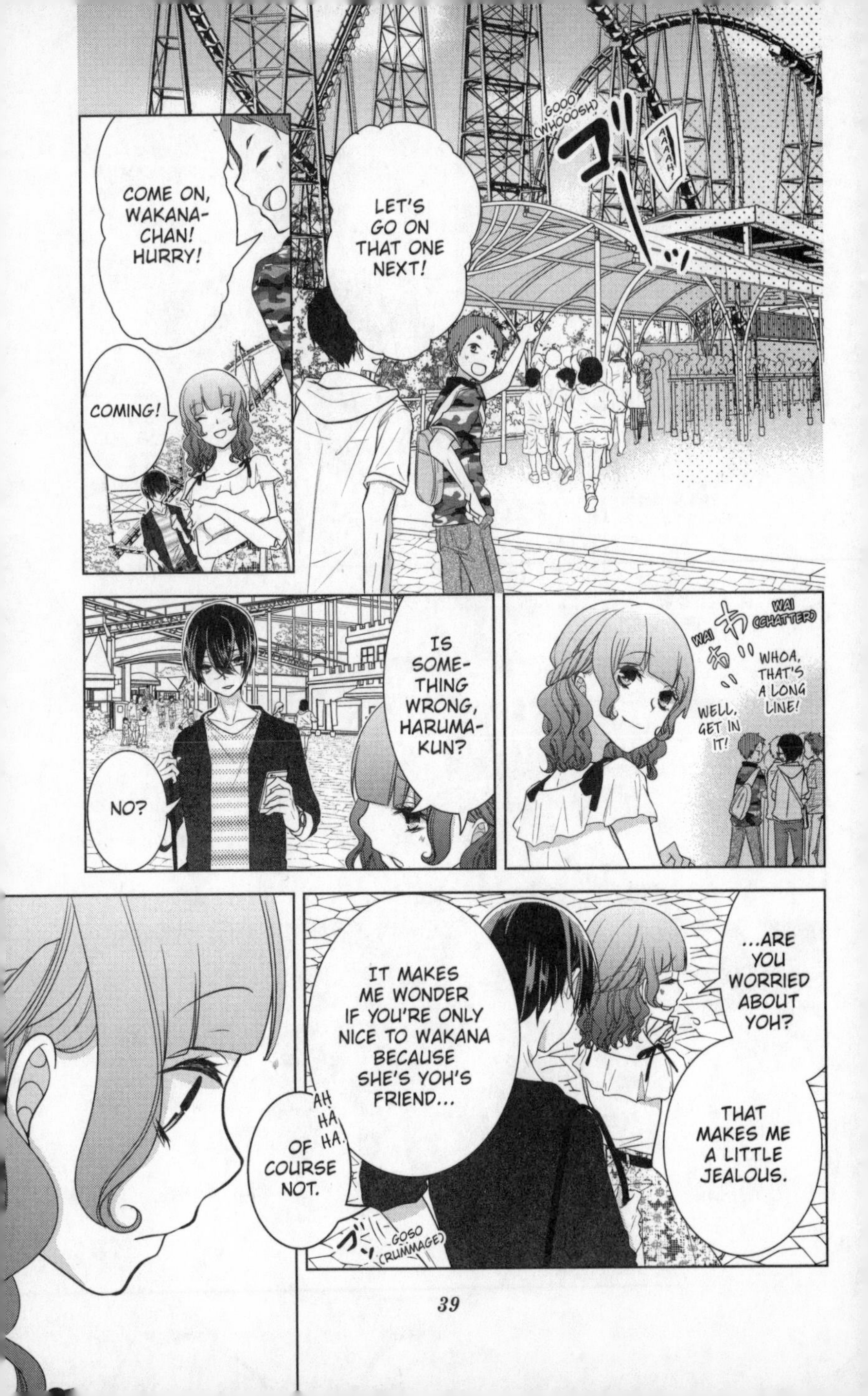
GOOO (WHOOOSH)
AAAAAH!
LET'S GO ON THAT ONE NEXT!
COME ON, WAKANA-CHAN! HURRY!
COMING!
WAI (CHATTER)
WAI
WHOA, THAT'S A LONG LINE!
WELL, GET IN IT!
IS SOMETHING WRONG, HARUMA-KUN?
NO?
...ARE YOU WORRIED ABOUT YOH?
THAT MAKES ME A LITTLE JEALOUS.
IT MAKES ME WONDER IF YOU'RE ONLY NICE TO WAKANA BECAUSE SHE'S YOH'S FRIEND...
AH HA HA!
OF COURSE NOT.
GOSO (RUMMAGE)

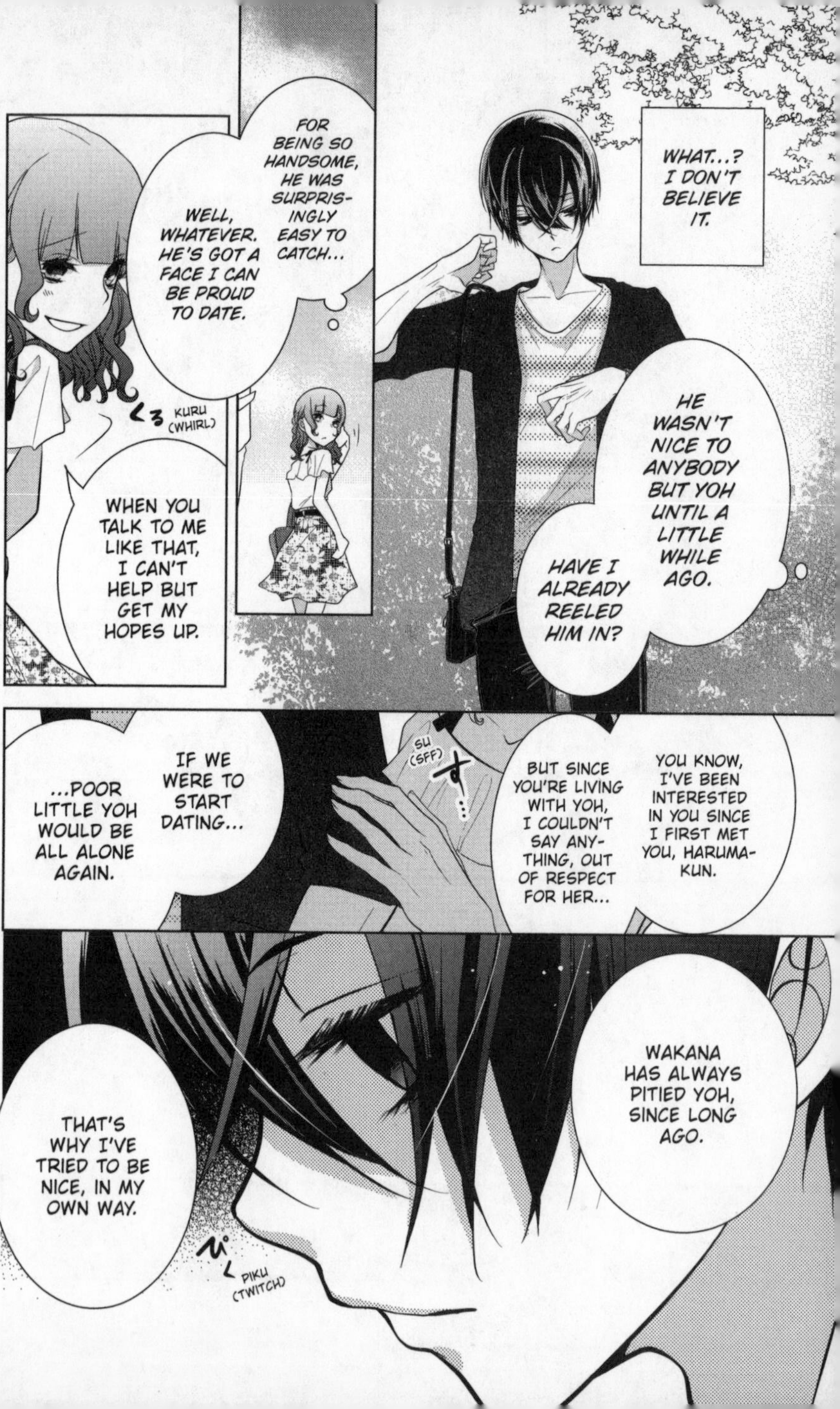
WHAT...? I DON'T BELIEVE IT.
HE WASN'T NICE TO ANYBODY BUT YOH UNTIL A LITTLE WHILE AGO.
HAVE I ALREADY REELED HIM IN?
FOR BEING SO HANDSOME, HE WAS SURPRIS-INGLY EASY TO CATCH...
WELL, WHATEVER. HE'S GOT A FACE I CAN BE PROUD TO DATE.
くる KURU (WHIRL)
WHEN YOU TALK TO ME LIKE THAT, I CAN'T HELP BUT GET MY HOPES UP.
YOU KNOW, I'VE BEEN INTERESTED IN YOU SINCE I FIRST MET YOU, HARUMA-KUN.
BUT SINCE YOU'RE LIVING WITH YOH, I COULDN'T SAY ANY-THING, OUT OF RESPECT FOR HER...
す... SU (SFF)
IF WE WERE TO START DATING...
...POOR LITTLE YOH WOULD BE ALL ALONE AGAIN.
WAKANA HAS ALWAYS PITIED YOH, SINCE LONG AGO.
ぴく PIKU (TWITCH)
THAT'S WHY I'VE TRIED TO BE NICE, IN MY OWN WAY.

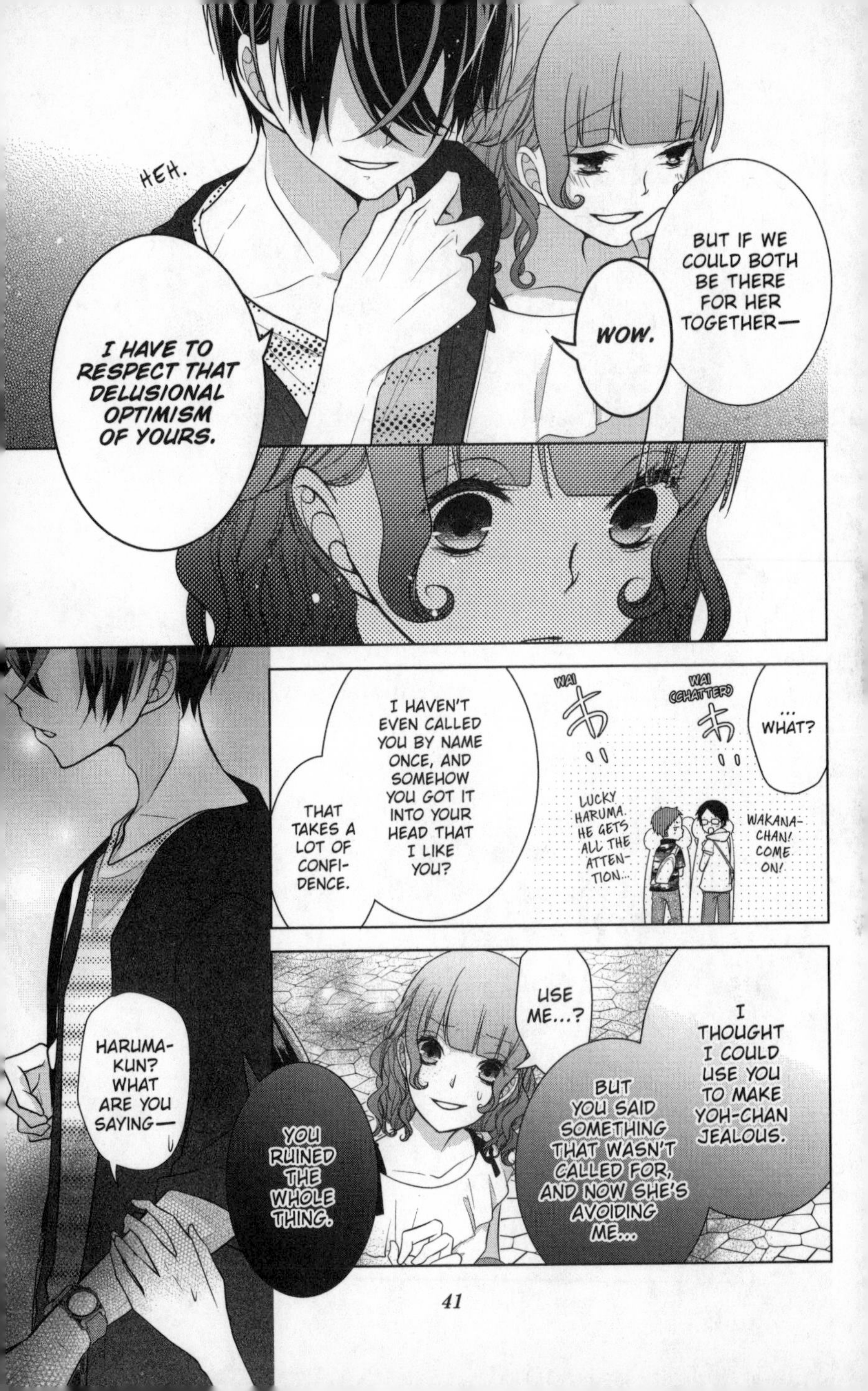
BUT IF WE COULD BOTH BE THERE FOR HER TOGETHER—
WOW.
HEH.
I HAVE TO RESPECT THAT DELUSIONAL OPTIMISM OF YOURS.
... WHAT?
WAI
WAI (CHATTER)
WAKANA-CHAN! COME ON!
LUCKY HARUMA. HE GETS ALL THE ATTENTION...
I HAVEN'T EVEN CALLED YOU BY NAME ONCE, AND SOMEHOW YOU GOT IT INTO YOUR HEAD THAT I LIKE YOU?
THAT TAKES A LOT OF CONFIDENCE.
I THOUGHT I COULD USE YOU TO MAKE YOH-CHAN JEALOUS.
USE ME...?
BUT YOU SAID SOMETHING THAT WASN'T CALLED FOR, AND NOW SHE'S AVOIDING ME...
YOU RUINED THE WHOLE THING.
HARUMA-KUN? WHAT ARE YOU SAYING—

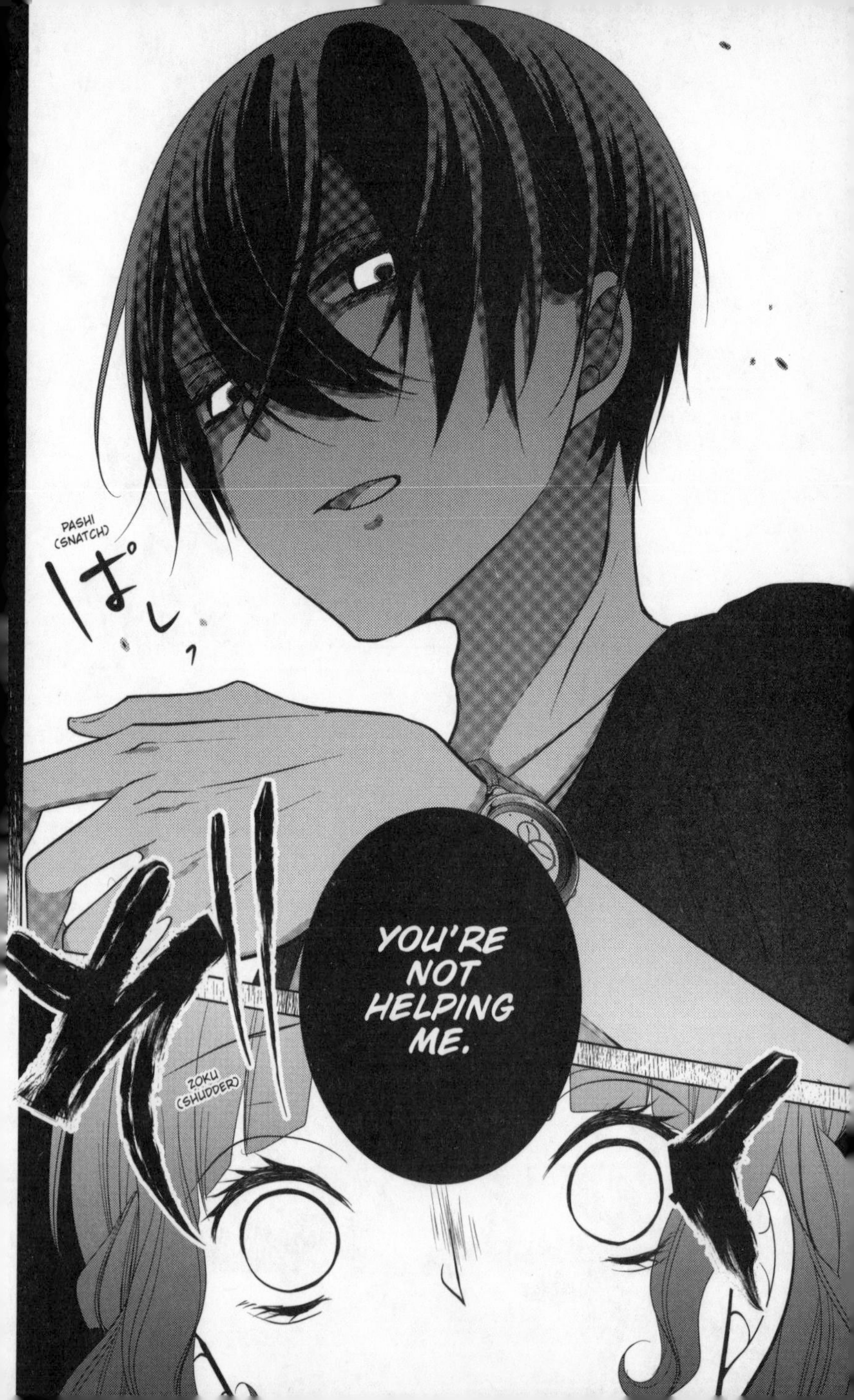
PASHI (SNATCH)
ぱしっ
ZOKU (SHUDDER)
YOU'RE NOT HELPING ME.

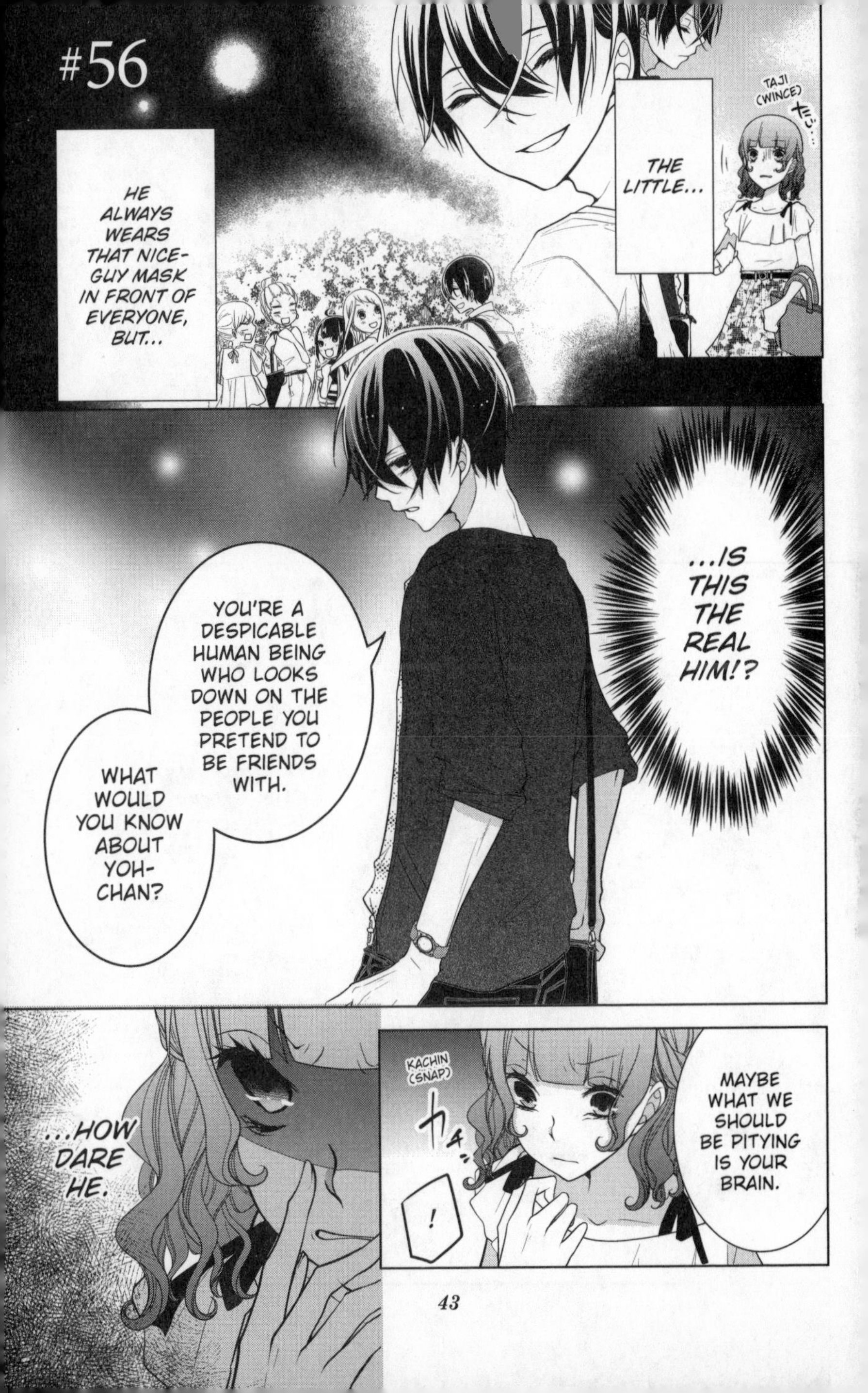
#56
TAJI (WINCE)
THE LITTLE...
HE ALWAYS WEARS THAT NICE-GUY MASK IN FRONT OF EVERYONE, BUT...
...IS THIS THE REAL HIM!?
YOU'RE A DESPICABLE HUMAN BEING WHO LOOKS DOWN ON THE PEOPLE YOU PRETEND TO BE FRIENDS WITH.
WHAT WOULD YOU KNOW ABOUT YOH-CHAN?
MAYBE WHAT WE SHOULD BE PITYING IS YOUR BRAIN.
KACHIN (SNAP)
!
...HOW DARE HE.

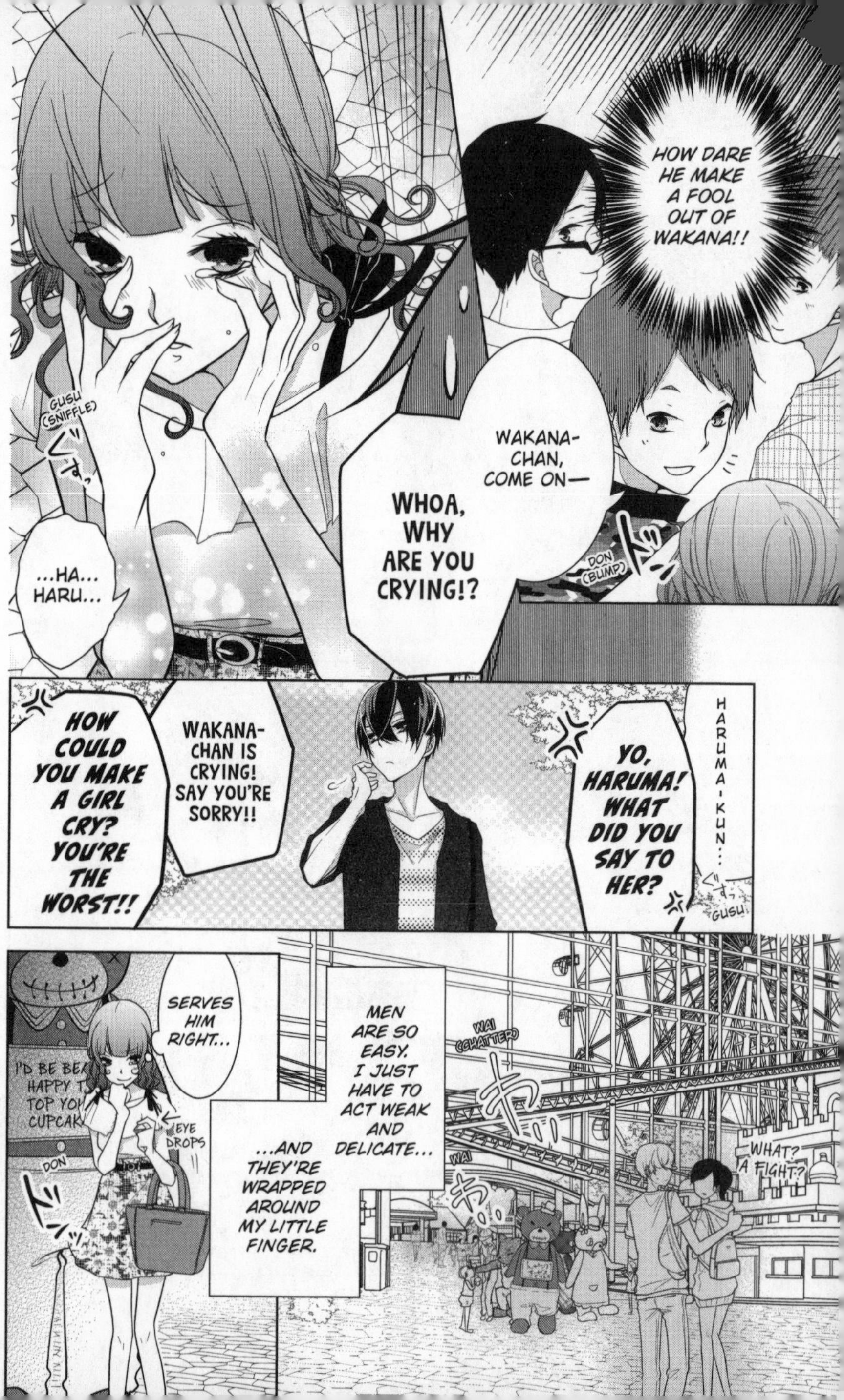
HOW DARE HE MAKE A FOOL OUT OF WAKANA!!
WAKANA-CHAN, COME ON—
DON (BUMP)
WHOA, WHY ARE YOU CRYING!?
GUSU (SNIFFLE)
...HA... HARU...
HARUMA-KUN...
GUSU
YO, HARUMA! WHAT DID YOU SAY TO HER?
WAKANA-CHAN IS CRYING! SAY YOU'RE SORRY!!
HOW COULD YOU MAKE A GIRL CRY? YOU'RE THE WORST!!
WHAT? A FIGHT!?
WAI (CHATTER)
WAI
MEN ARE SO EASY. I JUST HAVE TO ACT WEAK AND DELICATE...
...AND THEY'RE WRAPPED AROUND MY LITTLE FINGER.
SERVES HIM RIGHT...
EYE DROPS
DON

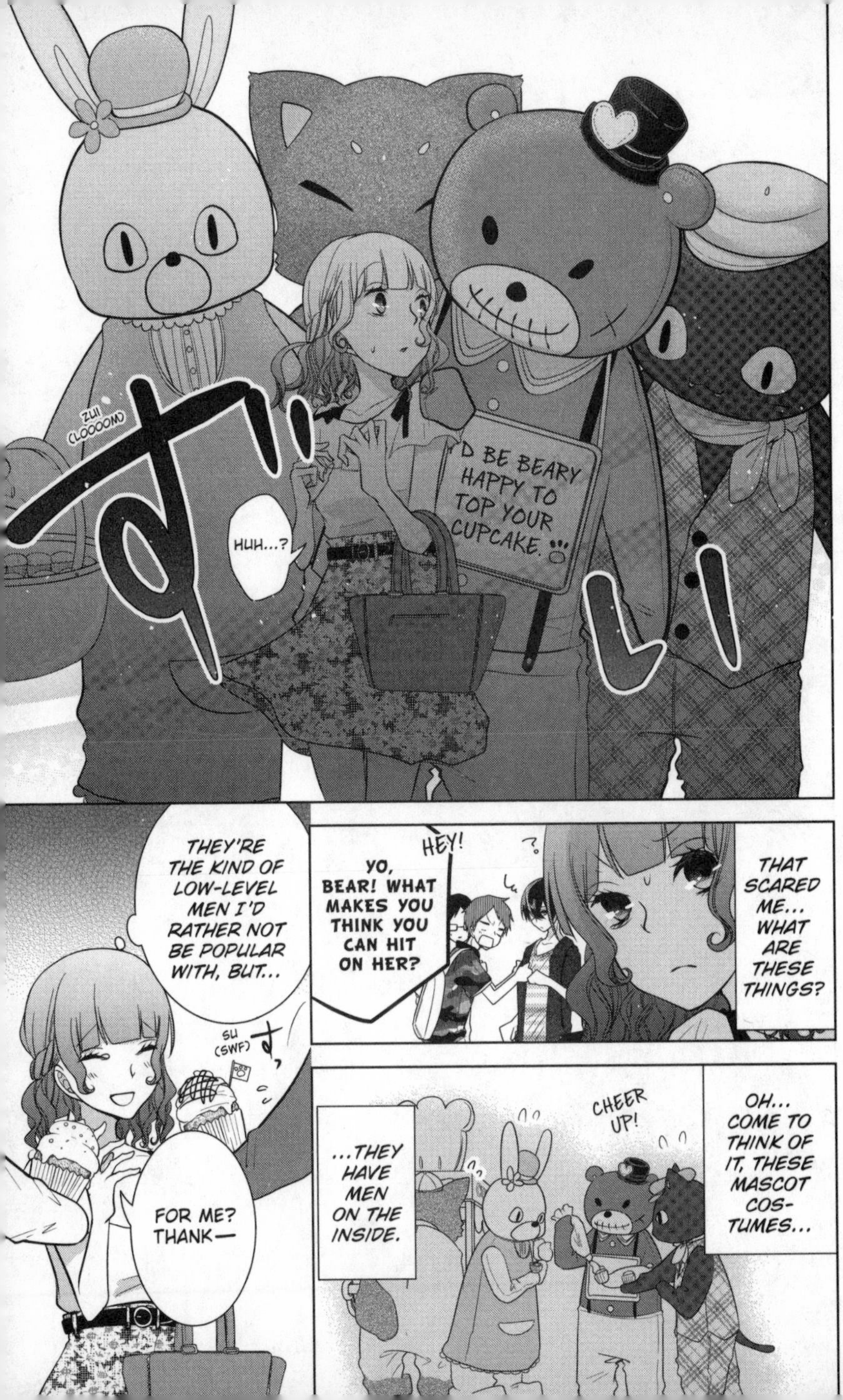
'D BE BEARY HAPPY TO TOP YOUR CUPCAKE.
HUH...?
ZUI (LOOOOM)
THAT SCARED ME... WHAT ARE THESE THINGS?
HEY!
YO, BEAR! WHAT MAKES YOU THINK YOU CAN HIT ON HER?
OH... COME TO THINK OF IT, THESE MASCOT COS-TUMES...
CHEER UP!
...THEY HAVE MEN ON THE INSIDE.
THEY'RE THE KIND OF LOW-LEVEL MEN I'D RATHER NOT BE POPULAR WITH, BUT...
SU (SWF)
FOR ME? THANK—

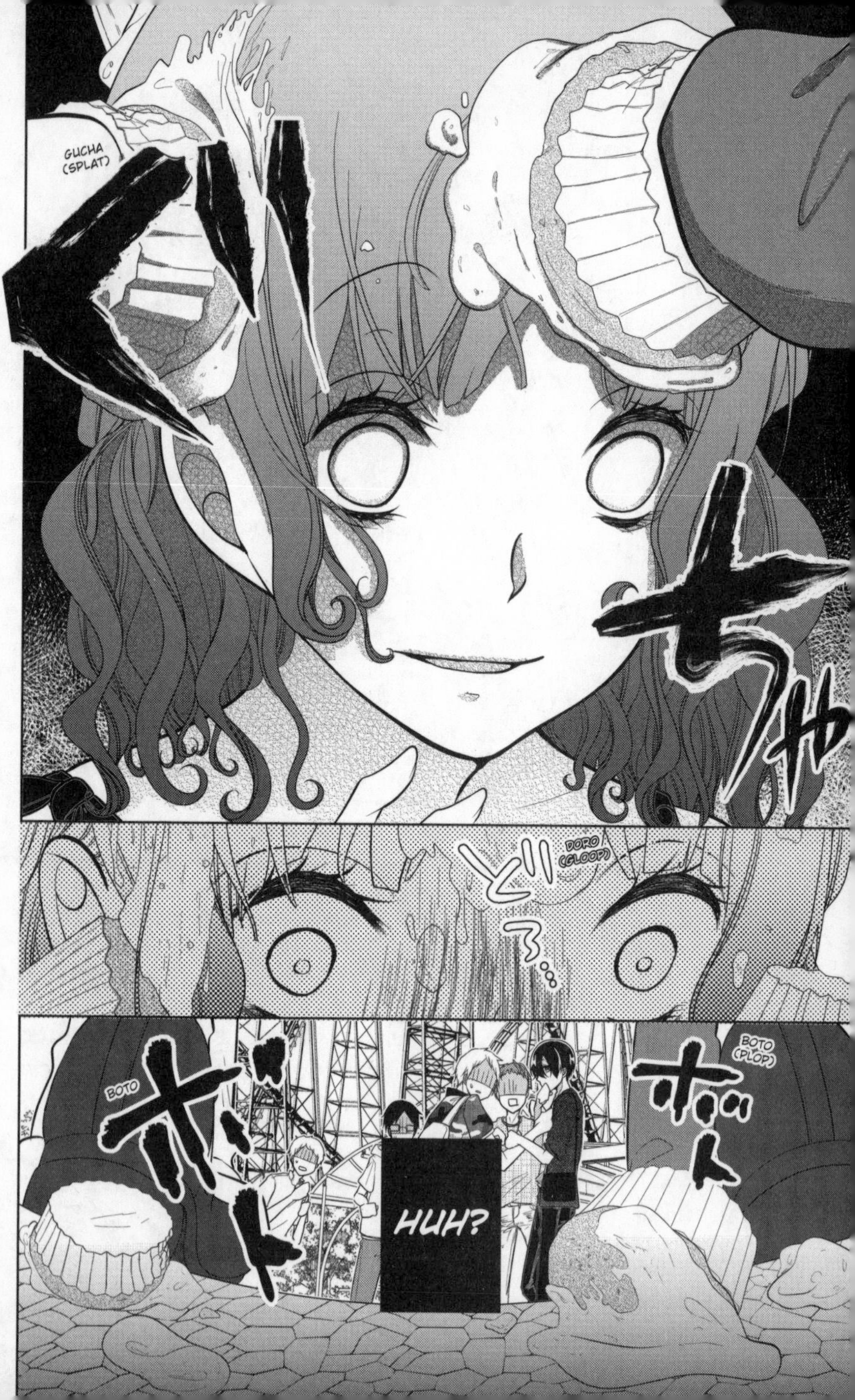

GUCHA (SPLAT)
DORO (GLOOP)
BOTO (PLOP)
HUH?
BOTO

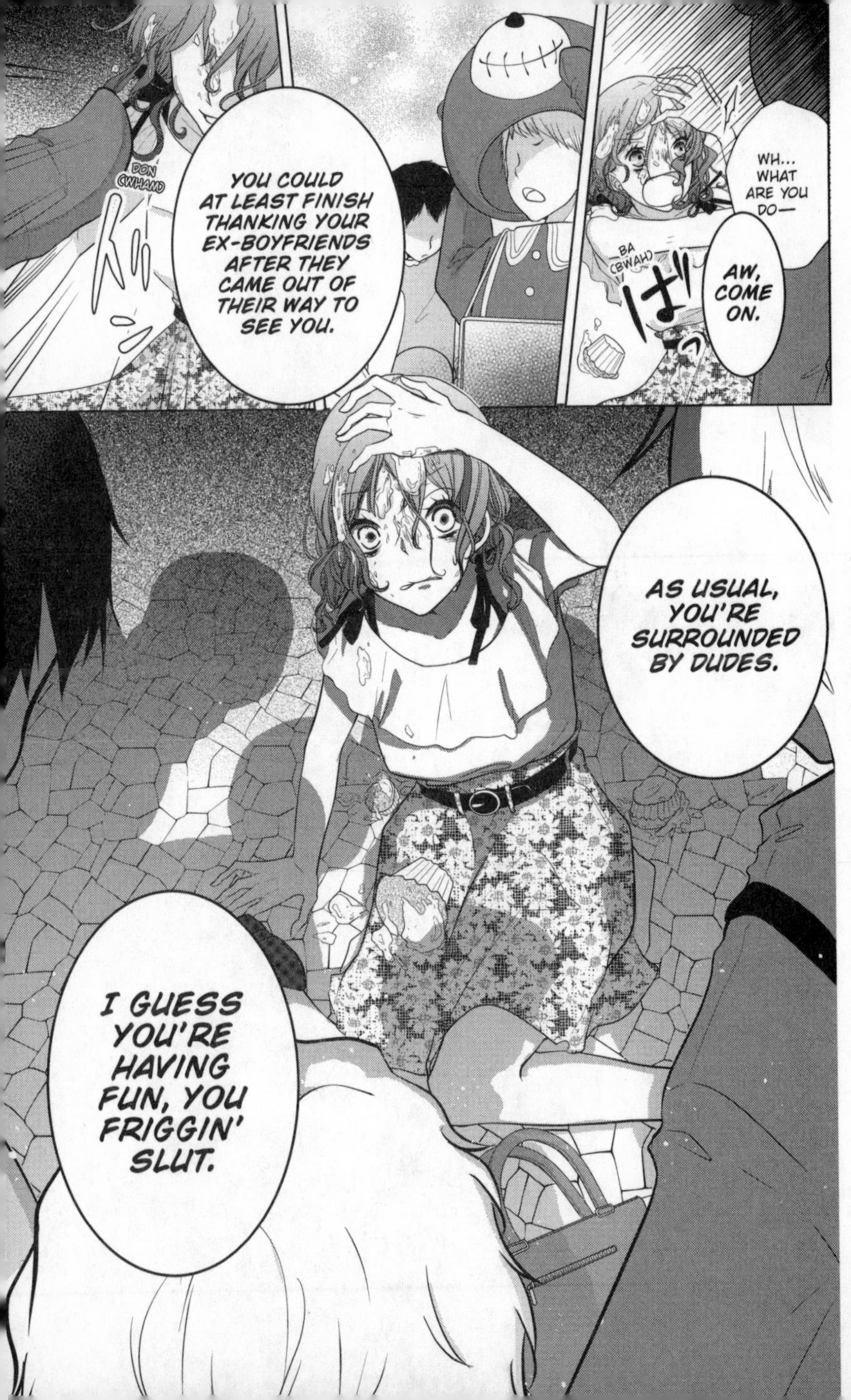
WH... WHAT ARE YOU DO—
BA (BWAH)
AW, COME ON.
DON (WHAM)
YOU COULD AT LEAST FINISH THANKING YOUR EX-BOYFRIENDS AFTER THEY CAME OUT OF THEIR WAY TO SEE YOU.
AS USUAL, YOU'RE SURROUNDED BY DUDES.
I GUESS YOU'RE HAVING FUN, YOU FRIGGIN' SLUT.

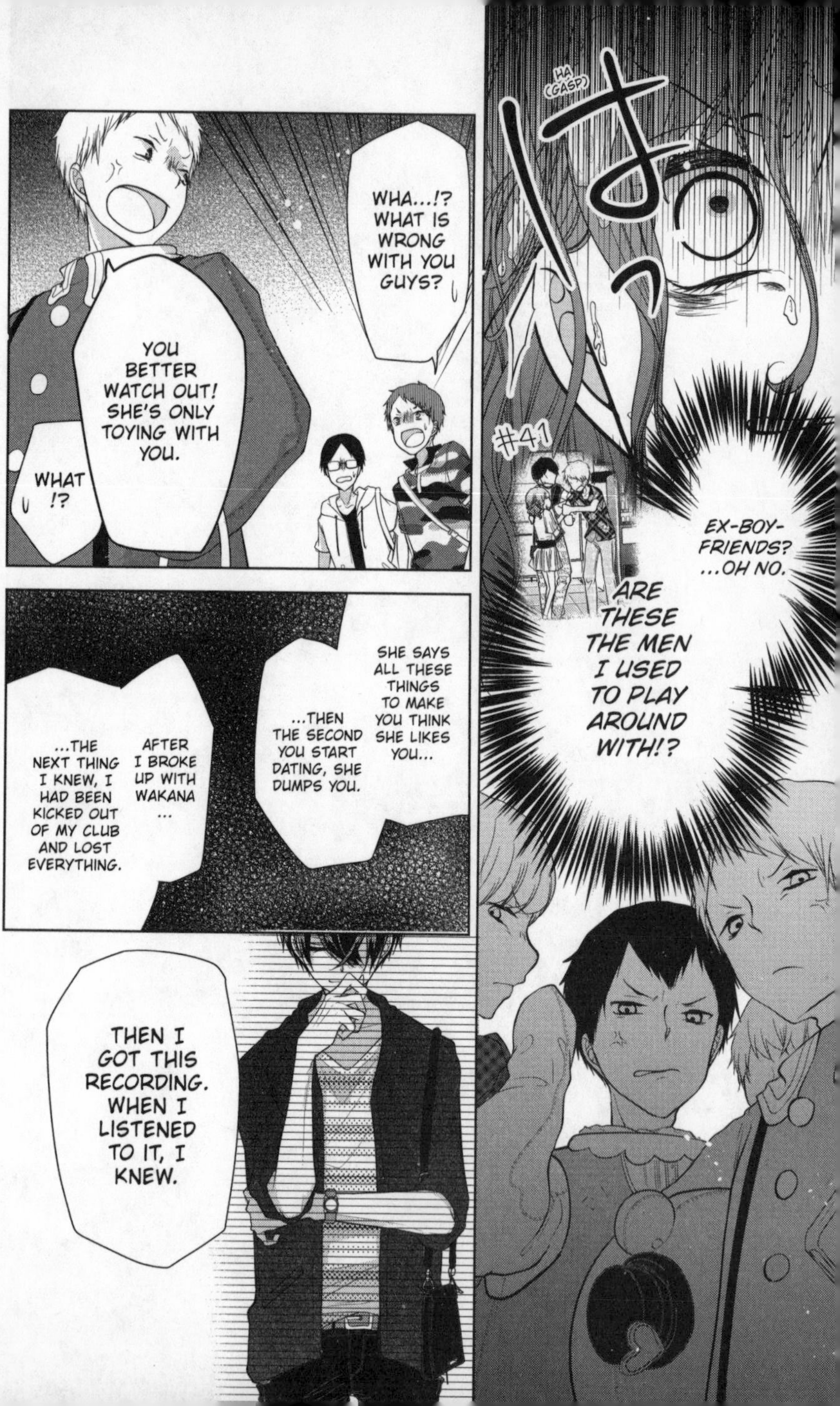
HA (GASP)
はっ
#41
EX-BOY-FRIENDS? ...OH NO.
ARE THESE THE MEN I USED TO PLAY AROUND WITH!?
WHA...!? WHAT IS WRONG WITH YOU GUYS?
YOU BETTER WATCH OUT! SHE'S ONLY TOYING WITH YOU.
WHAT !?
SHE SAYS ALL THESE THINGS TO MAKE YOU THINK SHE LIKES YOU...
...THEN THE SECOND YOU START DATING, SHE DUMPS YOU.
AFTER I BROKE UP WITH WAKANA ...
...THE NEXT THING I KNEW, I HAD BEEN KICKED OUT OF MY CLUB AND LOST EVERYTHING.
THEN I GOT THIS RECORDING. WHEN I LISTENED TO IT, I KNEW.

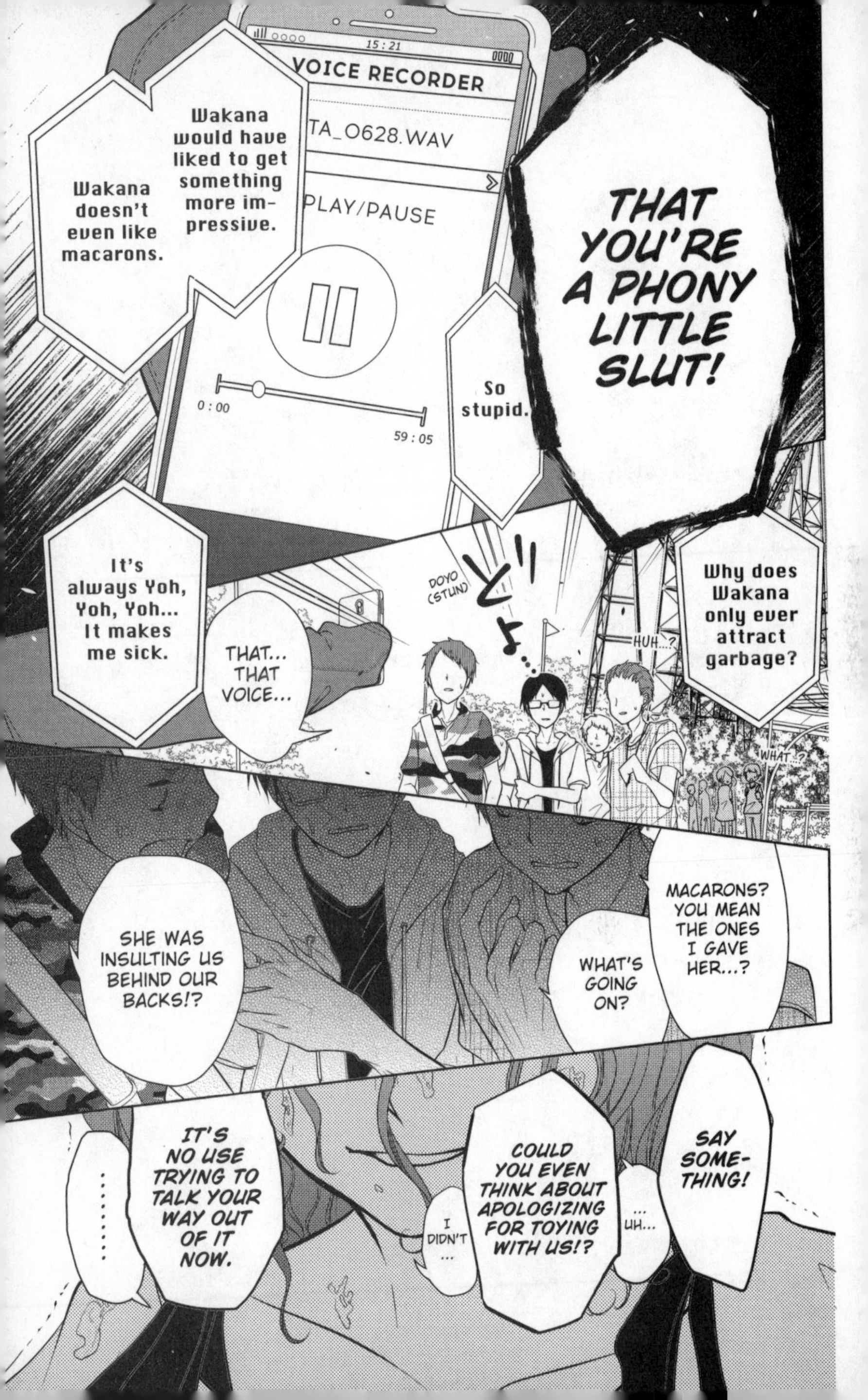
THAT YOU'RE A PHONY LITTLE SLUT!
Wakana would have liked to get something more impressive.
Wakana doesn't even like macarons.
VOICE RECORDER
TA_0628.WAV
PLAY/PAUSE
0 : 00
59 : 05
So stupid.
Why does Wakana only ever attract garbage?
HUH...?
DOYO (STUN)
THAT... THAT VOICE...
It's always Yoh, Yoh, Yoh... It makes me sick.
WHAT...?
MACARONS? YOU MEAN THE ONES I GAVE HER...?
WHAT'S GOING ON?
SHE WAS INSULTING US BEHIND OUR BACKS!?
SAY SOME-THING!
...UH...
COULD YOU EVEN THINK ABOUT APOLOGIZING FOR TOYING WITH US!?
I DIDN'T ...
IT'S NO USE TRYING TO TALK YOUR WAY OUT OF IT NOW.
......

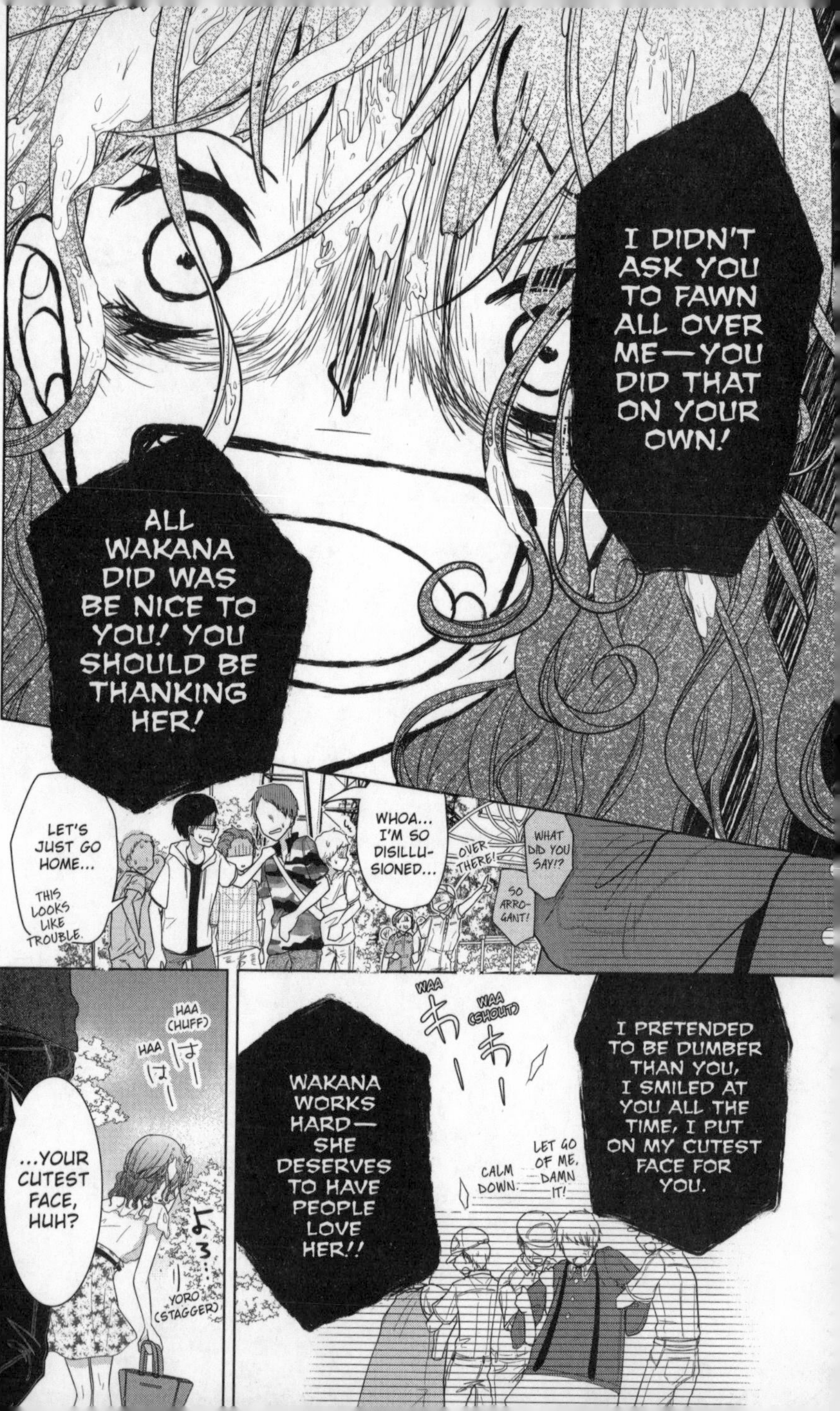
I DIDN'T ASK YOU TO FAWN ALL OVER ME—YOU DID THAT ON YOUR OWN!
ALL WAKANA DID WAS BE NICE TO YOU! YOU SHOULD BE THANKING HER!
WHAT DID YOU SAY!?
SO ARRO-GANT!
OVER THERE!
WHOA... I'M SO DISILLU-SIONED...
LET'S JUST GO HOME...
THIS LOOKS LIKE TROUBLE.
I PRETENDED TO BE DUMBER THAN YOU, I SMILED AT YOU ALL THE TIME, I PUT ON MY CUTEST FACE FOR YOU.
WAA (SHOUT)
WAA
LET GO OF ME, DAMN IT!
CALM DOWN.
WAKANA WORKS HARD—SHE DESERVES TO HAVE PEOPLE LOVE HER!!
HAA (CHUFF)
HAA
...YOUR CUTEST FACE, HUH?
YORO (STAGGER)

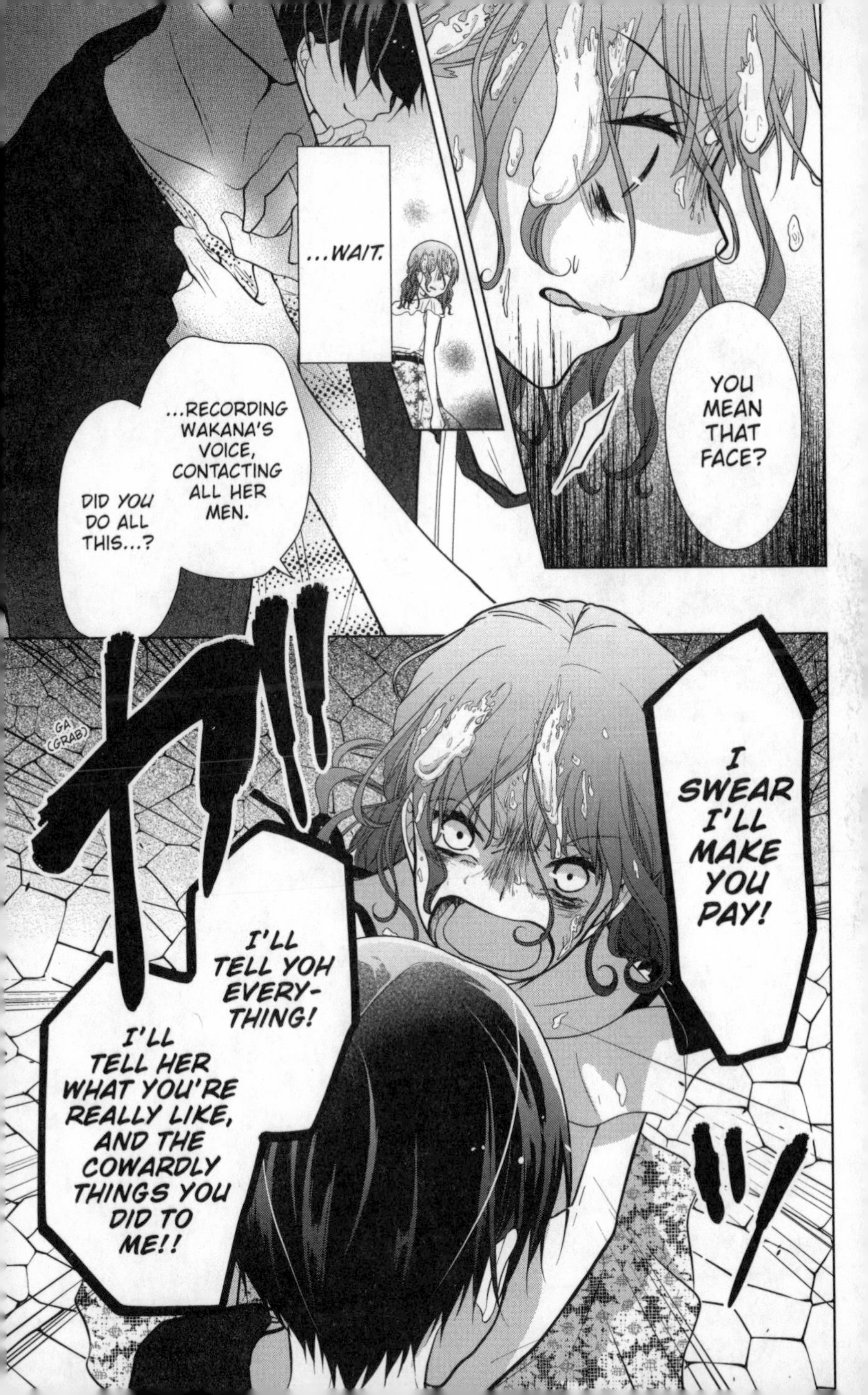
YOU MEAN THAT FACE?
...WAIT.
...RECORDING WAKANA'S VOICE, CONTACTING ALL HER MEN.
DID YOU DO ALL THIS...?
I SWEAR I'LL MAKE YOU PAY!
GA (GRAB)
I'LL TELL YOH EVERY-THING!
I'LL TELL HER WHAT YOU'RE REALLY LIKE, AND THE COWARDLY THINGS YOU DID TO ME!!

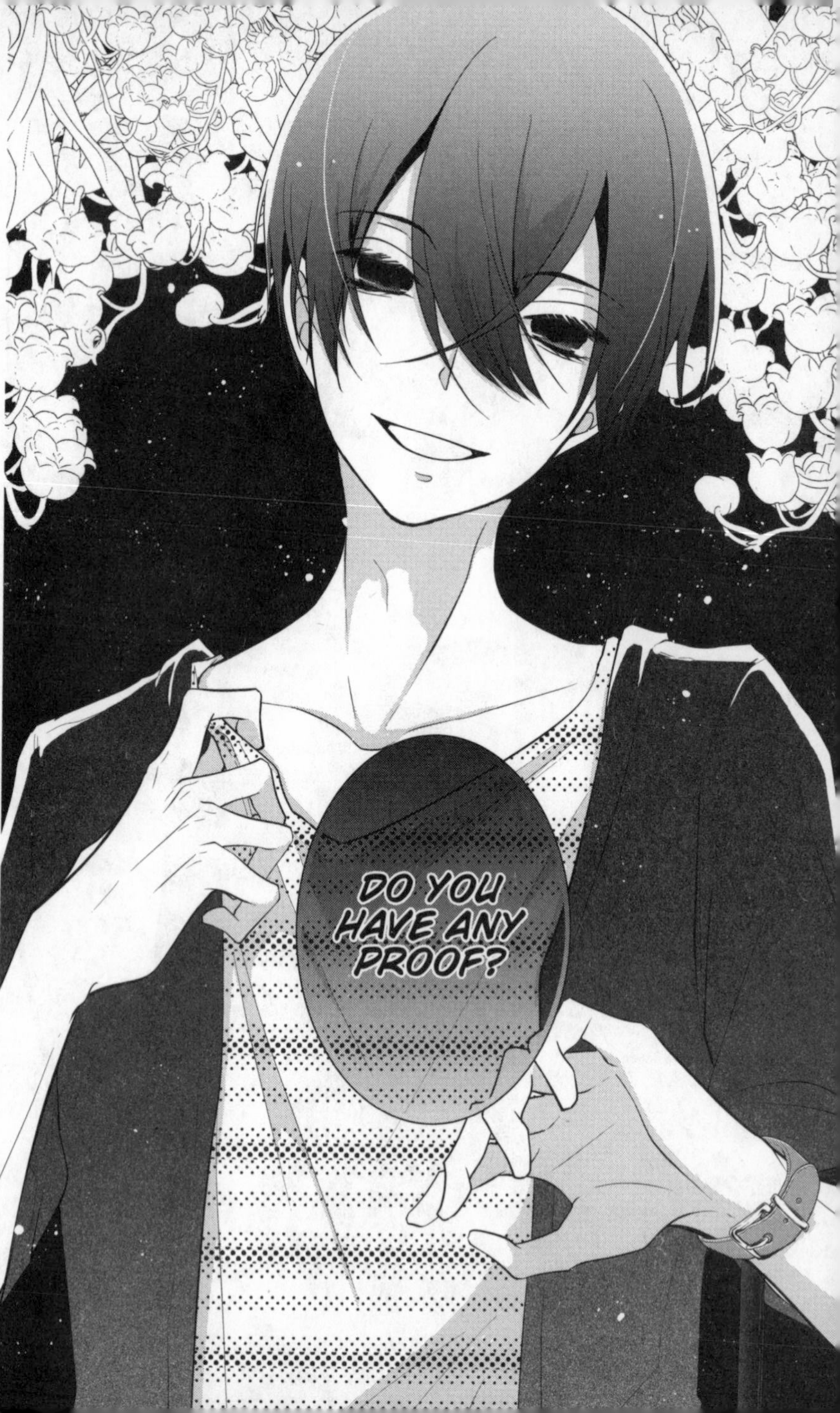
DO YOU HAVE ANY PROOF?

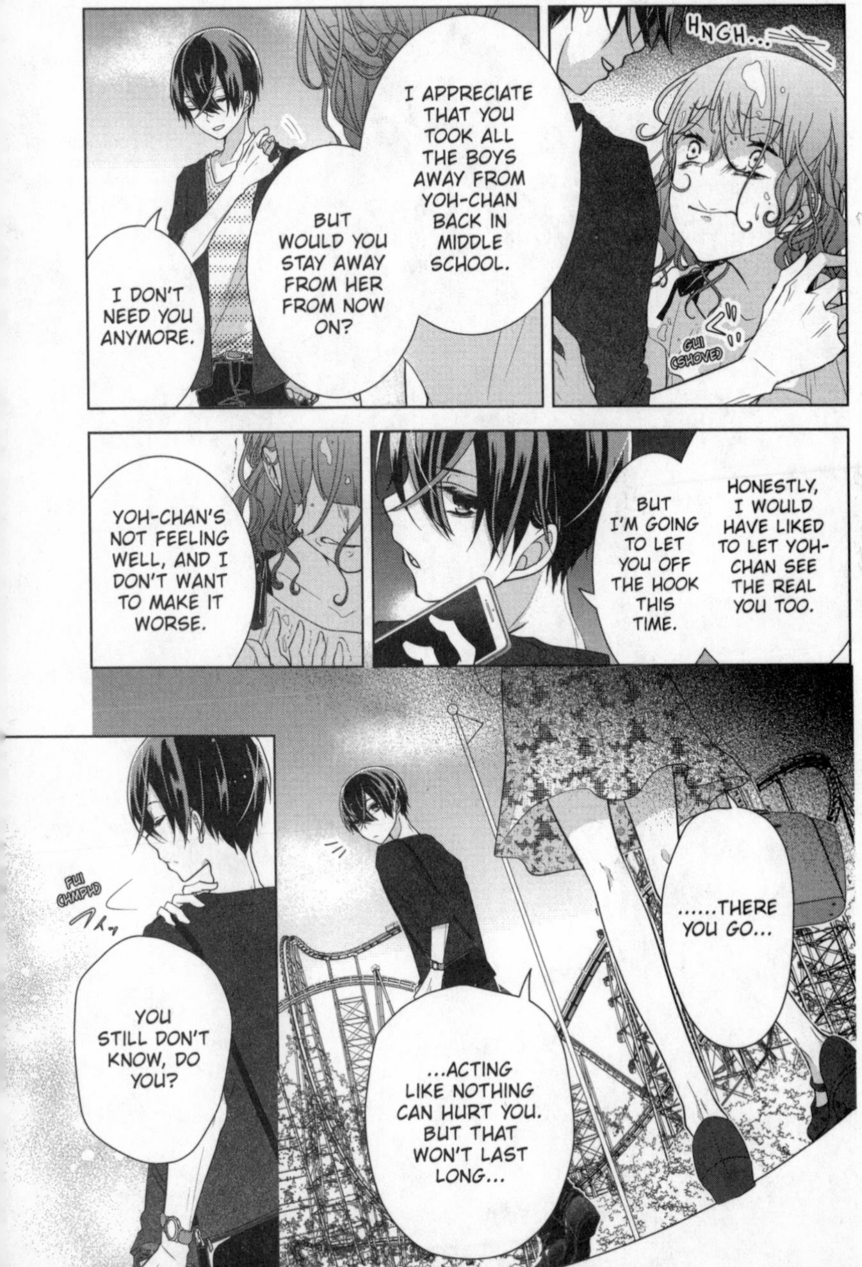
HNGH...
GUI (SHOVED)
I APPRECIATE THAT YOU TOOK ALL THE BOYS AWAY FROM YOH-CHAN BACK IN MIDDLE SCHOOL.
BUT WOULD YOU STAY AWAY FROM HER FROM NOW ON?
I DON'T NEED YOU ANYMORE.
HONESTLY, I WOULD HAVE LIKED TO LET YOH-CHAN SEE THE REAL YOU TOO.
BUT I'M GOING TO LET YOU OFF THE HOOK THIS TIME.
YOH-CHAN'S NOT FEELING WELL, AND I DON'T WANT TO MAKE IT WORSE.
......THERE YOU GO...
...ACTING LIKE NOTHING CAN HURT YOU. BUT THAT WON'T LAST LONG...
FUI CHMPHD
YOU STILL DON'T KNOW, DO YOU?

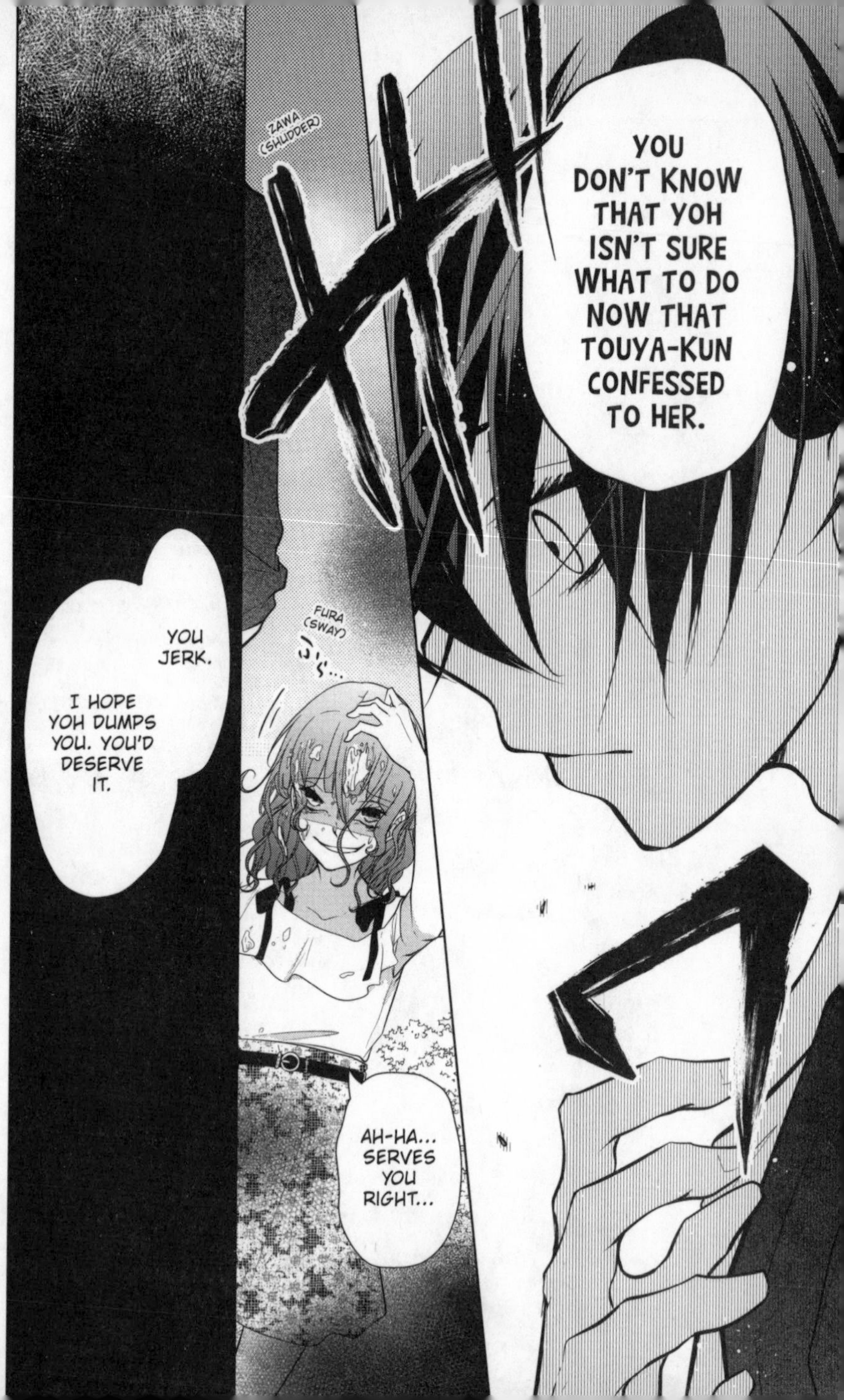
YOU DON'T KNOW THAT YOH ISN'T SURE WHAT TO DO NOW THAT TOUYA-KUN CONFESSED TO HER.
ZAWA (SHUDDER)
FURA (SWAY)
AH-HA... SERVES YOU RIGHT...
YOU JERK.
I HOPE YOH DUMPS YOU. YOU'D DESERVE IT.

#57

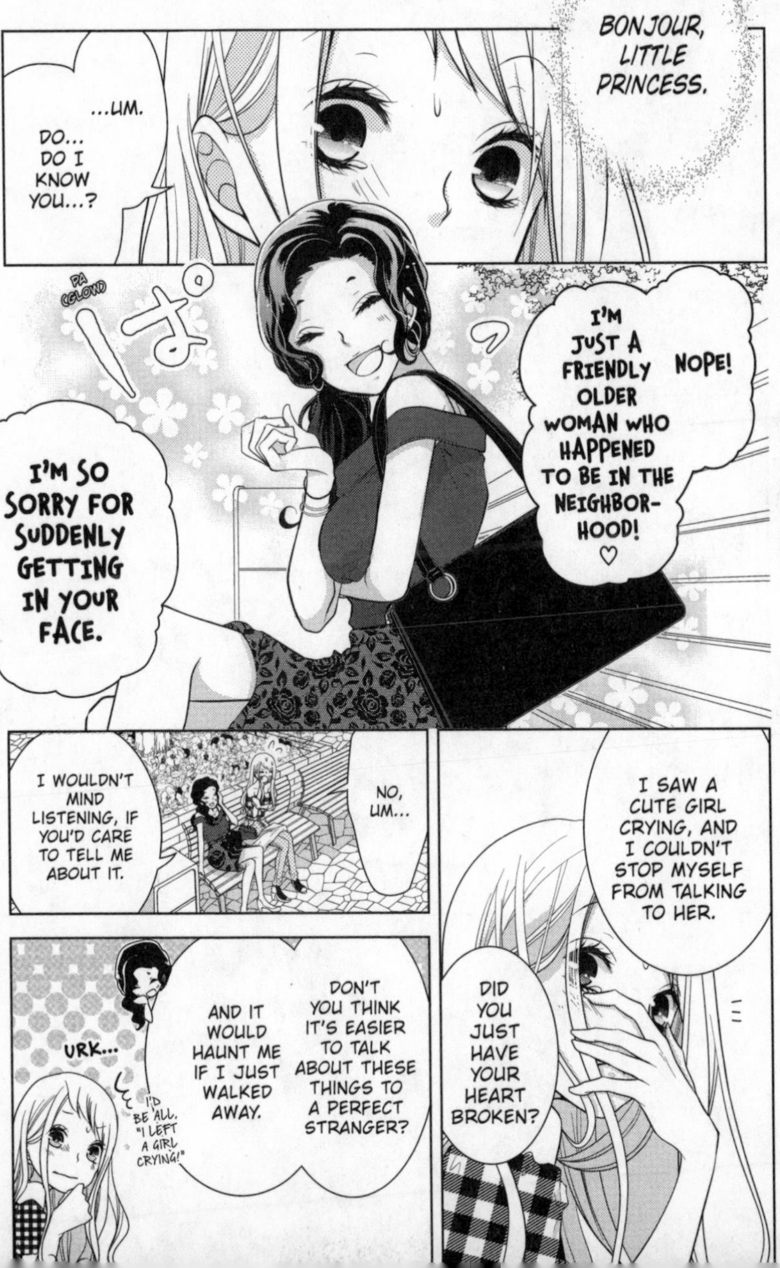
BONJOUR, LITTLE PRINCESS.
...UM.
DO... DO I KNOW YOU...?
PA (GLOW)
NOPE!
I'M JUST A FRIENDLY OLDER WOMAN WHO HAPPENED TO BE IN THE NEIGHBOR-HOOD! ♡
I'M SO SORRY FOR SUDDENLY GETTING IN YOUR FACE.
I SAW A CUTE GIRL CRYING, AND I COULDN'T STOP MYSELF FROM TALKING TO HER.
DID YOU JUST HAVE YOUR HEART BROKEN?
NO, UM...
I WOULDN'T MIND LISTENING, IF YOU'D CARE TO TELL ME ABOUT IT.
DON'T YOU THINK IT'S EASIER TO TALK ABOUT THESE THINGS TO A PERFECT STRANGER?
AND IT WOULD HAUNT ME IF I JUST WALKED AWAY.
URK...
I'D BE ALL, "I LEFT A GIRL CRYING!"

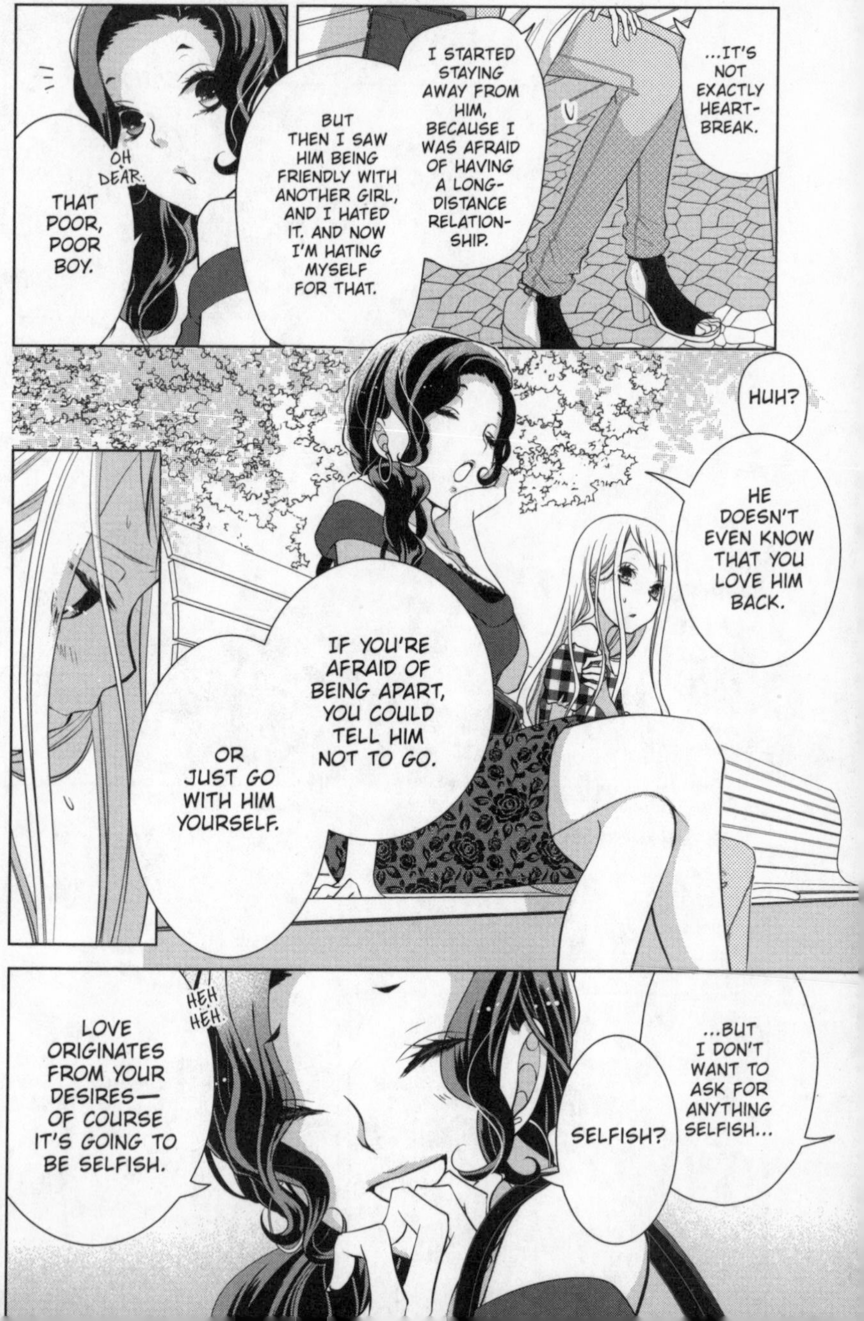

...IT'S NOT EXACTLY HEARTBREAK.
I STARTED STAYING AWAY FROM HIM, BECAUSE I WAS AFRAID OF HAVING A LONG-DISTANCE RELATIONSHIP.
BUT THEN I SAW HIM BEING FRIENDLY WITH ANOTHER GIRL, AND I HATED IT. AND NOW I'M HATING MYSELF FOR THAT.
OH DEAR.
THAT POOR, POOR BOY.
HUH?
HE DOESN'T EVEN KNOW THAT YOU LOVE HIM BACK.
IF YOU'RE AFRAID OF BEING APART, YOU COULD TELL HIM NOT TO GO.
OR JUST GO WITH HIM YOURSELF.
...BUT I DON'T WANT TO ASK FOR ANYTHING SELFISH...
SELFISH?
HEH HEH.
LOVE ORIGINATES FROM YOUR DESIRES— OF COURSE IT'S GOING TO BE SELFISH.

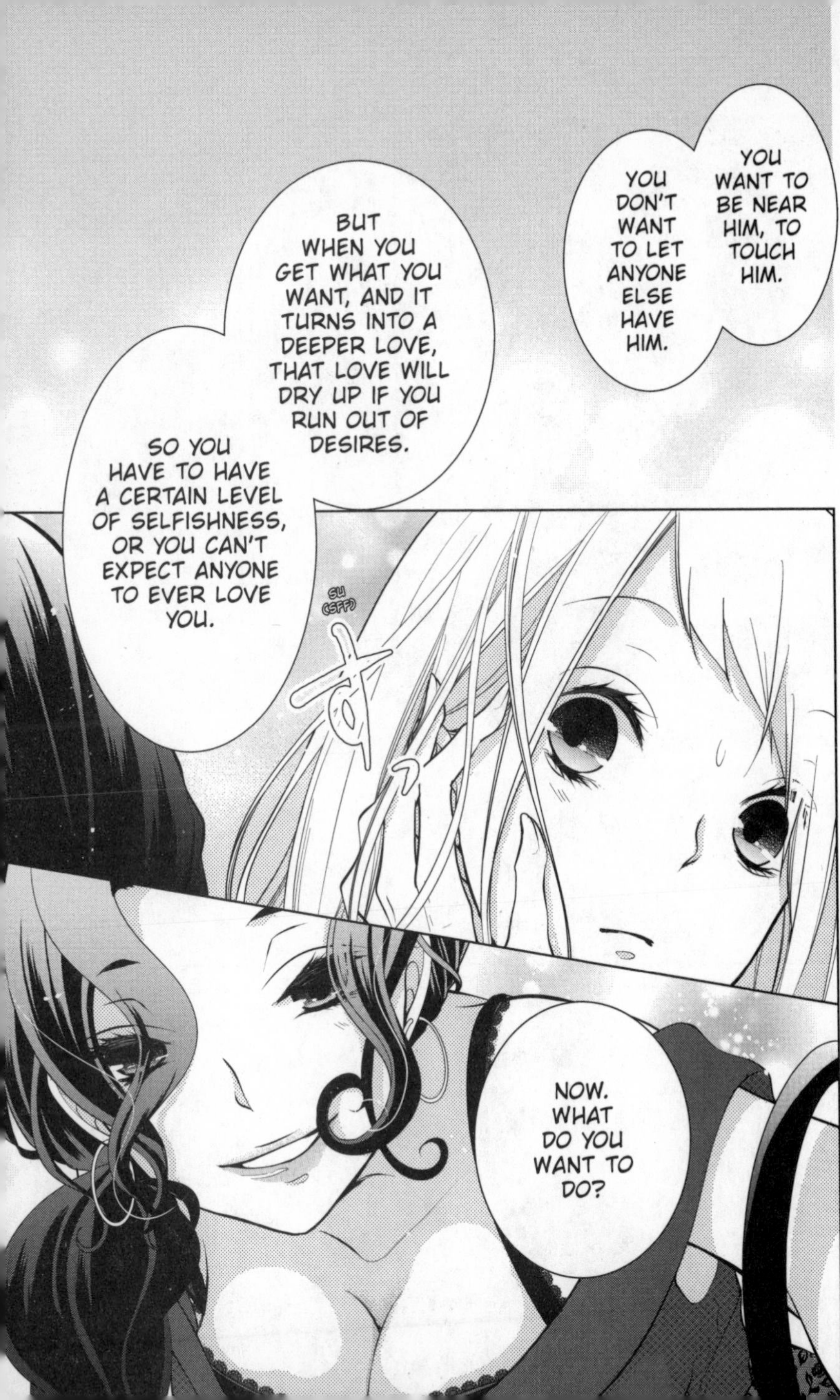
YOU WANT TO BE NEAR HIM, TO TOUCH HIM.
YOU DON'T WANT TO LET ANYONE ELSE HAVE HIM.
BUT WHEN YOU GET WHAT YOU WANT, AND IT TURNS INTO A DEEPER LOVE, THAT LOVE WILL DRY UP IF YOU RUN OUT OF DESIRES.
SO YOU HAVE TO HAVE A CERTAIN LEVEL OF SELFISHNESS, OR YOU CAN'T EXPECT ANYONE TO EVER LOVE YOU.
SU (SFF)
NOW. WHAT DO YOU WANT TO DO?

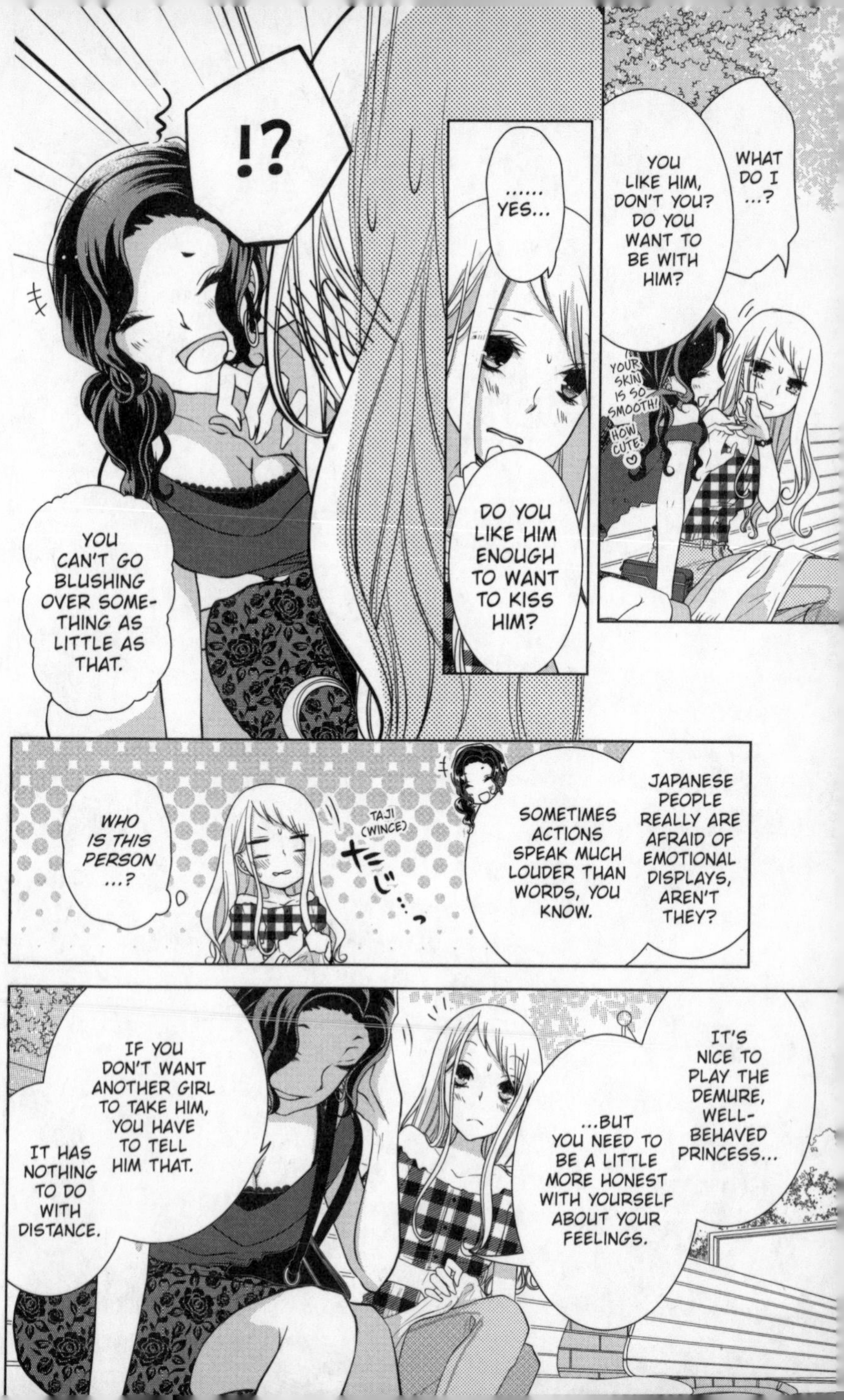
WHAT DO I ...?
YOU LIKE HIM, DON'T YOU? DO YOU WANT TO BE WITH HIM?
YOUR SKIN IS SO SMOOTH! HOW CUTE! ♡
...... YES...
DO YOU LIKE HIM ENOUGH TO WANT TO KISS HIM?
!?
YOU CAN'T GO BLUSHING OVER SOME-THING AS LITTLE AS THAT.
JAPANESE PEOPLE REALLY ARE AFRAID OF EMOTIONAL DISPLAYS, AREN'T THEY?
SOMETIMES ACTIONS SPEAK MUCH LOUDER THAN WORDS, YOU KNOW.
TAJI (WINCE)
WHO IS THIS PERSON ...?
IT'S NICE TO PLAY THE DEMURE, WELL-BEHAVED PRINCESS...
...BUT YOU NEED TO BE A LITTLE MORE HONEST WITH YOURSELF ABOUT YOUR FEELINGS.
IF YOU DON'T WANT ANOTHER GIRL TO TAKE HIM, YOU HAVE TO TELL HIM THAT.
IT HAS NOTHING TO DO WITH DISTANCE.

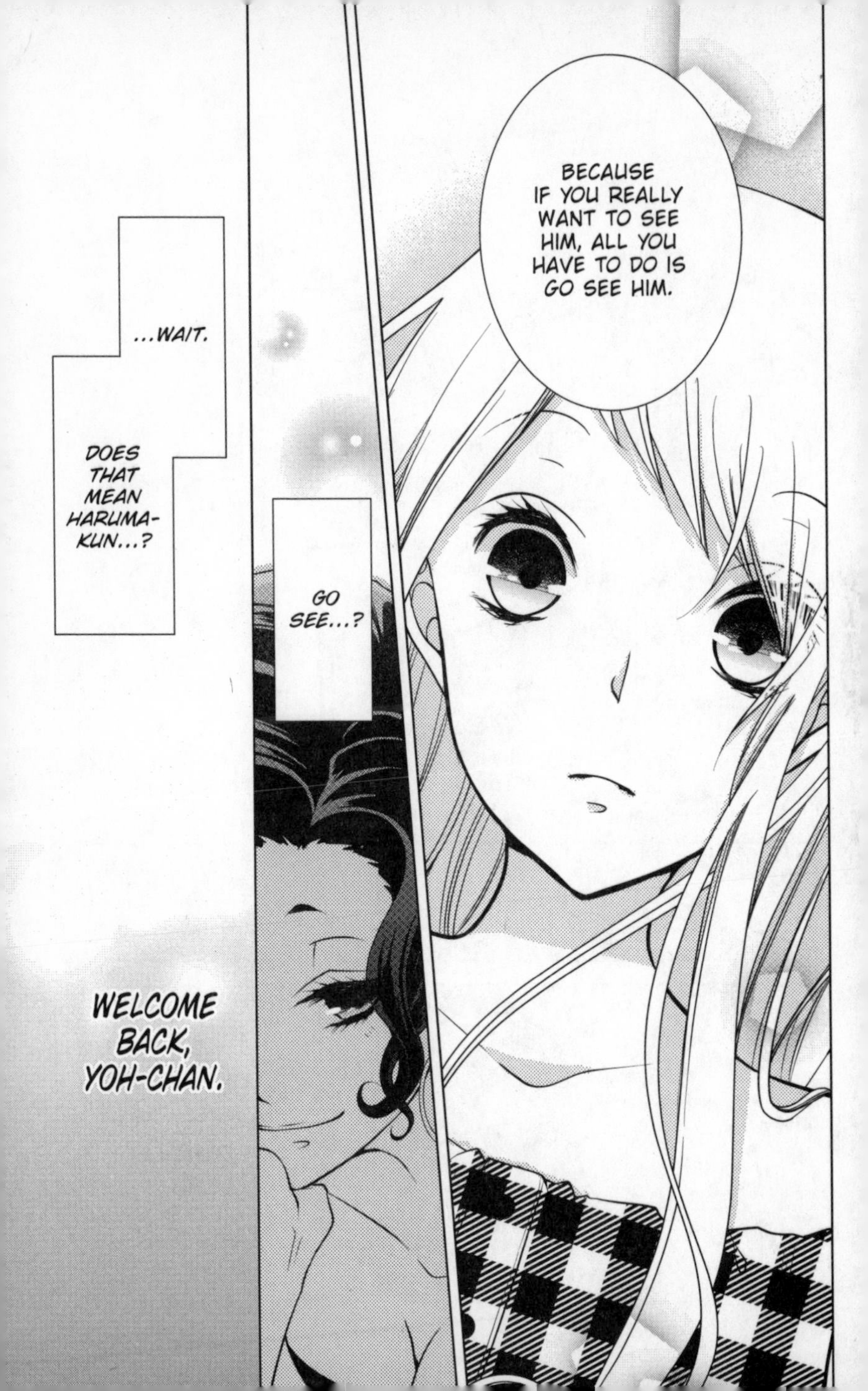
BECAUSE IF YOU REALLY WANT TO SEE HIM, ALL YOU HAVE TO DO IS GO SEE HIM.
GO SEE...?
...WAIT.
DOES THAT MEAN HARUMA-KUN...?
WELCOME BACK, YOH-CHAN.

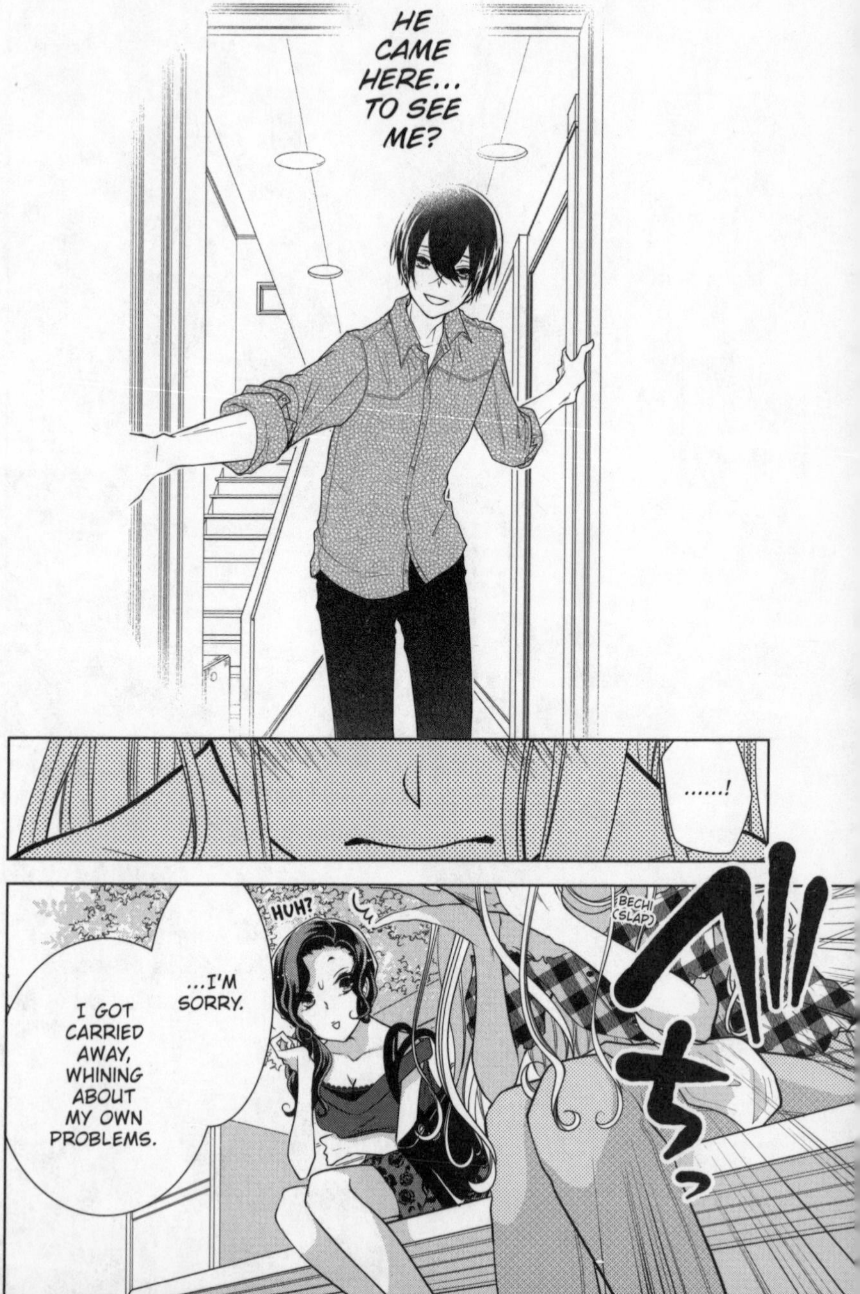
HE CAME HERE... TO SEE ME?
......!
BECHI (SLAP)
HUH?
...I'M SORRY.
I GOT CARRIED AWAY, WHINING ABOUT MY OWN PROBLEMS.

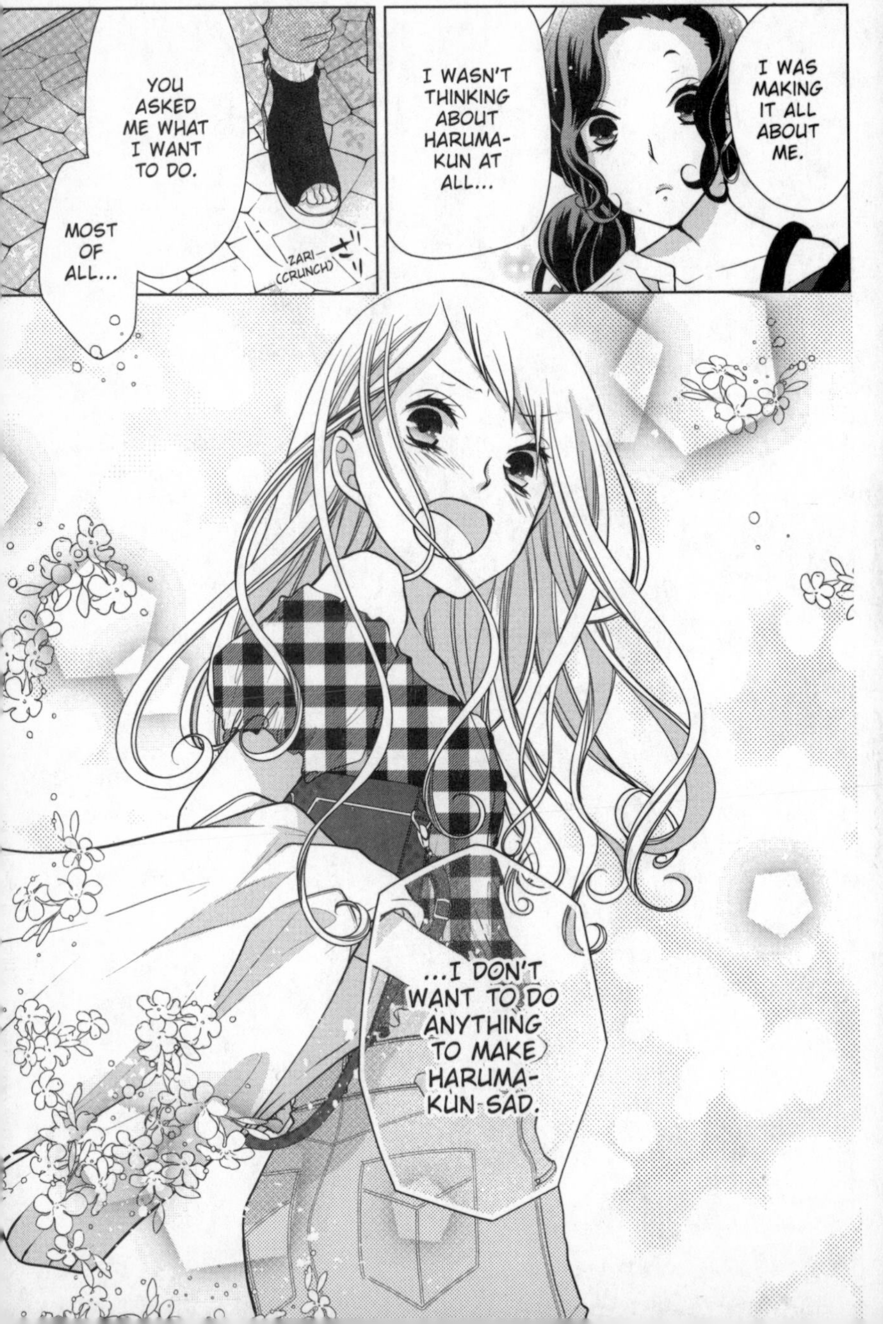
I WAS MAKING IT ALL ABOUT ME.
I WASN'T THINKING ABOUT HARUMA-KUN AT ALL...
YOU ASKED ME WHAT I WANT TO DO.
MOST OF ALL...
ザリ
ZARI (CRUNCH)
...I DON'T WANT TO DO ANYTHING TO MAKE HARUMA-KUN SAD.

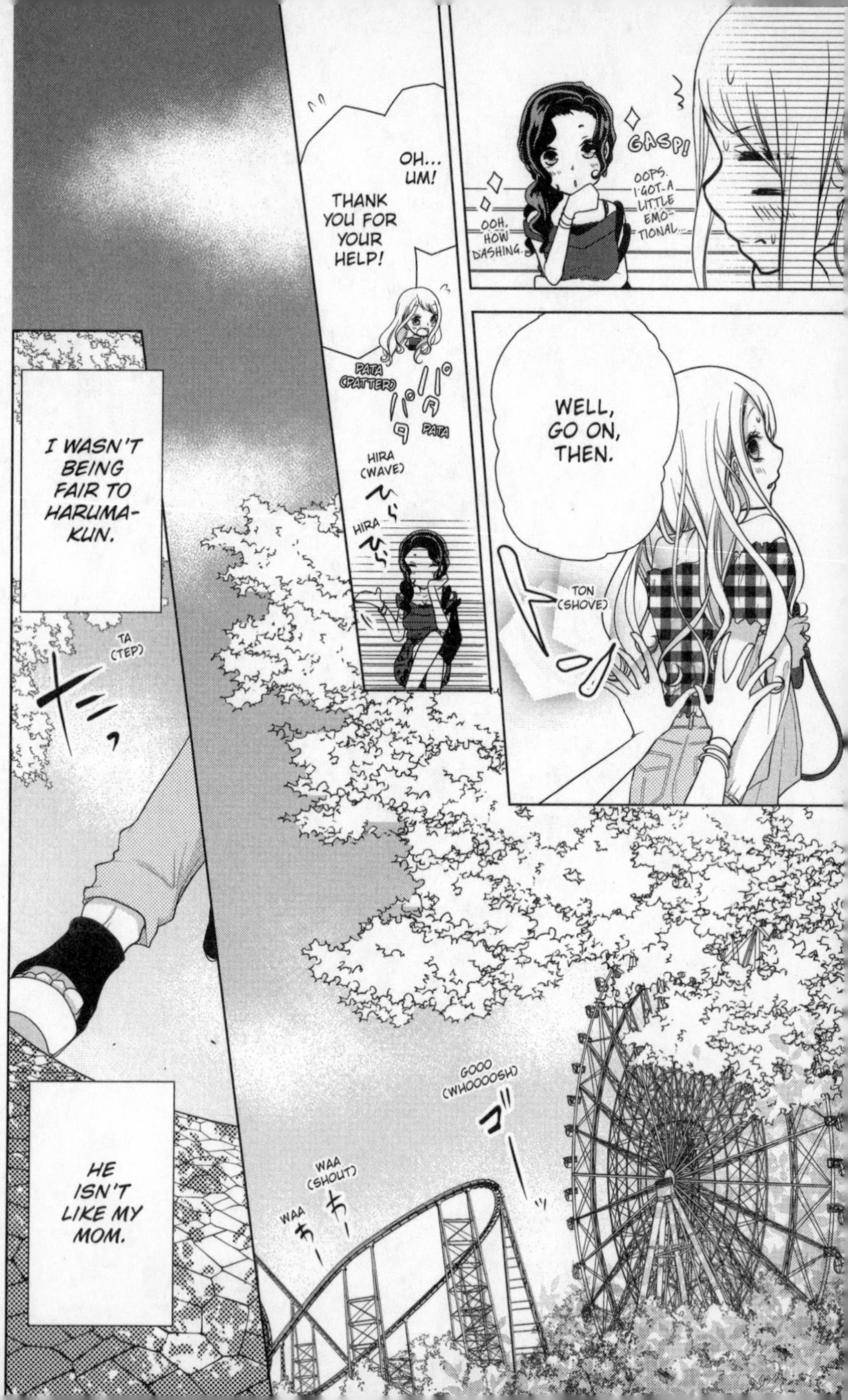
GASP!
OOPS. I GOT A LITTLE EMOTIONAL...
OOH, HOW DASHING.
OH... UM!
THANK YOU FOR YOUR HELP!
PATA (PATTER)
PATA
HIRA (WAVE)
HIRA
WELL, GO ON, THEN.
TON (SHOVE)
I WASN'T BEING FAIR TO HARUMA-KUN.
TA (TEP)
GOOO (WHOOOOSH)
WAA (SHOUT)
WAA
HE ISN'T LIKE MY MOM.

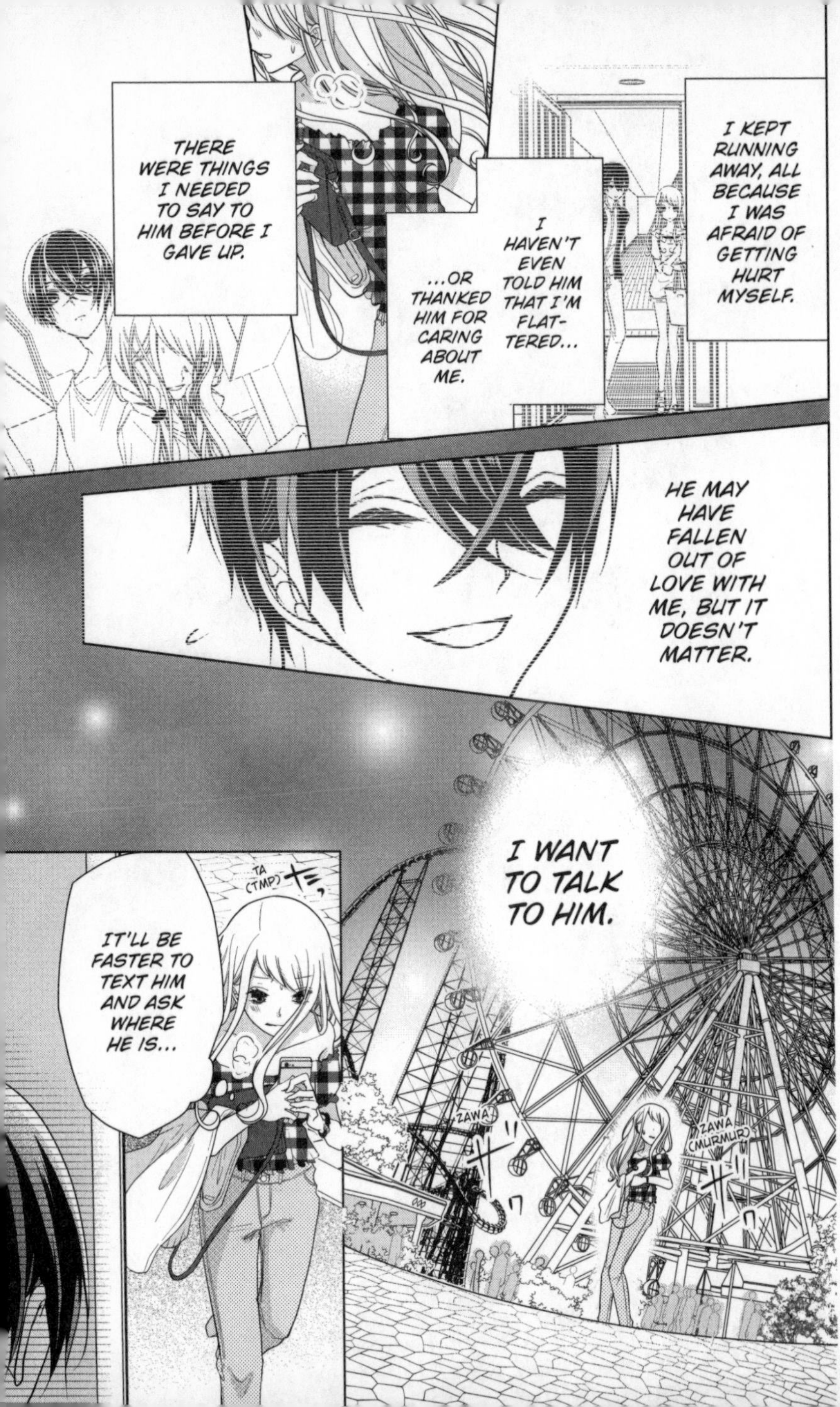

I KEPT RUNNING AWAY, ALL BECAUSE I WAS AFRAID OF GETTING HURT MYSELF.
I HAVEN'T EVEN TOLD HIM THAT I'M FLATTERED...
...OR THANKED HIM FOR CARING ABOUT ME.
THERE WERE THINGS I NEEDED TO SAY TO HIM BEFORE I GAVE UP.
HE MAY HAVE FALLEN OUT OF LOVE WITH ME, BUT IT DOESN'T MATTER.
I WANT TO TALK TO HIM.
ZAWA (MURMUR)
ZAWA
TA (TMP)
IT'LL BE FASTER TO TEXT HIM AND ASK WHERE HE IS...

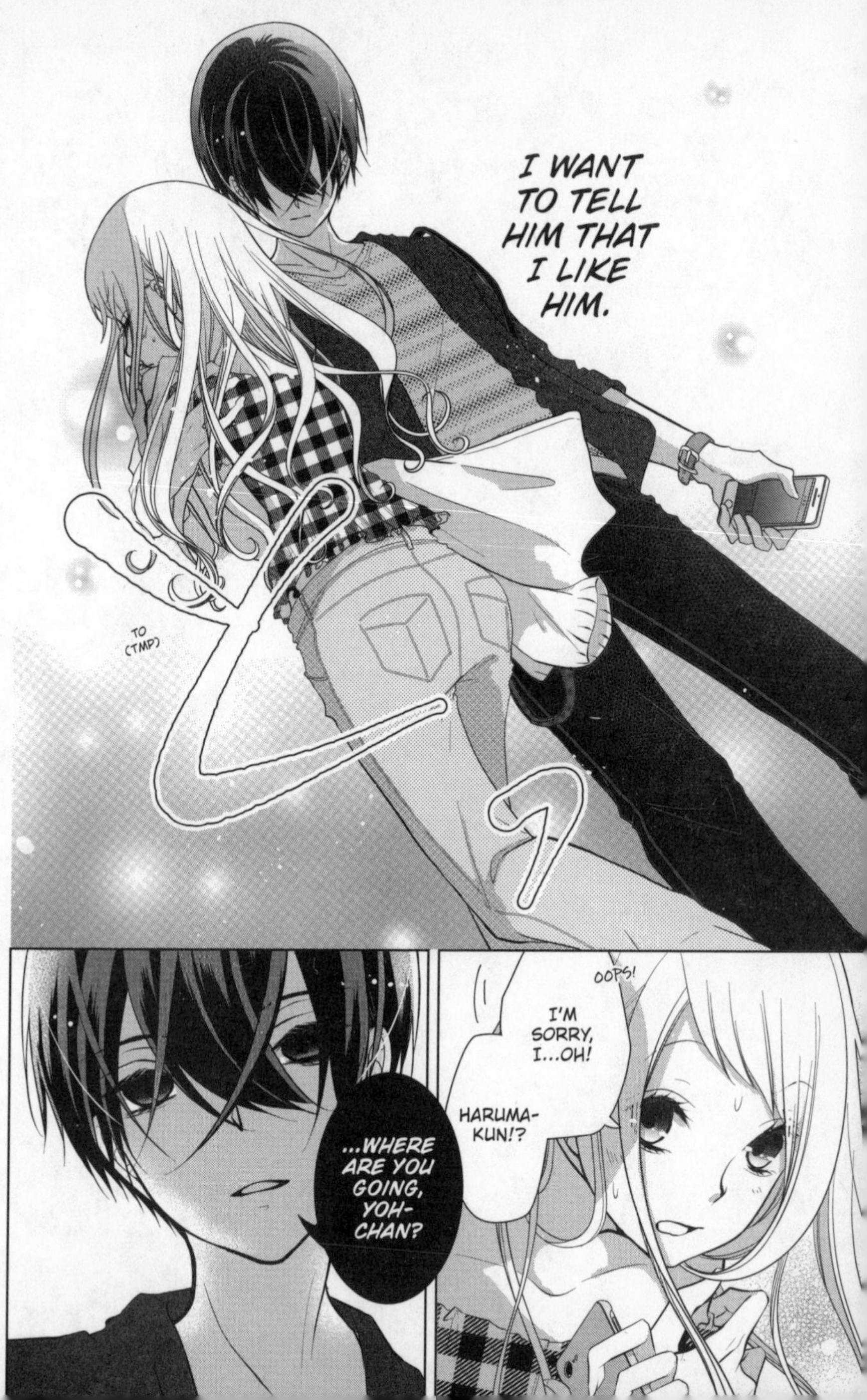
I WANT TO TELL HIM THAT I LIKE HIM.
TO (TMP)
OOPS!
I'M SORRY, I...OH!
HARUMA-KUN!?
...WHERE ARE YOU GOING, YOH-CHAN?

#58

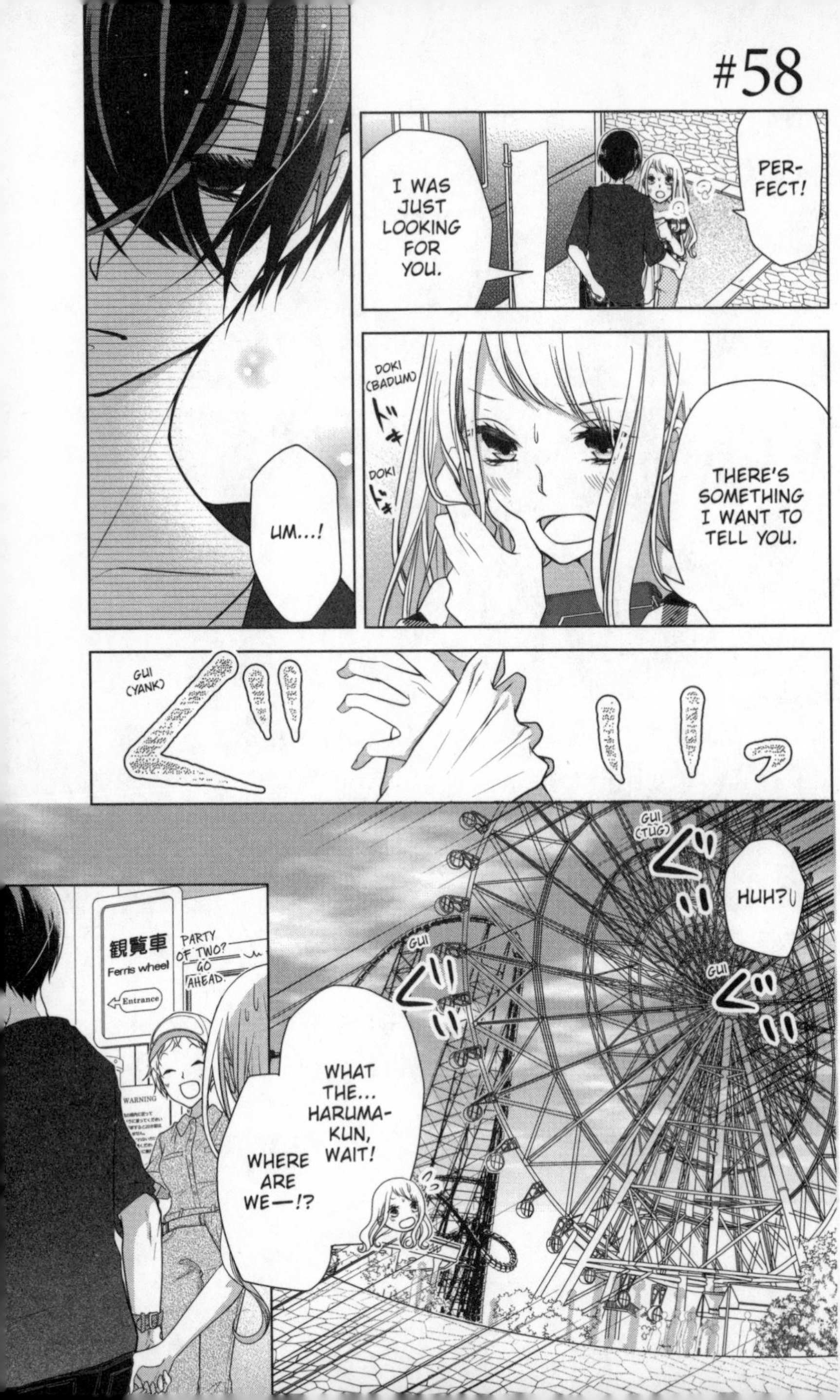
PER-FECT!
I WAS JUST LOOKING FOR YOU.
THERE'S SOMETHING I WANT TO TELL YOU.
DOKI (BADUM)
DOKI
UM...!
GUI (YANK)
GUI (TUG)
HUH?
GUI
GUI
WHAT THE... HARUMA-KUN, WAIT!
WHERE ARE WE—!?
観覧車
Ferris wheel
Entrance
WARNING
PARTY OF TWO? GO AHEAD.

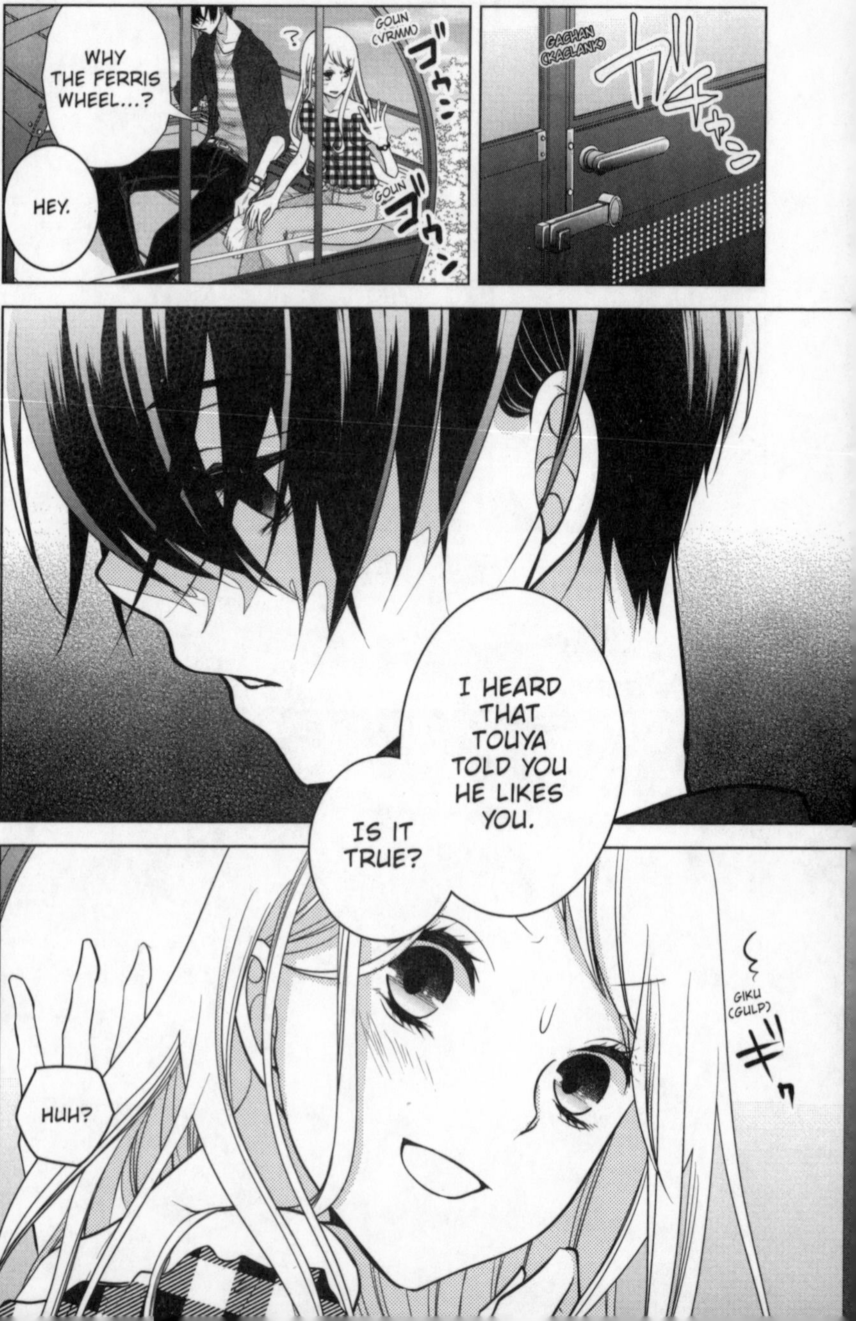

GACHAN (KACLANK)
?
GOUN (VRMM)
WHY THE FERRIS WHEEL...?
GOUN
HEY.
I HEARD THAT TOUYA TOLD YOU HE LIKES YOU.
IS IT TRUE?
GIKU (GULP)
HUH?

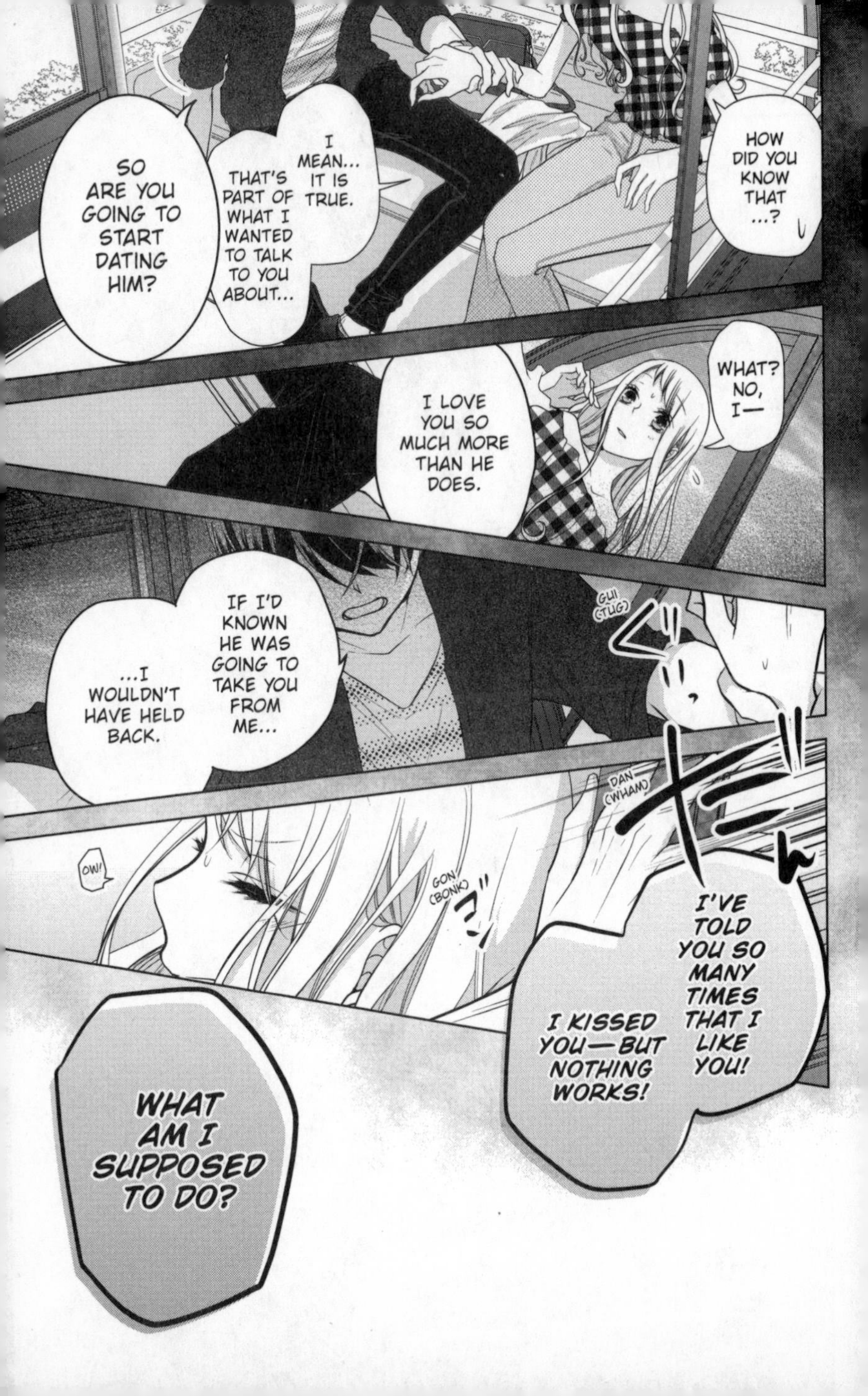
HOW DID YOU KNOW THAT ...?
I MEAN... IT IS TRUE.
THAT'S PART OF WHAT I WANTED TO TALK TO YOU ABOUT...
SO ARE YOU GOING TO START DATING HIM?
WHAT? NO, I—
I LOVE YOU SO MUCH MORE THAN HE DOES.
GUI (TUG)
IF I'D KNOWN HE WAS GOING TO TAKE YOU FROM ME...
...I WOULDN'T HAVE HELD BACK.
DAN (WHAM)
GON (BONK)
OW!
I'VE TOLD YOU SO MANY TIMES THAT I LIKE YOU!
I KISSED YOU—BUT NOTHING WORKS!
WHAT AM I SUPPOSED TO DO?

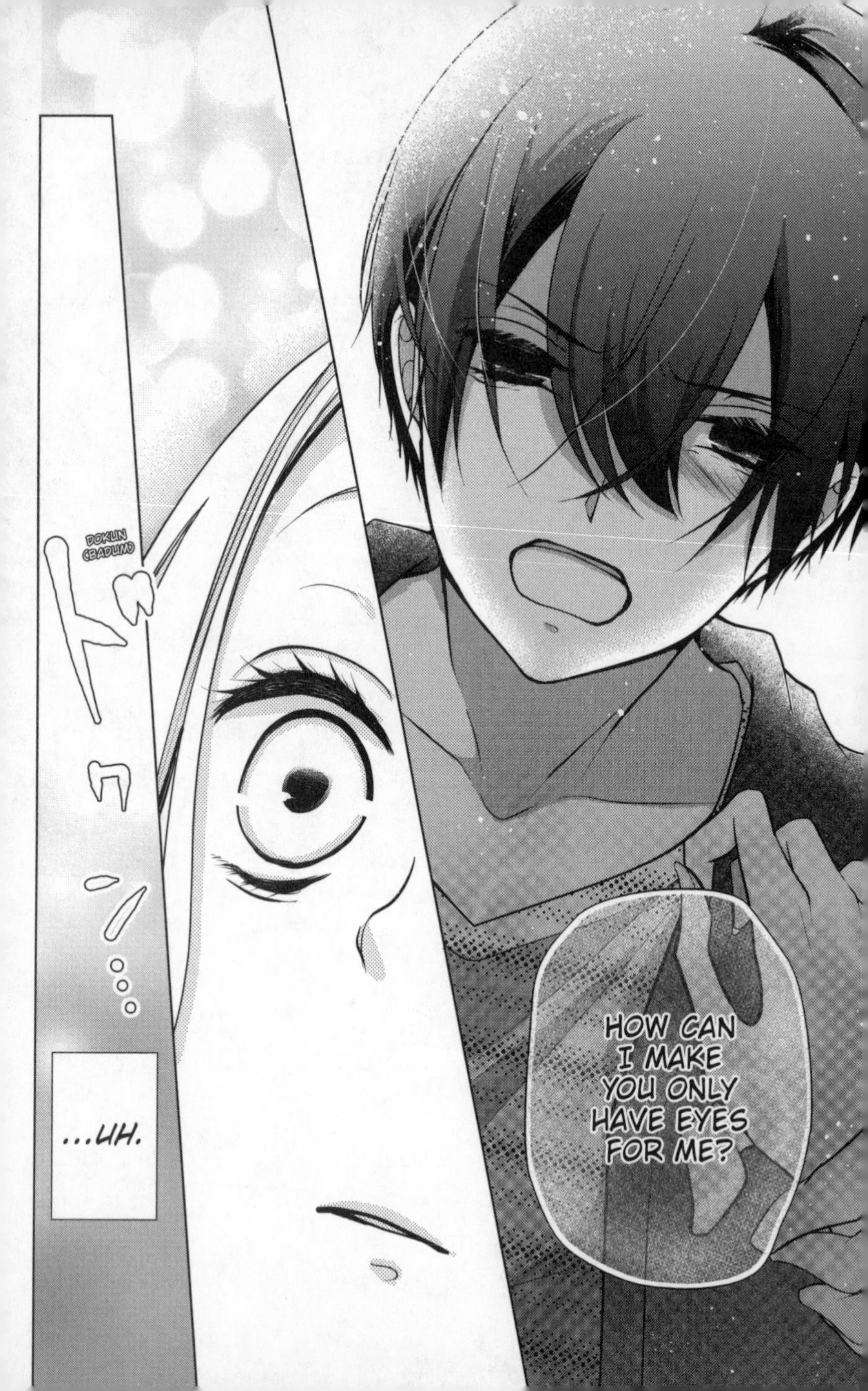
HOW CAN I MAKE YOU ONLY HAVE EYES FOR ME?
DOKUN (BADUM)
...UH.

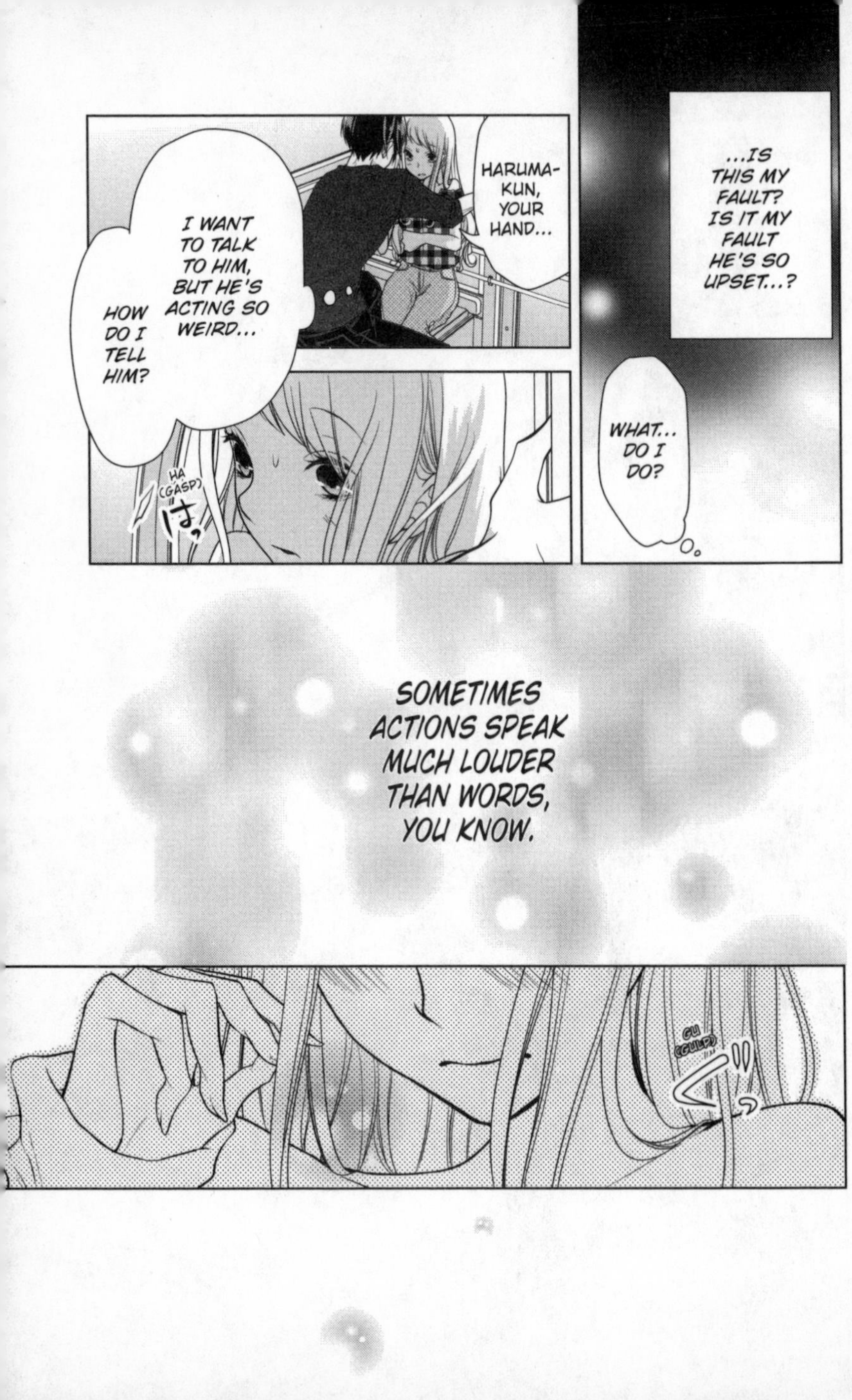
...IS THIS MY FAULT? IS IT MY FAULT HE'S SO UPSET...?
WHAT... DO I DO?
HARUMA-KUN, YOUR HAND...
I WANT TO TALK TO HIM, BUT HE'S ACTING SO WEIRD...
HOW DO I TELL HIM?
HA (GASP)
SOMETIMES ACTIONS SPEAK MUCH LOUDER THAN WORDS, YOU KNOW.
GU (GULP)

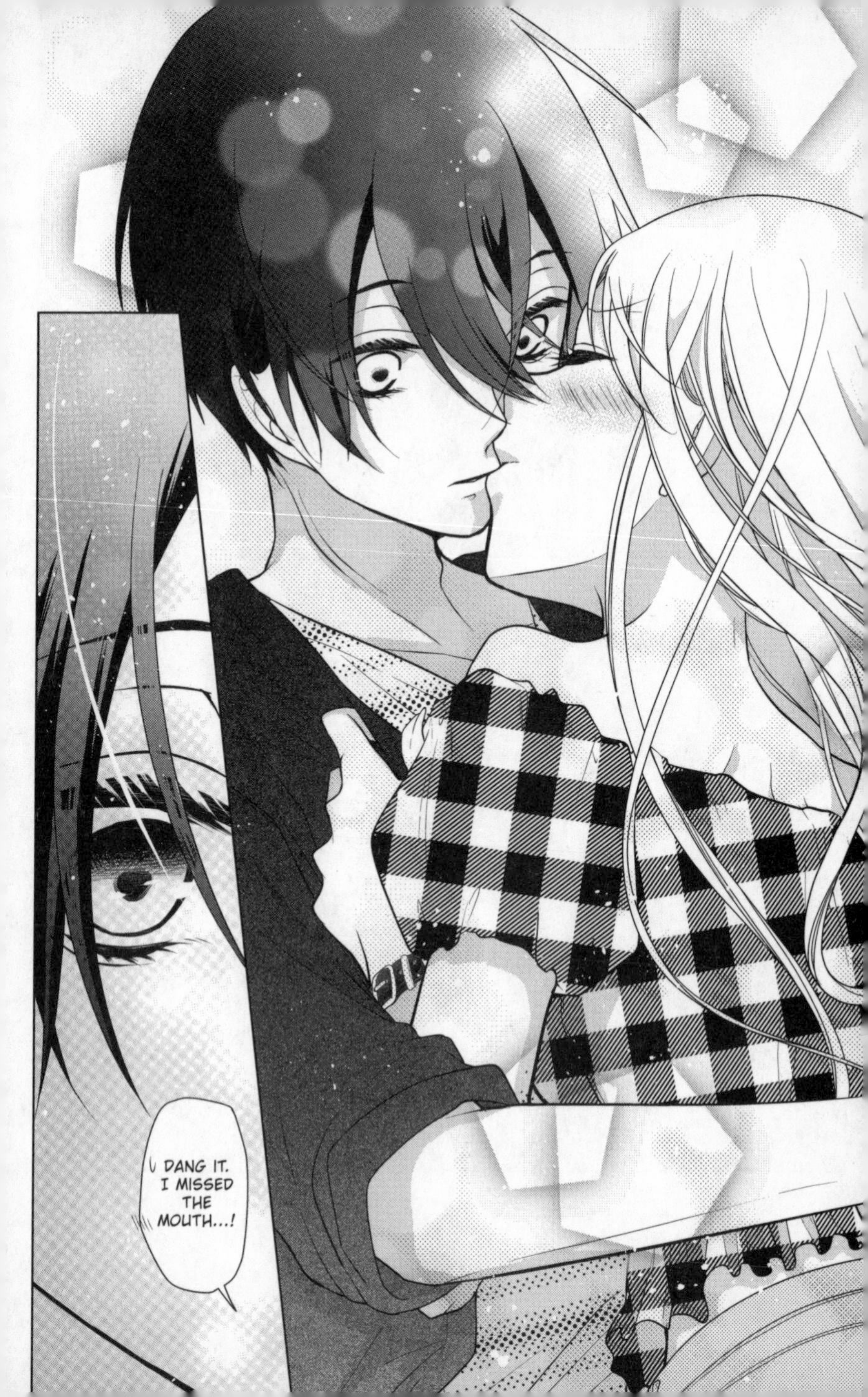
DANG IT. I MISSED THE MOUTH...!

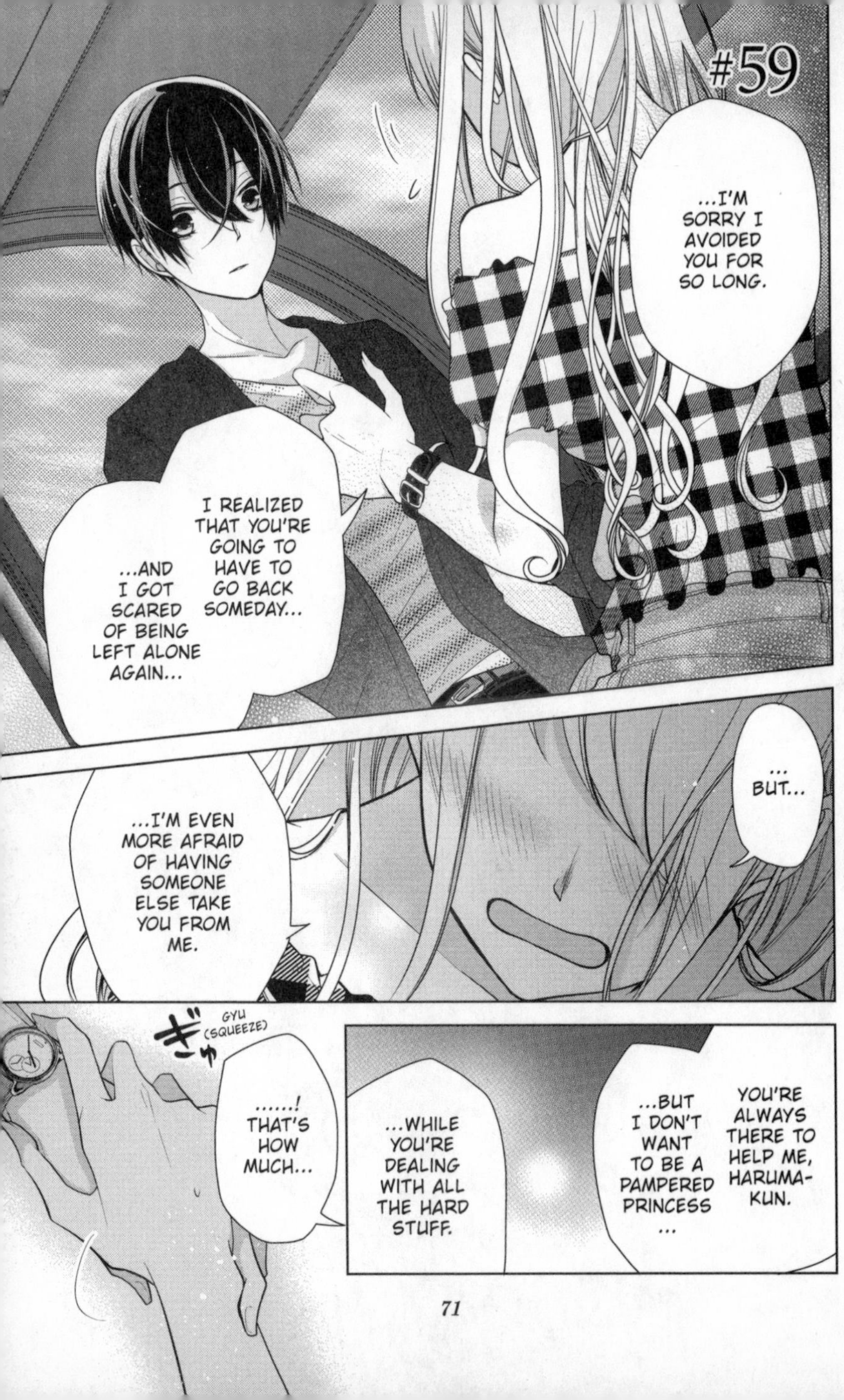

#59
...I'M SORRY I AVOIDED YOU FOR SO LONG.
I REALIZED THAT YOU'RE GOING TO HAVE TO GO BACK SOMEDAY...
...AND I GOT SCARED OF BEING LEFT ALONE AGAIN...
...BUT...
...I'M EVEN MORE AFRAID OF HAVING SOMEONE ELSE TAKE YOU FROM ME.
YOU'RE ALWAYS THERE TO HELP ME, HARUMA-KUN.
...BUT I DON'T WANT TO BE A PAMPERED PRINCESS...
...WHILE YOU'RE DEALING WITH ALL THE HARD STUFF.
ギュ
GYU (SQUEEZE)
......! THAT'S HOW MUCH...

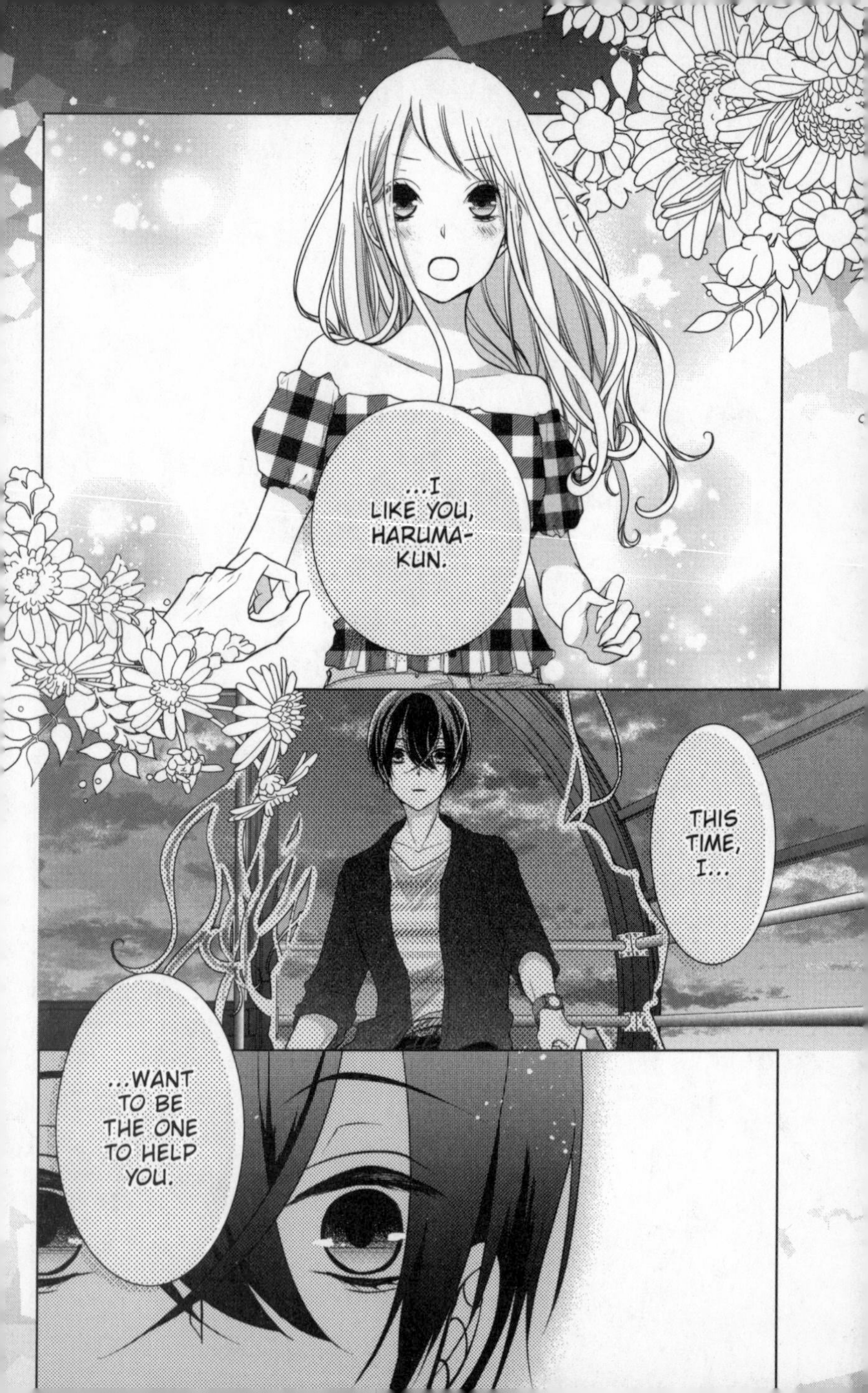
...I LIKE YOU, HARUMA-KUN.
THIS TIME, I...
...WANT TO BE THE ONE TO HELP YOU.

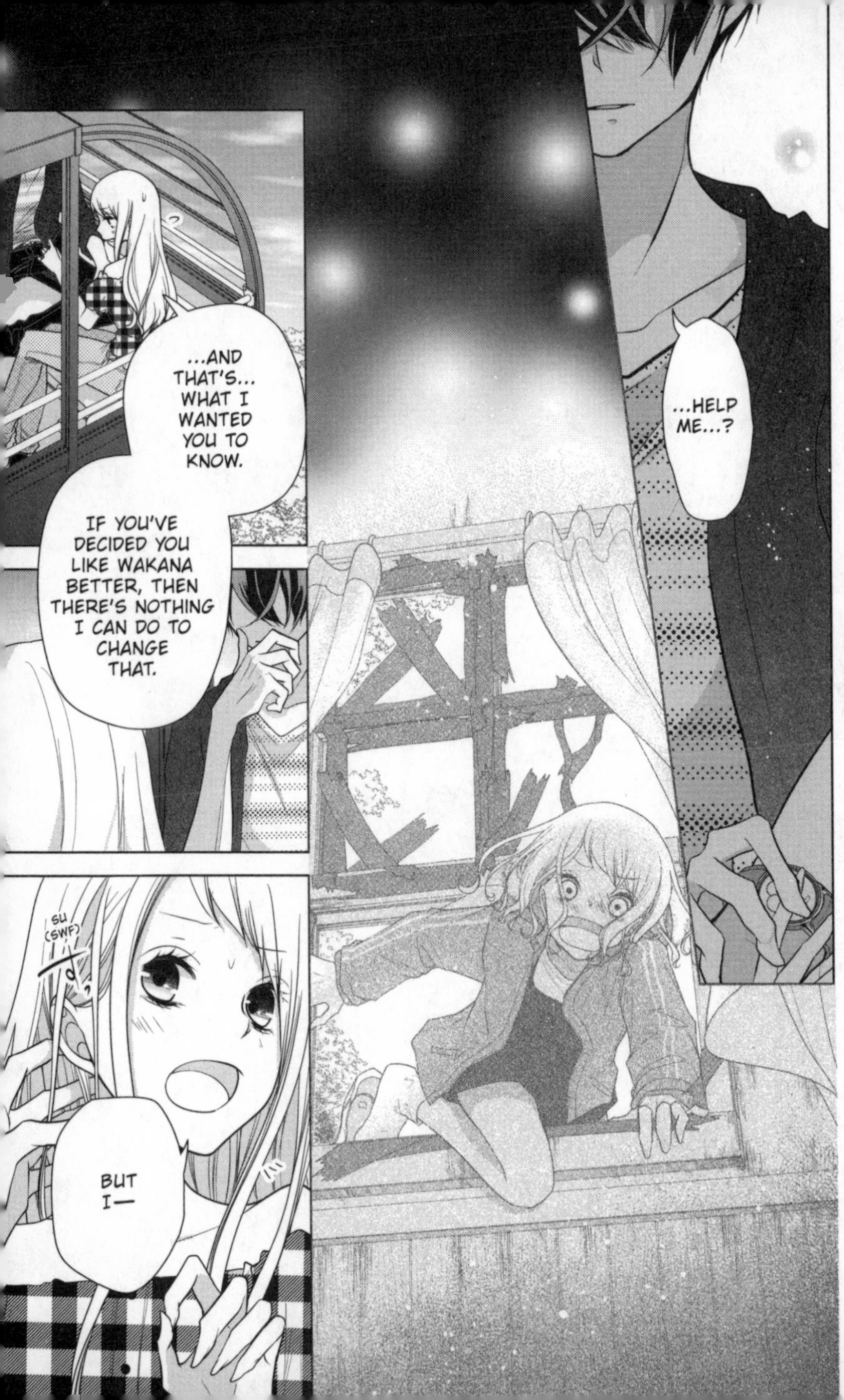
...HELP ME...?
...AND THAT'S... WHAT I WANTED YOU TO KNOW.
IF YOU'VE DECIDED YOU LIKE WAKANA BETTER, THEN THERE'S NOTHING I CAN DO TO CHANGE THAT.
SU (SWF)
BUT I—

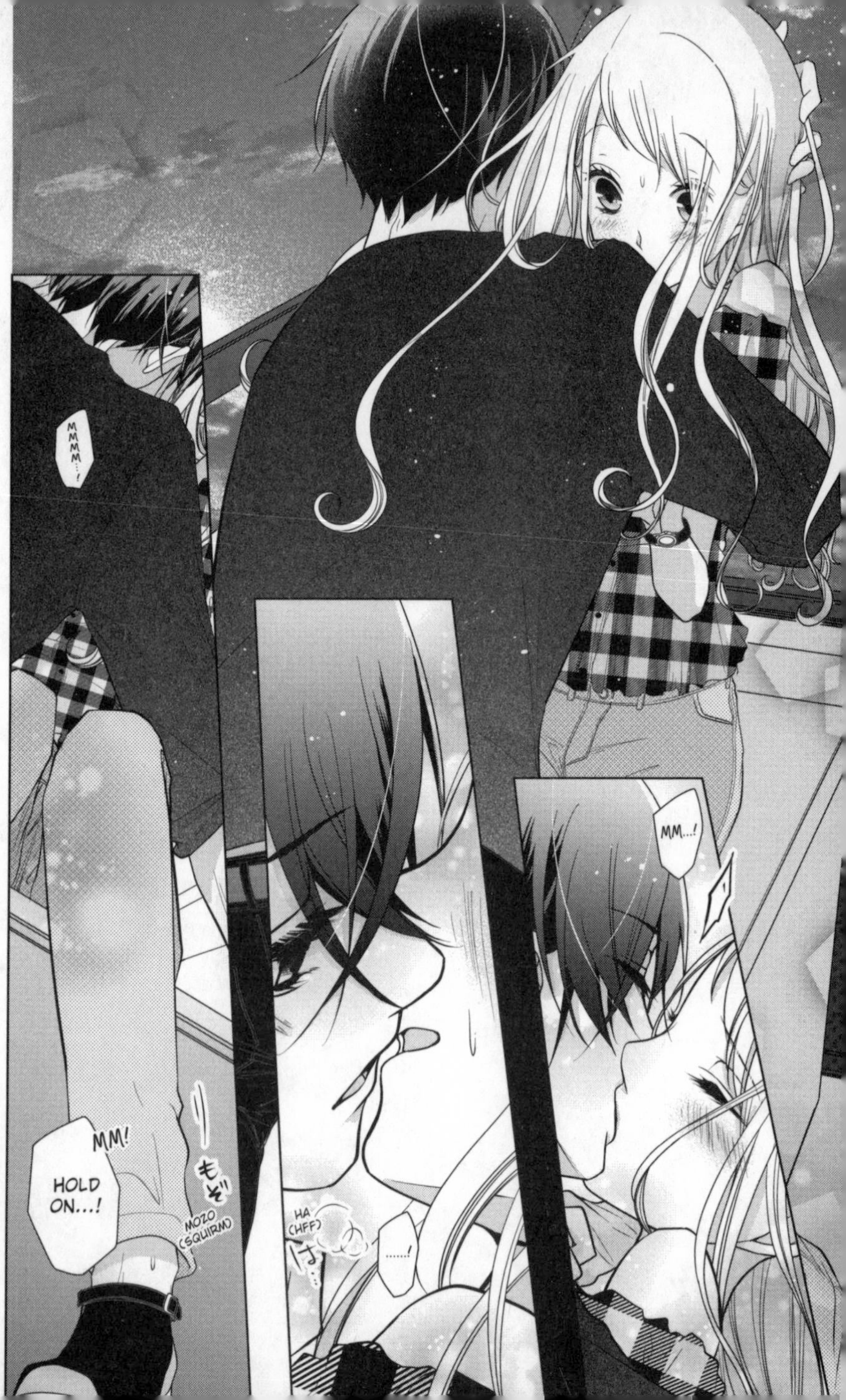

MM...!
HA (HFF)
は…
......!
MMMM...!
MM! HOLD ON...!
もぞ
MOZO (SQUIRM)

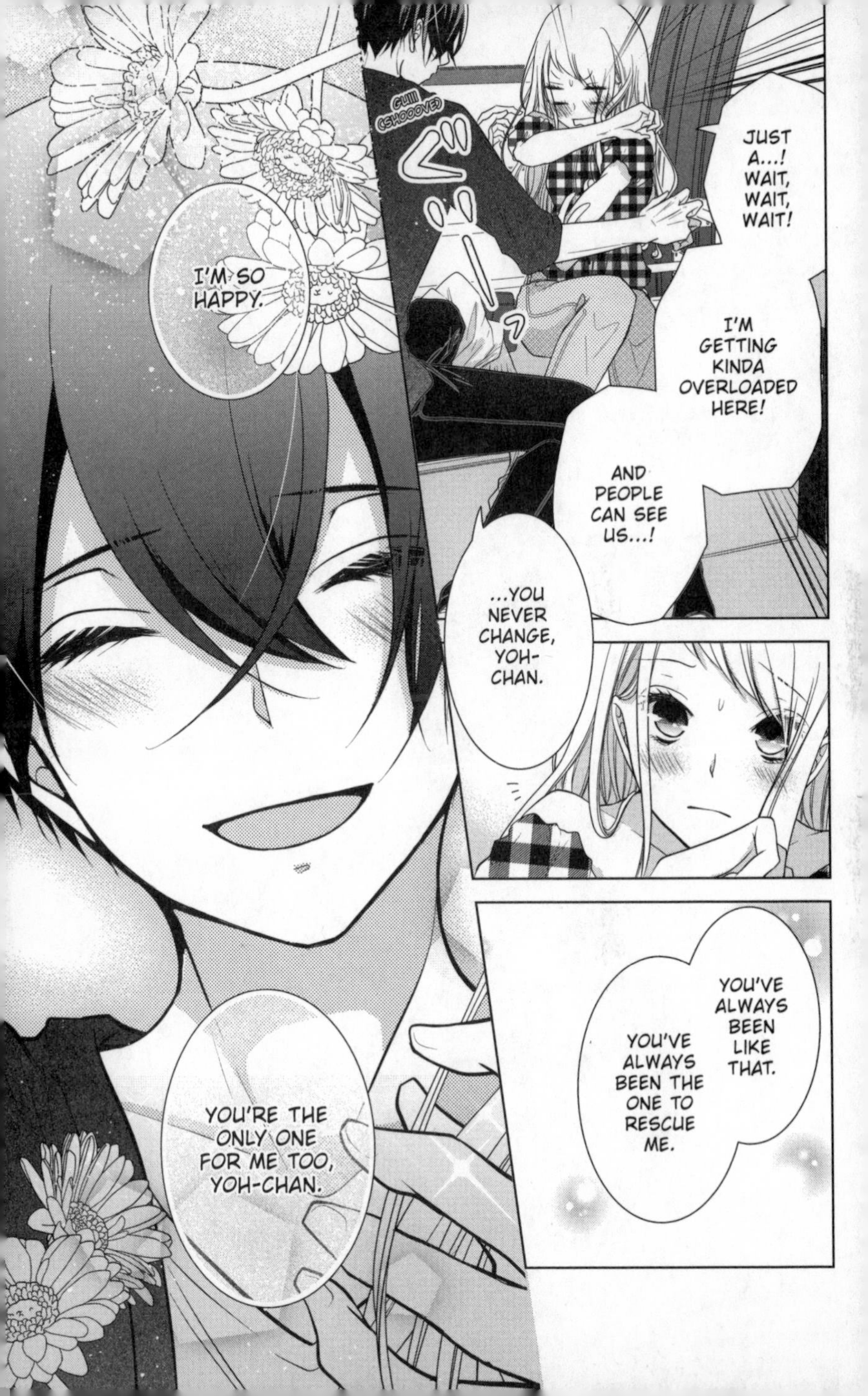
GUIII (SHOOOVE)
JUST A...! WAIT, WAIT, WAIT!
I'M GETTING KINDA OVERLOADED HERE!
AND PEOPLE CAN SEE US...!
...YOU NEVER CHANGE, YOH-CHAN.
YOU'VE ALWAYS BEEN LIKE THAT.
YOU'VE ALWAYS BEEN THE ONE TO RESCUE ME.
I'M SO HAPPY.
YOU'RE THE ONLY ONE FOR ME TOO, YOH-CHAN.

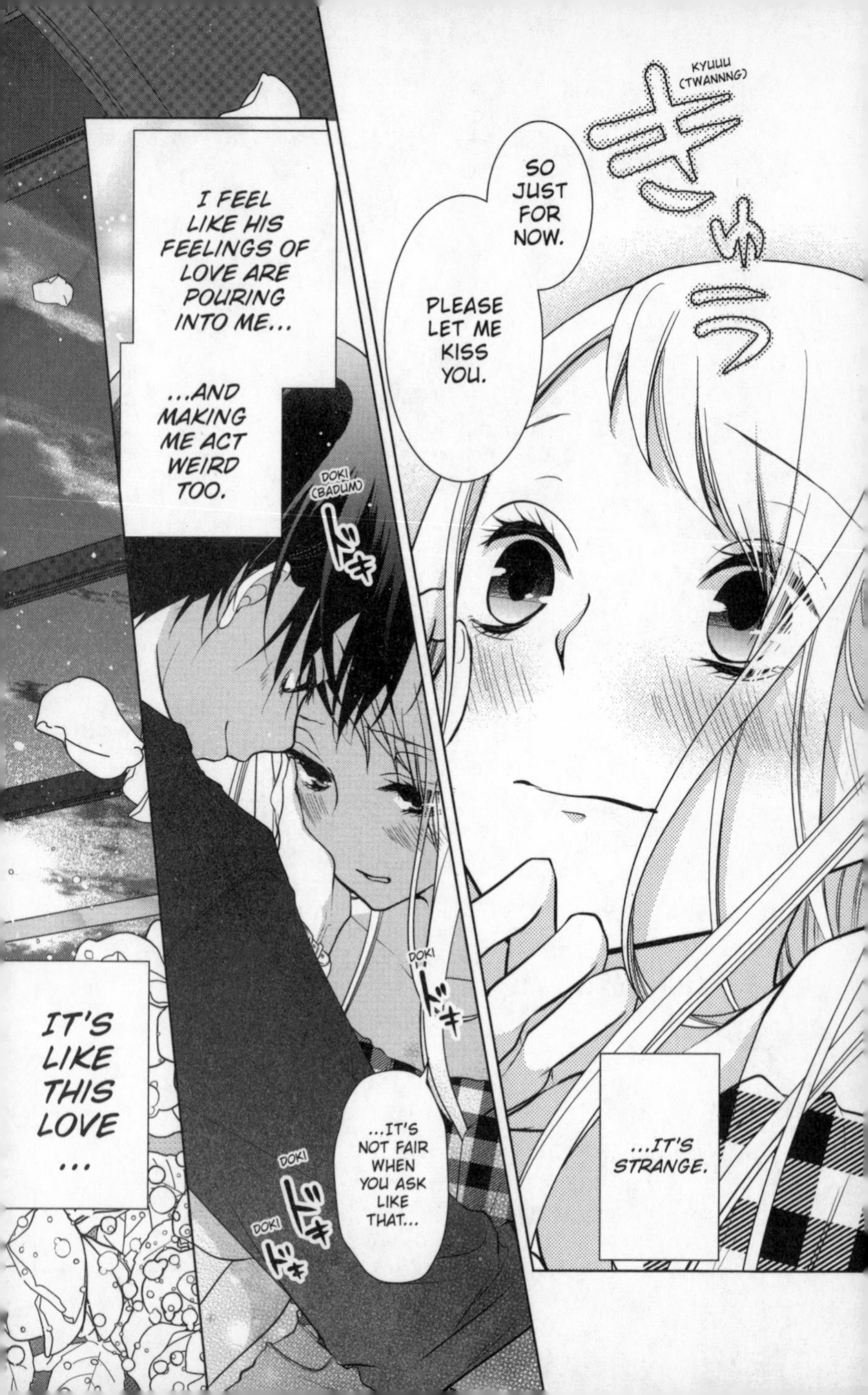
KYUUU (TWANNNG)
SO JUST FOR NOW.
PLEASE LET ME KISS YOU.
I FEEL LIKE HIS FEELINGS OF LOVE ARE POURING INTO ME...
...AND MAKING ME ACT WEIRD TOO.
DOKI (BADUM)
DOKI
...IT'S NOT FAIR WHEN YOU ASK LIKE THAT...
DOKI
DOKI
IT'S LIKE THIS LOVE...
...IT'S STRANGE.

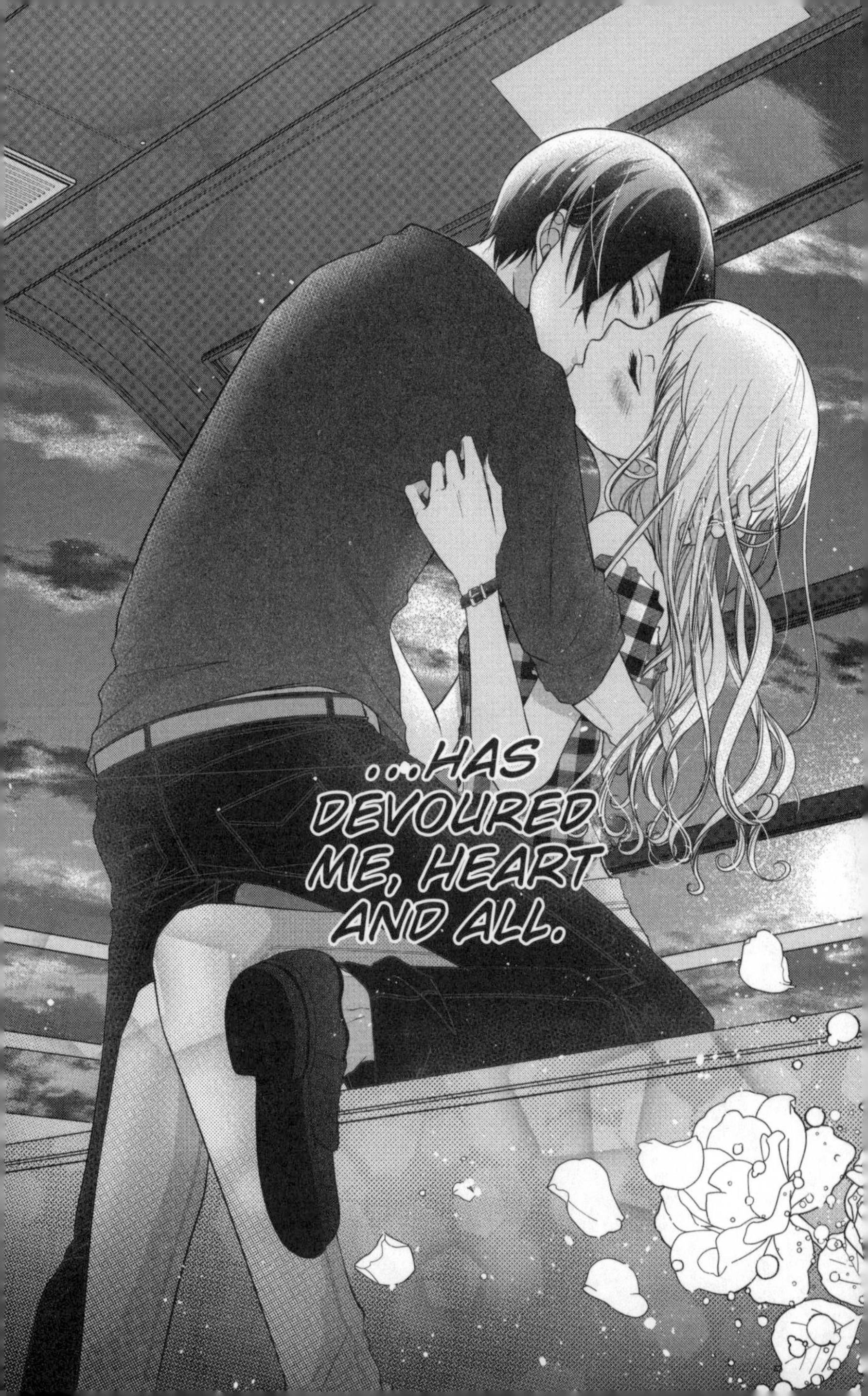
...HAS DEVOURED ME, HEART AND ALL.

#60

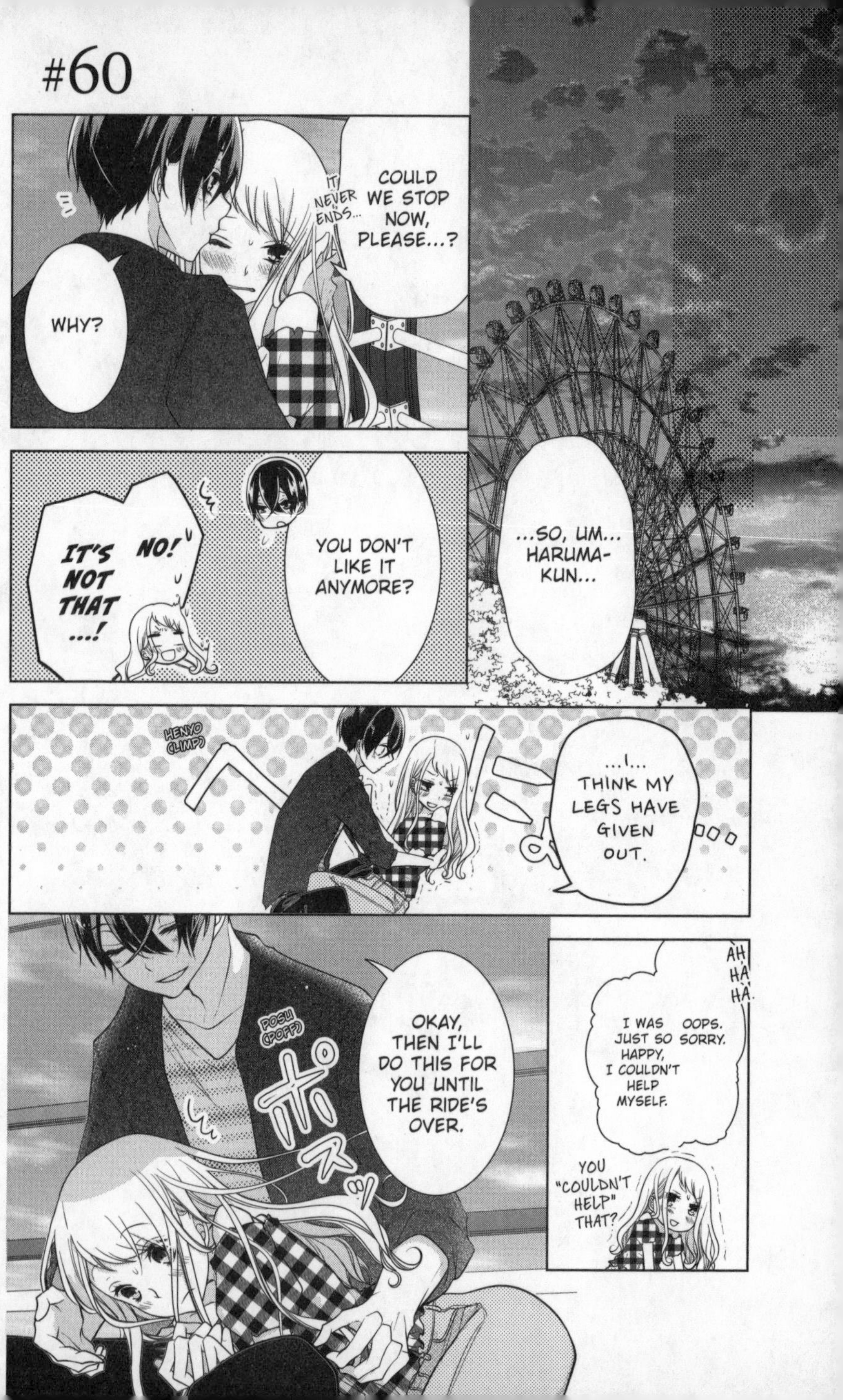
...SO, UM... HARUMA-KUN...
COULD WE STOP NOW, PLEASE...?
IT NEVER ENDS...
WHY?
YOU DON'T LIKE IT ANYMORE?
NO! IT'S NOT THAT....!
...I... THINK MY LEGS HAVE GIVEN OUT.
HENYO (LIMP)
AH HA HA.
OOPS. SORRY.
I WAS JUST SO HAPPY, I COULDN'T HELP MYSELF.
YOU "COULDN'T HELP" THAT?
OKAY, THEN I'LL DO THIS FOR YOU UNTIL THE RIDE'S OVER.
POSU (POFF)

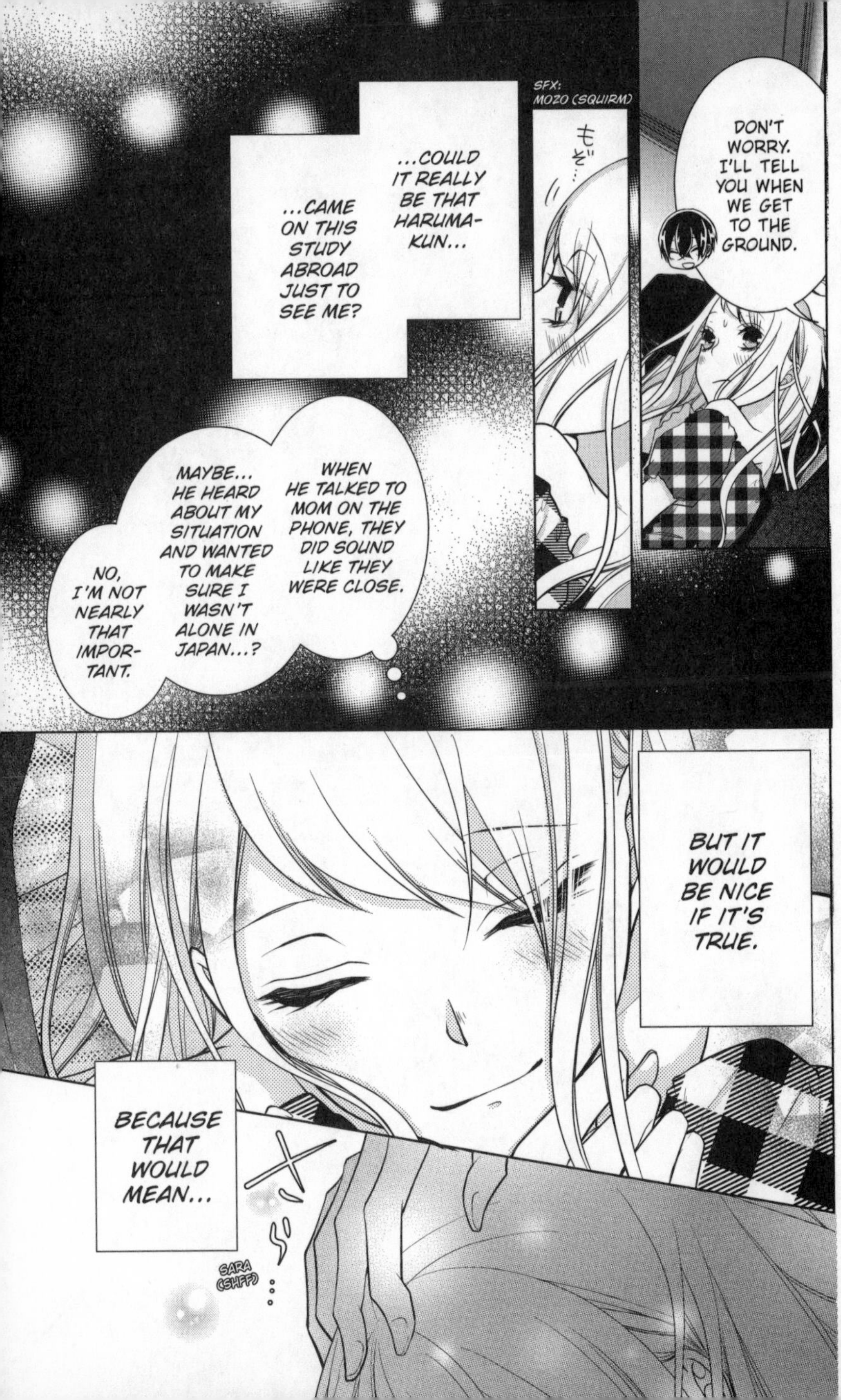
DON'T WORRY. I'LL TELL YOU WHEN WE GET TO THE GROUND.
SFX: MOZO (SQUIRM)
もぞ…
...COULD IT REALLY BE THAT HARUMA-KUN...
...CAME ON THIS STUDY ABROAD JUST TO SEE ME?
WHEN HE TALKED TO MOM ON THE PHONE, THEY DID SOUND LIKE THEY WERE CLOSE.
MAYBE... HE HEARD ABOUT MY SITUATION AND WANTED TO MAKE SURE I WASN'T ALONE IN JAPAN...?
NO, I'M NOT NEARLY THAT IMPOR-TANT.
BUT IT WOULD BE NICE IF IT'S TRUE.
BECAUSE THAT WOULD MEAN...
SARA (SHFF)

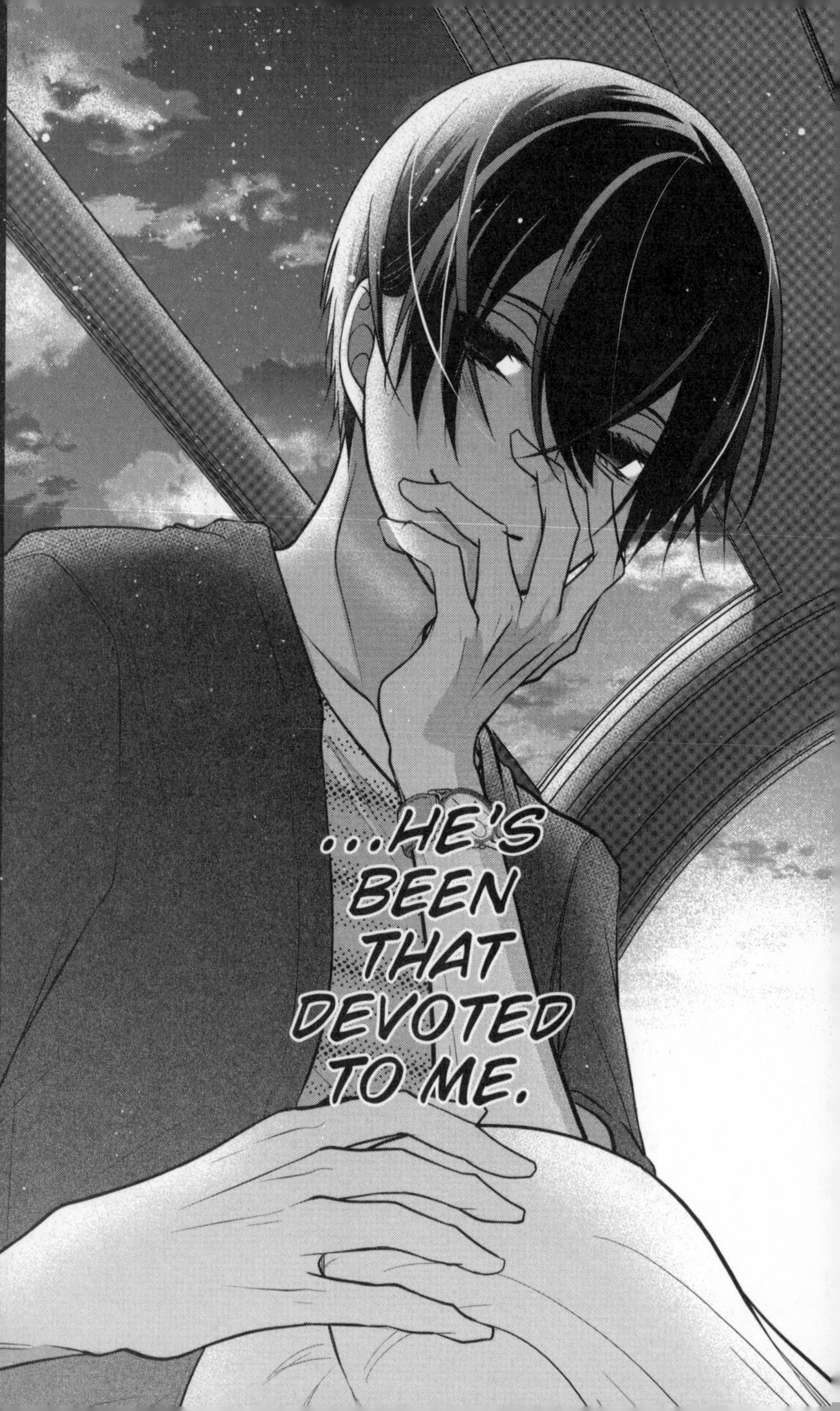
...HE'S BEEN THAT DEVOTED TO ME.

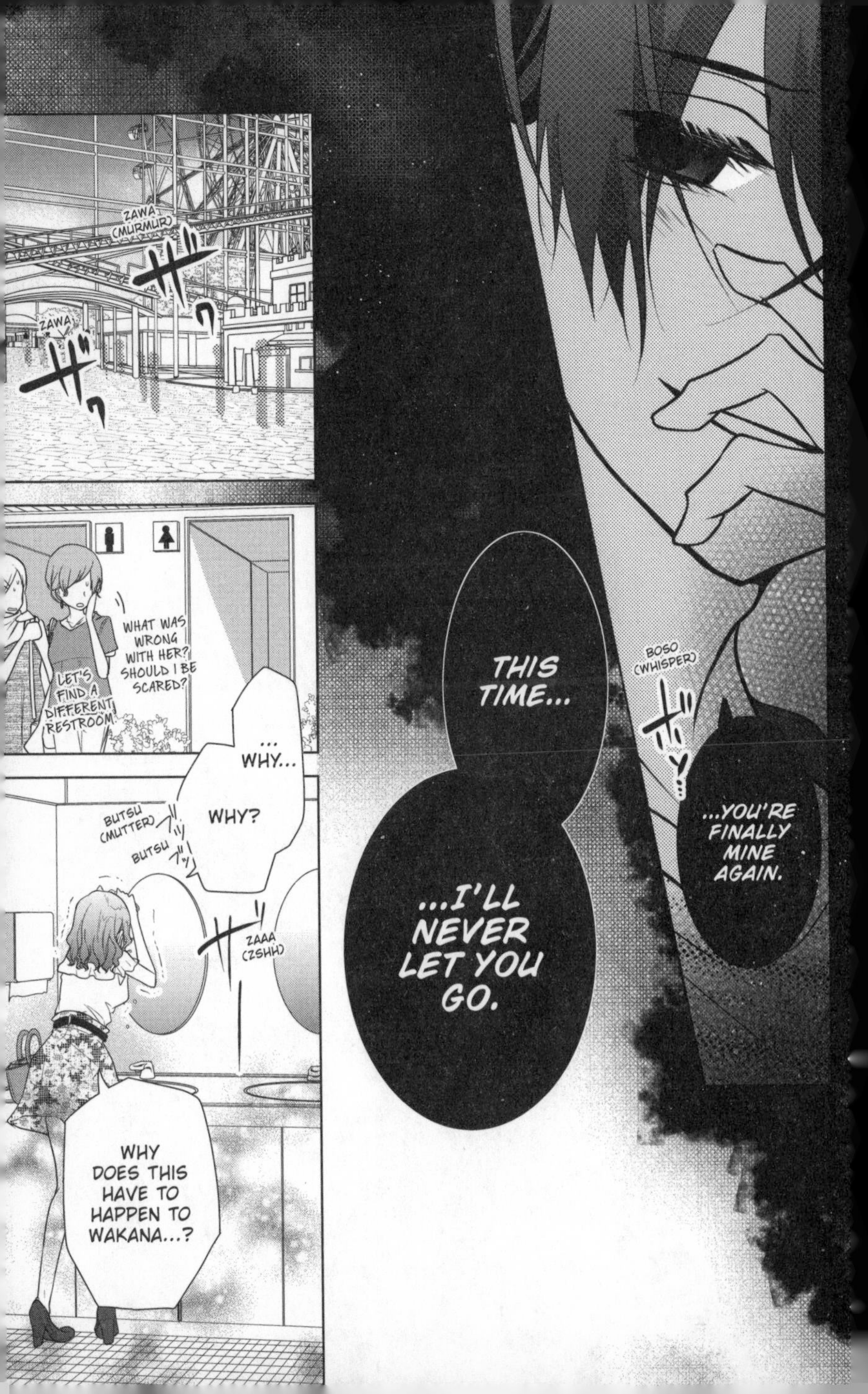
BOSO (WHISPER)
THIS TIME...
...YOU'RE FINALLY MINE AGAIN.
...I'LL NEVER LET YOU GO.
ZAWA (MURMUR)
ZAWA
WHAT WAS WRONG WITH HER? SHOULD I BE SCARED?
LET'S FIND A DIFFERENT RESTROOM.
... WHY...
WHY?
BUTSU (MUTTER)
BUTSU
ZAAA (ZSHH)
WHY DOES THIS HAVE TO HAPPEN TO WAKANA...?

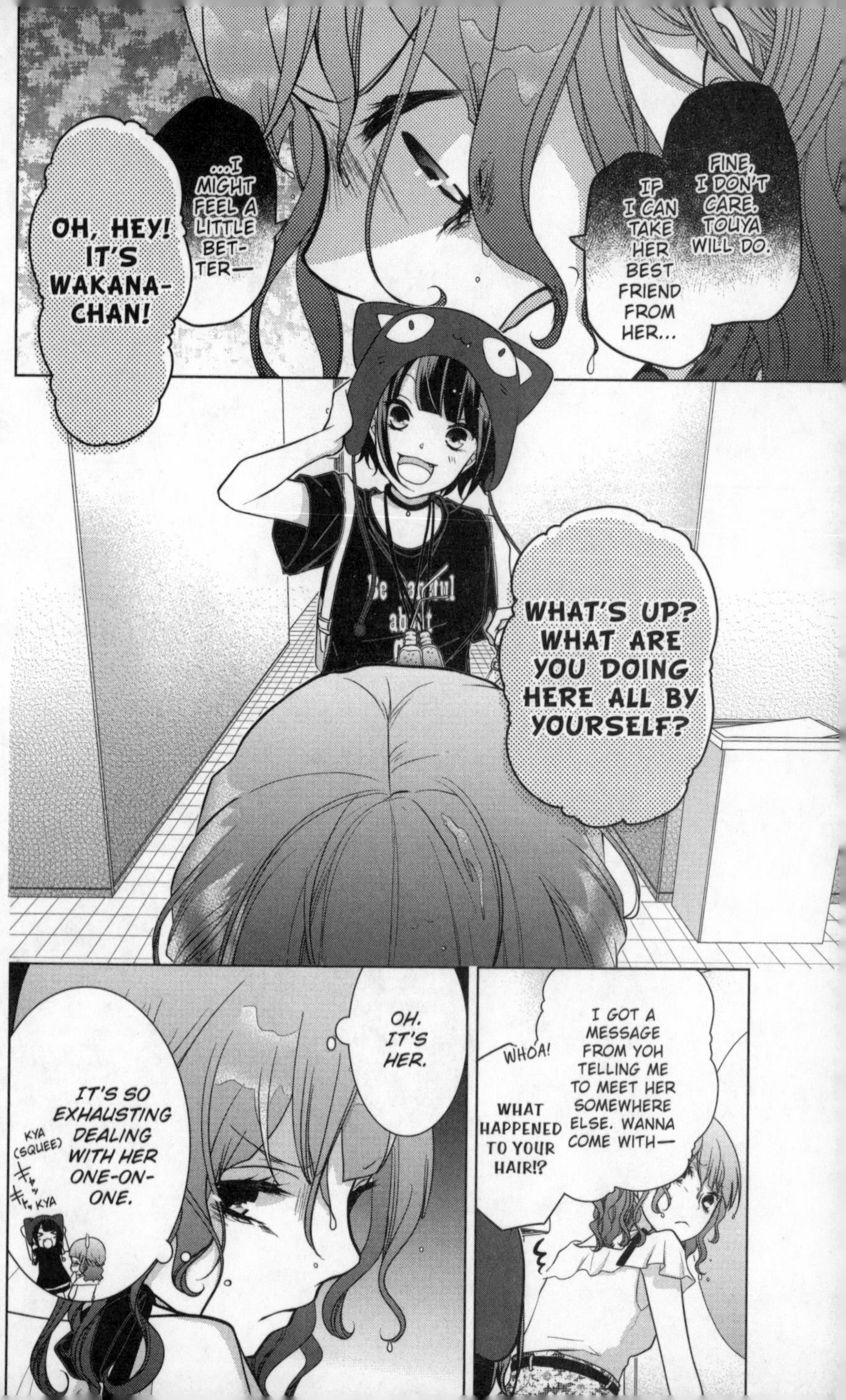
FINE, I DON'T CARE. TOUYA WILL DO.
IF I CAN TAKE HER BEST FRIEND FROM HER...
...I MIGHT FEEL A LITTLE BET-TER—
OH, HEY! IT'S WAKANA-CHAN!
WHAT'S UP? WHAT ARE YOU DOING HERE ALL BY YOURSELF?
I GOT A MESSAGE FROM YOH TELLING ME TO MEET HER SOMEWHERE ELSE. WANNA COME WITH—
WHOA!
WHAT HAPPENED TO YOUR HAIR!?
OH. IT'S HER.
IT'S SO EXHAUSTING DEALING WITH HER ONE-ON-ONE.
KYA (SQUEE)
KYA

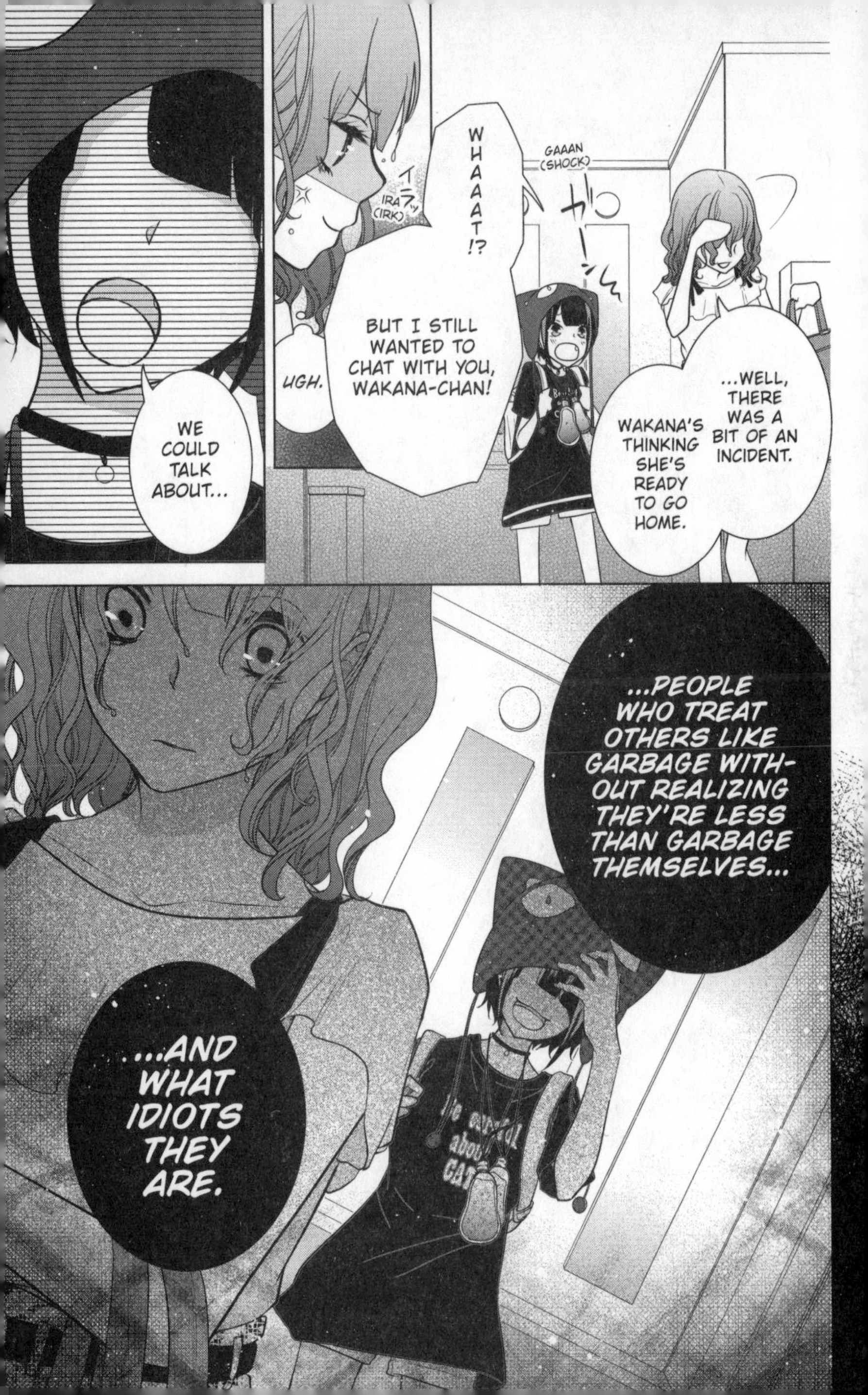
...WELL, THERE WAS A BIT OF AN INCIDENT.
WAKANA'S THINKING SHE'S READY TO GO HOME.
GAAAN (SHOCK)
WHAAAAT!?
IRA (IRK)
BUT I STILL WANTED TO CHAT WITH YOU, WAKANA-CHAN!
UGH.
WE COULD TALK ABOUT...
...PEOPLE WHO TREAT OTHERS LIKE GARBAGE WITH-OUT REALIZING THEY'RE LESS THAN GARBAGE THEMSELVES...
...AND WHAT IDIOTS THEY ARE.

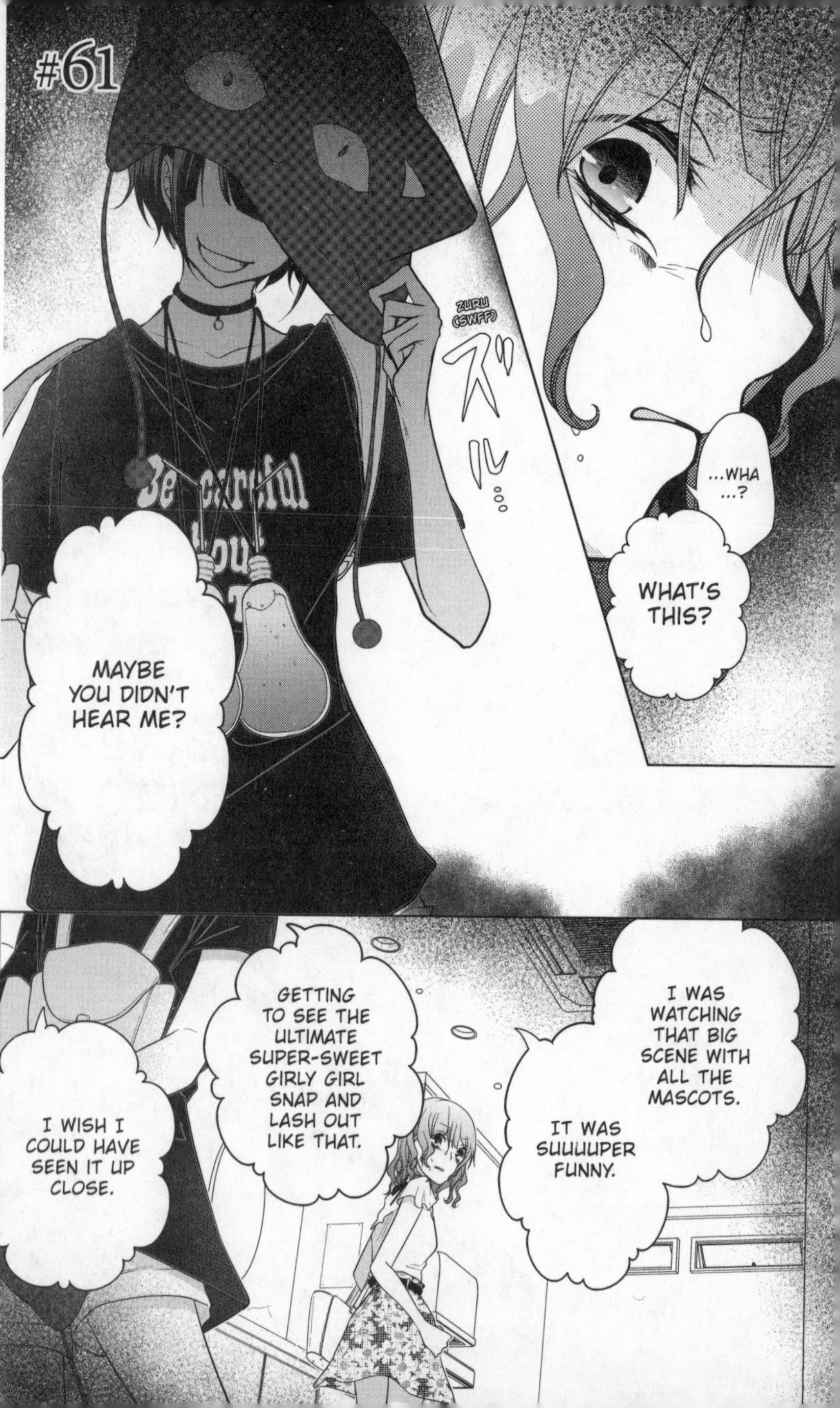
#61
...WHA ...?
WHAT'S THIS?
ZURU (SWFF)
ズル
MAYBE YOU DIDN'T HEAR ME?
I WAS WATCHING THAT BIG SCENE WITH ALL THE MASCOTS.
IT WAS SUUUUPER FUNNY.
GETTING TO SEE THE ULTIMATE SUPER-SWEET GIRLY GIRL SNAP AND LASH OUT LIKE THAT.
I WISH I COULD HAVE SEEN IT UP CLOSE.

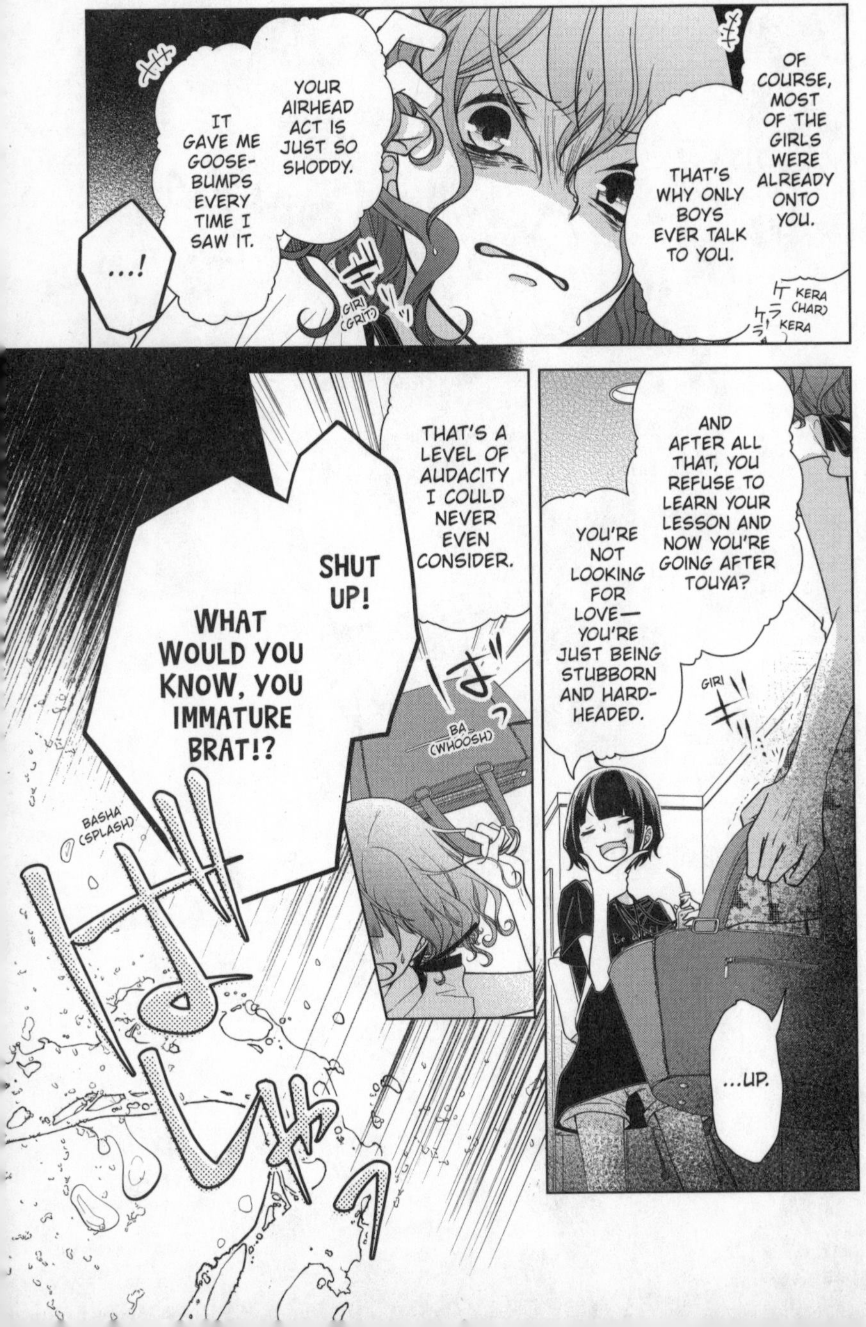
OF COURSE, MOST OF THE GIRLS WERE ALREADY ONTO YOU.
THAT'S WHY ONLY BOYS EVER TALK TO YOU.
KERA KERA (HAR)
YOUR AIRHEAD ACT IS JUST SO SHODDY.
IT GAVE ME GOOSE-BUMPS EVERY TIME I SAW IT.
GIRI (GRIT)
...!
AND AFTER ALL THAT, YOU REFUSE TO LEARN YOUR LESSON AND NOW YOU'RE GOING AFTER TOUYA?
YOU'RE NOT LOOKING FOR LOVE— YOU'RE JUST BEING STUBBORN AND HARD-HEADED.
GIRI
...UP.
THAT'S A LEVEL OF AUDACITY I COULD NEVER EVEN CONSIDER.
SHUT UP!
BA (WHOOSH)
WHAT WOULD YOU KNOW, YOU IMMATURE BRAT!?
BASHA (SPLASH)

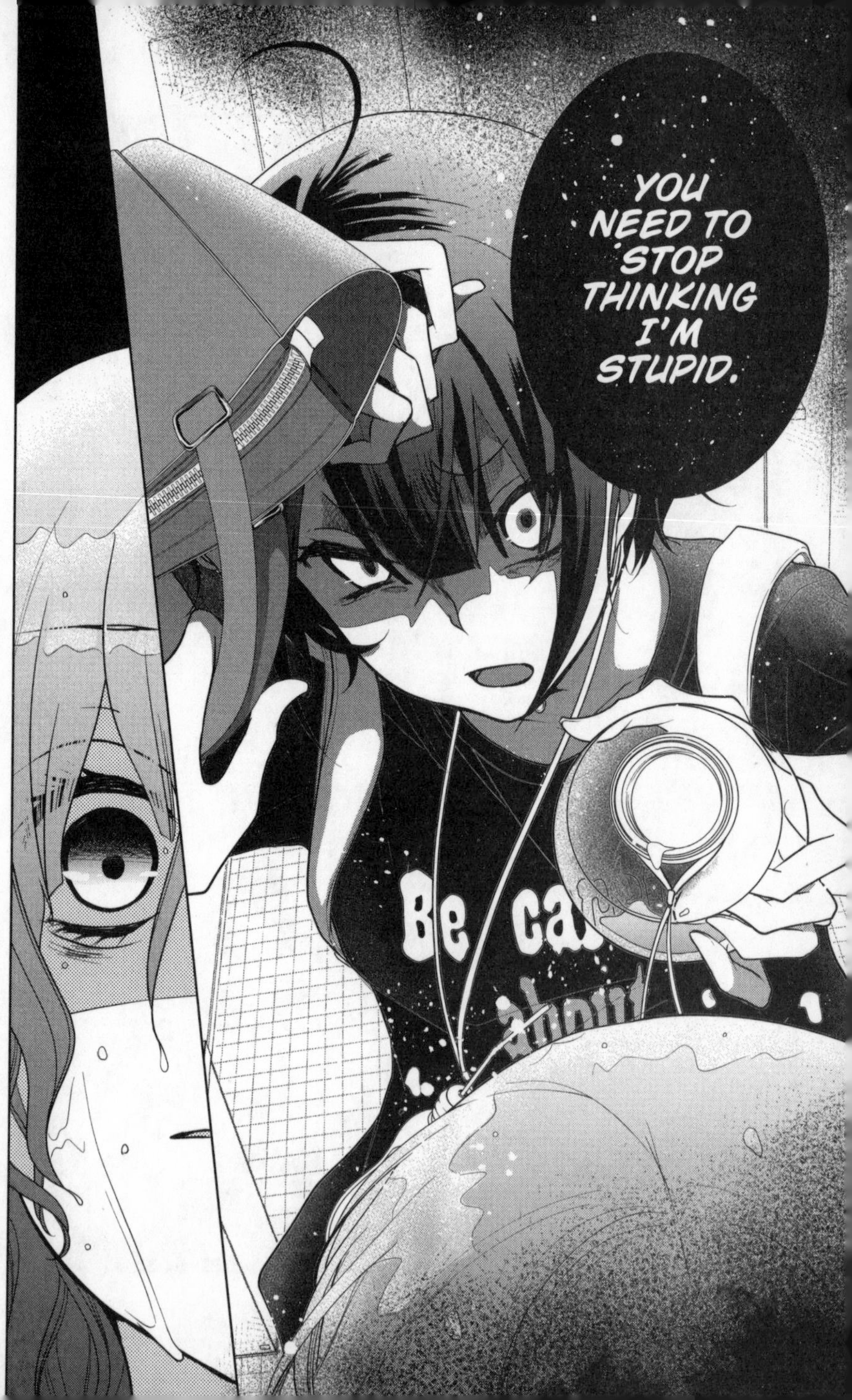
YOU NEED TO STOP THINKING I'M STUPID.

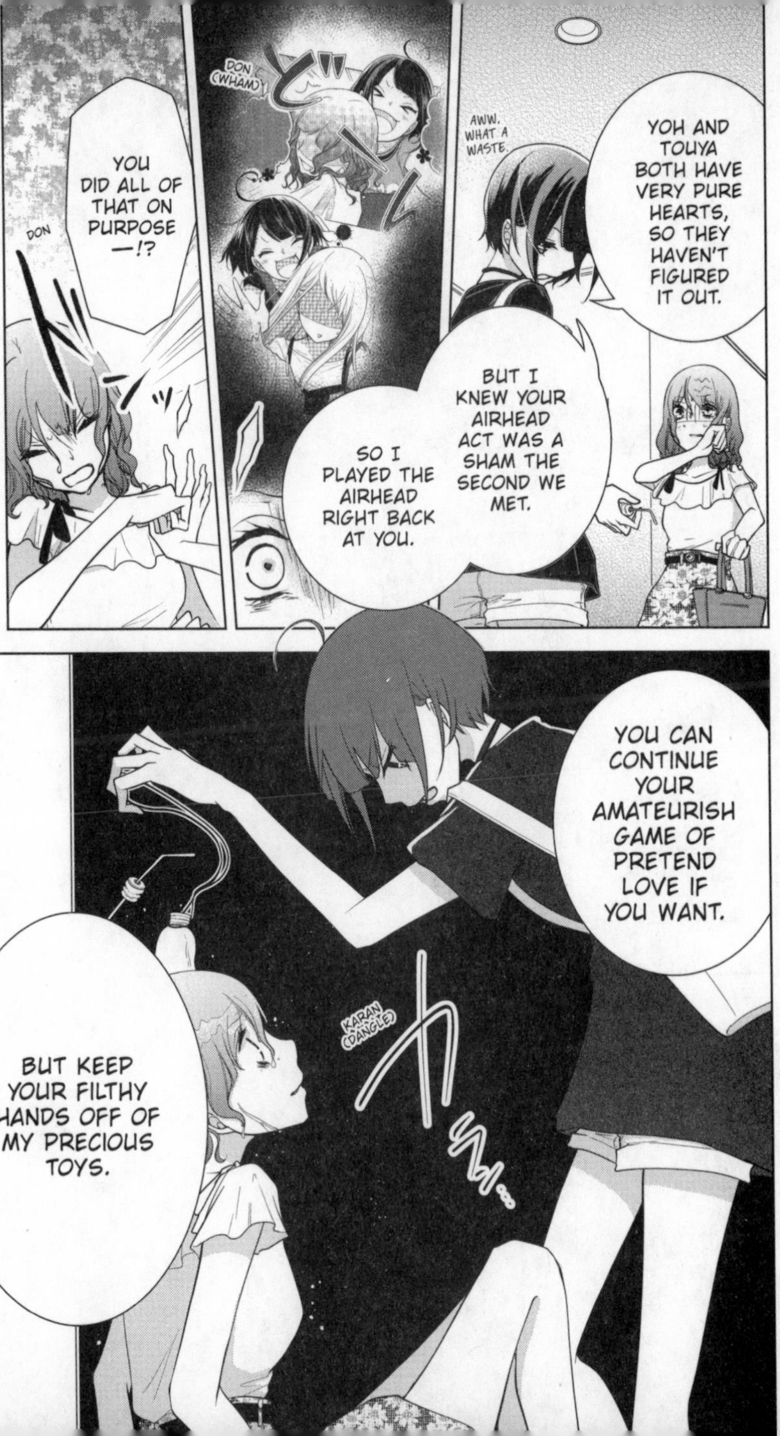
YOH AND TOUYA BOTH HAVE VERY PURE HEARTS, SO THEY HAVEN'T FIGURED IT OUT.
AWW, WHAT A WASTE.
BUT I KNEW YOUR AIRHEAD ACT WAS A SHAM THE SECOND WE MET.
SO I PLAYED THE AIRHEAD RIGHT BACK AT YOU.
DON (WHAM)
YOU DID ALL OF THAT ON PURPOSE —!?
DON
YOU CAN CONTINUE YOUR AMATEURISH GAME OF PRETEND LOVE IF YOU WANT.
KARAN (DANGLE)
BUT KEEP YOUR FILTHY HANDS OFF OF MY PRECIOUS TOYS.

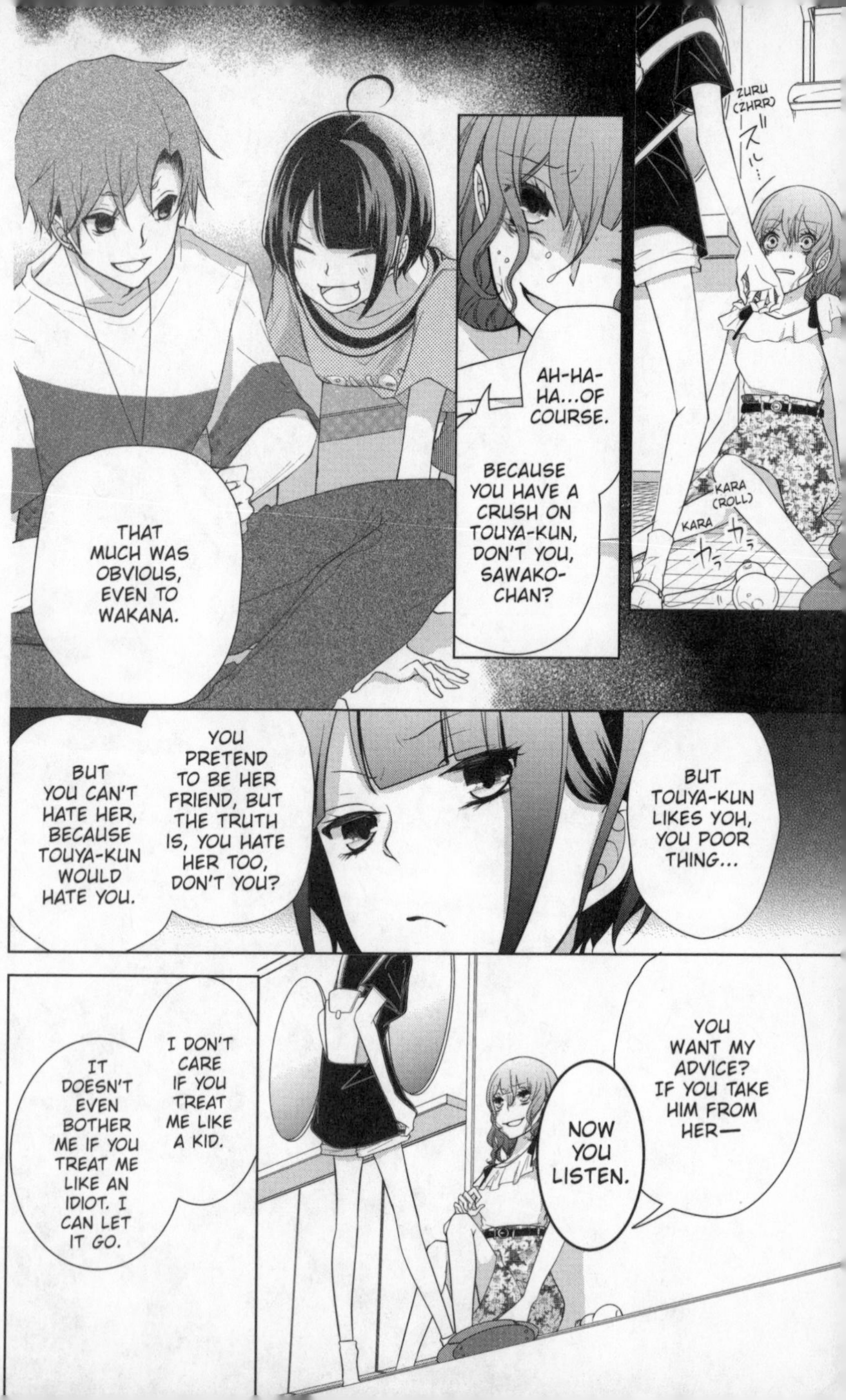
ZURU (ZHRR)
ズル…
KARA (ROLL)
KARA
カラ
カラ
AH-HA-HA...OF COURSE.
BECAUSE YOU HAVE A CRUSH ON TOUYA-KUN, DON'T YOU, SAWAKO-CHAN?
THAT MUCH WAS OBVIOUS, EVEN TO WAKANA.
BUT TOUYA-KUN LIKES YOH, YOU POOR THING...
YOU PRETEND TO BE HER FRIEND, BUT THE TRUTH IS, YOU HATE HER TOO, DON'T YOU?
BUT YOU CAN'T HATE HER, BECAUSE TOUYA-KUN WOULD HATE YOU.
YOU WANT MY ADVICE? IF YOU TAKE HIM FROM HER—
NOW YOU LISTEN.
I DON'T CARE IF YOU TREAT ME LIKE A KID.
IT DOESN'T EVEN BOTHER ME IF YOU TREAT ME LIKE AN IDIOT. I CAN LET IT GO.

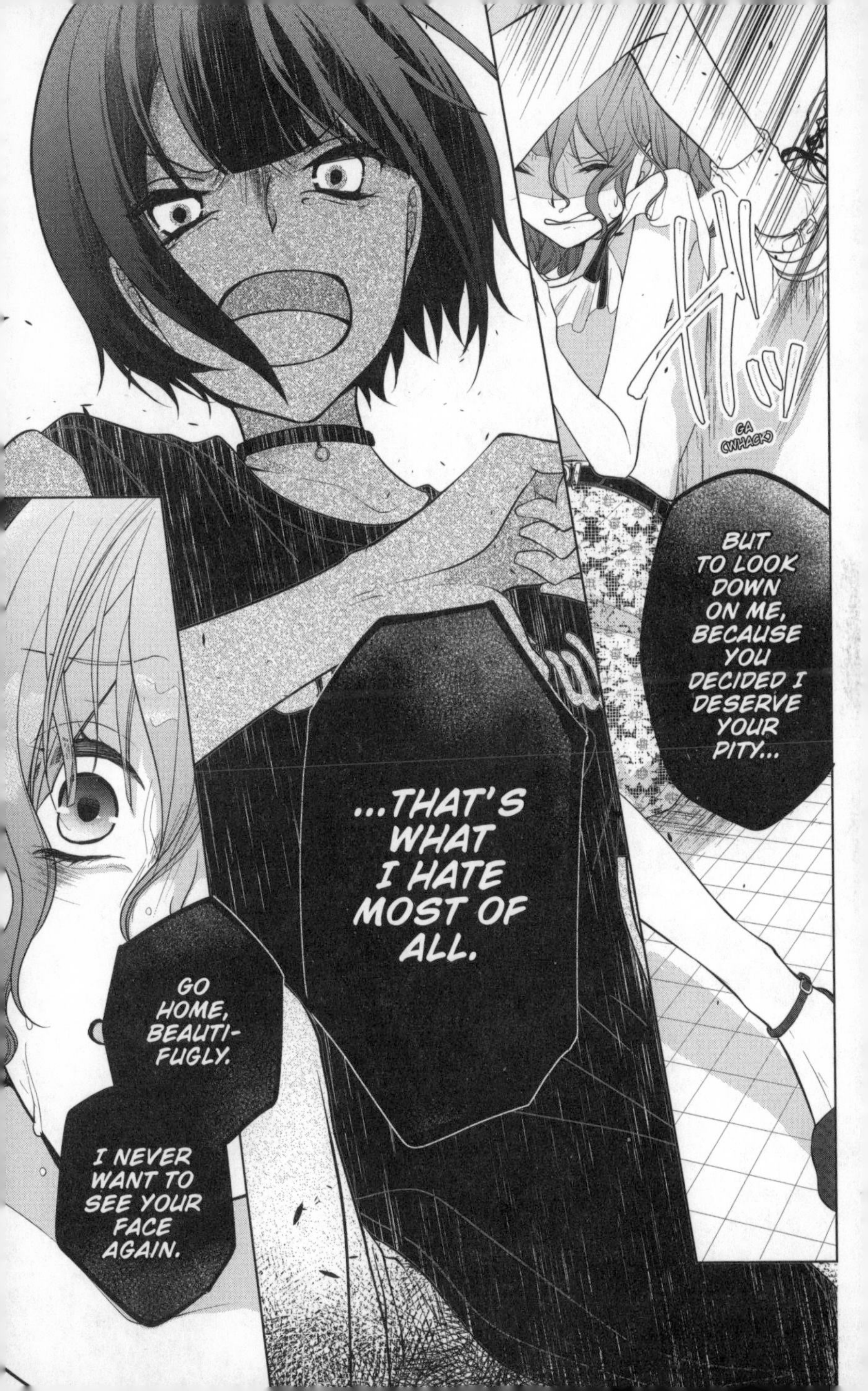
GA (WHACK)
BUT TO LOOK DOWN ON ME, BECAUSE YOU DECIDED I DESERVE YOUR PITY...
...THAT'S WHAT I HATE MOST OF ALL.
GO HOME, BEAUTI-FUGLY.
I NEVER WANT TO SEE YOUR FACE AGAIN.

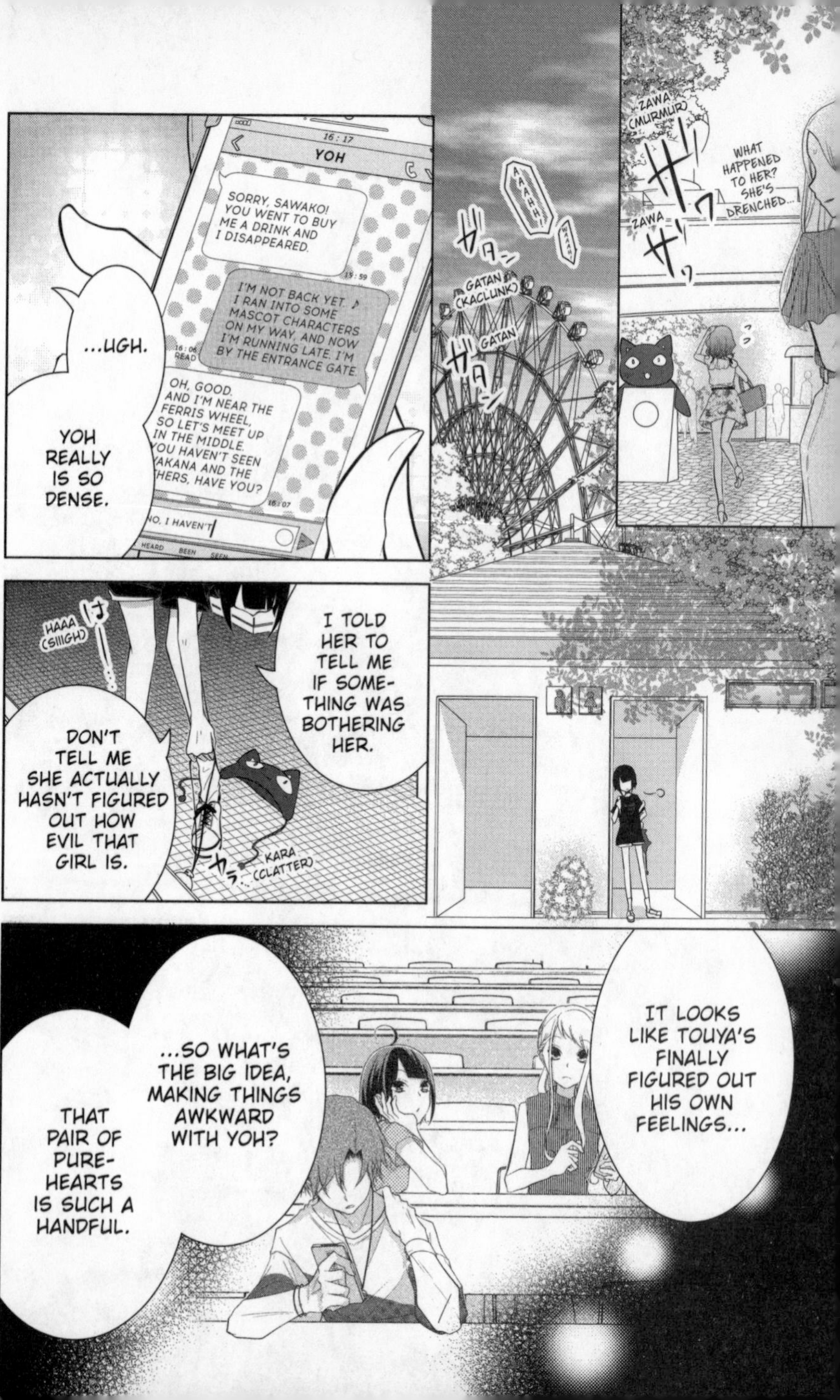
ZAWA (MURMUR)
ZAWA
WHAT HAPPENED TO HER? SHE'S DRENCHED...
AAAHH!
WAAAH!
GATAN (KACLUNK)
GATAN
16:17
YOH
SORRY, SAWAKO! YOU WENT TO BUY ME A DRINK AND I DISAPPEARED.
15:59
I'M NOT BACK YET. ♪ I RAN INTO SOME MASCOT CHARACTERS ON MY WAY, AND NOW I'M RUNNING LATE. I'M BY THE ENTRANCE GATE.
16:06 READ
OH, GOOD. AND I'M NEAR THE FERRIS WHEEL, SO LET'S MEET UP IN THE MIDDLE. YOU HAVEN'T SEEN YAKANA AND THE OTHERS, HAVE YOU?
16:07
NO, I HAVEN'T
HEARD BEEN SEEN
...UGH.
YOH REALLY IS SO DENSE.
I TOLD HER TO TELL ME IF SOME-THING WAS BOTHERING HER.
HAAA (SIIIGH)
DON'T TELL ME SHE ACTUALLY HASN'T FIGURED OUT HOW EVIL THAT GIRL IS.
KARA (CLATTER)
IT LOOKS LIKE TOUYA'S FINALLY FIGURED OUT HIS OWN FEELINGS...
...SO WHAT'S THE BIG IDEA, MAKING THINGS AWKWARD WITH YOH?
THAT PAIR OF PURE-HEARTS IS SUCH A HANDFUL.

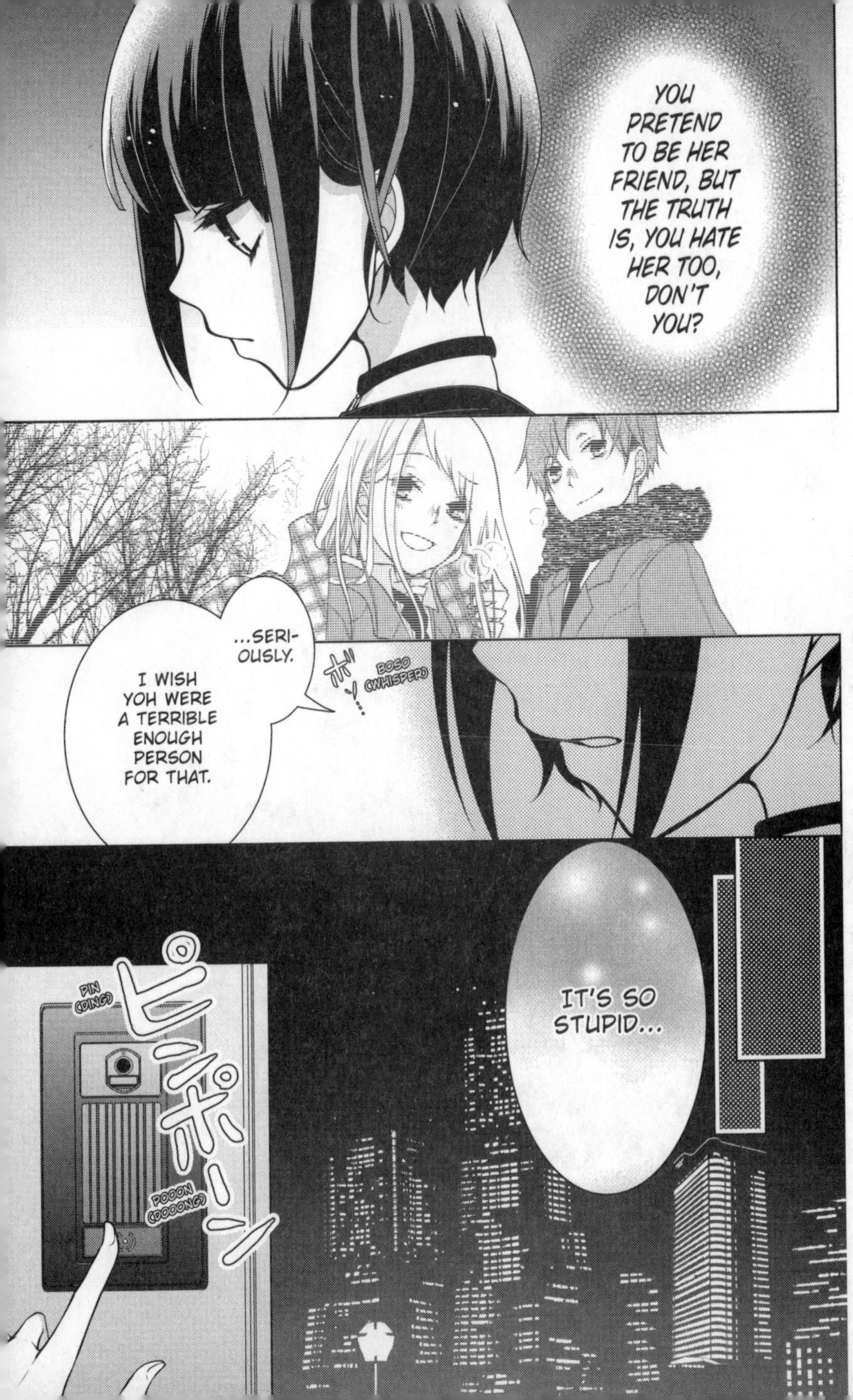
YOU PRETEND TO BE HER FRIEND, BUT THE TRUTH IS, YOU HATE HER TOO, DON'T YOU?
BOSO (WHISPER)
...SERI-OUSLY.
I WISH YOH WERE A TERRIBLE ENOUGH PERSON FOR THAT.
IT'S SO STUPID...
PIN (DING)
POOON (DOOONG)

#62

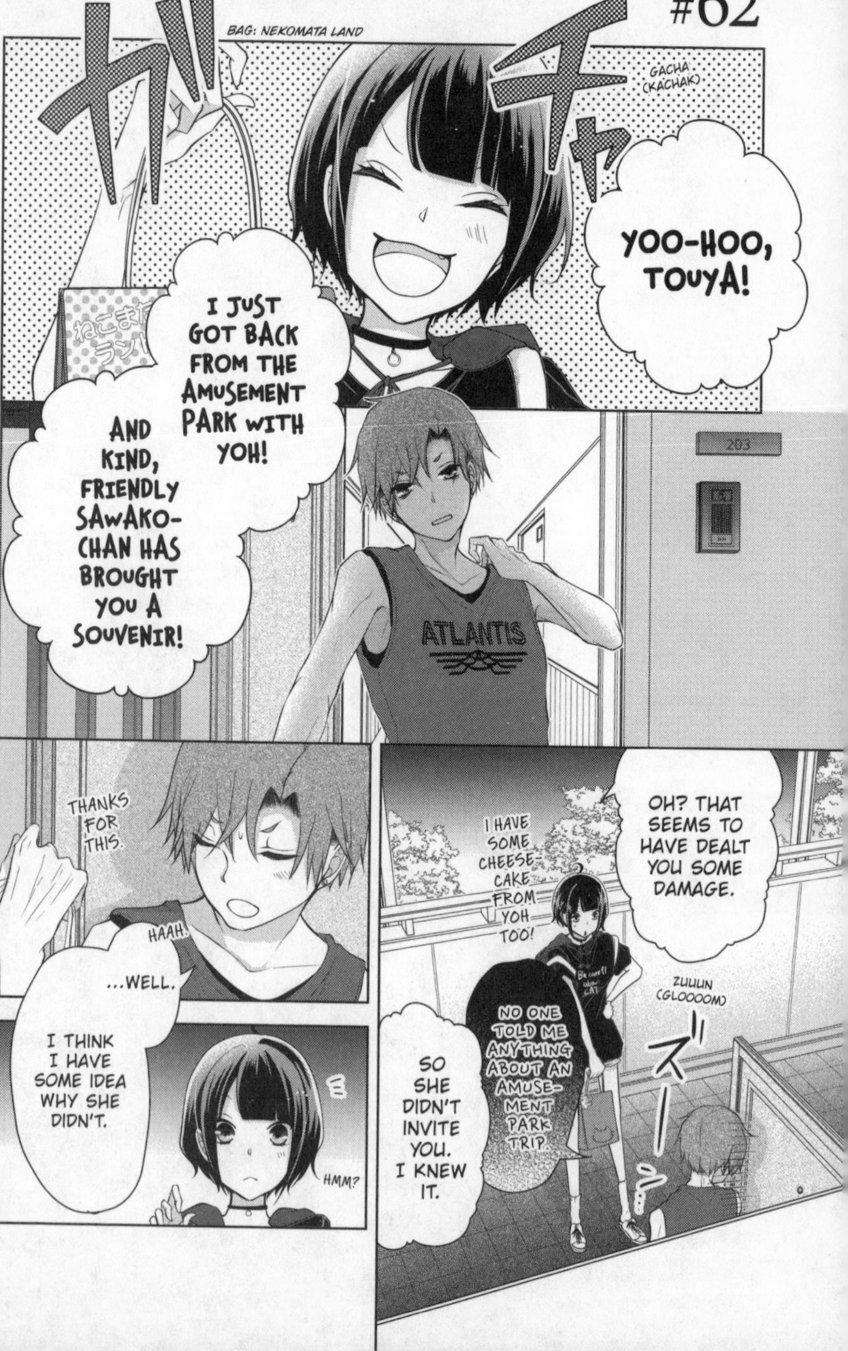
GACHA (KACHAK)
BAG: NEKOMATA LAND
YOO-HOO, TOUYA!
I JUST GOT BACK FROM THE AMUSEMENT PARK WITH YOH!
AND KIND, FRIENDLY SAWAKO-CHAN HAS BROUGHT YOU A SOUVENIR!
OH? THAT SEEMS TO HAVE DEALT YOU SOME DAMAGE.
I HAVE SOME CHEESE-CAKE FROM YOH TOO!
ZUUUN (GLOOOOM)
NO ONE TOLD ME ANYTHING ABOUT AN AMUSE-MENT PARK TRIP.
SO SHE DIDN'T INVITE YOU. I KNEW IT.
THANKS FOR THIS.
HAAH.
...WELL.
I THINK I HAVE SOME IDEA WHY SHE DIDN'T.
HMM?

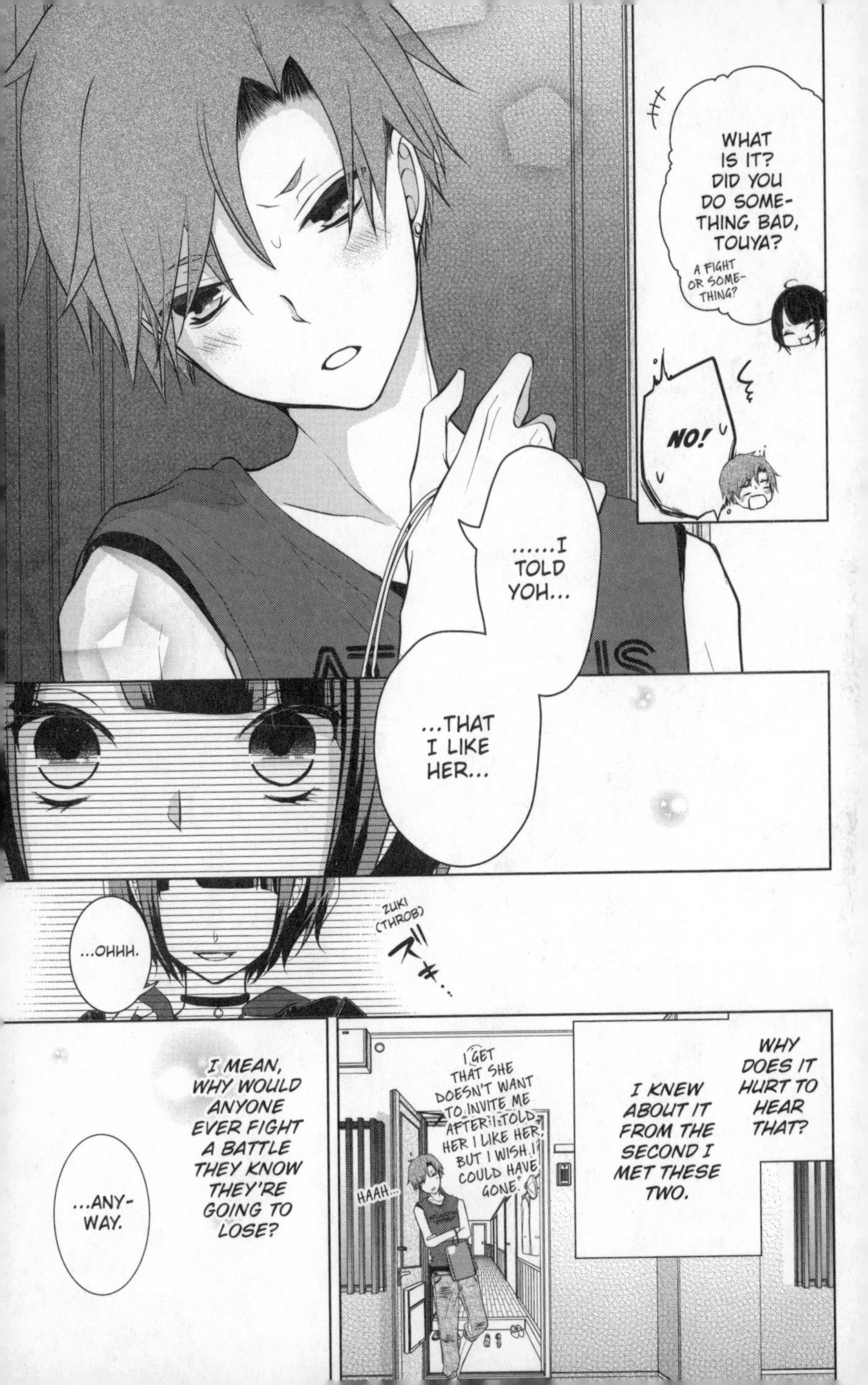
WHAT IS IT? DID YOU DO SOME-THING BAD, TOUYA?
A FIGHT OR SOME-THING?
NO!
......I TOLD YOH...
...THAT I LIKE HER...
ZUKI (THROB)
...OHHH.
WHY DOES IT HURT TO HEAR THAT?
I KNEW ABOUT IT FROM THE SECOND I MET THESE TWO.
I GET THAT SHE DOESN'T WANT TO INVITE ME AFTER I TOLD HER I LIKE HER, BUT I WISH I COULD HAVE GONE.
HAAH...
I MEAN, WHY WOULD ANYONE EVER FIGHT A BATTLE THEY KNOW THEY'RE GOING TO LOSE?
...ANY-WAY.

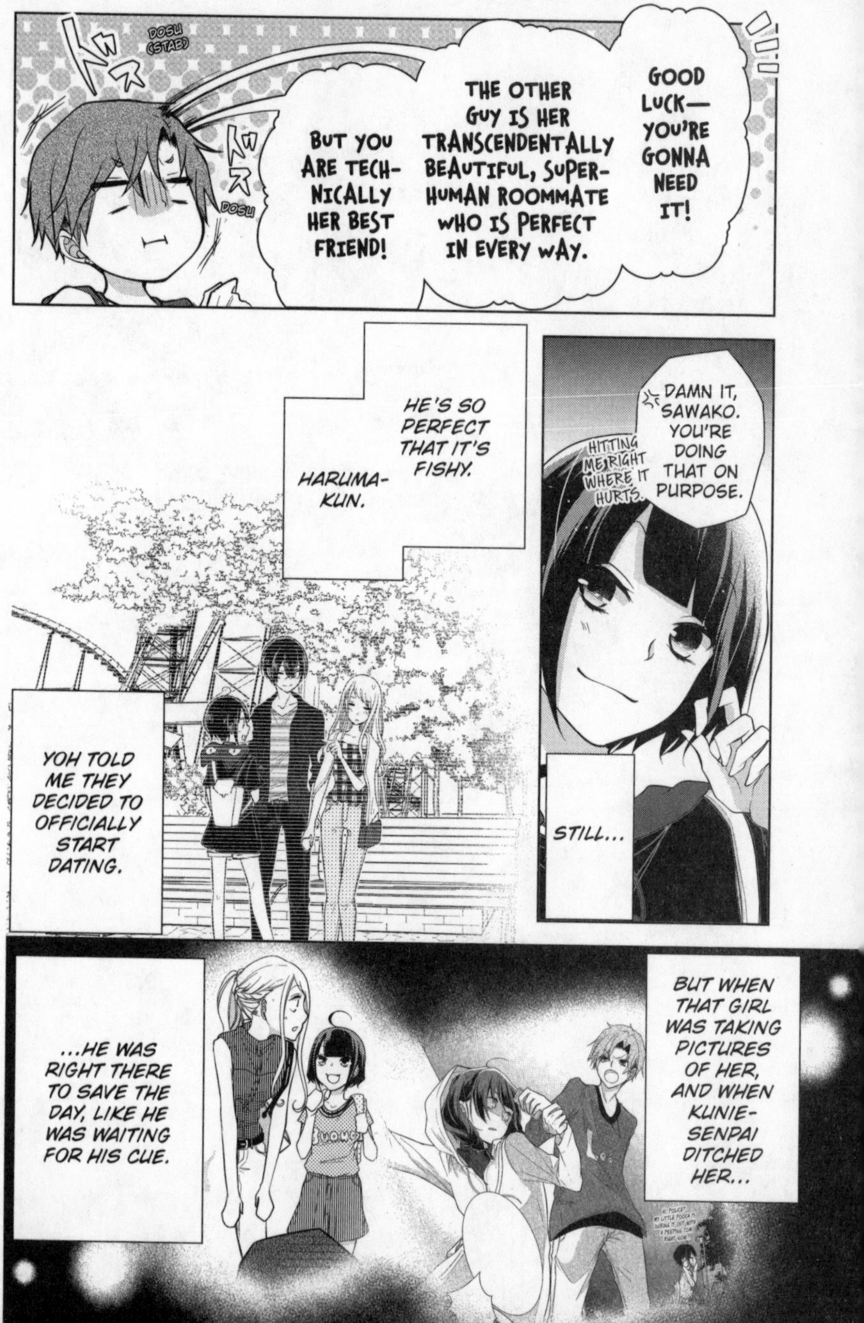
DOSU (STAB)
DOSU
GOOD LUCK—YOU'RE GONNA NEED IT!
THE OTHER GUY IS HER TRANSCENDENTALLY BEAUTIFUL, SUPER-HUMAN ROOMMATE WHO IS PERFECT IN EVERY WAY.
BUT YOU ARE TECH-NICALLY HER BEST FRIEND!
DAMN IT, SAWAKO. YOU'RE DOING THAT ON PURPOSE.
HITTING ME RIGHT WHERE IT HURTS.
STILL...
HE'S SO PERFECT THAT IT'S FISHY.
HARUMA-KUN.
YOH TOLD ME THEY DECIDED TO OFFICIALLY START DATING.
BUT WHEN THAT GIRL WAS TAKING PICTURES OF HER, AND WHEN KUNIE-SENPAI DITCHED HER...
...HE WAS RIGHT THERE TO SAVE THE DAY, LIKE HE WAS WAITING FOR HIS CUE.

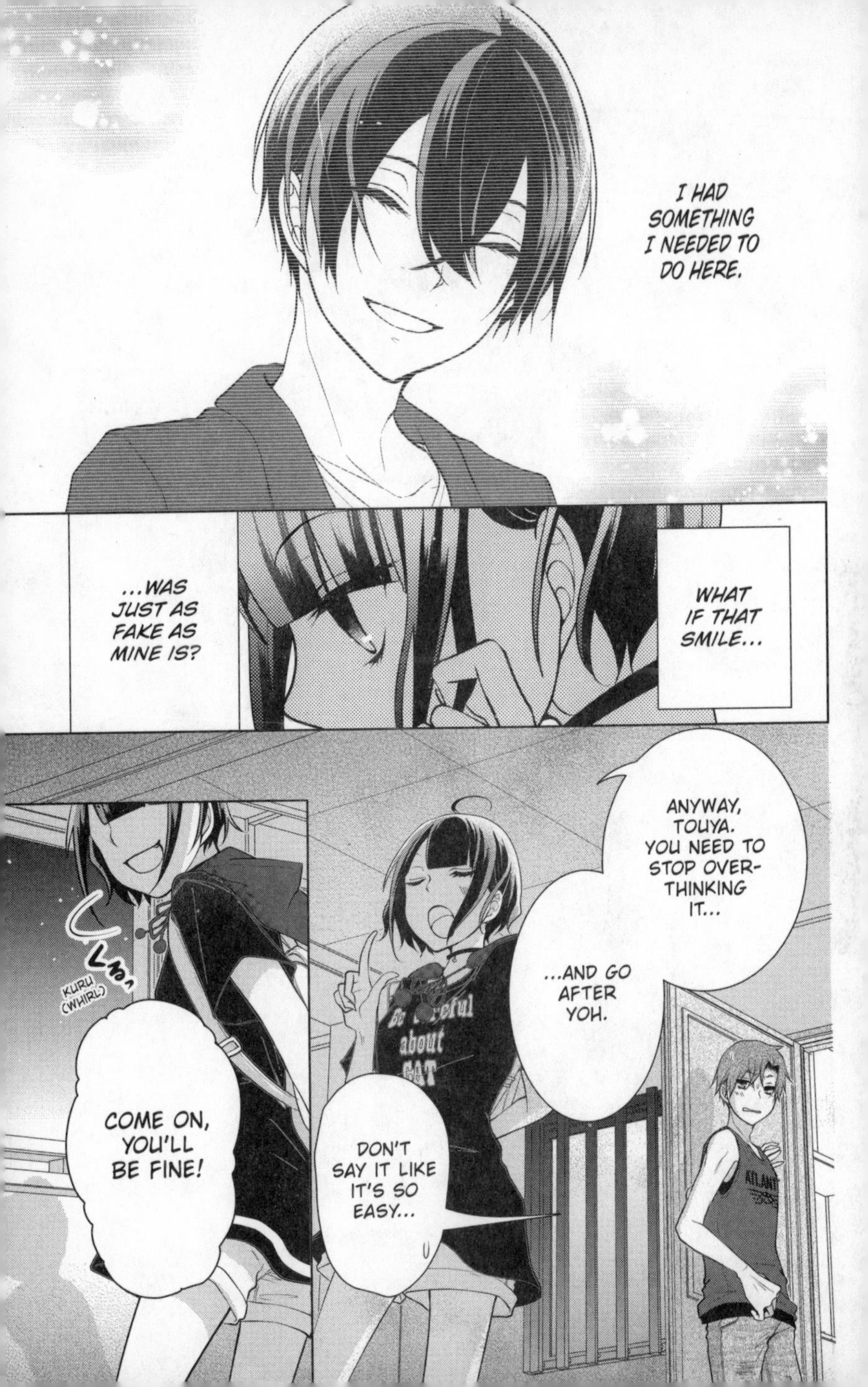
I HAD SOMETHING I NEEDED TO DO HERE.
WHAT IF THAT SMILE...
...WAS JUST AS FAKE AS MINE IS?
ANYWAY, TOUYA. YOU NEED TO STOP OVER-THINKING IT...
...AND GO AFTER YOH.
DON'T SAY IT LIKE IT'S SO EASY...
KURU (WHIRL)
COME ON, YOU'LL BE FINE!

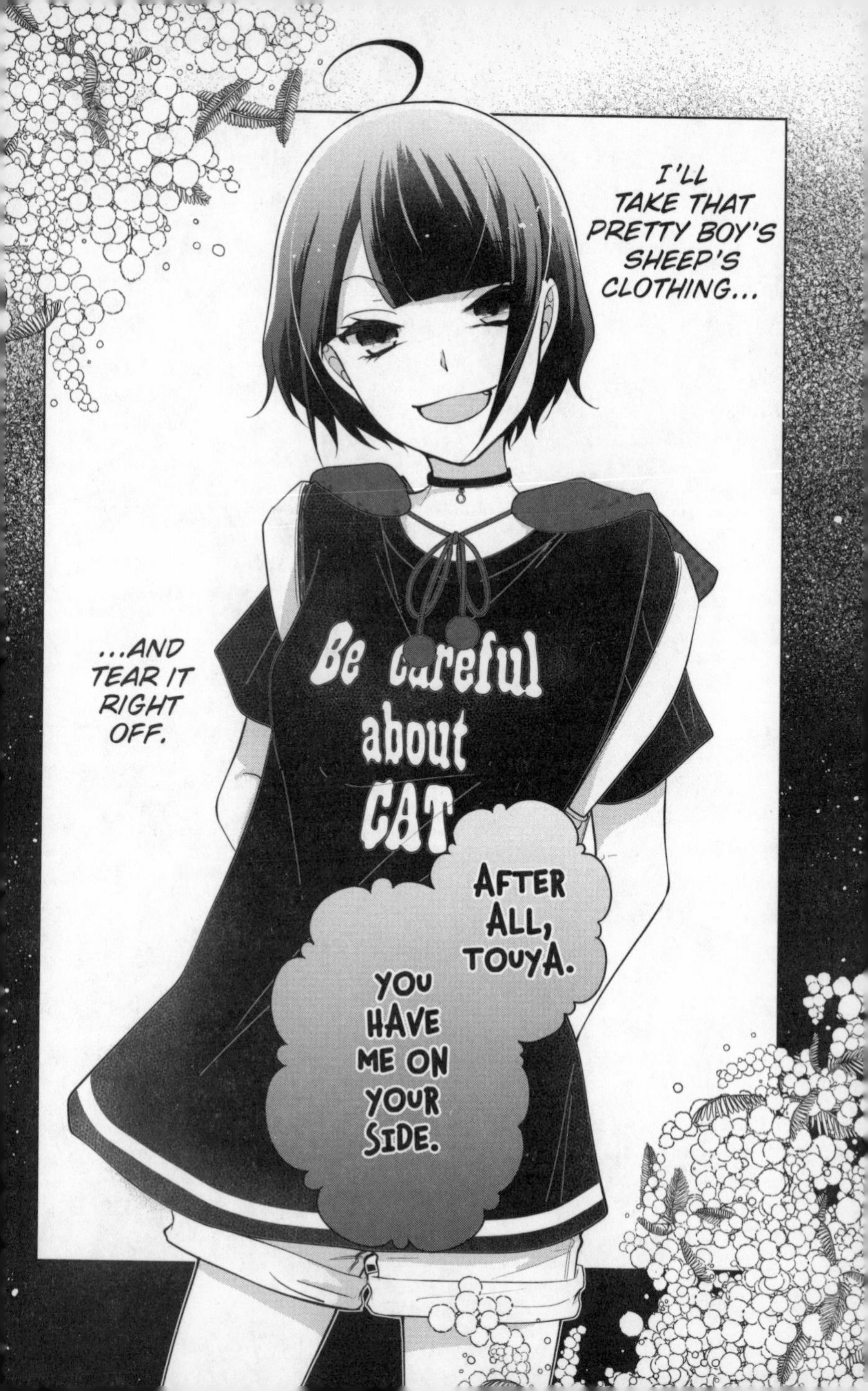
I'LL TAKE THAT PRETTY BOY'S SHEEP'S CLOTHING...
...AND TEAR IT RIGHT OFF.
Be careful about CAT
AFTER ALL, TOUYA.
YOU HAVE ME ON YOUR SIDE.

ONE PHRASE THAT CAN ERASE ALL THE DISCONTENT

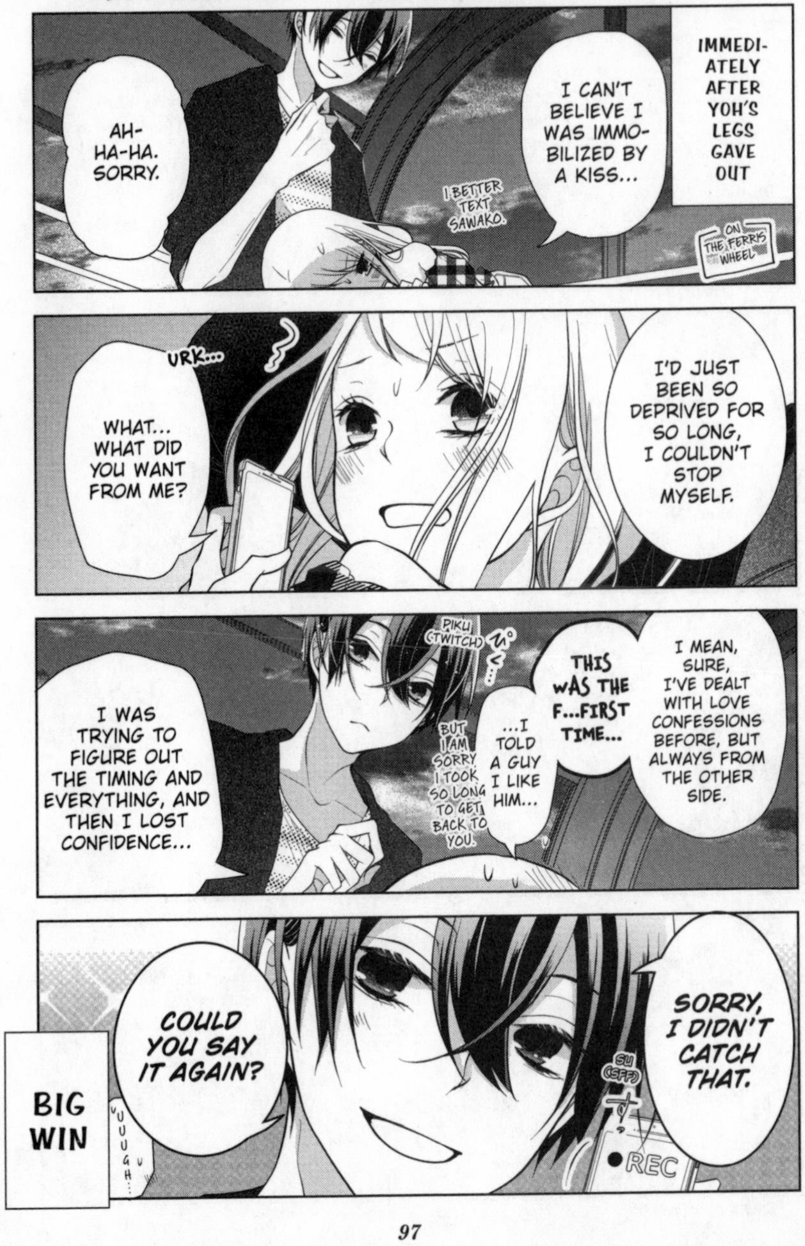
IMMEDIATELY AFTER YOH'S LEGS GAVE OUT
ON THE FERRIS WHEEL
I CAN'T BELIEVE I WAS IMMOBILIZED BY A KISS...
I BETTER TEXT SAWAKO.
AH-HA-HA. SORRY.
I'D JUST BEEN SO DEPRIVED FOR SO LONG, I COULDN'T STOP MYSELF.
URK...
WHAT... WHAT DID YOU WANT FROM ME?
I MEAN, SURE, I'VE DEALT WITH LOVE CONFESSIONS BEFORE, BUT ALWAYS FROM THE OTHER SIDE.
THIS WAS THE F...FIRST TIME...
...I TOLD A GUY I LIKE HIM...
PIKU (TWITCH)
BUT I AM SORRY I TOOK SO LONG TO GET BACK TO YOU.
I WAS TRYING TO FIGURE OUT THE TIMING AND EVERYTHING, AND THEN I LOST CONFIDENCE...
SORRY, I DIDN'T CATCH THAT.
SU (SFF)
REC
COULD YOU SAY IT AGAIN?
UUUGH...
BIG WIN

UNPRECEDENTEDLY LARGE BREASTS

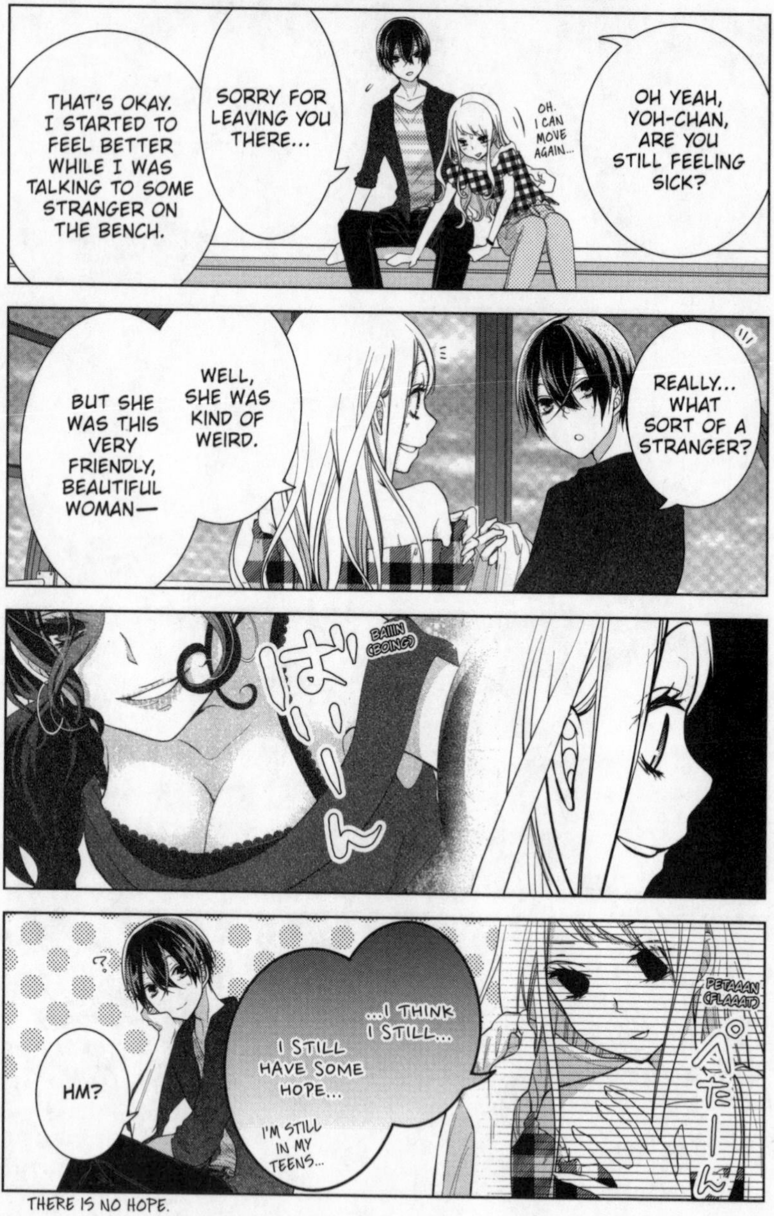
OH YEAH, YOH-CHAN, ARE YOU STILL FEELING SICK?
OH. I CAN MOVE AGAIN...
SORRY FOR LEAVING YOU THERE...
THAT'S OKAY. I STARTED TO FEEL BETTER WHILE I WAS TALKING TO SOME STRANGER ON THE BENCH.
REALLY... WHAT SORT OF A STRANGER?
WELL, SHE WAS KIND OF WEIRD.
BUT SHE WAS THIS VERY FRIENDLY, BEAUTIFUL WOMAN—
BAIIIN (BOING)
ばいーん
PETAAAN (FLAAAT)
ぺたーん
...I THINK I STILL...
I STILL HAVE SOME HOPE...
I'M STILL IN MY TEENS...
HM?

THERE IS NO HOPE.

WAY WORSE THAN BEFORE

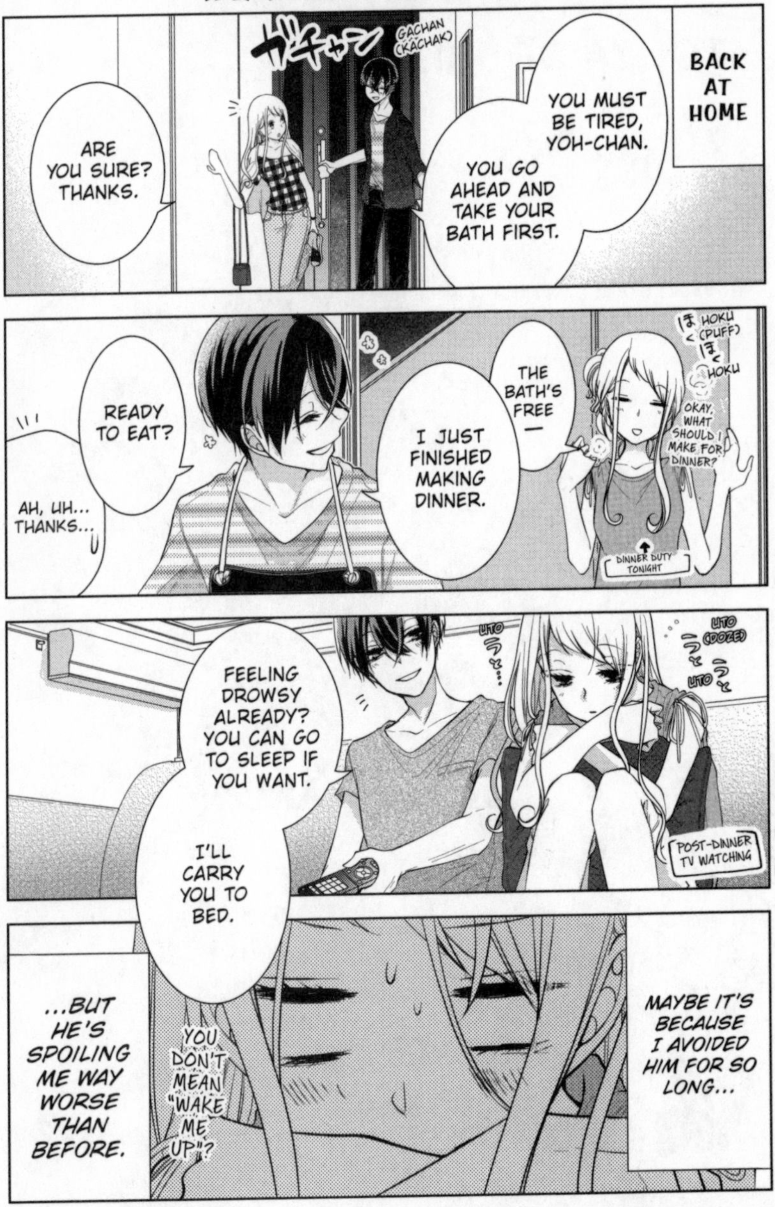
BACK AT HOME
YOU MUST BE TIRED, YOH-CHAN.
YOU GO AHEAD AND TAKE YOUR BATH FIRST.
GACHAN (KACHAK)
ARE YOU SURE? THANKS.
HOKU (PUFF) HOKU
OKAY, WHAT SHOULD I MAKE FOR DINNER?
DINNER DUTY TONIGHT
THE BATH'S FREE—
I JUST FINISHED MAKING DINNER.
READY TO EAT?
AH, UH... THANKS...
UTO (DOZE) UTO
UTO
POST-DINNER TV WATCHING
FEELING DROWSY ALREADY? YOU CAN GO TO SLEEP IF YOU WANT.
I'LL CARRY YOU TO BED.
MAYBE IT'S BECAUSE I AVOIDED HIM FOR SO LONG...
YOU DON'T MEAN "WAKE ME UP"?
...BUT HE'S SPOILING ME WAY WORSE THAN BEFORE.

TOUYA OOSHIMA

Age: 18
Birthday: December 21
Zodiac Sign: Sagittarius
Blood Type: B
Height: 180 cm [5′11″]
Weight: 65 kg [143 lbs.]
Family: Father, mother, younger sister
Hobbies: Video games, shopping
Special Skills: Basketball (was on the team in elementary and middle school)
Likes: Soba, accessories, shoes
Dislikes: Anything sweet, girl fights
Current Desire: His own apartment

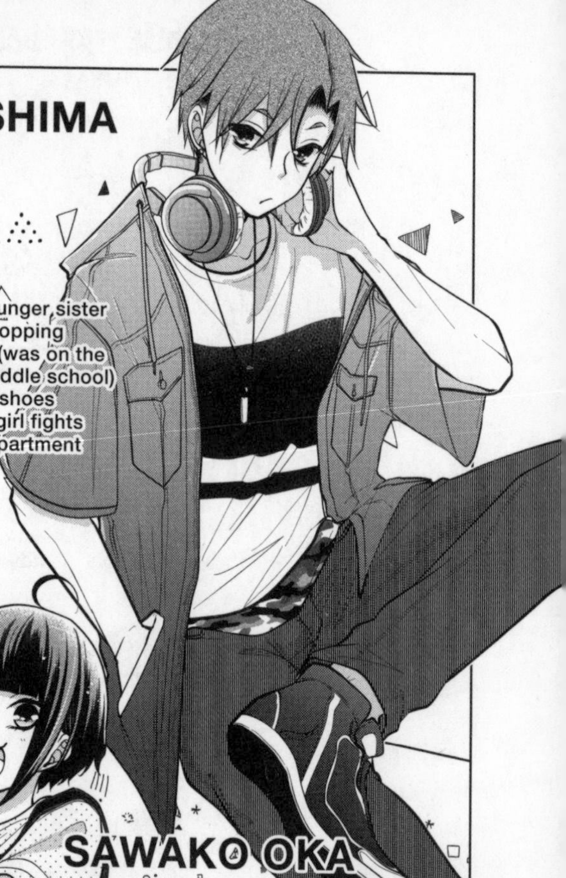

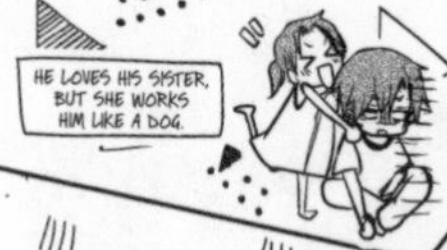
HE LOVES HIS SISTER, BUT SHE WORKS HIM LIKE A DOG.

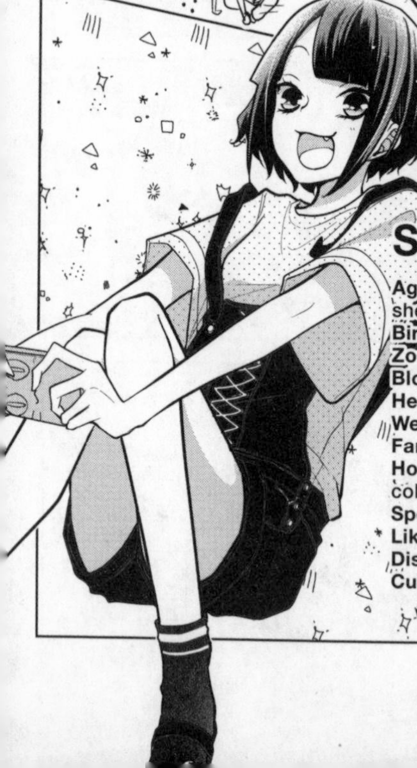

SAWAKO OKA

Age: 18 (but when the story got to June, she turned 19)
Birthday: June 6
Zodiac Sign: Gemini
Blood Type: O
Height: 150 cm [4′11″]
Weight: 45 kg [99 lbs.]
Family: Father, mother, two older sisters
Hobbies: Video games, collecting cat-themed merch
Special Skills: Worldly wisdom
Likes: Sweets such as ice cream, cat stuff
Dislikes: Spicy food
Current Desire: A crepe food truck

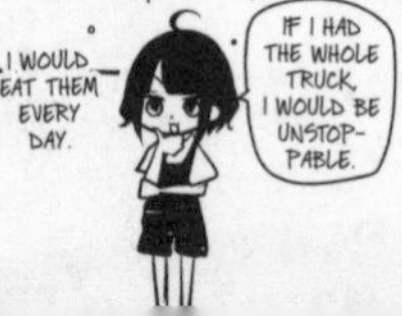
IF I HAD THE WHOLE TRUCK, I WOULD BE UNSTOP-PABLE.
I WOULD EAT THEM EVERY DAY.

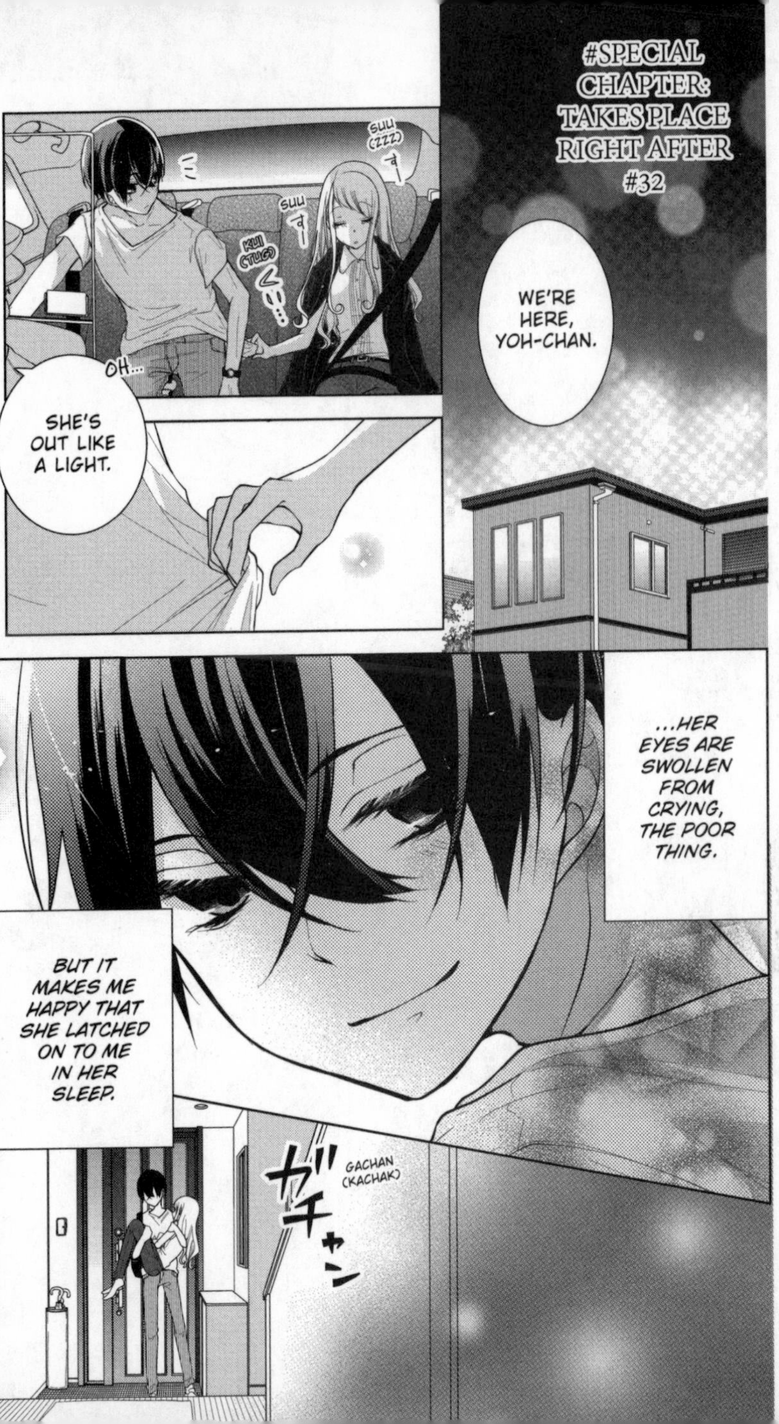
#SPECIAL CHAPTER: TAKES PLACE RIGHT AFTER #32
WE'RE HERE, YOH-CHAN.
SUU (ZZZ)
すー
SUU
す
KUI (TUG)
くい…
OH...
SHE'S OUT LIKE A LIGHT.
...HER EYES ARE SWOLLEN FROM CRYING, THE POOR THING.
BUT IT MAKES ME HAPPY THAT SHE LATCHED ON TO ME IN HER SLEEP.
GACHAN (KACHAK)
ガチャン

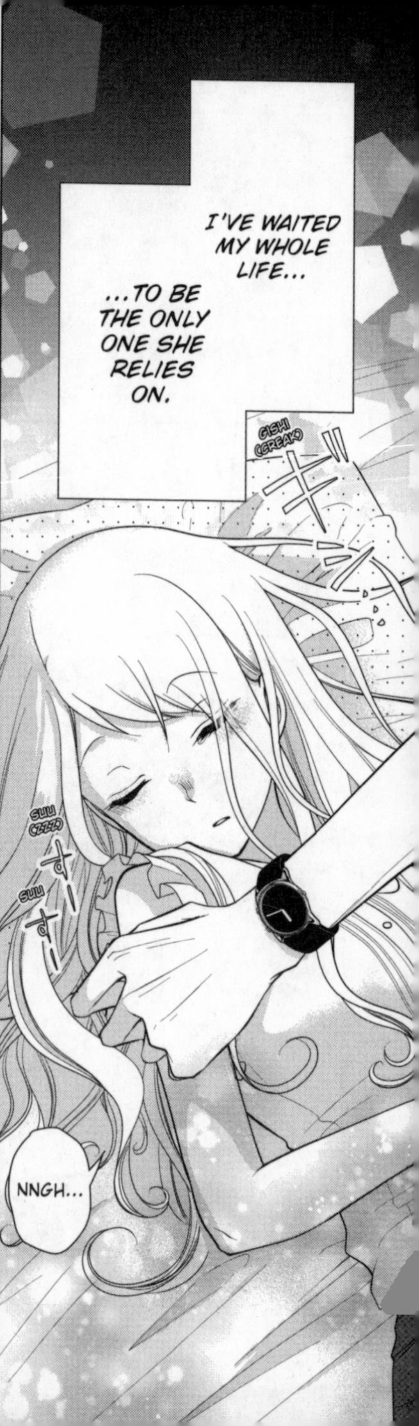
I'VE WAITED MY WHOLE LIFE...
...TO BE THE ONLY ONE SHE RELIES ON.
GISHI (CREAK)
ギシッ
SUU (ZZZ)
すー
SUU
すー
NNGH...
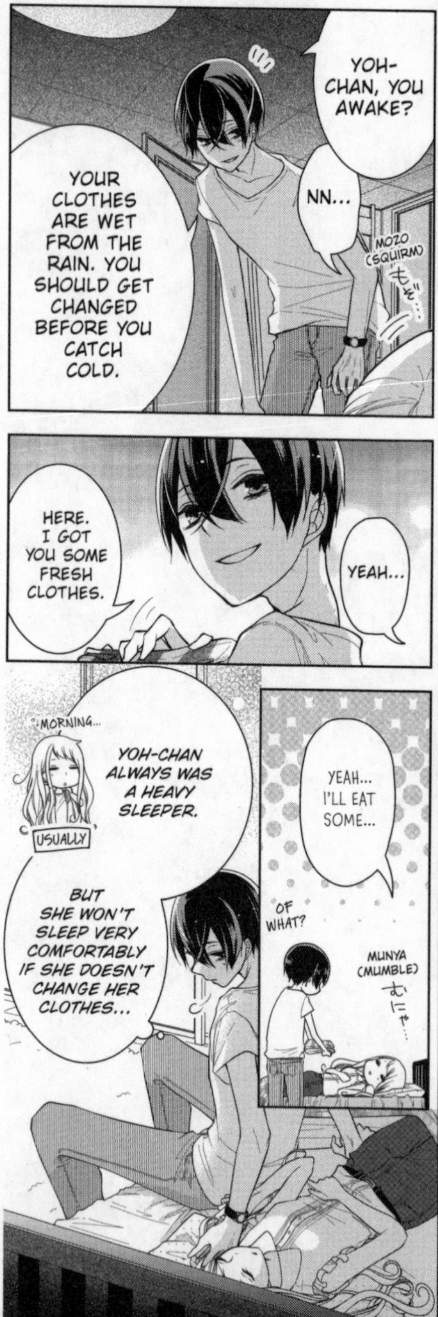
YOH-CHAN, YOU AWAKE?
NN...
MOZO (SQUIRM)
もぞ...
YOUR CLOTHES ARE WET FROM THE RAIN. YOU SHOULD GET CHANGED BEFORE YOU CATCH COLD.
HERE. I GOT YOU SOME FRESH CLOTHES.
YEAH...
YEAH... I'LL EAT SOME...
OF WHAT?
MUNYA (MUMBLE)
むにゃ...
MORNING...
USUALLY
YOH-CHAN ALWAYS WAS A HEAVY SLEEPER.
BUT SHE WON'T SLEEP VERY COMFORTABLY IF SHE DOESN'T CHANGE HER CLOTHES...

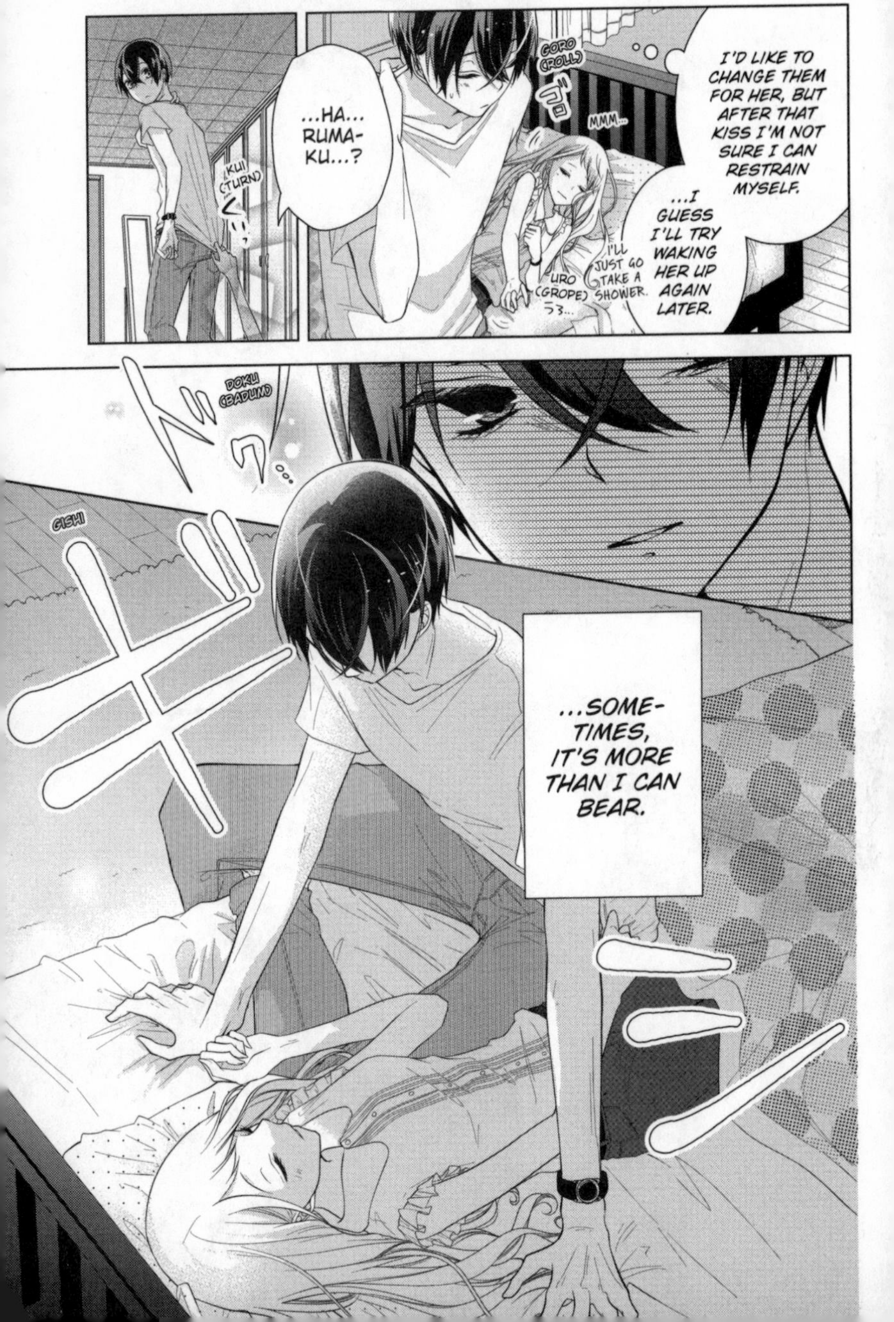
I'D LIKE TO CHANGE THEM FOR HER, BUT AFTER THAT KISS I'M NOT SURE I CAN RESTRAIN MYSELF.
...I GUESS I'LL TRY WAKING HER UP AGAIN LATER.
GORO (ROLL)
MMM...
I'LL JUST GO TAKE A SHOWER.
URO (GROPE)
...HA... RUMA-KU...?
KUI (TURN)
...SOME-TIMES, IT'S MORE THAN I CAN BEAR.
DOKU (BADUM)
GISHI

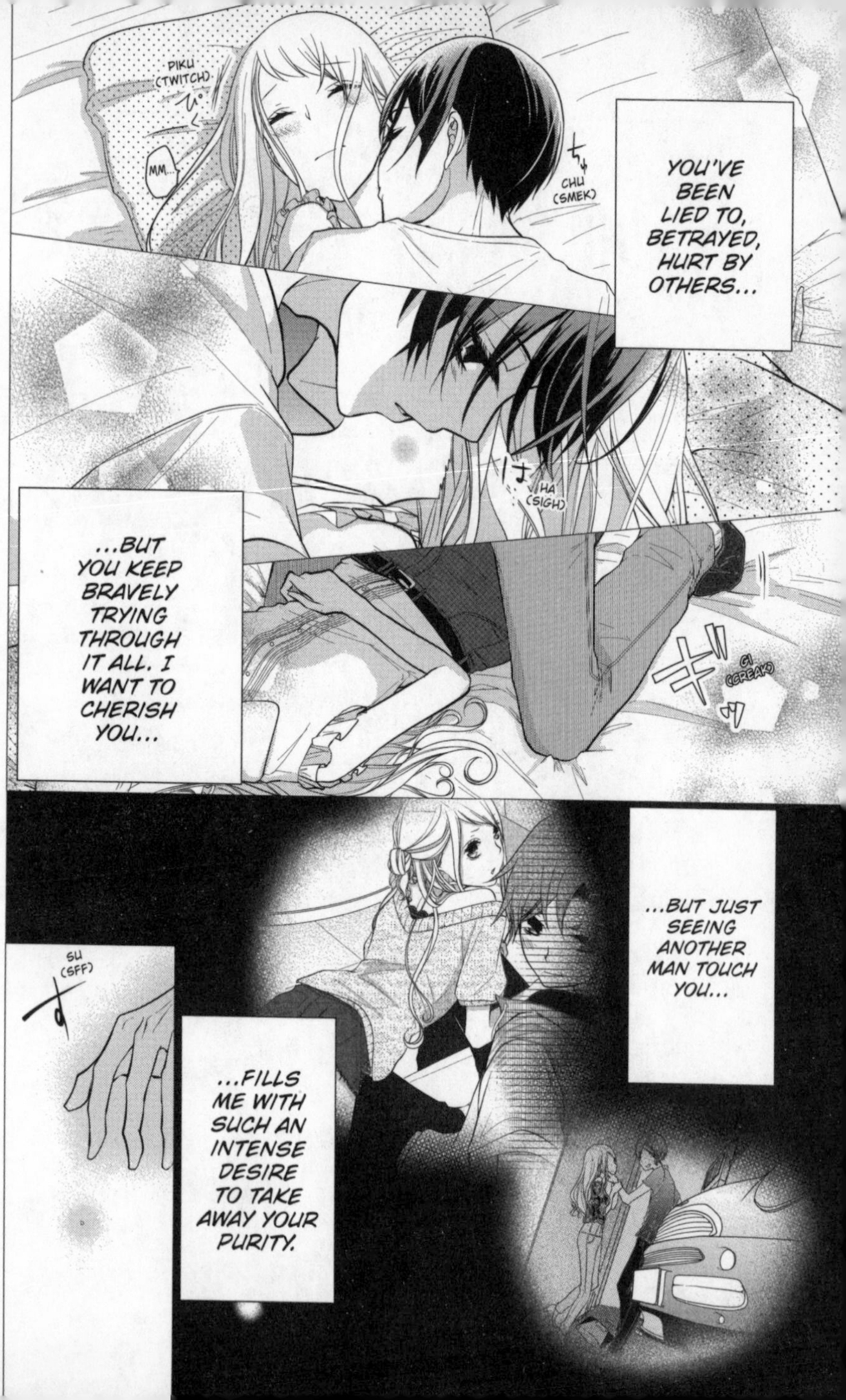
YOU'VE BEEN LIED TO, BETRAYED, HURT BY OTHERS...
CHU (SMEK)
PIKU (TWITCH)
MM...
HA (SIGH)
GI (CREAK)
...BUT YOU KEEP BRAVELY TRYING THROUGH IT ALL. I WANT TO CHERISH YOU...
...BUT JUST SEEING ANOTHER MAN TOUCH YOU...
...FILLS ME WITH SUCH AN INTENSE DESIRE TO TAKE AWAY YOUR PURITY.
SU (SFF)

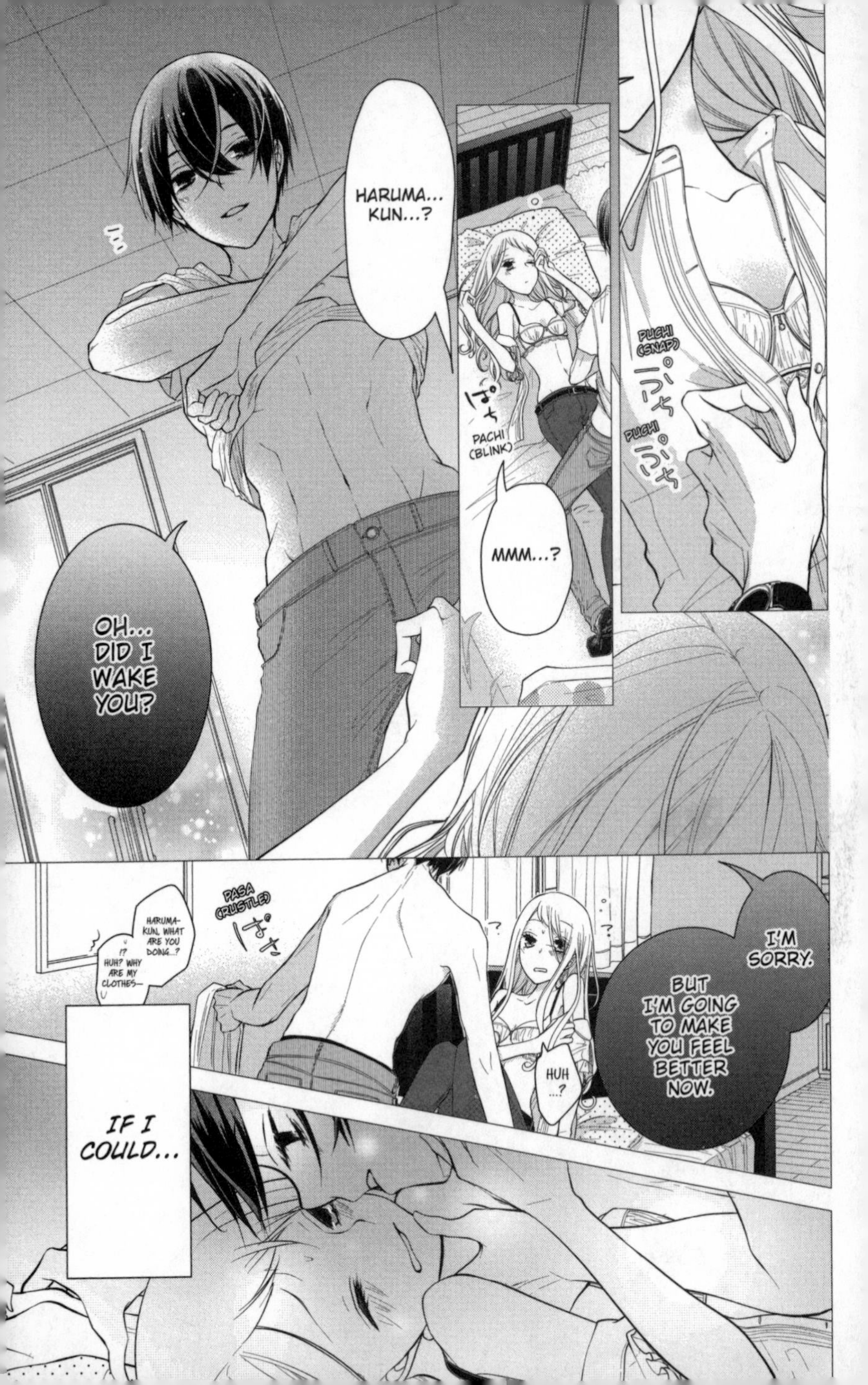
PUCHI (SNAP)
ぷち
PUCHI
ぷち
ぱち
PACHI (BLINK)
MMM...?
HARUMA... KUN...?
OH... DID I WAKE YOU?
...
I'M SORRY.
BUT I'M GOING TO MAKE YOU FEEL BETTER NOW.
HUH ...?
PASA (RUSTLE)
ぱさ
HARUMA-KUN, WHAT ARE YOU DOING...?
!? HUH? WHY ARE MY CLOTHES—
IF I COULD...

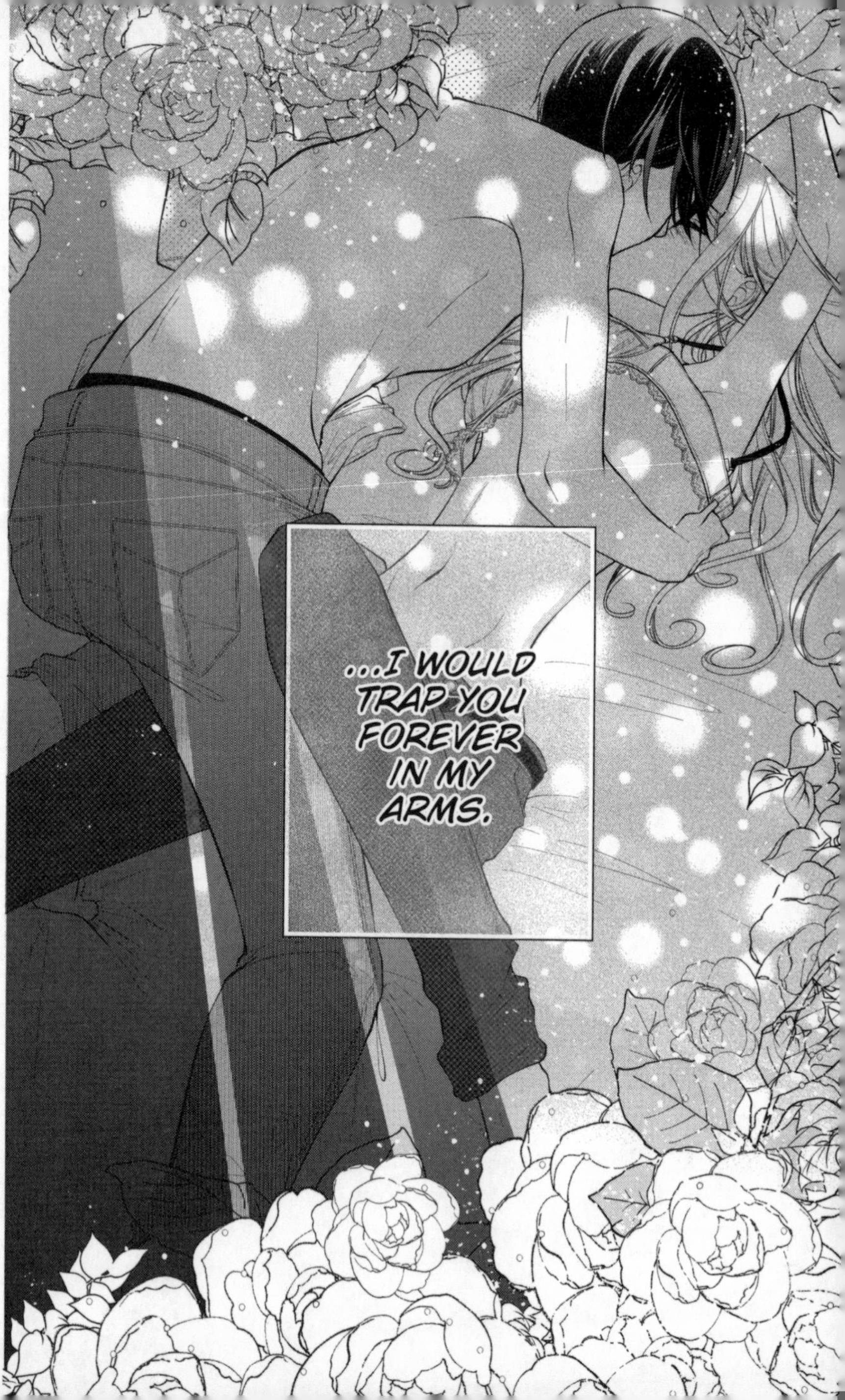
...I WOULD TRAP YOU FOREVER IN MY ARMS.

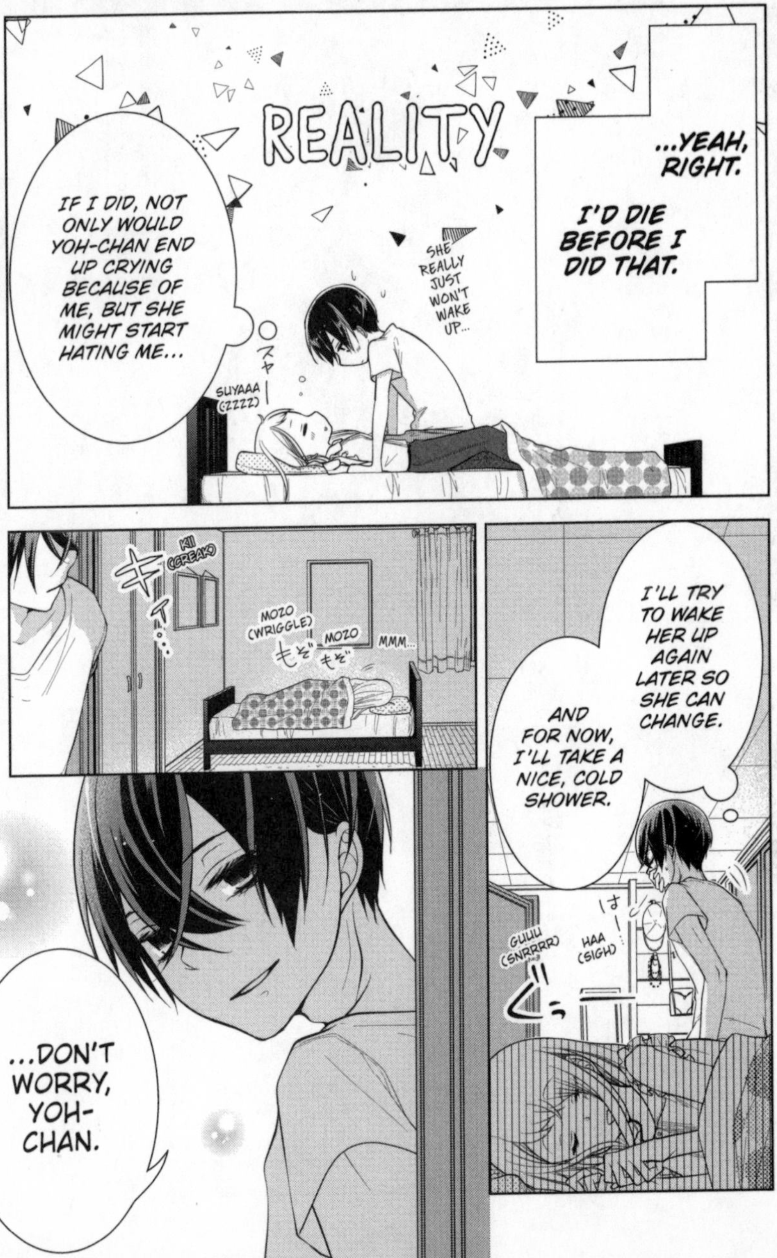

...YEAH, RIGHT.
I'D DIE BEFORE I DID THAT.
REALITY
SHE REALLY JUST WON'T WAKE UP...
IF I DID, NOT ONLY WOULD YOH-CHAN END UP CRYING BECAUSE OF ME, BUT SHE MIGHT START HATING ME...
SUYAAA (ZZZZ)
I'LL TRY TO WAKE HER UP AGAIN LATER SO SHE CAN CHANGE.
AND FOR NOW, I'LL TAKE A NICE, COLD SHOWER.
HAA (SIGH)
GUUU (SNRRRR)
KII (CREAK)
MOZO (WRIGGLE)
MOZO
MMM...
...DON'T WORRY, YOH-CHAN.

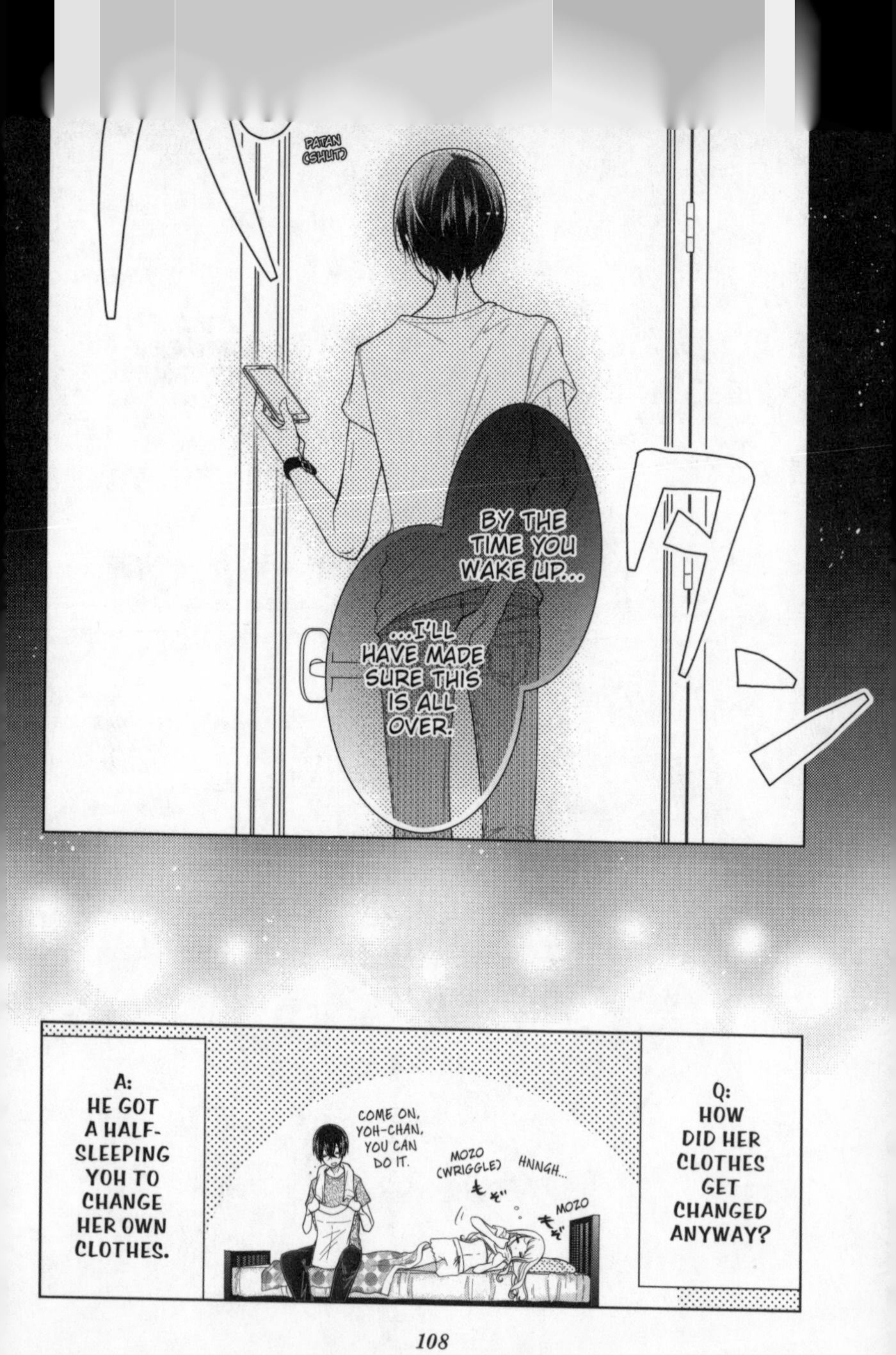
PATAN (SHUT)
BY THE TIME YOU WAKE UP...
...I'LL HAVE MADE SURE THIS IS ALL OVER.
Q: HOW DID HER CLOTHES GET CHANGED ANYWAY?
COME ON, YOH-CHAN, YOU CAN DO IT.
MOZO (WRIGGLE)
HNNGH...
MOZO
A: HE GOT A HALF-SLEEPING YOH TO CHANGE HER OWN CLOTHES.

#63

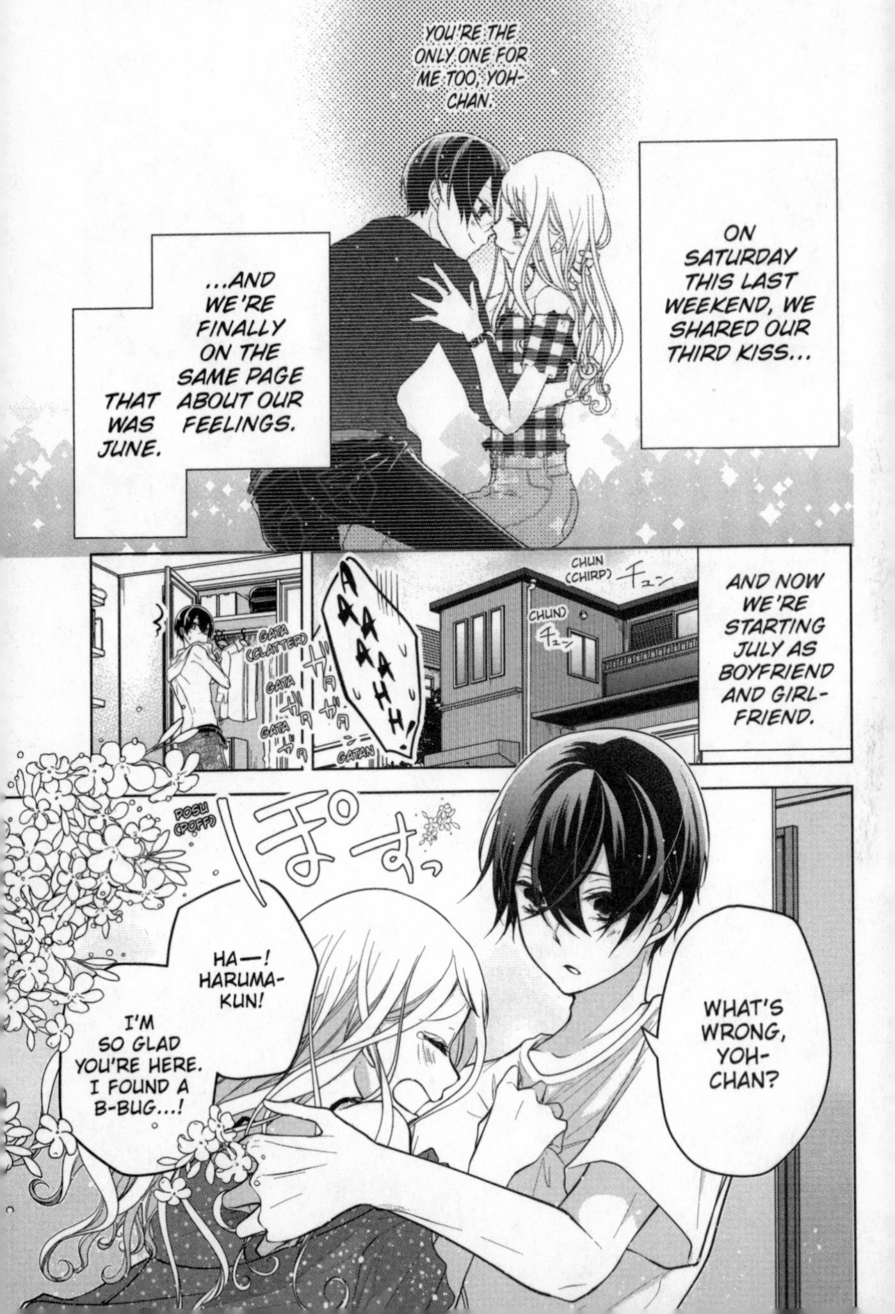
YOU'RE THE ONLY ONE FOR ME TOO, YOH-CHAN.
ON SATURDAY THIS LAST WEEKEND, WE SHARED OUR THIRD KISS...
...AND WE'RE FINALLY ON THE SAME PAGE ABOUT OUR FEELINGS.
THAT WAS JUNE.
AND NOW WE'RE STARTING JULY AS BOYFRIEND AND GIRL-FRIEND.
CHUN (CHIRP)
CHUN
AAAAAHH!
GATAN
GATA (CLATTER)
GATA
GATA
WHAT'S WRONG, YOH-CHAN?
POSU (POFF)
HA—! HARUMA-KUN!
I'M SO GLAD YOU'RE HERE. I FOUND A B-BUG...!

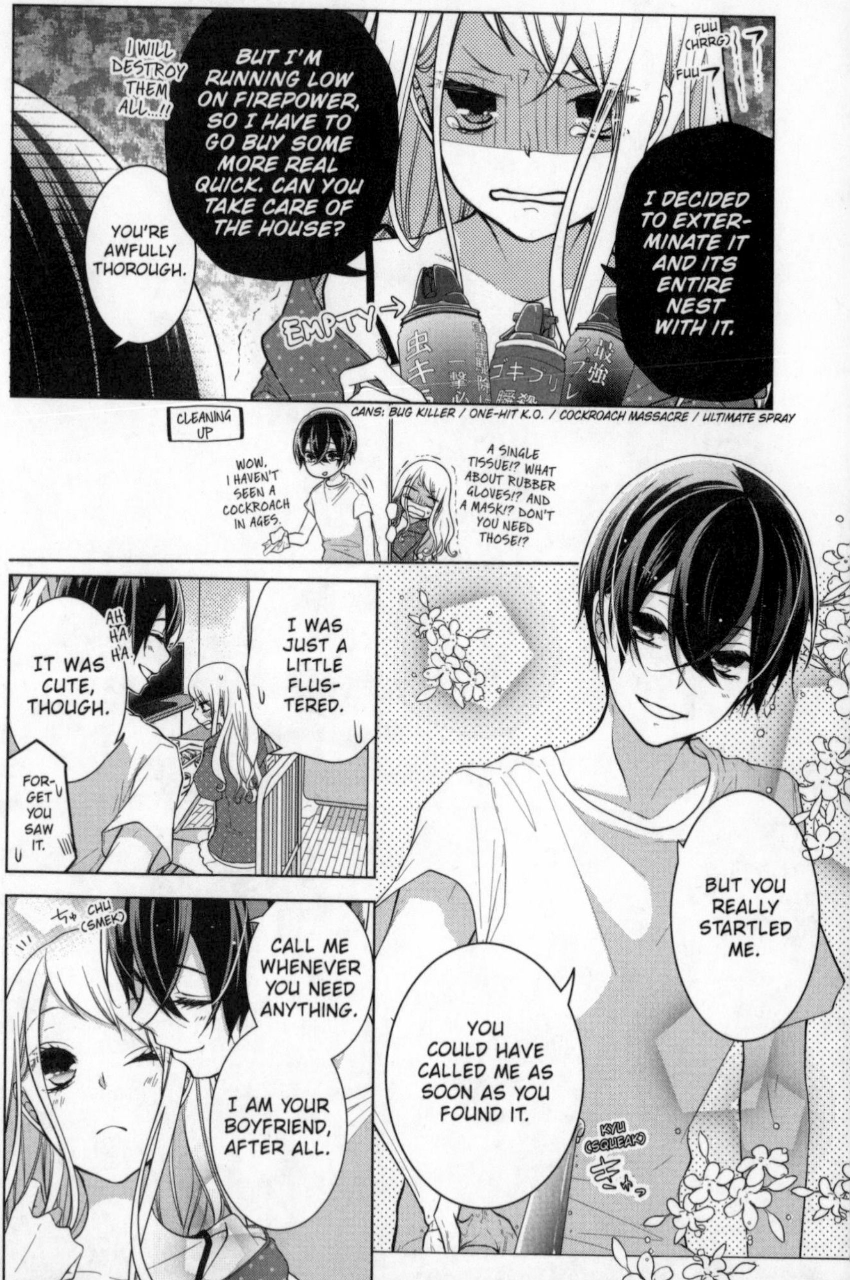
FUU (CHRRG)
FUU
I DECIDED TO EXTERMINATE IT AND ITS ENTIRE NEST WITH IT.
EMPTY
BUT I'M RUNNING LOW ON FIREPOWER, SO I HAVE TO GO BUY SOME MORE REAL QUICK. CAN YOU TAKE CARE OF THE HOUSE?
I WILL DESTROY THEM ALL...!!!
YOU'RE AWFULLY THOROUGH.
CANS: BUG KILLER / ONE-HIT K.O. / COCKROACH MASSACRE / ULTIMATE SPRAY
CLEANING UP
A SINGLE TISSUE!? WHAT ABOUT RUBBER GLOVES!? AND A MASK!? DON'T YOU NEED THOSE!?
WOW. I HAVEN'T SEEN A COCKROACH IN AGES.
BUT YOU REALLY STARTLED ME.
YOU COULD HAVE CALLED ME AS SOON AS YOU FOUND IT.
KYU (SQUEAK)
I WAS JUST A LITTLE FLUSTERED.
AH HA HA.
IT WAS CUTE, THOUGH.
FORGET YOU SAW IT.
CALL ME WHENEVER YOU NEED ANYTHING.
I AM YOUR BOYFRIEND, AFTER ALL.
CHU (SMEK)

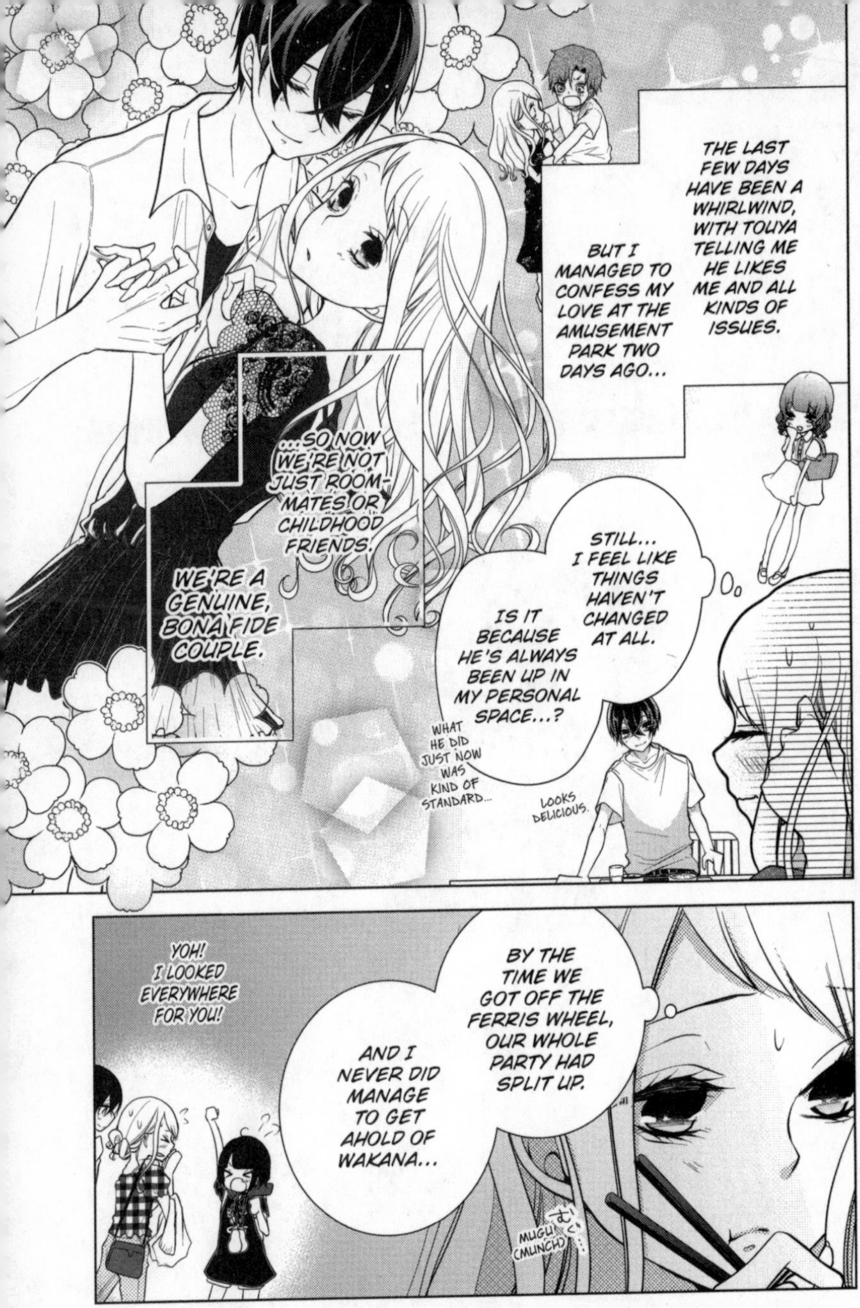
THE LAST FEW DAYS HAVE BEEN A WHIRLWIND, WITH TOUYA TELLING ME HE LIKES ME AND ALL KINDS OF ISSUES.
BUT I MANAGED TO CONFESS MY LOVE AT THE AMUSEMENT PARK TWO DAYS AGO...
...SO NOW WE'RE NOT JUST ROOM-MATES OR CHILDHOOD FRIENDS.
WE'RE A GENUINE, BONA FIDE COUPLE.
STILL... I FEEL LIKE THINGS HAVEN'T CHANGED AT ALL.
IS IT BECAUSE HE'S ALWAYS BEEN UP IN MY PERSONAL SPACE...?
WHAT HE DID JUST NOW WAS KIND OF STANDARD...
LOOKS DELICIOUS.
BY THE TIME WE GOT OFF THE FERRIS WHEEL, OUR WHOLE PARTY HAD SPLIT UP.
AND I NEVER DID MANAGE TO GET AHOLD OF WAKANA...
YOH! I LOOKED EVERYWHERE FOR YOU!
むぐ…
MUGU (MUNCH)

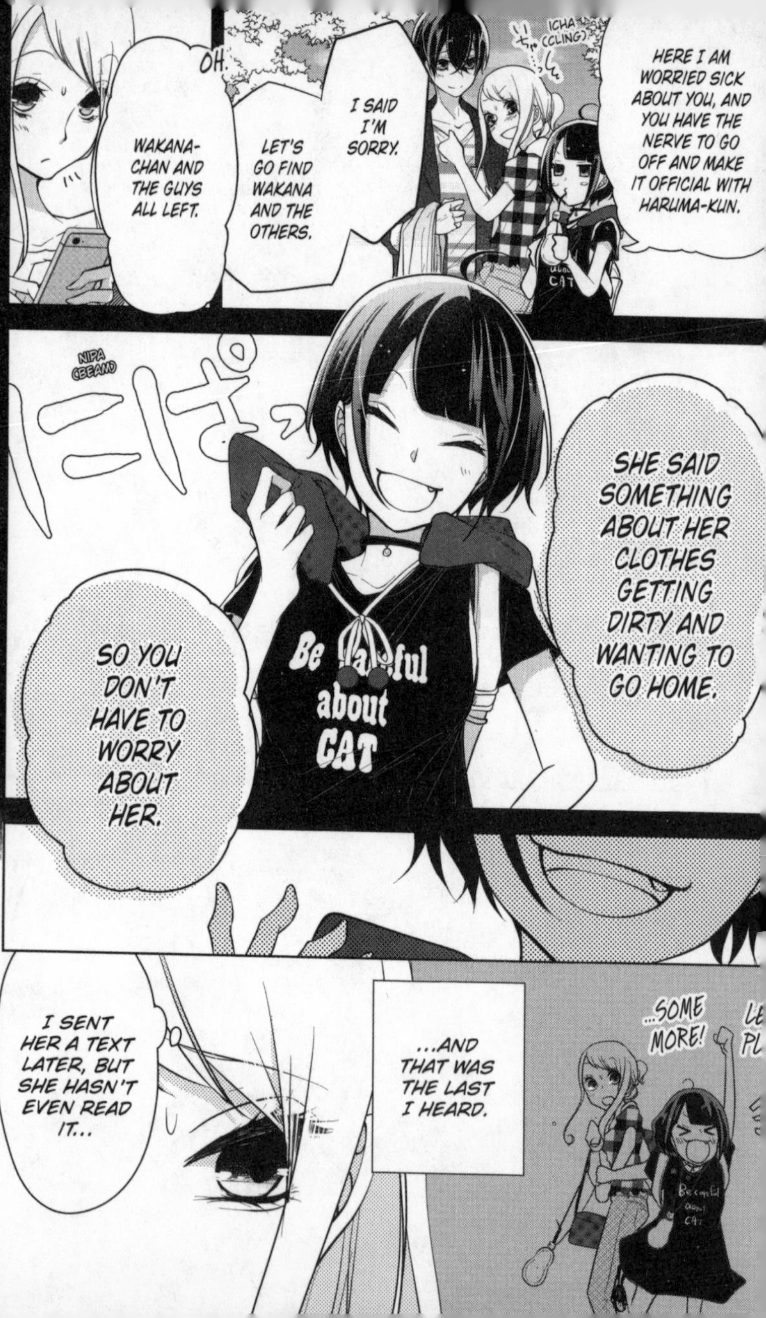
ICHA (CLING)
HERE I AM WORRIED SICK ABOUT YOU, AND YOU HAVE THE NERVE TO GO OFF AND MAKE IT OFFICIAL WITH HARUMA-KUN.
I SAID I'M SORRY.
LET'S GO FIND WAKANA AND THE OTHERS.
OH.
WAKANA-CHAN AND THE GUYS ALL LEFT.
NIPA (BEAM)
SHE SAID SOMETHING ABOUT HER CLOTHES GETTING DIRTY AND WANTING TO GO HOME.
SO YOU DON'T HAVE TO WORRY ABOUT HER.
...SOME MORE!
...AND THAT WAS THE LAST I HEARD.
I SENT HER A TEXT LATER, BUT SHE HASN'T EVEN READ IT...

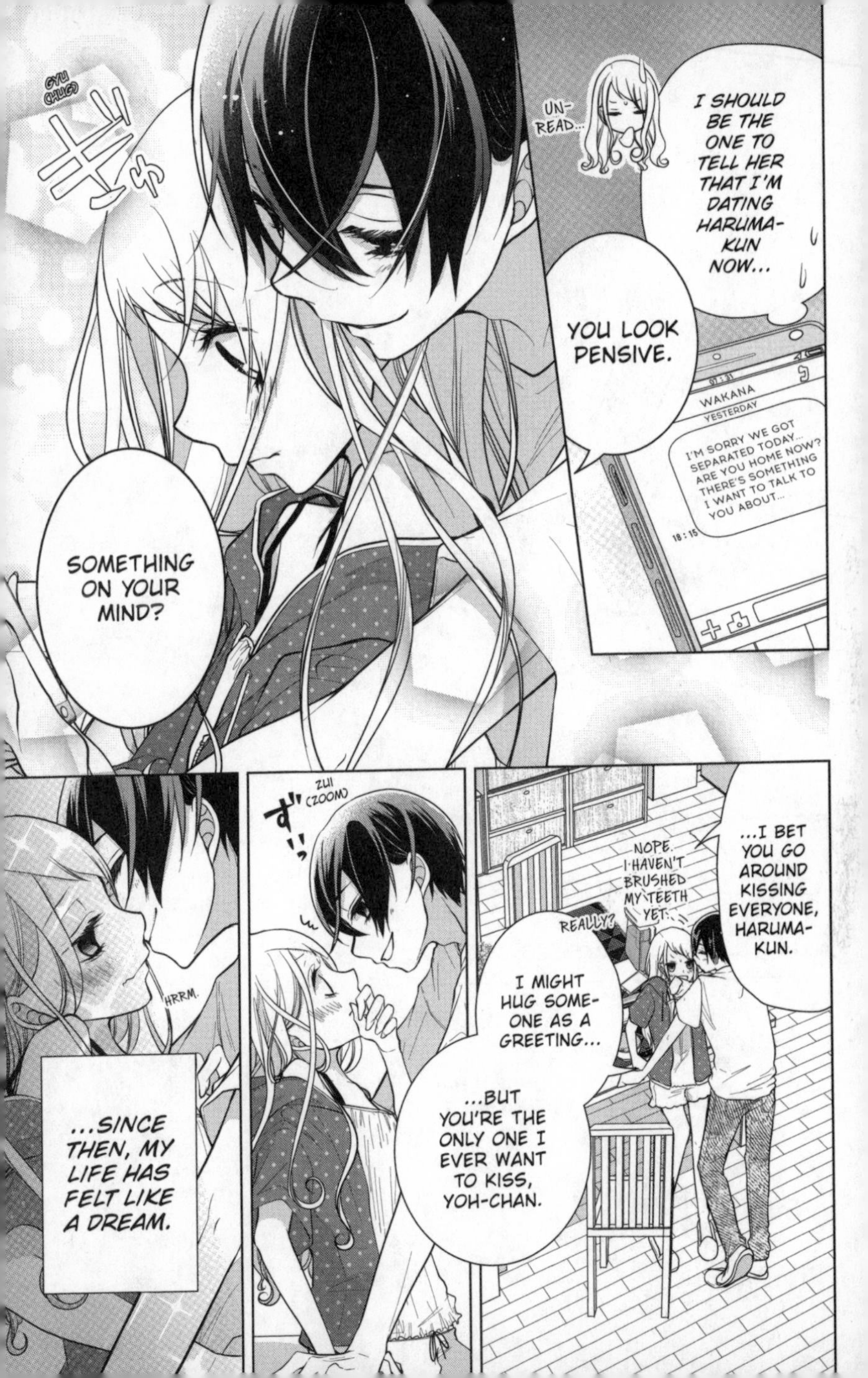
I SHOULD BE THE ONE TO TELL HER THAT I'M DATING HARUMA-KUN NOW...
UN-READ...
WAKANA
YESTERDAY
I'M SORRY WE GOT SEPARATED TODAY... ARE YOU HOME NOW? THERE'S SOMETHING I WANT TO TALK TO YOU ABOUT...
18:15
YOU LOOK PENSIVE.
GYU (HUG)
SOMETHING ON YOUR MIND?
...I BET YOU GO AROUND KISSING EVERYONE, HARUMA-KUN.
NOPE. I HAVEN'T BRUSHED MY TEETH YET.
REALLY?
I MIGHT HUG SOME-ONE AS A GREETING...
...BUT YOU'RE THE ONLY ONE I EVER WANT TO KISS, YOH-CHAN.
ZUI (ZOOM)
HRRM.
...SINCE THEN, MY LIFE HAS FELT LIKE A DREAM.

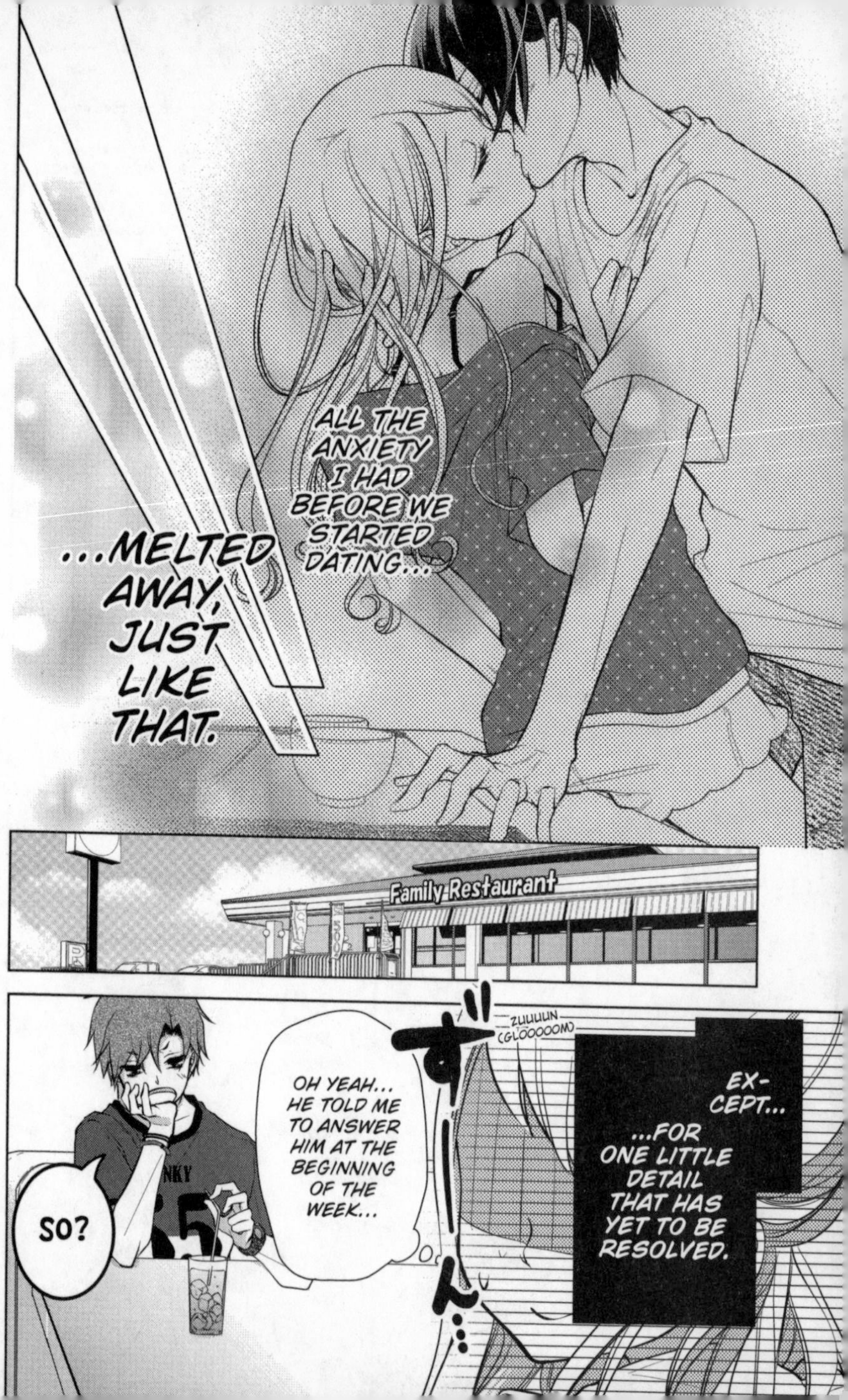
ALL THE ANXIETY I HAD BEFORE WE STARTED DATING...
...MELTED AWAY, JUST LIKE THAT.
Family Restaurant
EX-CEPT...
...FOR ONE LITTLE DETAIL THAT HAS YET TO BE RESOLVED.
ZUUUUN (GLOOOOOM)
OH YEAH... HE TOLD ME TO ANSWER HIM AT THE BEGINNING OF THE WEEK...
SO?

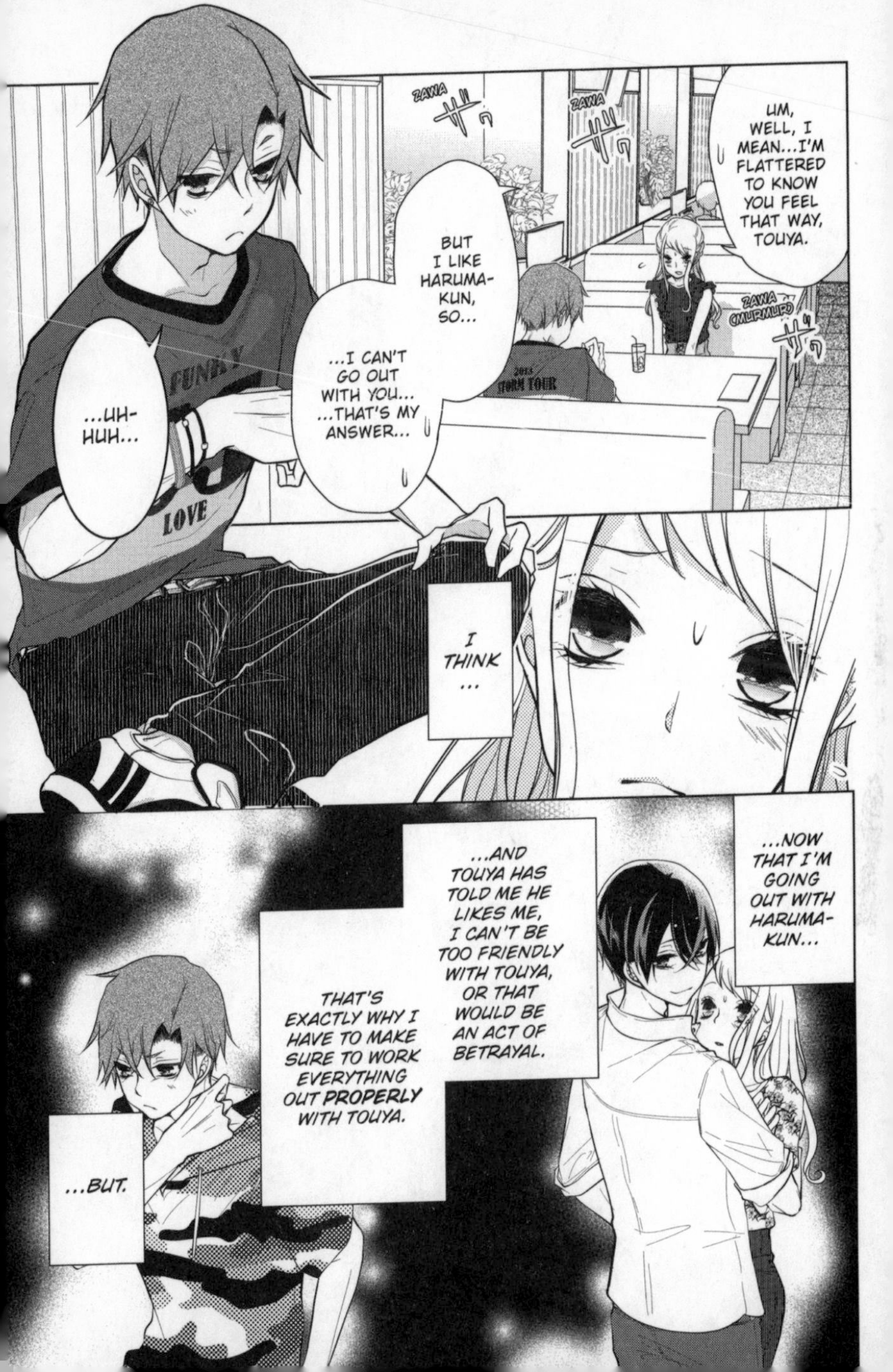
ZAWA
ZAWA
UM, WELL, I MEAN...I'M FLATTERED TO KNOW YOU FEEL THAT WAY, TOUYA.
ZAWA (MURMUR)
BUT I LIKE HARUMA-KUN, SO...
...I CAN'T GO OUT WITH YOU... ...THAT'S MY ANSWER...
...UH-HUH...
I THINK...
...NOW THAT I'M GOING OUT WITH HARUMA-KUN...
...AND TOUYA HAS TOLD ME HE LIKES ME, I CAN'T BE TOO FRIENDLY WITH TOUYA, OR THAT WOULD BE AN ACT OF BETRAYAL.
THAT'S EXACTLY WHY I HAVE TO MAKE SURE TO WORK EVERYTHING OUT PROPERLY WITH TOUYA.
...BUT.

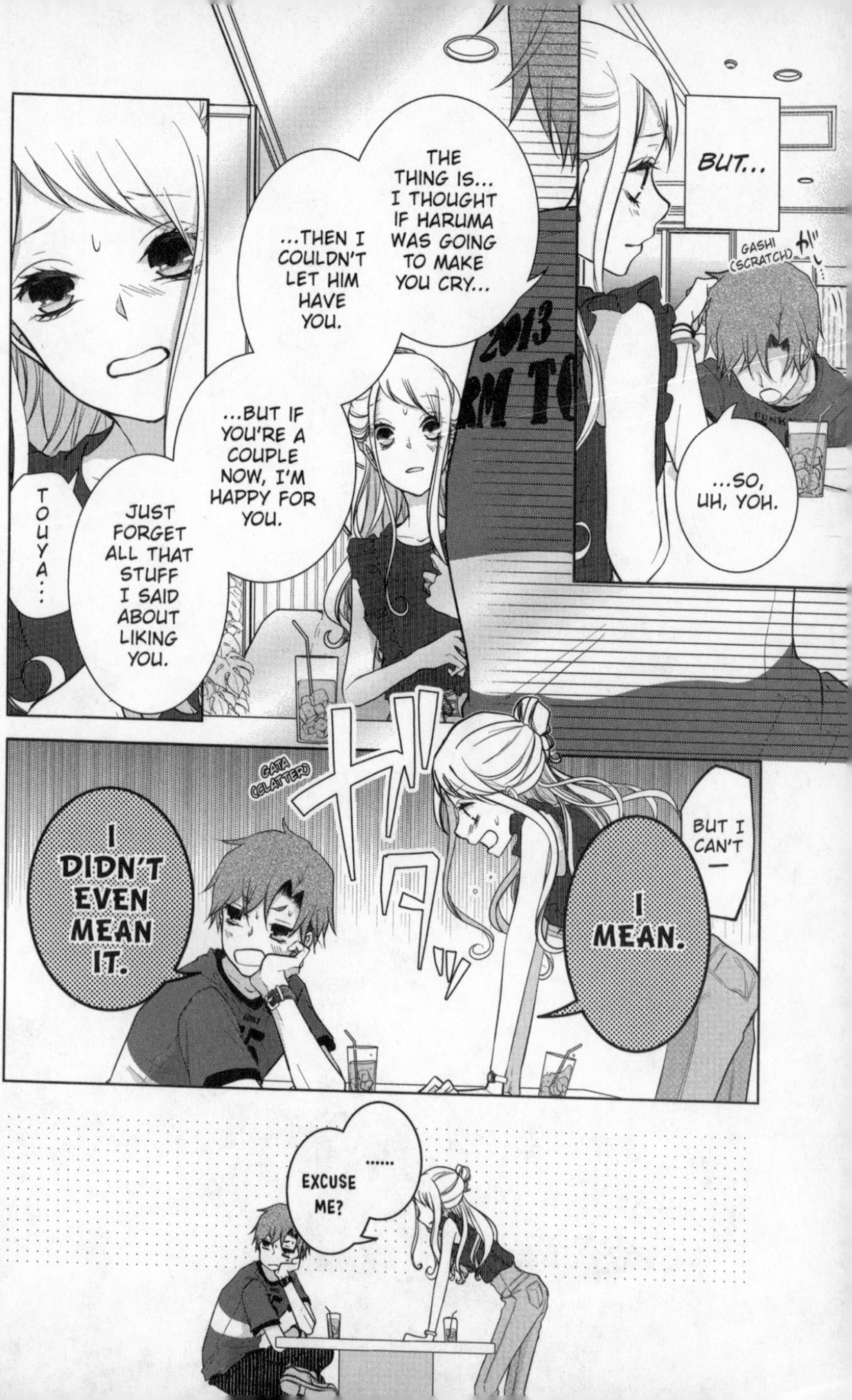
BUT...
GASHI (SCRATCH)
...SO, UH, YOH.
THE THING IS... I THOUGHT IF HARUMA WAS GOING TO MAKE YOU CRY...
...THEN I COULDN'T LET HIM HAVE YOU.
...BUT IF YOU'RE A COUPLE NOW, I'M HAPPY FOR YOU.
JUST FORGET ALL THAT STUFF I SAID ABOUT LIKING YOU.
TOUYA...
BUT I CAN'T —
I MEAN.
GATA (CLATTER)
I DIDN'T EVEN MEAN IT.
......
EXCUSE ME?

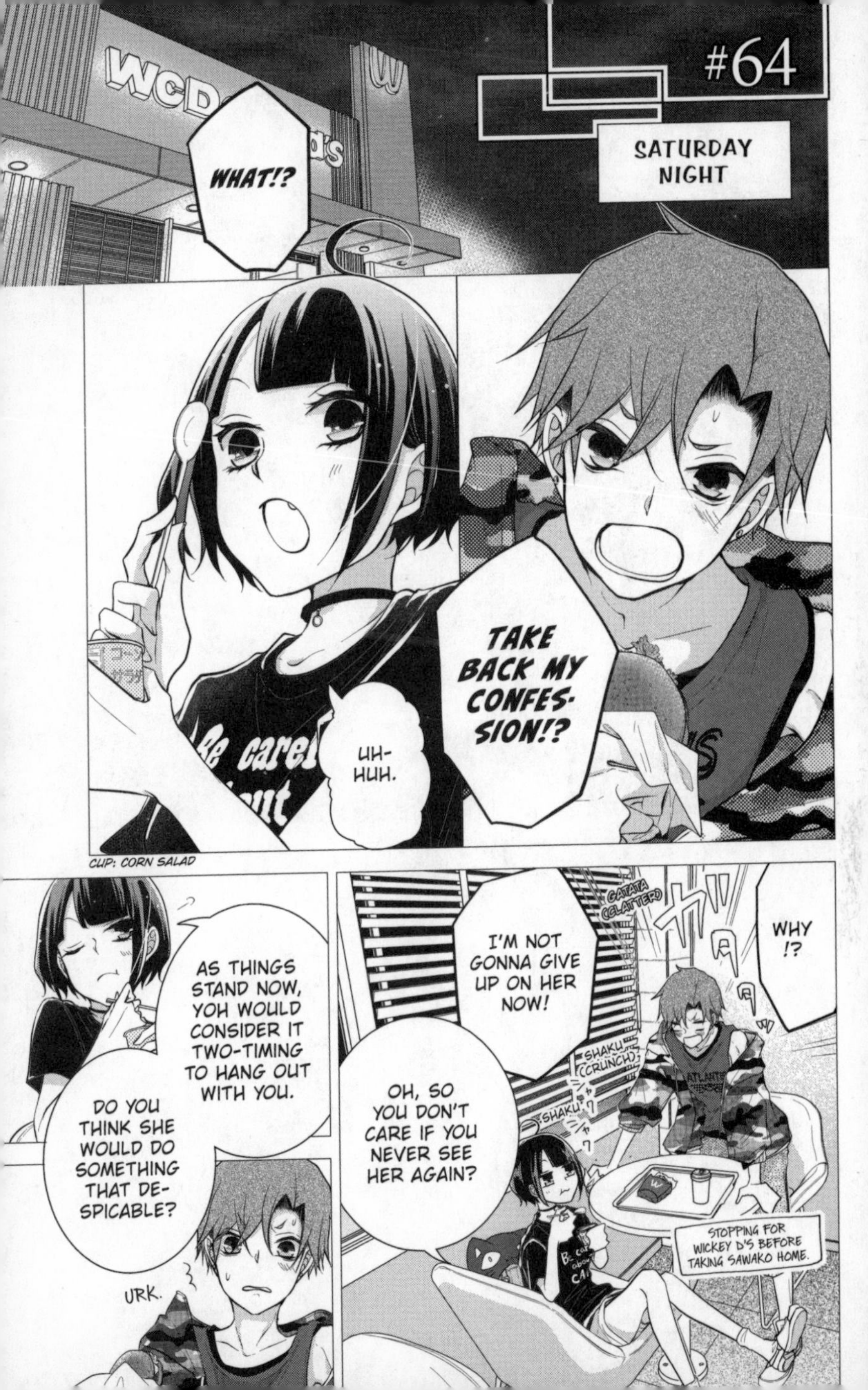
#64
SATURDAY NIGHT
WHAT!?
TAKE BACK MY CONFES-SION!?
UH-HUH.
CUP: CORN SALAD
WHY!?
GATATA (CLATTER)
I'M NOT GONNA GIVE UP ON HER NOW!
SHAKU (CRUNCH)
SHAKU
OH, SO YOU DON'T CARE IF YOU NEVER SEE HER AGAIN?
STOPPING FOR WICKEY D'S BEFORE TAKING SAWAKO HOME.
AS THINGS STAND NOW, YOH WOULD CONSIDER IT TWO-TIMING TO HANG OUT WITH YOU.
DO YOU THINK SHE WOULD DO SOMETHING THAT DE-SPICABLE?
URK.

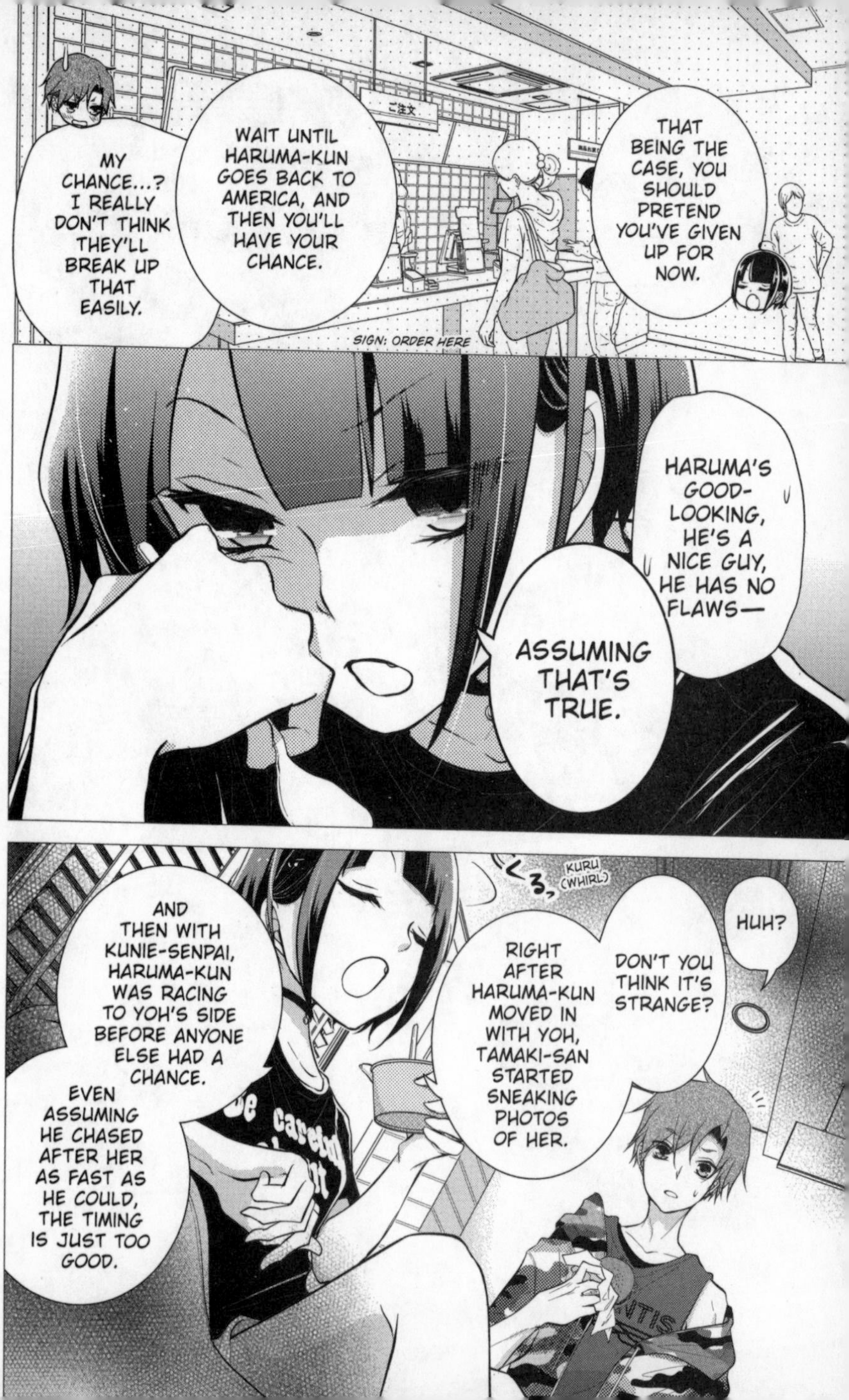
THAT BEING THE CASE, YOU SHOULD PRETEND YOU'VE GIVEN UP FOR NOW.
ご注文
WAIT UNTIL HARUMA-KUN GOES BACK TO AMERICA, AND THEN YOU'LL HAVE YOUR CHANCE.
MY CHANCE...? I REALLY DON'T THINK THEY'LL BREAK UP THAT EASILY.
SIGN: ORDER HERE
HARUMA'S GOOD-LOOKING, HE'S A NICE GUY, HE HAS NO FLAWS—
ASSUMING THAT'S TRUE.
HUH?
DON'T YOU THINK IT'S STRANGE?
RIGHT AFTER HARUMA-KUN MOVED IN WITH YOH, TAMAKI-SAN STARTED SNEAKING PHOTOS OF HER.
くる
KURU (WHIRL)
AND THEN WITH KUNIE-SENPAI, HARUMA-KUN WAS RACING TO YOH'S SIDE BEFORE ANYONE ELSE HAD A CHANCE.
EVEN ASSUMING HE CHASED AFTER HER AS FAST AS HE COULD, THE TIMING IS JUST TOO GOOD.

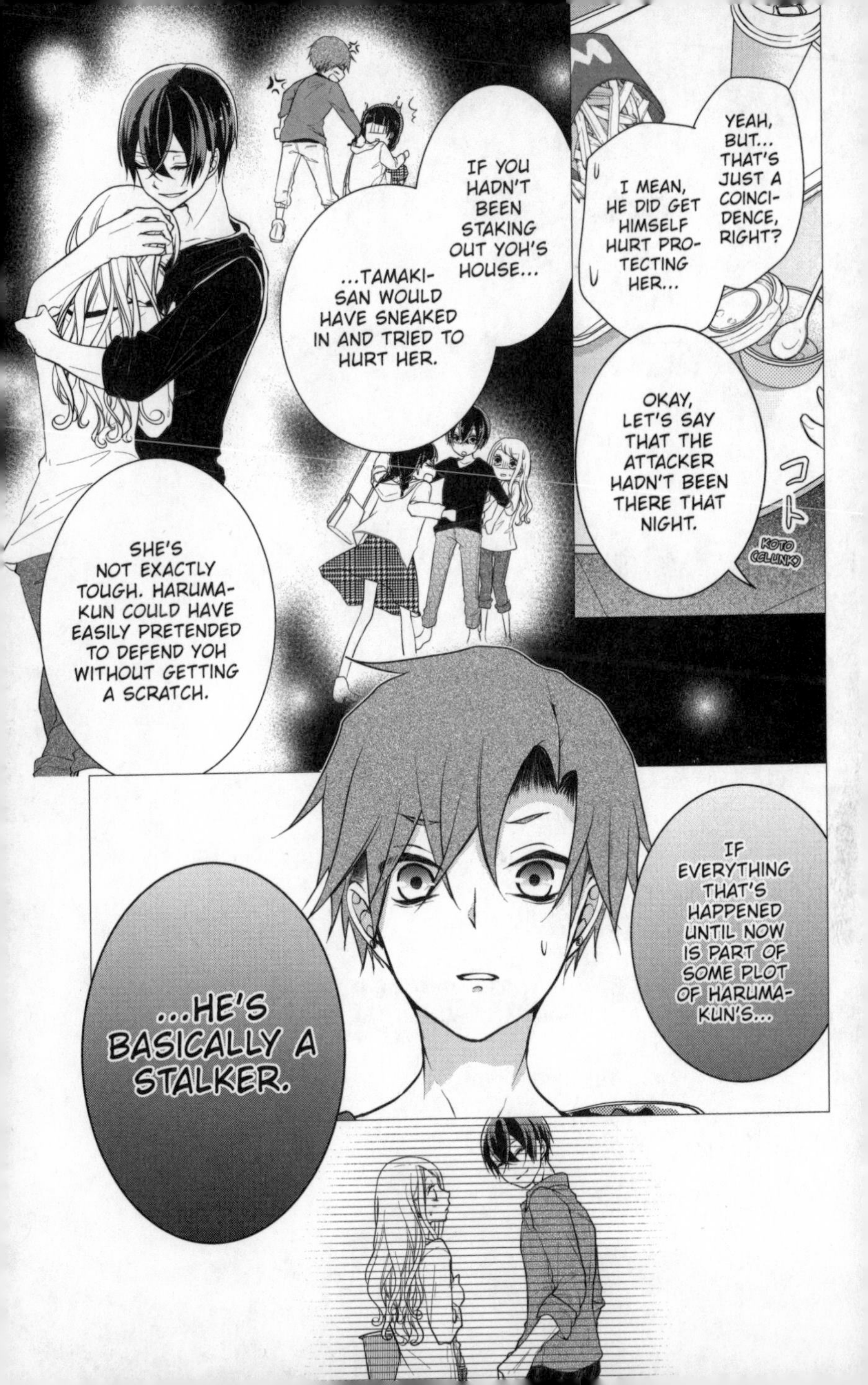
YEAH, BUT... THAT'S JUST A COINCIDENCE, RIGHT?
I MEAN, HE DID GET HIMSELF HURT PROTECTING HER...
OKAY, LET'S SAY THAT THE ATTACKER HADN'T BEEN THERE THAT NIGHT.
KOTO (CLUNK)
IF YOU HADN'T BEEN STAKING OUT YOH'S HOUSE...
...TAMAKI-SAN WOULD HAVE SNEAKED IN AND TRIED TO HURT HER.
SHE'S NOT EXACTLY TOUGH. HARUMA-KUN COULD HAVE EASILY PRETENDED TO DEFEND YOH WITHOUT GETTING A SCRATCH.
IF EVERYTHING THAT'S HAPPENED UNTIL NOW IS PART OF SOME PLOT OF HARUMA-KUN'S...
...HE'S BASICALLY A STALKER.

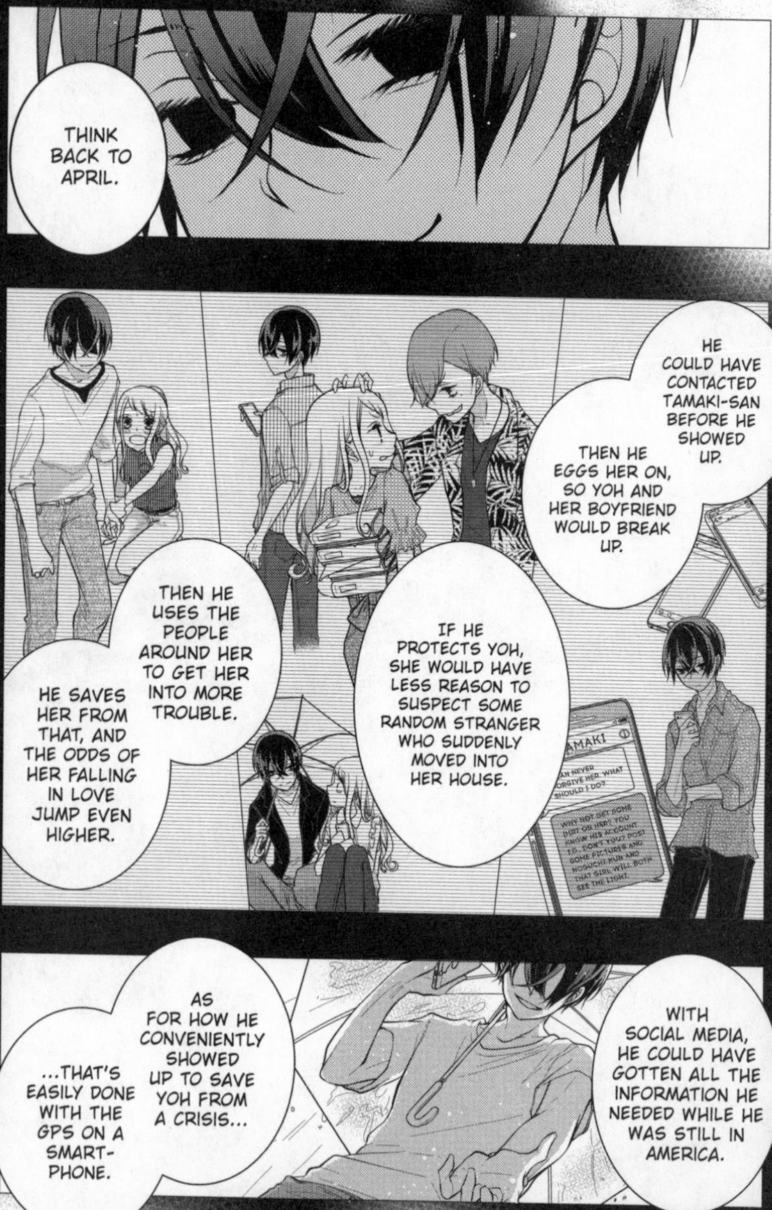
THINK BACK TO APRIL.
HE COULD HAVE CONTACTED TAMAKI-SAN BEFORE HE SHOWED UP.
THEN HE EGGS HER ON, SO YOH AND HER BOYFRIEND WOULD BREAK UP.
WHY NOT GET SOME DIRT ON HER? YOU KNOW HIS ACCOUNT TOO, DON'T YOU? POST SOME PICTURES AND NOGUCHI-KUN AND THAT GIRL WILL BOTH SEE THE LIGHT.
IF HE PROTECTS YOH, SHE WOULD HAVE LESS REASON TO SUSPECT SOME RANDOM STRANGER WHO SUDDENLY MOVED INTO HER HOUSE.
THEN HE USES THE PEOPLE AROUND HER TO GET HER INTO MORE TROUBLE.
HE SAVES HER FROM THAT, AND THE ODDS OF HER FALLING IN LOVE JUMP EVEN HIGHER.
WITH SOCIAL MEDIA, HE COULD HAVE GOTTEN ALL THE INFORMATION HE NEEDED WHILE HE WAS STILL IN AMERICA.
AS FOR HOW HE CONVENIENTLY SHOWED UP TO SAVE YOH FROM A CRISIS...
...THAT'S EASILY DONE WITH THE GPS ON A SMART-PHONE.

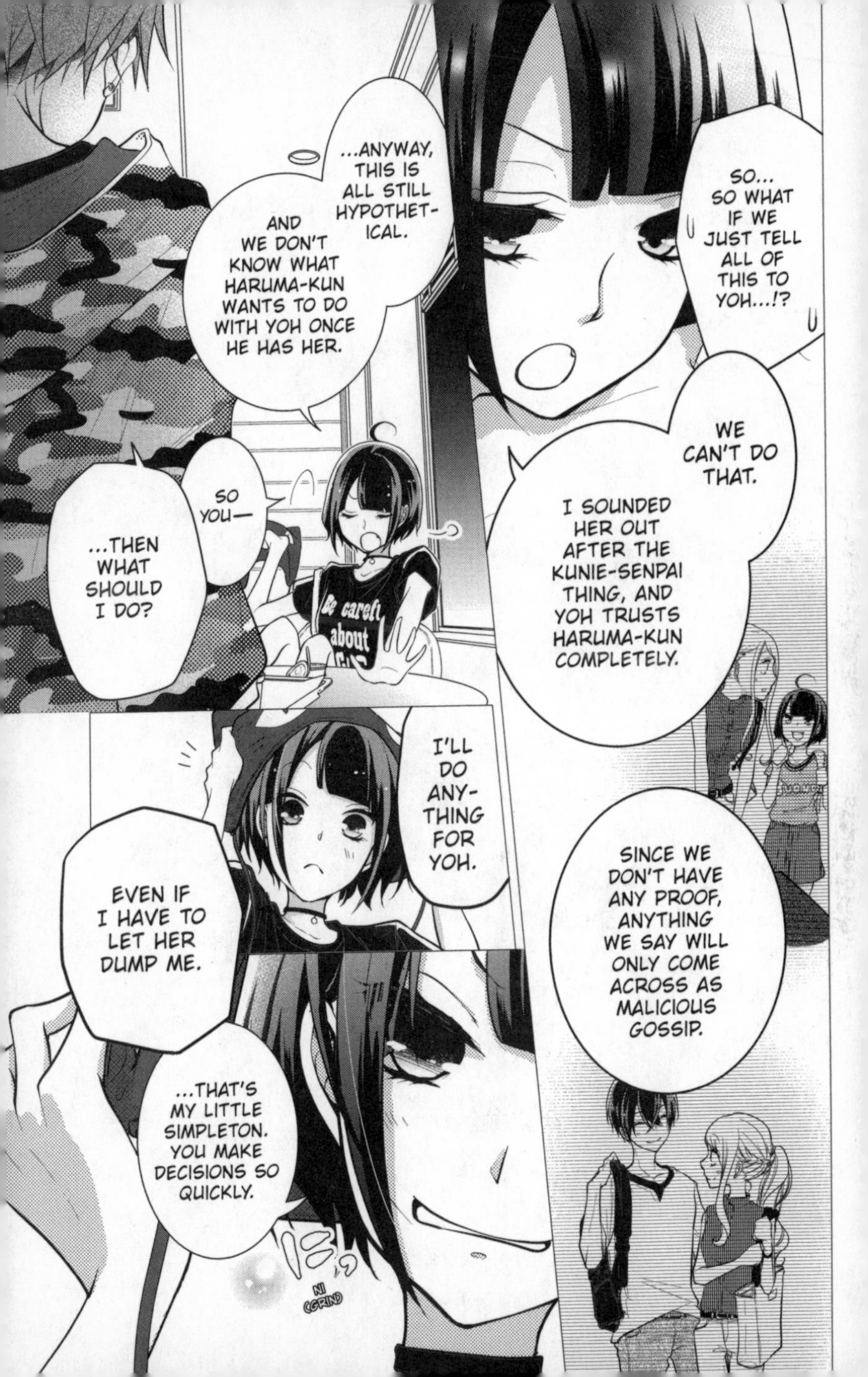
SO... SO WHAT IF WE JUST TELL ALL OF THIS TO YOH...!?
WE CAN'T DO THAT.
I SOUNDED HER OUT AFTER THE KUNIE-SENPAI THING, AND YOH TRUSTS HARUMA-KUN COMPLETELY.
SINCE WE DON'T HAVE ANY PROOF, ANYTHING WE SAY WILL ONLY COME ACROSS AS MALICIOUS GOSSIP.
...ANYWAY, THIS IS ALL STILL HYPOTHET-ICAL.
AND WE DON'T KNOW WHAT HARUMA-KUN WANTS TO DO WITH YOH ONCE HE HAS HER.
SO YOU—
...THEN WHAT SHOULD I DO?
I'LL DO ANY-THING FOR YOH.
EVEN IF I HAVE TO LET HER DUMP ME.
...THAT'S MY LITTLE SIMPLETON. YOU MAKE DECISIONS SO QUICKLY.
NI (GRIND)

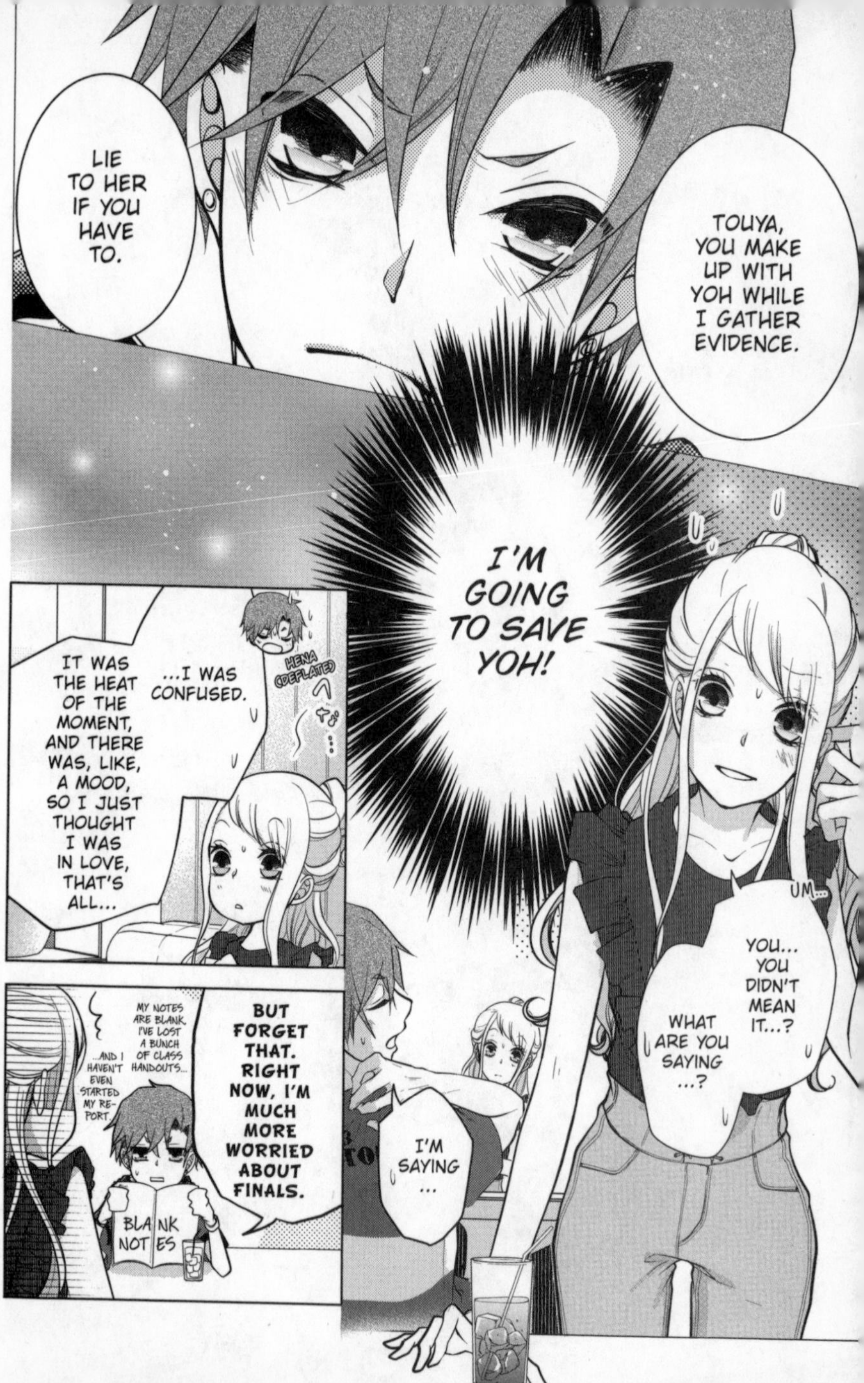
TOUYA, YOU MAKE UP WITH YOH WHILE I GATHER EVIDENCE.
LIE TO HER IF YOU HAVE TO.
I'M GOING TO SAVE YOH!
UM...
YOU... YOU DIDN'T MEAN IT...?
WHAT ARE YOU SAYING ...?
I'M SAYING ...
...I WAS CONFUSED.
IT WAS THE HEAT OF THE MOMENT, AND THERE WAS, LIKE, A MOOD, SO I JUST THOUGHT I WAS IN LOVE, THAT'S ALL...
HENA (DEFLATED)
BUT FORGET THAT. RIGHT NOW, I'M MUCH MORE WORRIED ABOUT FINALS.
MY NOTES ARE BLANK. I'VE LOST A BUNCH OF CLASS HANDOUTS...
...AND I HAVEN'T EVEN STARTED MY RE-PORT.
BLANK NOTES

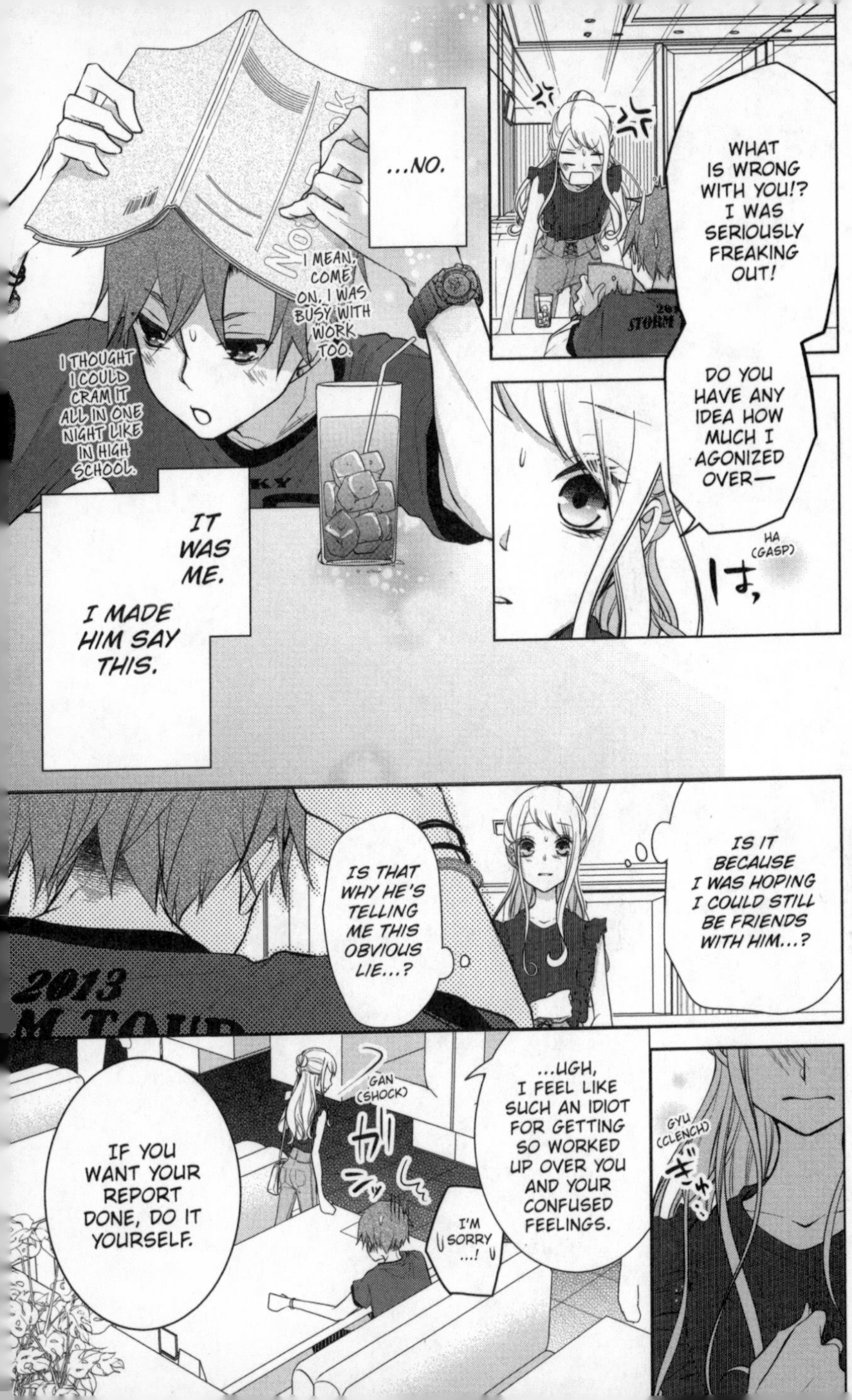
WHAT IS WRONG WITH YOU!? I WAS SERIOUSLY FREAKING OUT!
DO YOU HAVE ANY IDEA HOW MUCH I AGONIZED OVER—
HA (GASP)
...NO.
I MEAN, COME ON, I WAS BUSY WITH WORK TOO.
I THOUGHT I COULD CRAM IT ALL IN ONE NIGHT LIKE IN HIGH SCHOOL.
IT WAS ME.
I MADE HIM SAY THIS.
IS IT BECAUSE I WAS HOPING I COULD STILL BE FRIENDS WITH HIM...?
IS THAT WHY HE'S TELLING ME THIS OBVIOUS LIE...?
GYU (CLENCH)
...UGH, I FEEL LIKE SUCH AN IDIOT FOR GETTING SO WORKED UP OVER YOU AND YOUR CONFUSED FEELINGS.
GAN (SHOCK)
I'M SORRY ...!
IF YOU WANT YOUR REPORT DONE, DO IT YOURSELF.

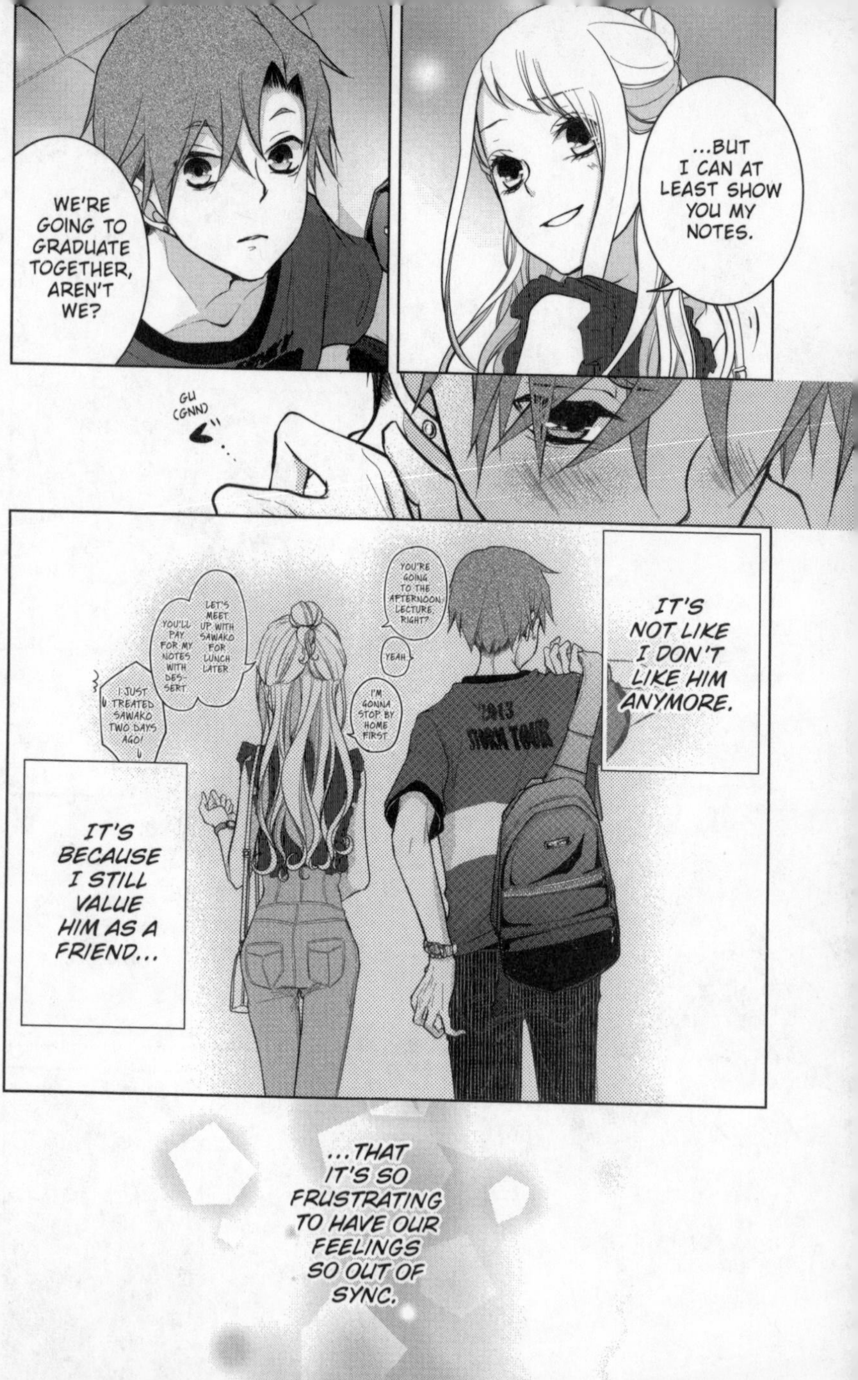
...BUT I CAN AT LEAST SHOW YOU MY NOTES.
WE'RE GOING TO GRADUATE TOGETHER, AREN'T WE?
GU (GNN)
IT'S NOT LIKE I DON'T LIKE HIM ANYMORE.
YOU'RE GOING TO THE AFTERNOON LECTURE, RIGHT?
YEAH
I'M GONNA STOP BY HOME FIRST
LET'S MEET UP WITH SAWAKO FOR LUNCH LATER
YOU'LL PAY FOR MY NOTES WITH DES-SERT.
I JUST TREATED SAWAKO TWO DAYS AGO!
IT'S BECAUSE I STILL VALUE HIM AS A FRIEND...
...THAT IT'S SO FRUSTRATING TO HAVE OUR FEELINGS SO OUT OF SYNC.

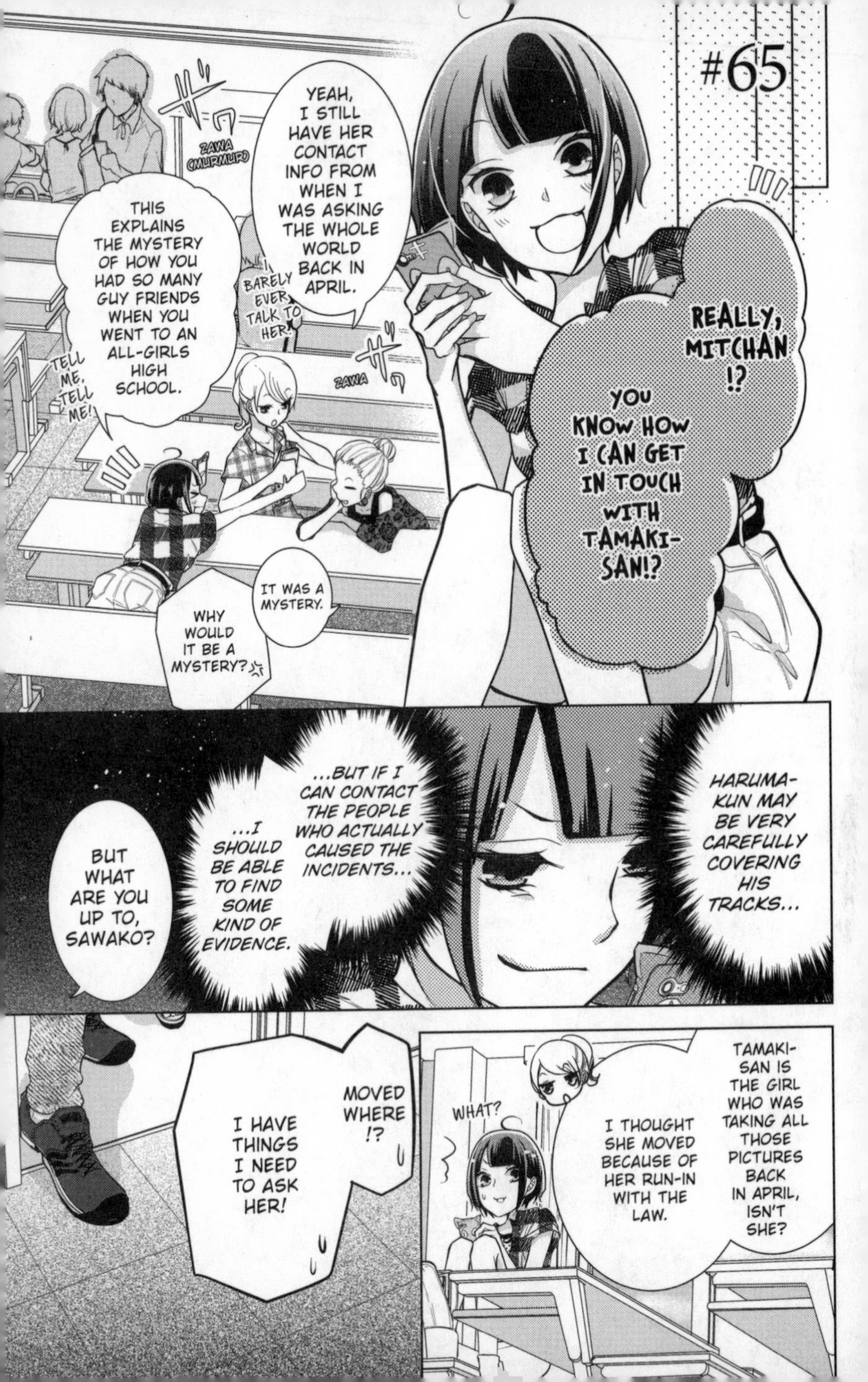
#65
REALLY, MITCHAN!?
YOU KNOW HOW I CAN GET IN TOUCH WITH TAMAKI-SAN!?
YEAH, I STILL HAVE HER CONTACT INFO FROM WHEN I WAS ASKING THE WHOLE WORLD BACK IN APRIL.
ZAWA (MURMUR)
BARELY EVER TALK TO HER!
THIS EXPLAINS THE MYSTERY OF HOW YOU HAD SO MANY GUY FRIENDS WHEN YOU WENT TO AN ALL-GIRLS HIGH SCHOOL.
ZAWA
TELL ME, TELL ME!
IT WAS A MYSTERY.
WHY WOULD IT BE A MYSTERY?
HARUMA-KUN MAY BE VERY CAREFULLY COVERING HIS TRACKS...
...BUT IF I CAN CONTACT THE PEOPLE WHO ACTUALLY CAUSED THE INCIDENTS...
...I SHOULD BE ABLE TO FIND SOME KIND OF EVIDENCE.
BUT WHAT ARE YOU UP TO, SAWAKO?
TAMAKI-SAN IS THE GIRL WHO WAS TAKING ALL THOSE PICTURES BACK IN APRIL, ISN'T SHE?
I THOUGHT SHE MOVED BECAUSE OF HER RUN-IN WITH THE LAW.
WHAT?
MOVED WHERE!?
I HAVE THINGS I NEED TO ASK HER!

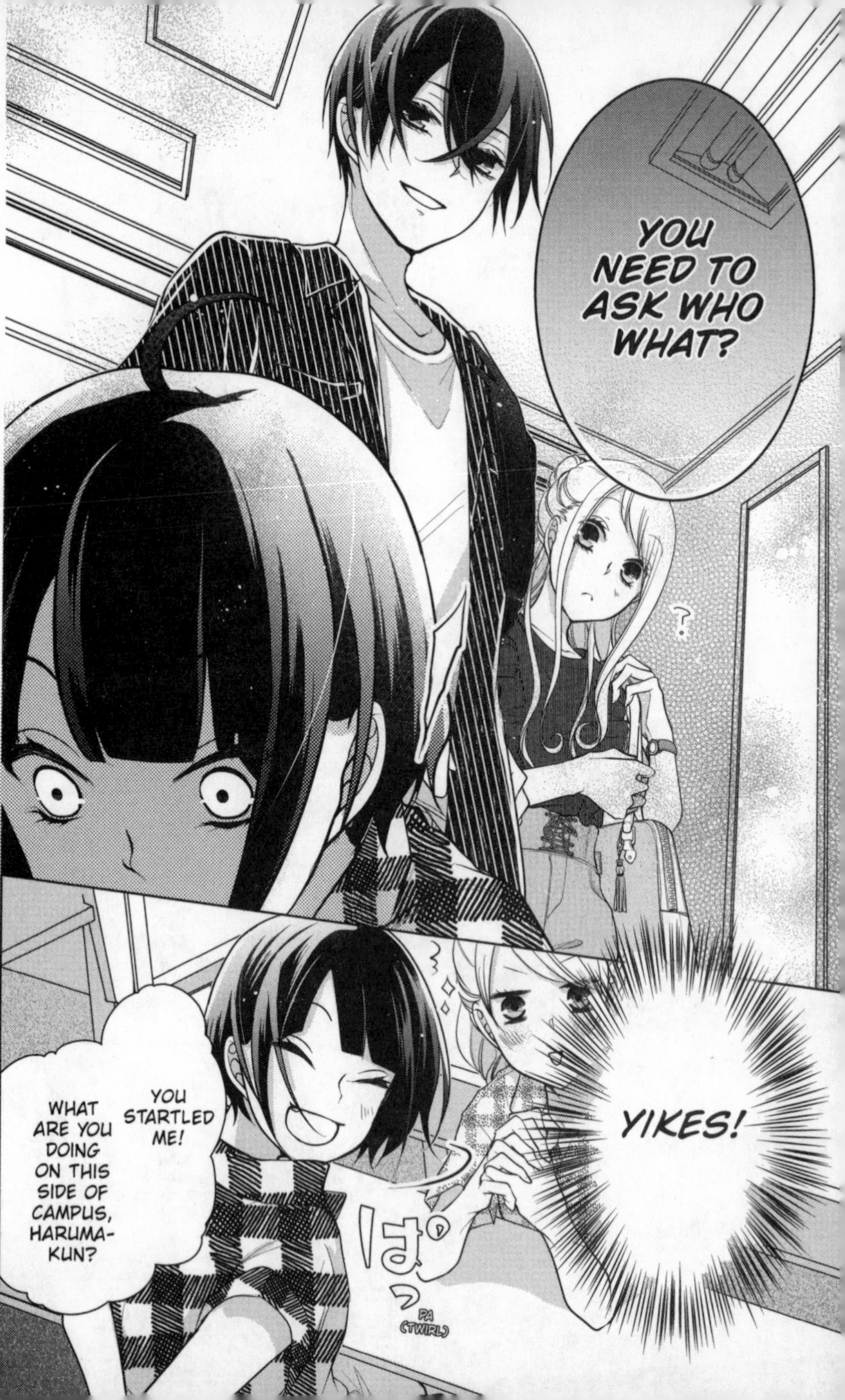
YOU NEED TO ASK WHO WHAT?
?
YIKES!
ぱっ
PA (TWIRL)
YOU STARTLED ME!
WHAT ARE YOU DOING ON THIS SIDE OF CAMPUS, HARUMA-KUN?

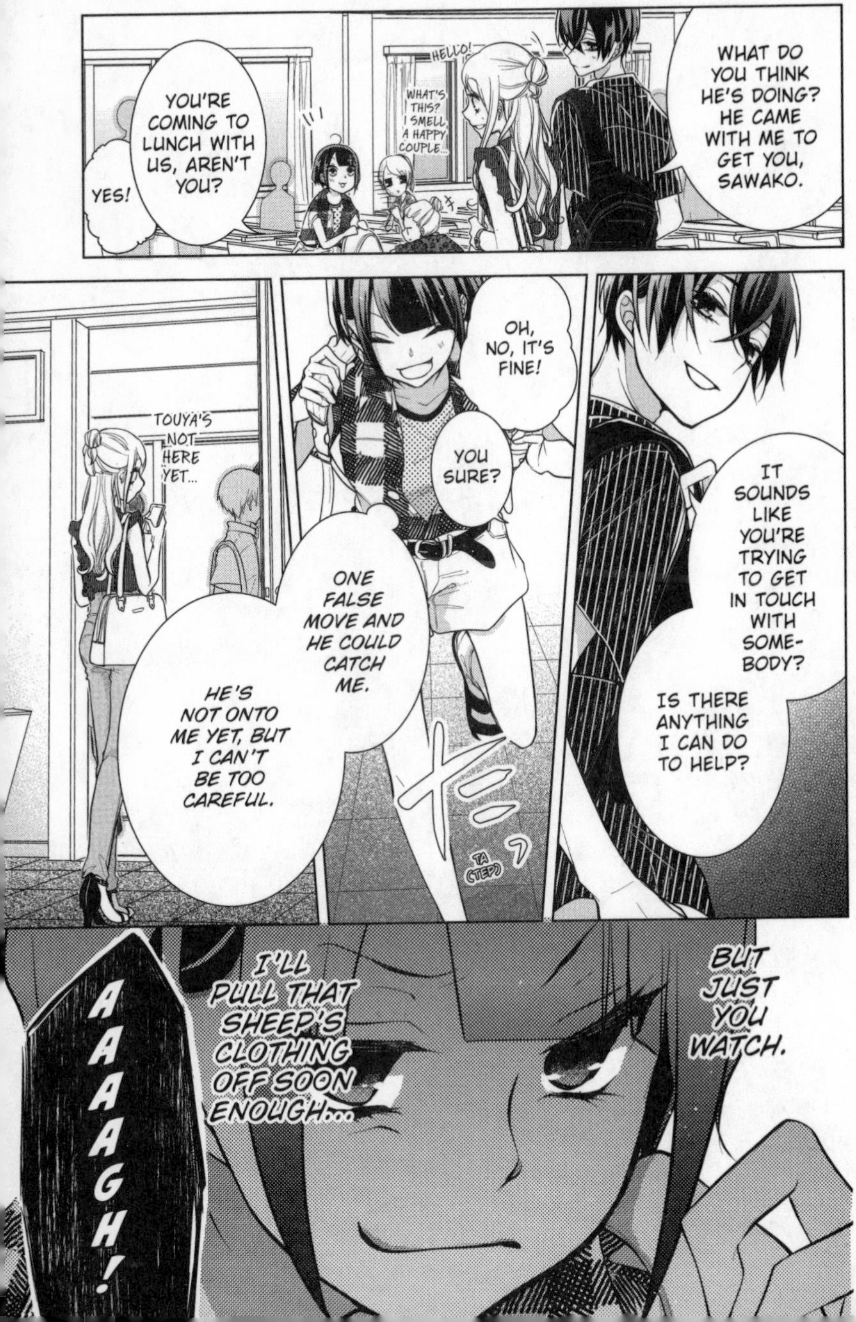
WHAT DO YOU THINK HE'S DOING? HE CAME WITH ME TO GET YOU, SAWAKO.
HELLO!
WHAT'S THIS? I SMELL A HAPPY COUPLE...
YOU'RE COMING TO LUNCH WITH US, AREN'T YOU?
YES!
IT SOUNDS LIKE YOU'RE TRYING TO GET IN TOUCH WITH SOME-BODY?
IS THERE ANYTHING I CAN DO TO HELP?
OH, NO, IT'S FINE!
YOU SURE?
TA (TEP)
ONE FALSE MOVE AND HE COULD CATCH ME.
HE'S NOT ONTO ME YET, BUT I CAN'T BE TOO CAREFUL.
TOUYA'S NOT HERE YET...
BUT JUST YOU WATCH.
I'LL PULL THAT SHEEP'S CLOTHING OFF SOON ENOUGH...
AAAAAAGH!

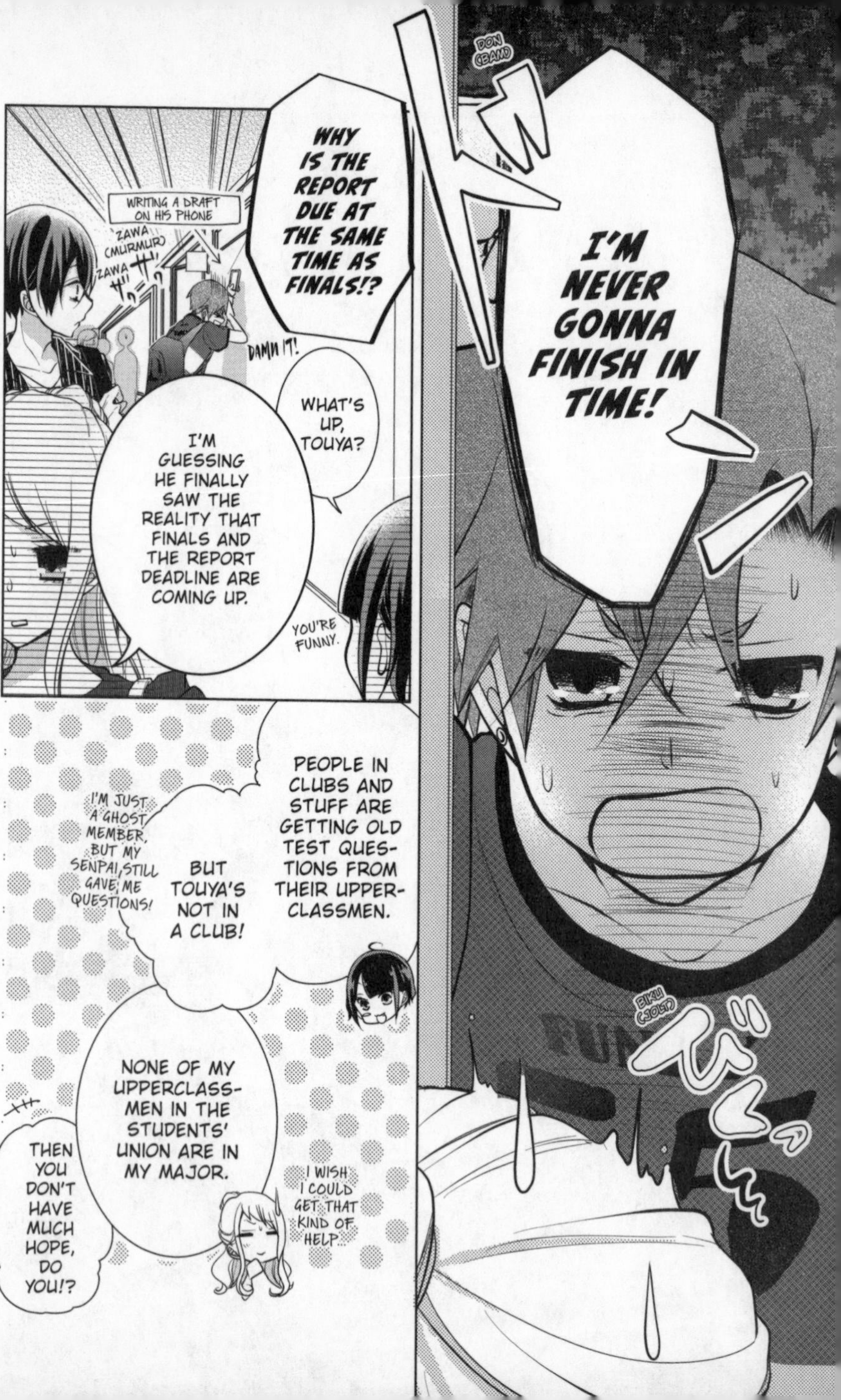
DON (BAM)
I'M NEVER GONNA FINISH IN TIME!
BIKU (JOLT)
WHY IS THE REPORT DUE AT THE SAME TIME AS FINALS!?
WRITING A DRAFT ON HIS PHONE
ZAWA (MURMUR) ZAWA
DAMN IT!
WHAT'S UP, TOUYA?
I'M GUESSING HE FINALLY SAW THE REALITY THAT FINALS AND THE REPORT DEADLINE ARE COMING UP.
YOU'RE FUNNY.
PEOPLE IN CLUBS AND STUFF ARE GETTING OLD TEST QUESTIONS FROM THEIR UPPERCLASSMEN.
BUT TOUYA'S NOT IN A CLUB!
I'M JUST A GHOST MEMBER, BUT MY SENPAI STILL GAVE ME QUESTIONS!
NONE OF MY UPPERCLASSMEN IN THE STUDENTS' UNION ARE IN MY MAJOR.
I WISH I COULD GET THAT KIND OF HELP...
THEN YOU DON'T HAVE MUCH HOPE, DO YOU!?

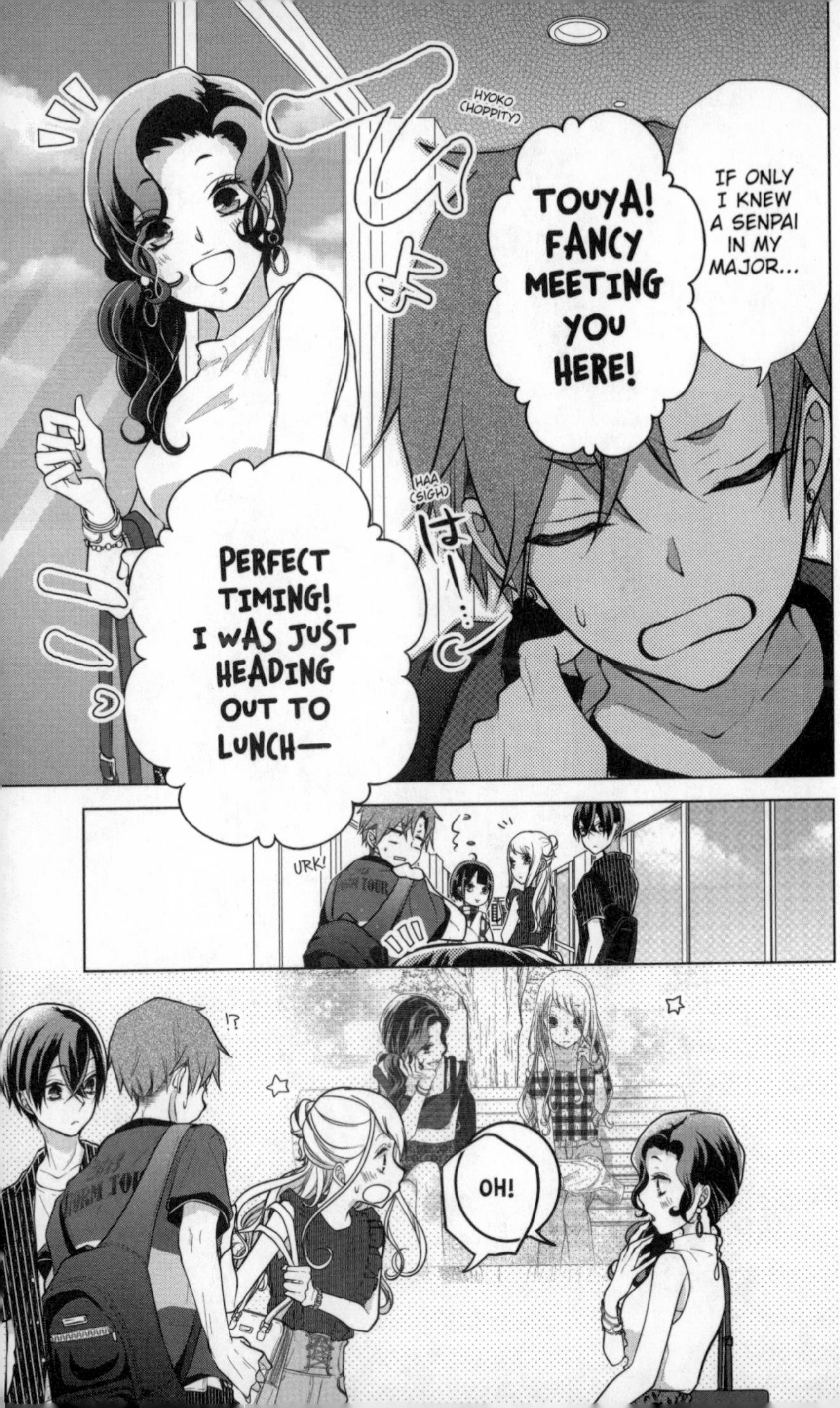
IF ONLY I KNEW A SENPAI IN MY MAJOR...
HYOKO (HOPPITY)
TOUYA! FANCY MEETING YOU HERE!
HAA (SIGH)
PERFECT TIMING! I WAS JUST HEADING OUT TO LUNCH—
URK!
OH!

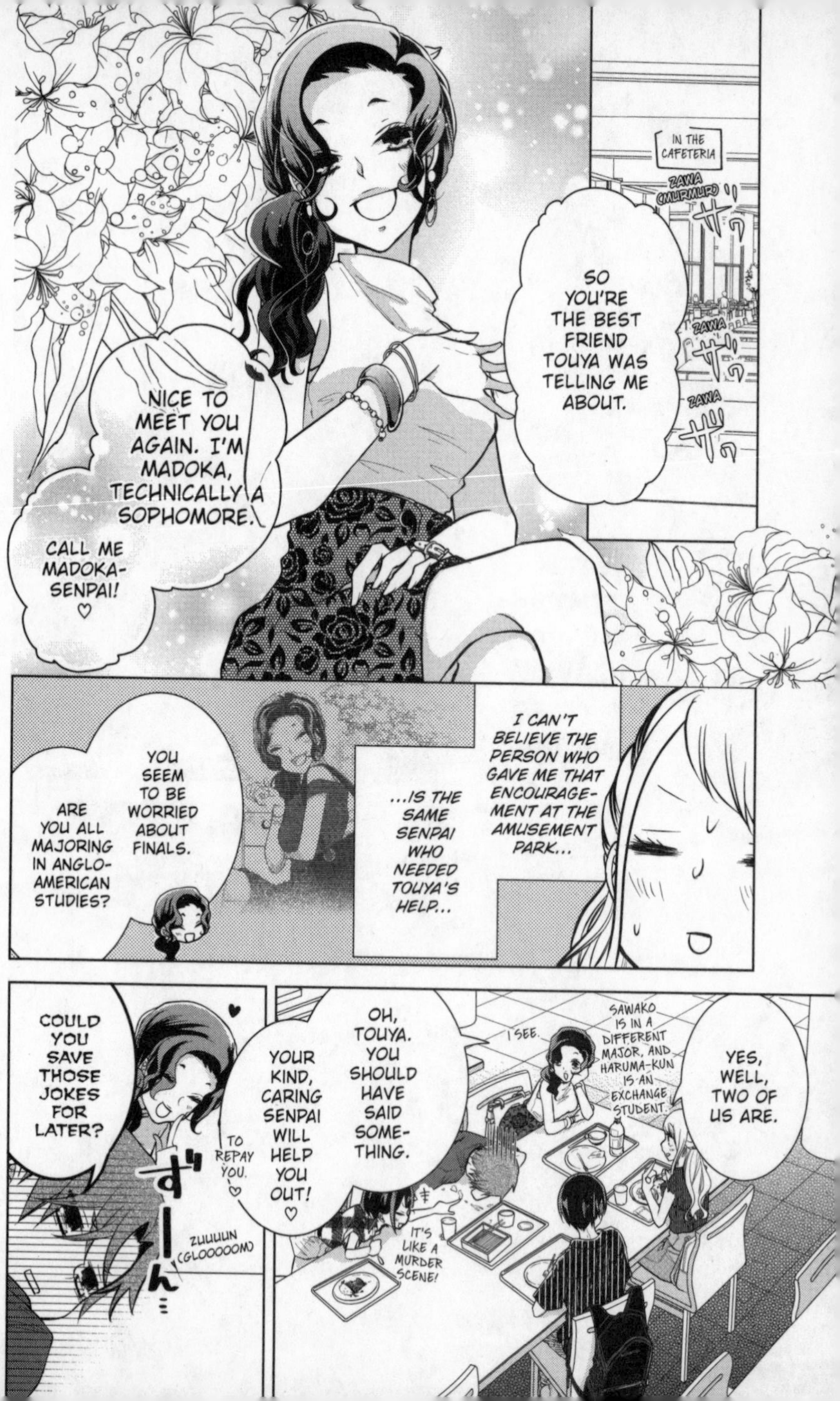
IN THE CAFETERIA
ZAWA (MURMUR)
ZAWA
ZAWA
SO YOU'RE THE BEST FRIEND TOUYA WAS TELLING ME ABOUT.
NICE TO MEET YOU AGAIN. I'M MADOKA, TECHNICALLY A SOPHOMORE.
CALL ME MADOKA-SENPAI! ♡
I CAN'T BELIEVE THE PERSON WHO GAVE ME THAT ENCOURAGEMENT AT THE AMUSEMENT PARK...
...IS THE SAME SENPAI WHO NEEDED TOUYA'S HELP...
YOU SEEM TO BE WORRIED ABOUT FINALS.
ARE YOU ALL MAJORING IN ANGLO-AMERICAN STUDIES?
YES, WELL, TWO OF US ARE.
SAWAKO IS IN A DIFFERENT MAJOR, AND HARUMA-KUN IS AN EXCHANGE STUDENT.
I SEE.
OH, TOUYA. YOU SHOULD HAVE SAID SOMETHING.
YOUR KIND, CARING SENPAI WILL HELP YOU OUT! ♡
TO REPAY YOU. ♡
IT'S LIKE A MURDER SCENE!
COULD YOU SAVE THOSE JOKES FOR LATER?
ZUUUUN (GLOOOOOM)

PAPER: FRESHMAN FINAL EXAM / ENGLISH GRAMMAR I

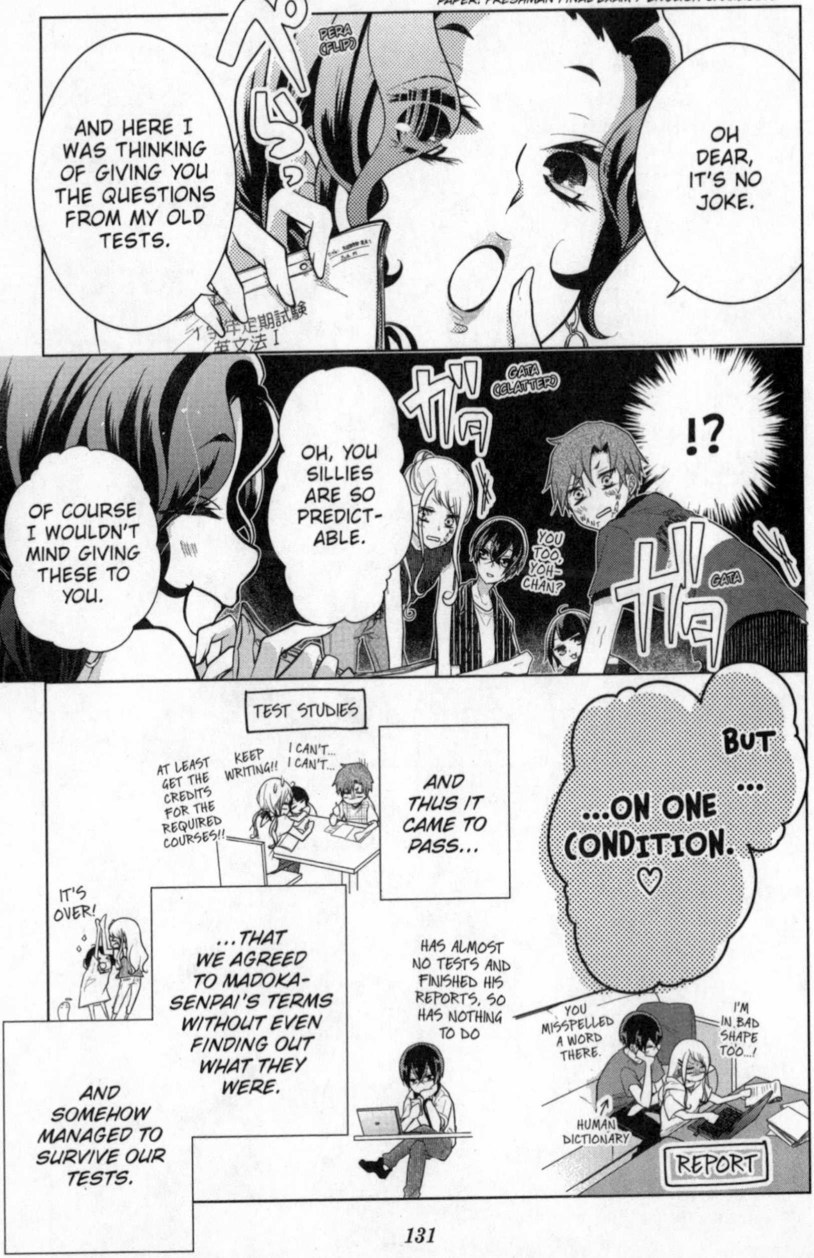

OH DEAR, IT'S NO JOKE.
PERA (FLIP)
AND HERE I WAS THINKING OF GIVING YOU THE QUESTIONS FROM MY OLD TESTS.
!?
GATA
YOU TOO, YOH-CHAN?
GATA (CLATTER)
OH, YOU SILLIES ARE SO PREDICTABLE.
OF COURSE I WOULDN'T MIND GIVING THESE TO YOU.
BUT...
...ON ONE CONDITION. ♥
AND THUS IT CAME TO PASS...
TEST STUDIES
I CAN'T... I CAN'T...
KEEP WRITING!!
AT LEAST GET THE CREDITS FOR THE REQUIRED COURSES!!
...THAT WE AGREED TO MADOKA-SENPAI'S TERMS WITHOUT EVEN FINDING OUT WHAT THEY WERE.
I'M IN BAD SHAPE TOO...!
YOU MISSPELLED A WORD THERE.
HUMAN DICTIONARY
REPORT
HAS ALMOST NO TESTS AND FINISHED HIS REPORTS, SO HAS NOTHING TO DO
IT'S OVER!
AND SOMEHOW MANAGED TO SURVIVE OUR TESTS.

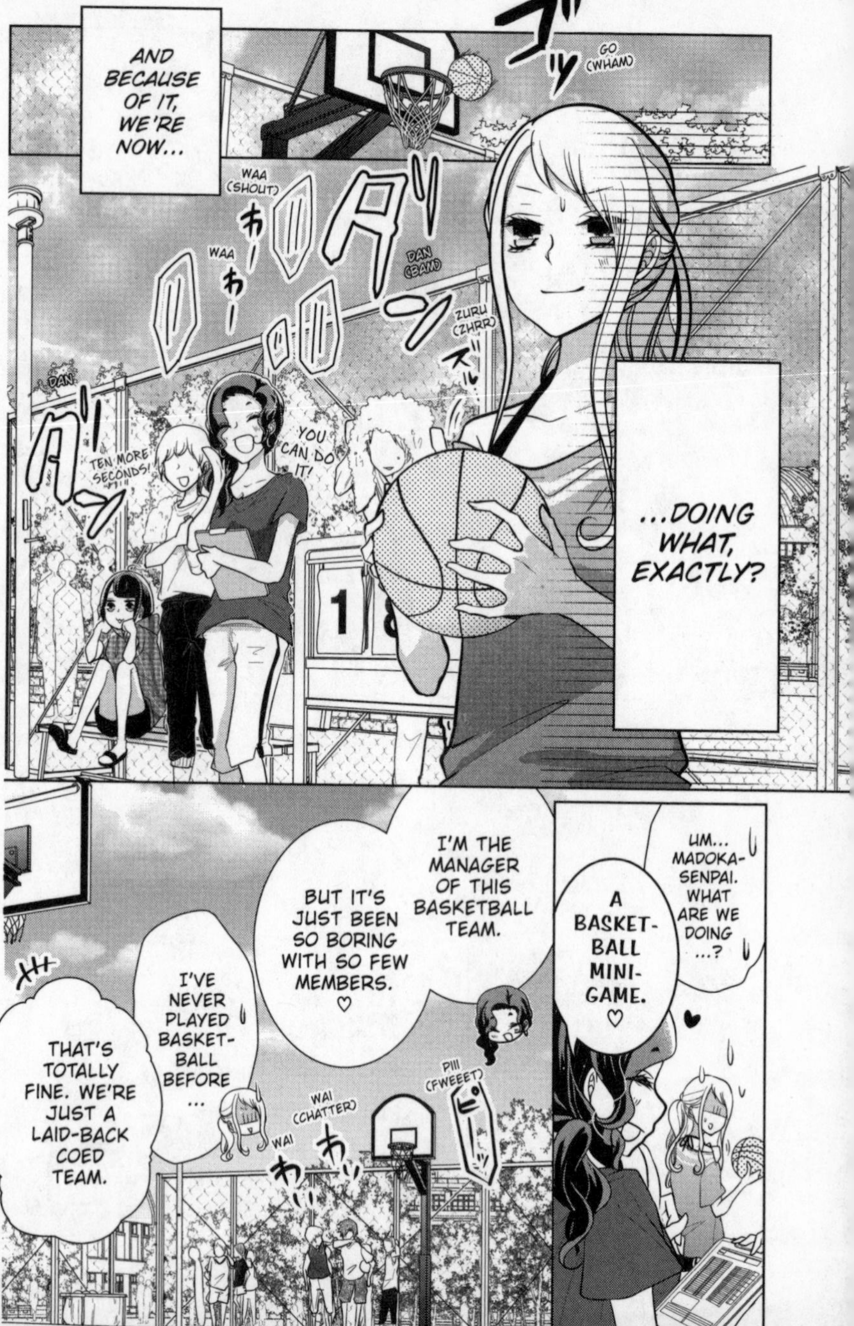
GO (WHAM)
AND BECAUSE OF IT, WE'RE NOW...
WAA (SHOUT)
DAN (BAM)
WAA
ZURU (ZHRR)
...DOING WHAT, EXACTLY?
YOU CAN DO IT!
TEN MORE SECONDS!
DAN
UM... MADOKA-SENPAI. WHAT ARE WE DOING ...?
A BASKET-BALL MINI-GAME. ♡
I'M THE MANAGER OF THIS BASKETBALL TEAM.
BUT IT'S JUST BEEN SO BORING WITH SO FEW MEMBERS. ♡
I'VE NEVER PLAYED BASKET-BALL BEFORE ...
THAT'S TOTALLY FINE. WE'RE JUST A LAID-BACK COED TEAM.
PIII (FWEEET)
WAI (CHATTER)
WAI

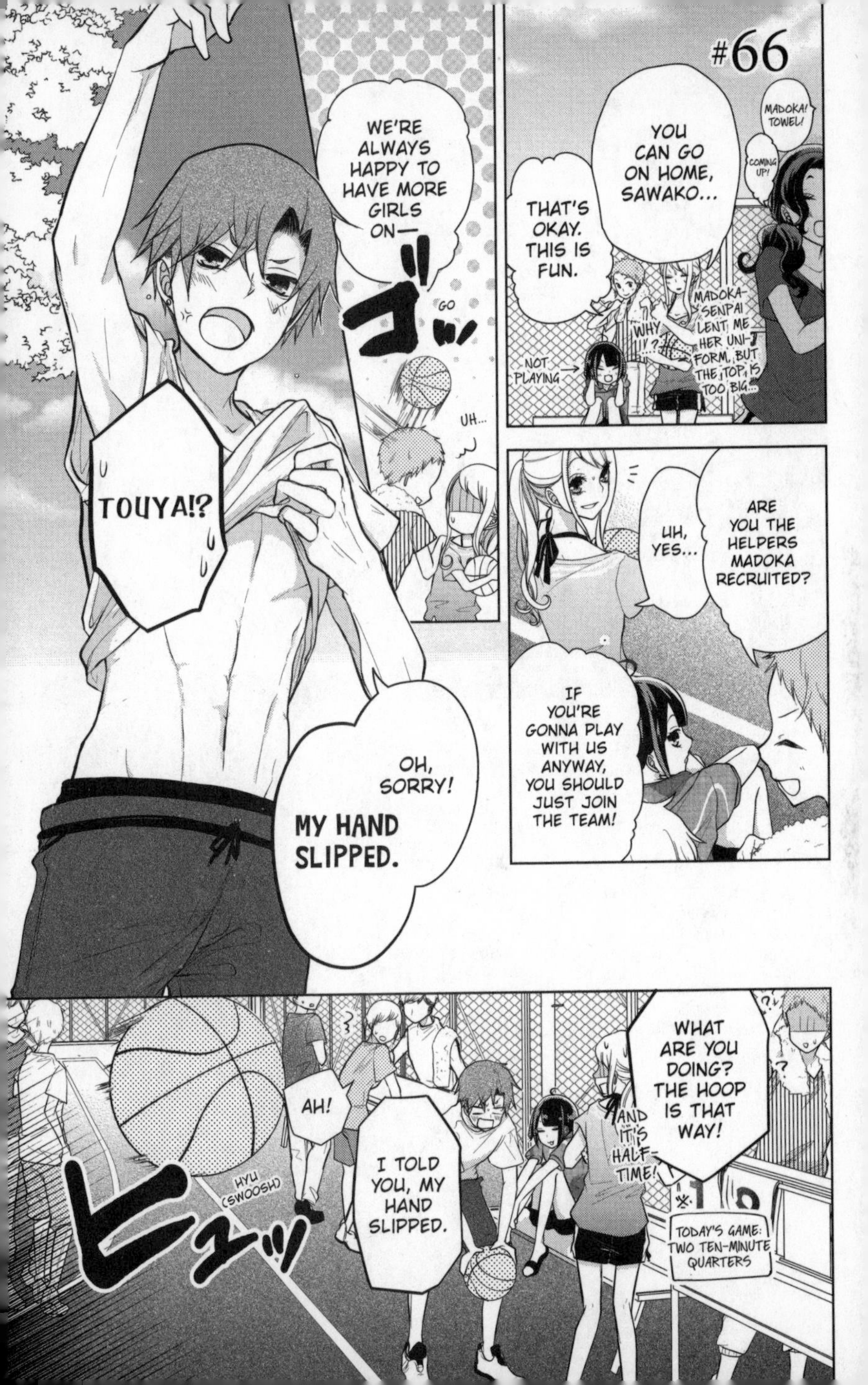
#66
MADOKA! TOWEL!
COMING UP!
YOU CAN GO ON HOME, SAWAKO...
THAT'S OKAY. THIS IS FUN.
MADOKA-SENPAI LENT ME HER UNIFORM, BUT THE TOP IS TOO BIG...
WHY!?
NOT PLAYING
ARE YOU THE HELPERS MADOKA RECRUITED?
UH, YES...
IF YOU'RE GONNA PLAY WITH US ANYWAY, YOU SHOULD JUST JOIN THE TEAM!
WE'RE ALWAYS HAPPY TO HAVE MORE GIRLS ON—
GO
UH...
TOUYA!?
OH, SORRY!
MY HAND SLIPPED.
WHAT ARE YOU DOING? THE HOOP IS THAT WAY!
AND IT'S HALF-TIME!
TODAY'S GAME: TWO TEN-MINUTE QUARTERS
I TOLD YOU, MY HAND SLIPPED.
AH!
HYU (SWOOSH)

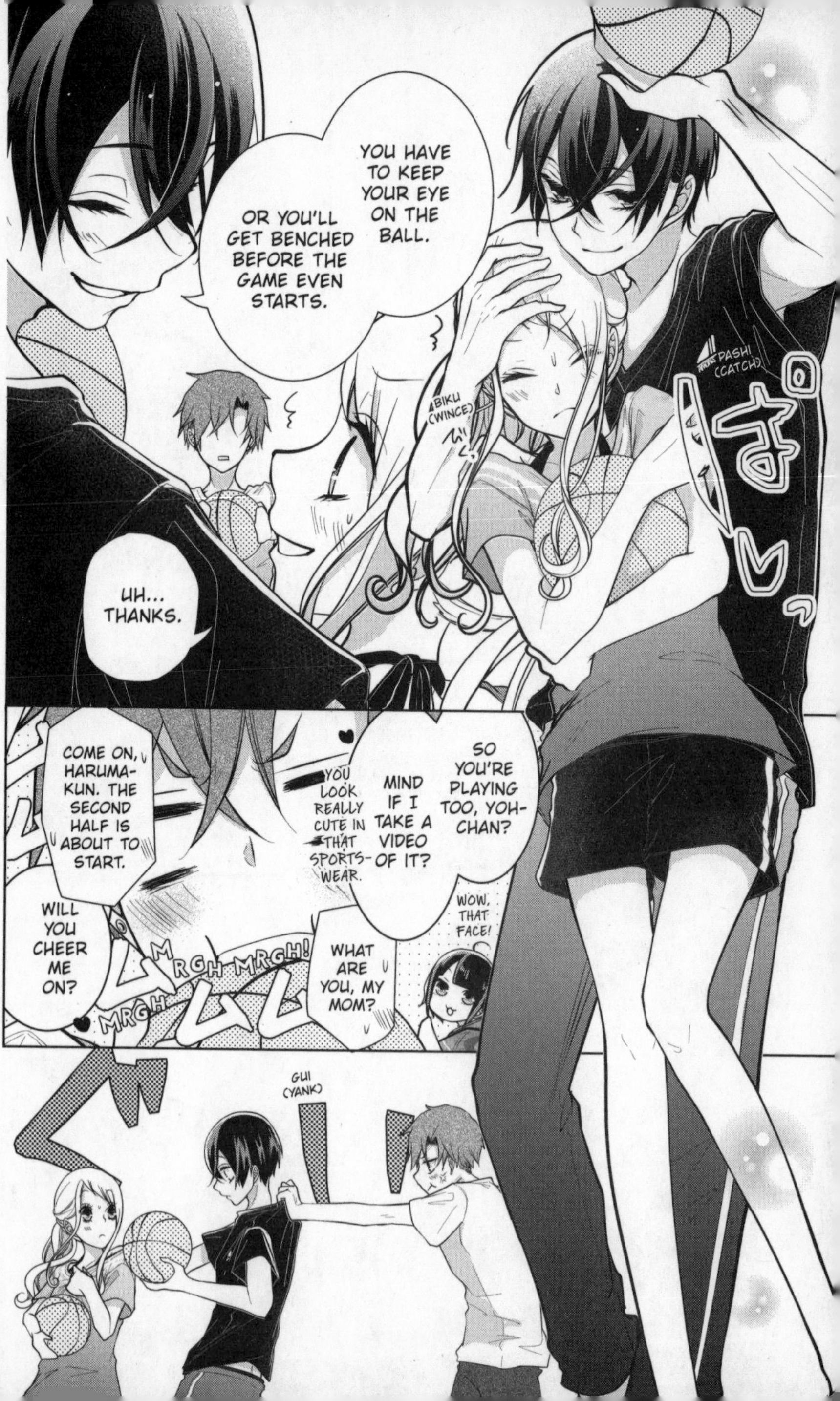
PASHI (CATCH)
YOU HAVE TO KEEP YOUR EYE ON THE BALL.
OR YOU'LL GET BENCHED BEFORE THE GAME EVEN STARTS.
BIKU (WINCE)
UH... THANKS.
SO YOU'RE PLAYING TOO, YOH-CHAN?
MIND IF I TAKE A VIDEO OF IT?
YOU LOOK REALLY CUTE IN THAT SPORTS-WEAR.
COME ON, HARUMA-KUN. THE SECOND HALF IS ABOUT TO START.
WOW, THAT FACE!
WHAT ARE YOU, MY MOM?
WILL YOU CHEER ME ON?
MRGH MRGH MRGH!
GUI (YANK)

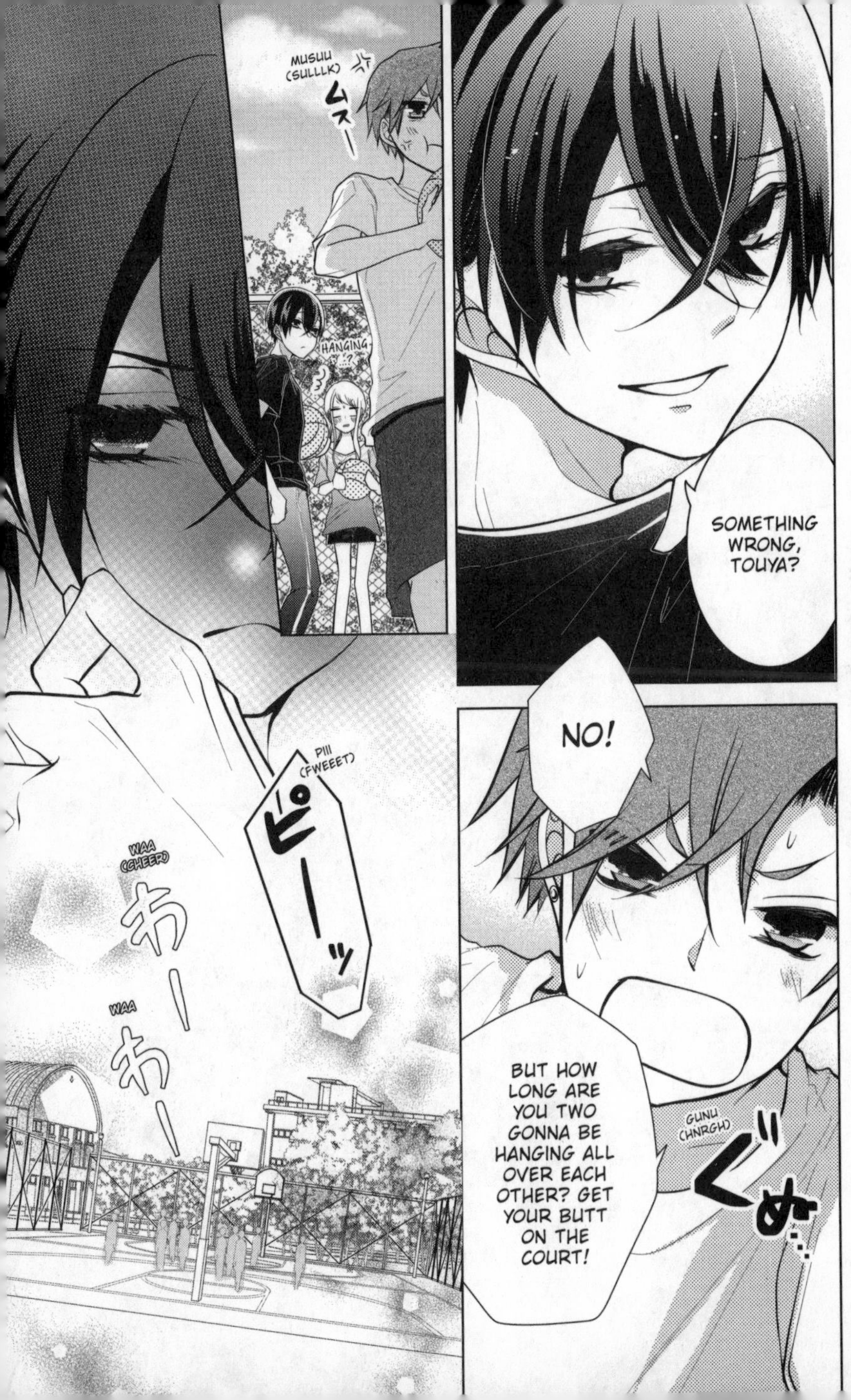
SOMETHING WRONG, TOUYA?
NO!
BUT HOW LONG ARE YOU TWO GONNA BE HANGING ALL OVER EACH OTHER? GET YOUR BUTT ON THE COURT!
GUNU (HNRGH)
ぐぬ…
MUSUU (SULLLK)
ムスー
HANGING...?
PIII (FWEEET)
ピーッ
WAA (CHEER)
わー
WAA
わー

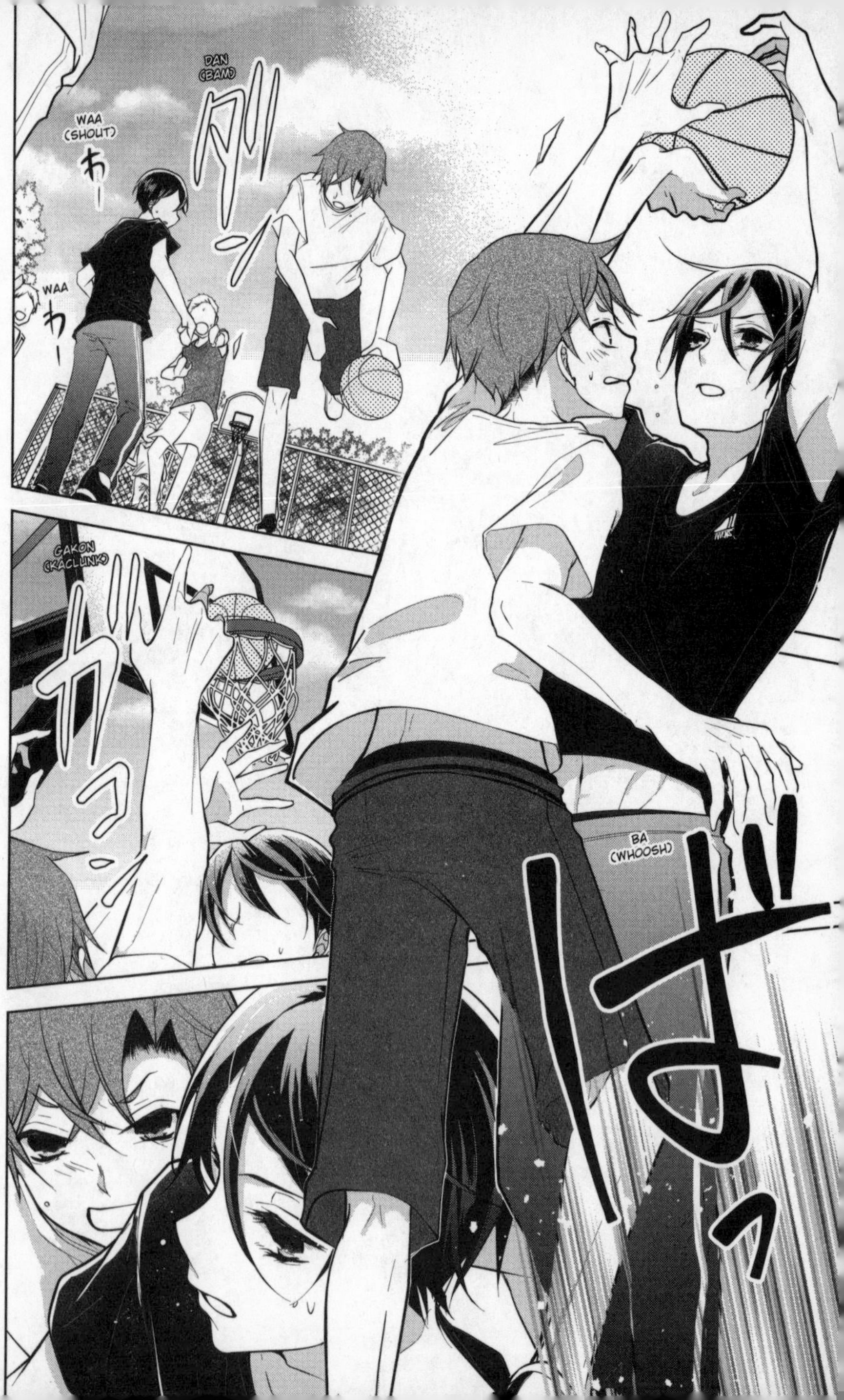
BA (WHOOSH)
DAN (BAM)
WAA (SHOUT)
WAA
GAKON (KACLUNK)

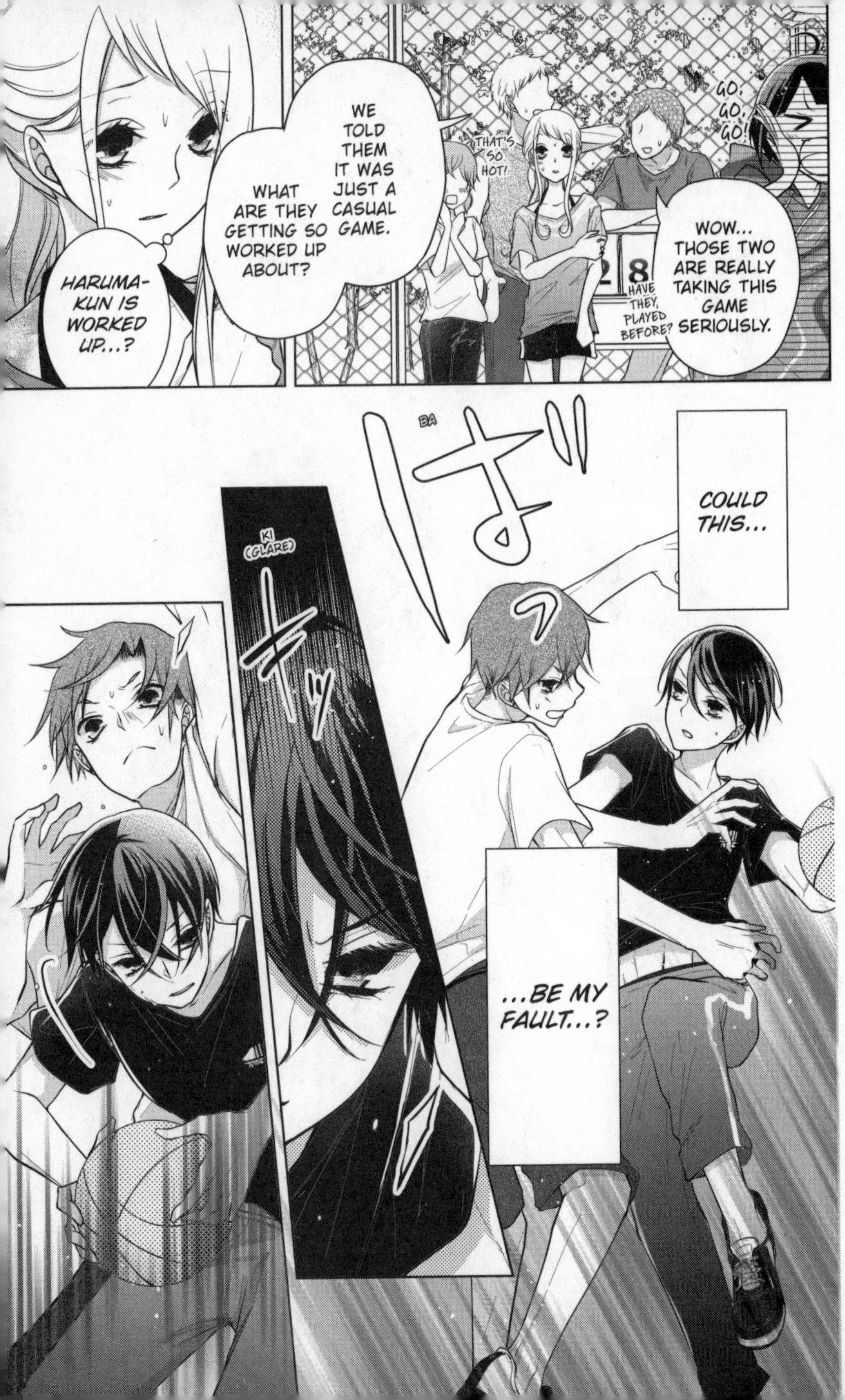
GO, GO, GO!
WOW... THOSE TWO ARE REALLY TAKING THIS GAME SERIOUSLY.
HAVE THEY, PLAYED BEFORE?
THAT'S SO HOT!
WE TOLD THEM IT WAS JUST A CASUAL GAME.
WHAT ARE THEY GETTING SO WORKED UP ABOUT?
HARUMA-KUN IS WORKED UP...?
BA
COULD THIS...
KI (GLARE)
...BE MY FAULT...?

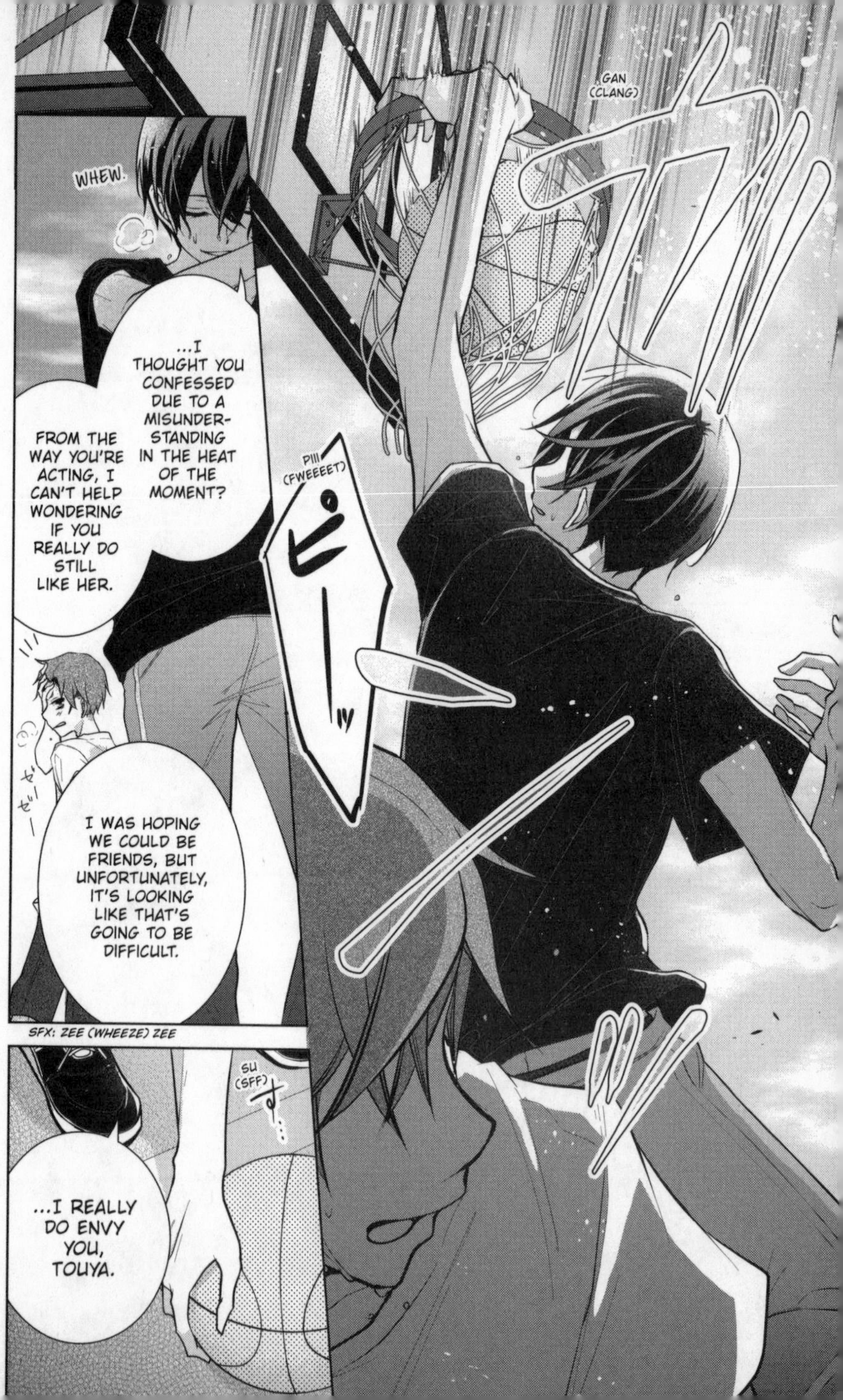
GAN (CLANG)
PIII (FWEEEET)
WHEW.
...I THOUGHT YOU CONFESSED DUE TO A MISUNDER-STANDING IN THE HEAT OF THE MOMENT?
FROM THE WAY YOU'RE ACTING, I CAN'T HELP WONDERING IF YOU REALLY DO STILL LIKE HER.
I WAS HOPING WE COULD BE FRIENDS, BUT UNFORTUNATELY, IT'S LOOKING LIKE THAT'S GOING TO BE DIFFICULT.
SFX: ZEE (WHEEZE) ZEE
SU (SFF)
...I REALLY DO ENVY YOU, TOUYA.

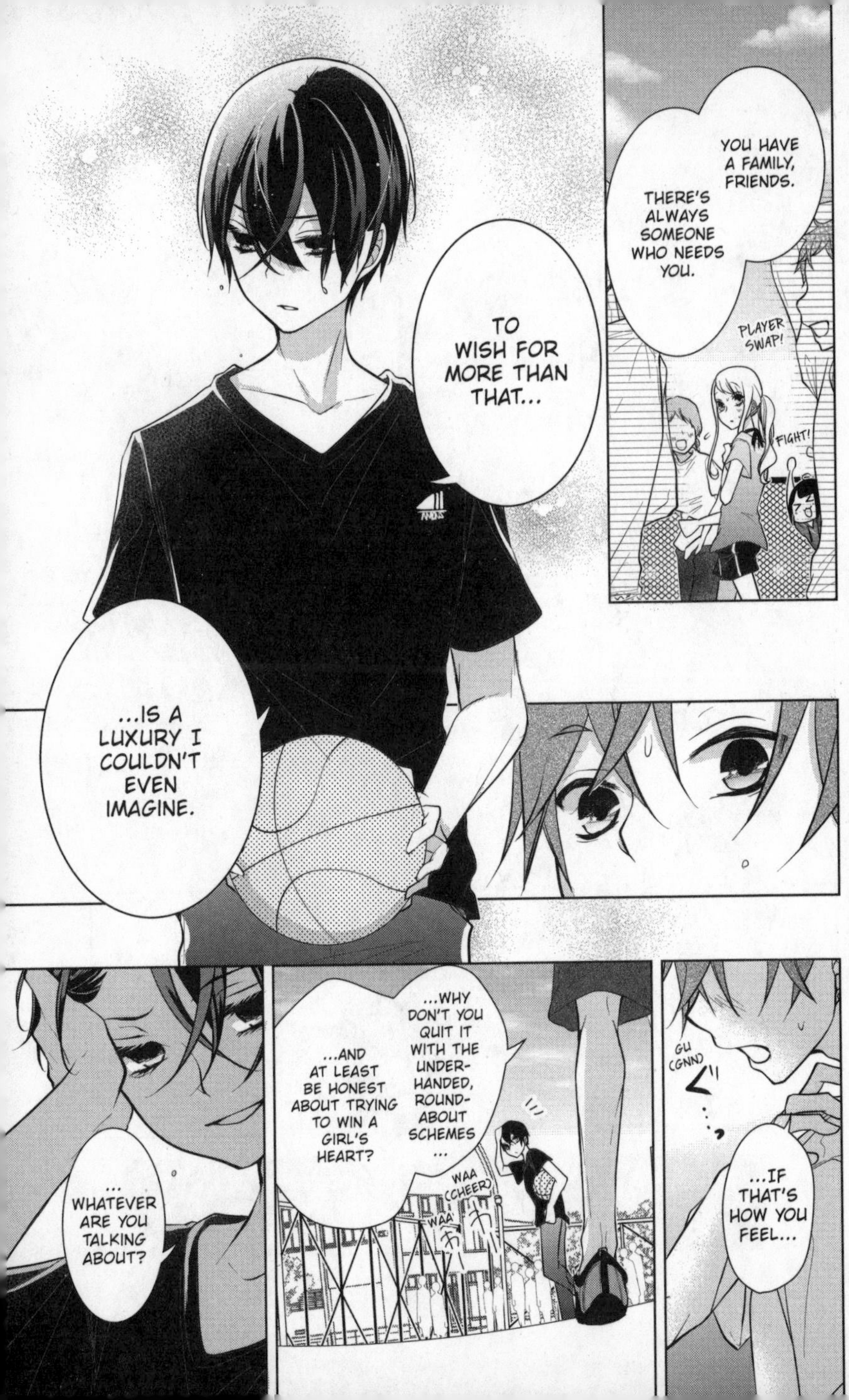
YOU HAVE A FAMILY, FRIENDS.
THERE'S ALWAYS SOMEONE WHO NEEDS YOU.
PLAYER SWAP!
FIGHT!
TO WISH FOR MORE THAN THAT...
...IS A LUXURY I COULDN'T EVEN IMAGINE.
GU (GNN)
...IF THAT'S HOW YOU FEEL...
...WHY DON'T YOU QUIT IT WITH THE UNDER-HANDED, ROUND-ABOUT SCHEMES...
...AND AT LEAST BE HONEST ABOUT TRYING TO WIN A GIRL'S HEART?
WAA (CHEER)
WAA
... WHATEVER ARE YOU TALKING ABOUT?

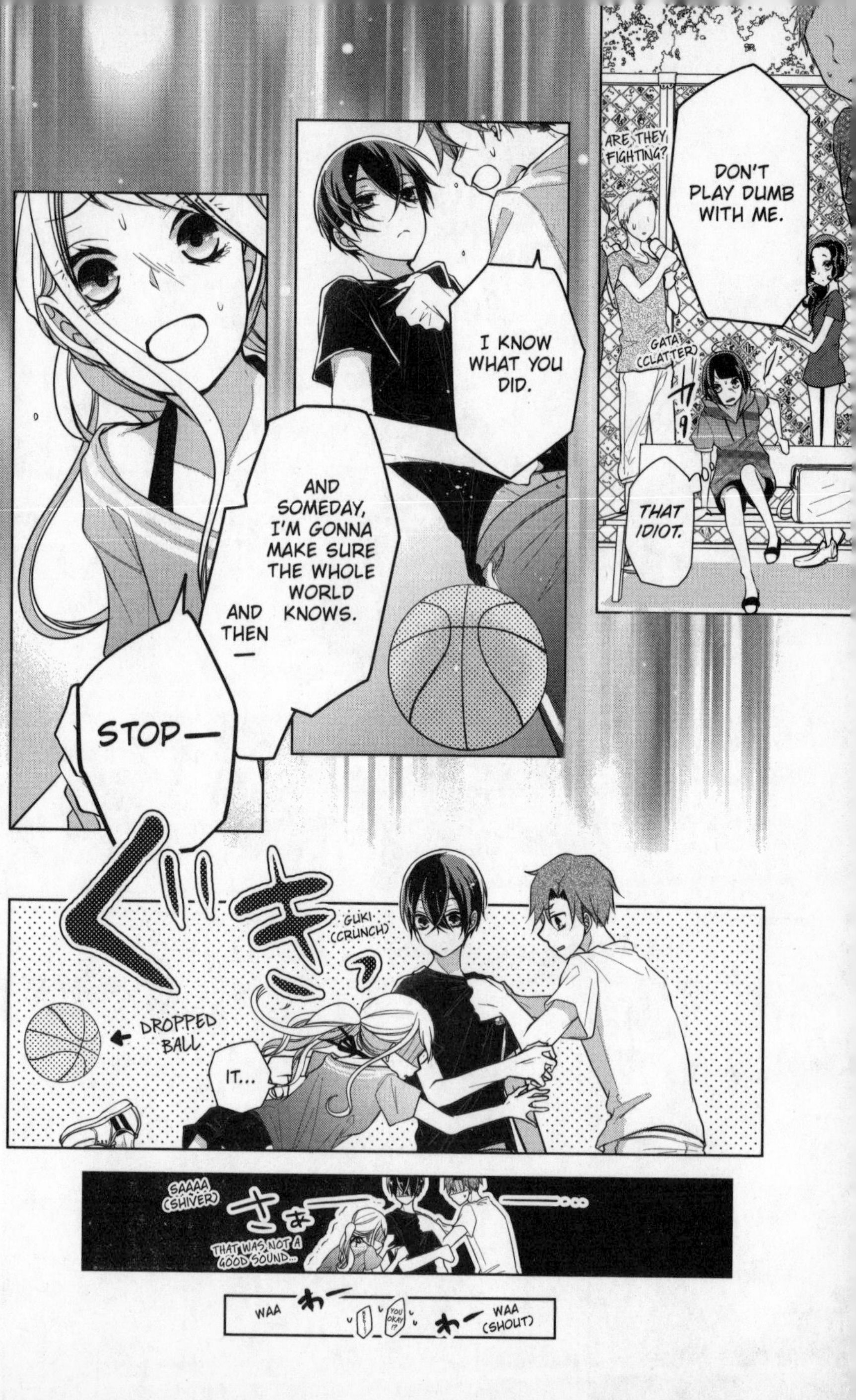
ARE THEY FIGHTING?
DON'T PLAY DUMB WITH ME.
GATA (CLATTER)
THAT IDIOT.
I KNOW WHAT YOU DID.
AND SOMEDAY, I'M GONNA MAKE SURE THE WHOLE WORLD KNOWS.
AND THEN —
STOP—
GUKI (CRUNCH)
DROPPED BALL
IT...
SAAAA (SHIVER)
THAT WAS NOT A GOOD SOUND...
WAA
YOU OKAY!?
WAA (SHOUT)

#67

SIGN: GENERAL HOSPITAL
IT'S A SPRAIN.
IT IS A SPECTACULAR SPRAIN, THOUGH.
BUT THERE WAS NO DAMAGE TO THE BONE.
IF SHE STAYS OFF IT FOR A WHILE, THE SWELLING WILL GO DOWN.
I FEEL BAD FOR HER, WITH SUMMER VACATION JUST STARTING FOR YOU COLLEGE KIDS.
OWWW...
YOH IS GETTING TREATMENT IN ANOTHER ROOM
...NO, THIS TIMING IS PERFECT.
NOW I HAVE A GOOD REASON NOT TO LET HER SEE ANYONE ELSE.
BOSO (WHISPER)
LET ME GET YOU THOSE PAINKILLERS AND COMPRESSES.
HM?
NIKO (GRIND)

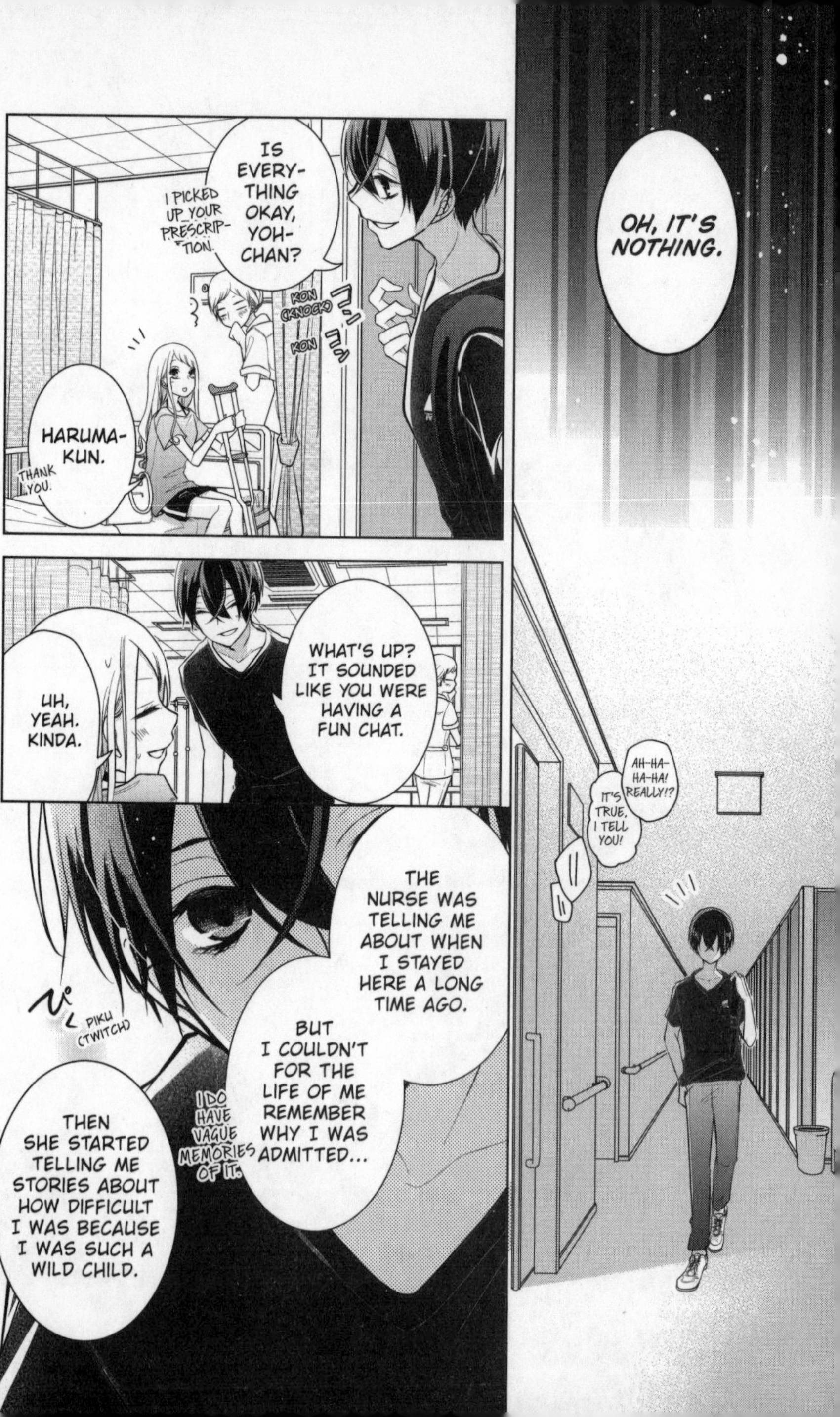
OH, IT'S NOTHING.
AH-HA-HA-HA! REALLY!?
IT'S TRUE, I TELL YOU!
IS EVERY-THING OKAY, YOH-CHAN?
KON (KNOCK) KON
I PICKED UP YOUR PRESCRIP-TION.
HARUMA-KUN.
THANK YOU.
WHAT'S UP? IT SOUNDED LIKE YOU WERE HAVING A FUN CHAT.
UH, YEAH. KINDA.
THE NURSE WAS TELLING ME ABOUT WHEN I STAYED HERE A LONG TIME AGO.
BUT I COULDN'T FOR THE LIFE OF ME REMEMBER WHY I WAS ADMITTED...
I DO HAVE VAGUE MEMORIES OF IT.
PIKU (TWITCH)
THEN SHE STARTED TELLING ME STORIES ABOUT HOW DIFFICULT I WAS BECAUSE I WAS SUCH A WILD CHILD.

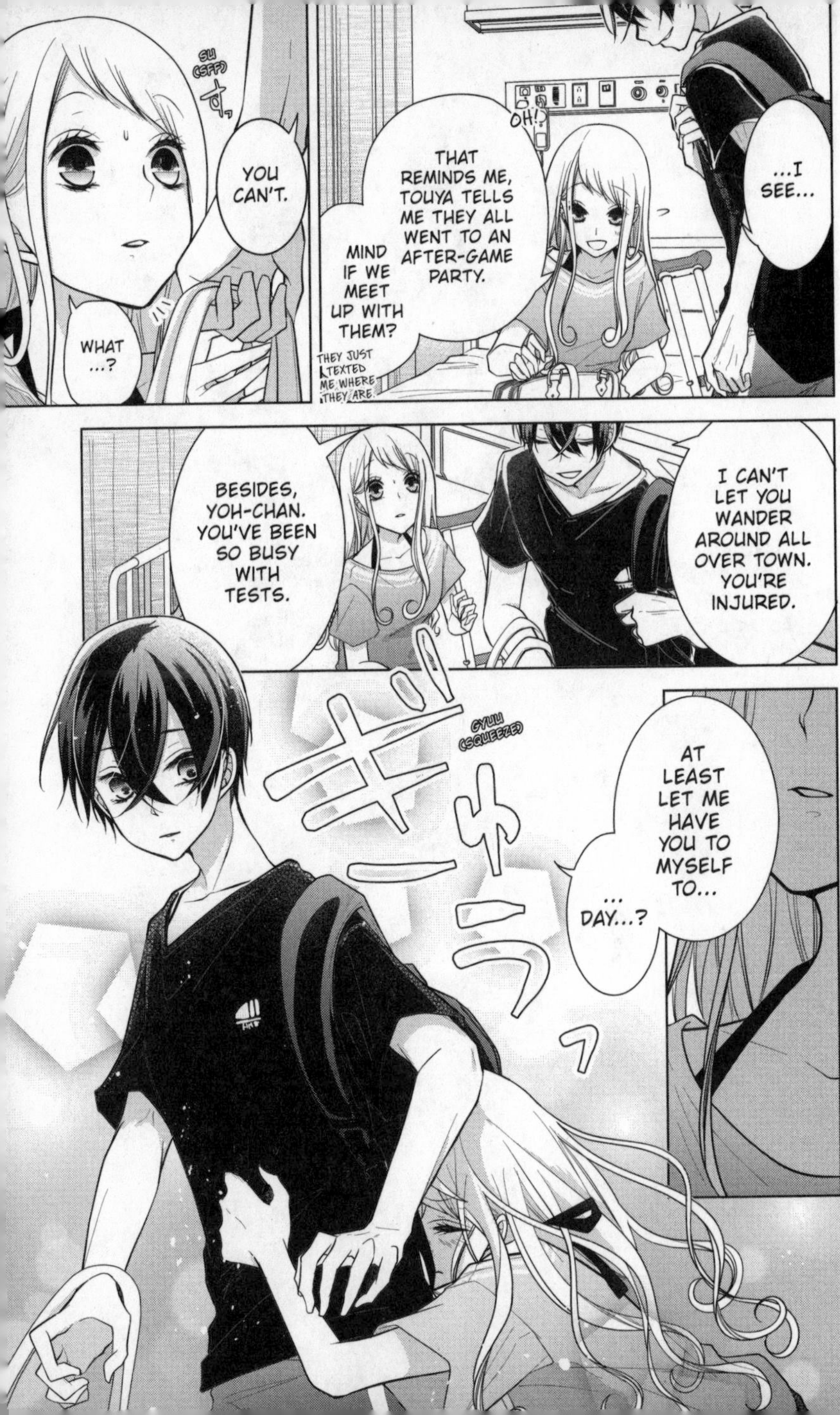
...I SEE...
OH!?
THAT REMINDS ME, TOUYA TELLS ME THEY ALL WENT TO AN AFTER-GAME PARTY.
MIND IF WE MEET UP WITH THEM?
THEY JUST TEXTED ME WHERE THEY ARE.
SU (SFF)
す
YOU CAN'T.
WHAT ...?
I CAN'T LET YOU WANDER AROUND ALL OVER TOWN. YOU'RE INJURED.
BESIDES, YOH-CHAN. YOU'VE BEEN SO BUSY WITH TESTS.
AT LEAST LET ME HAVE YOU TO MYSELF TO...
... DAY...?
GYUU (SQUEEZE)
ぎゅーっ

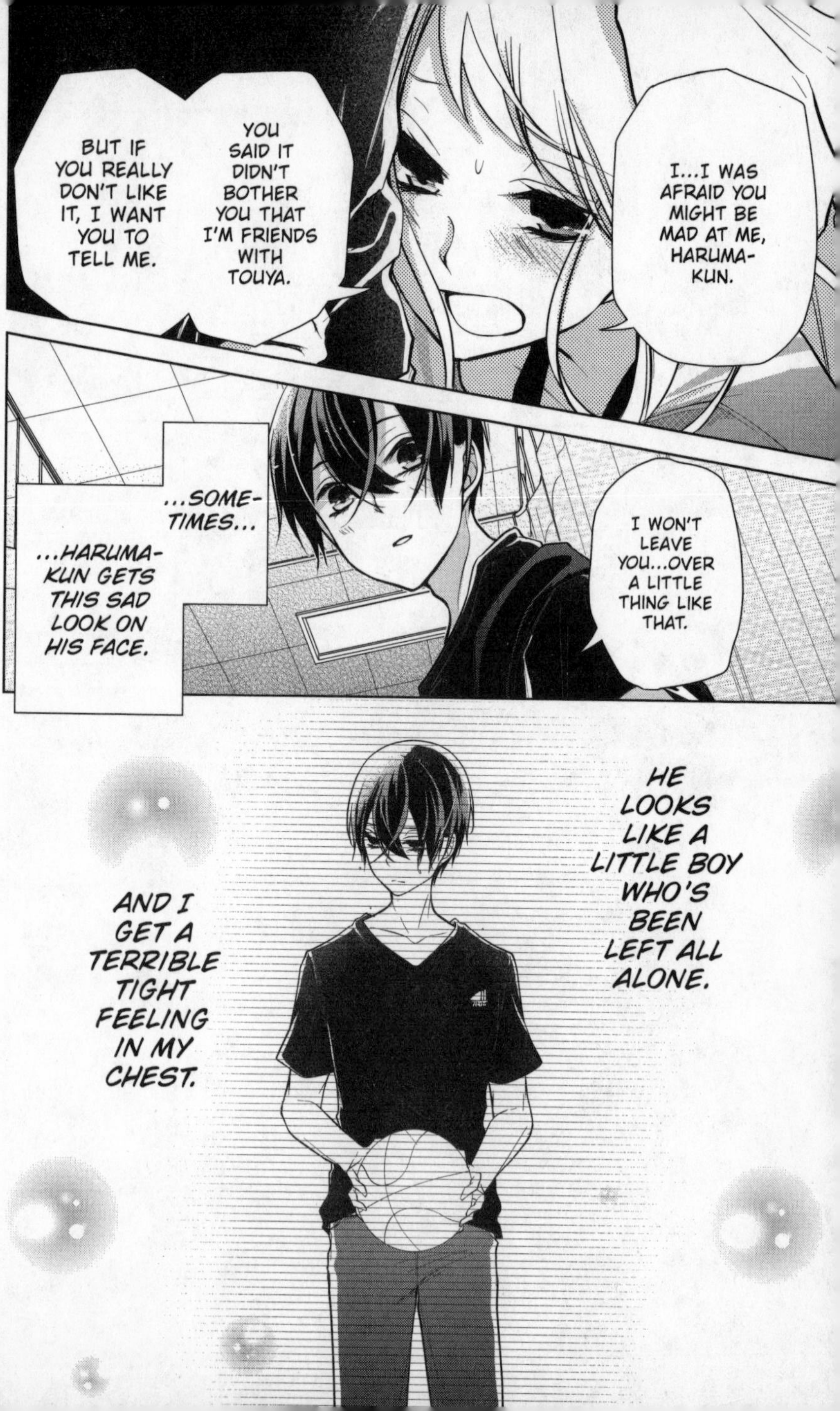
I...I WAS AFRAID YOU MIGHT BE MAD AT ME, HARUMA-KUN.
YOU SAID IT DIDN'T BOTHER YOU THAT I'M FRIENDS WITH TOUYA.
BUT IF YOU REALLY DON'T LIKE IT, I WANT YOU TO TELL ME.
I WON'T LEAVE YOU...OVER A LITTLE THING LIKE THAT.
...SOME-TIMES...
...HARUMA-KUN GETS THIS SAD LOOK ON HIS FACE.
HE LOOKS LIKE A LITTLE BOY WHO'S BEEN LEFT ALL ALONE.
AND I GET A TERRIBLE TIGHT FEELING IN MY CHEST.

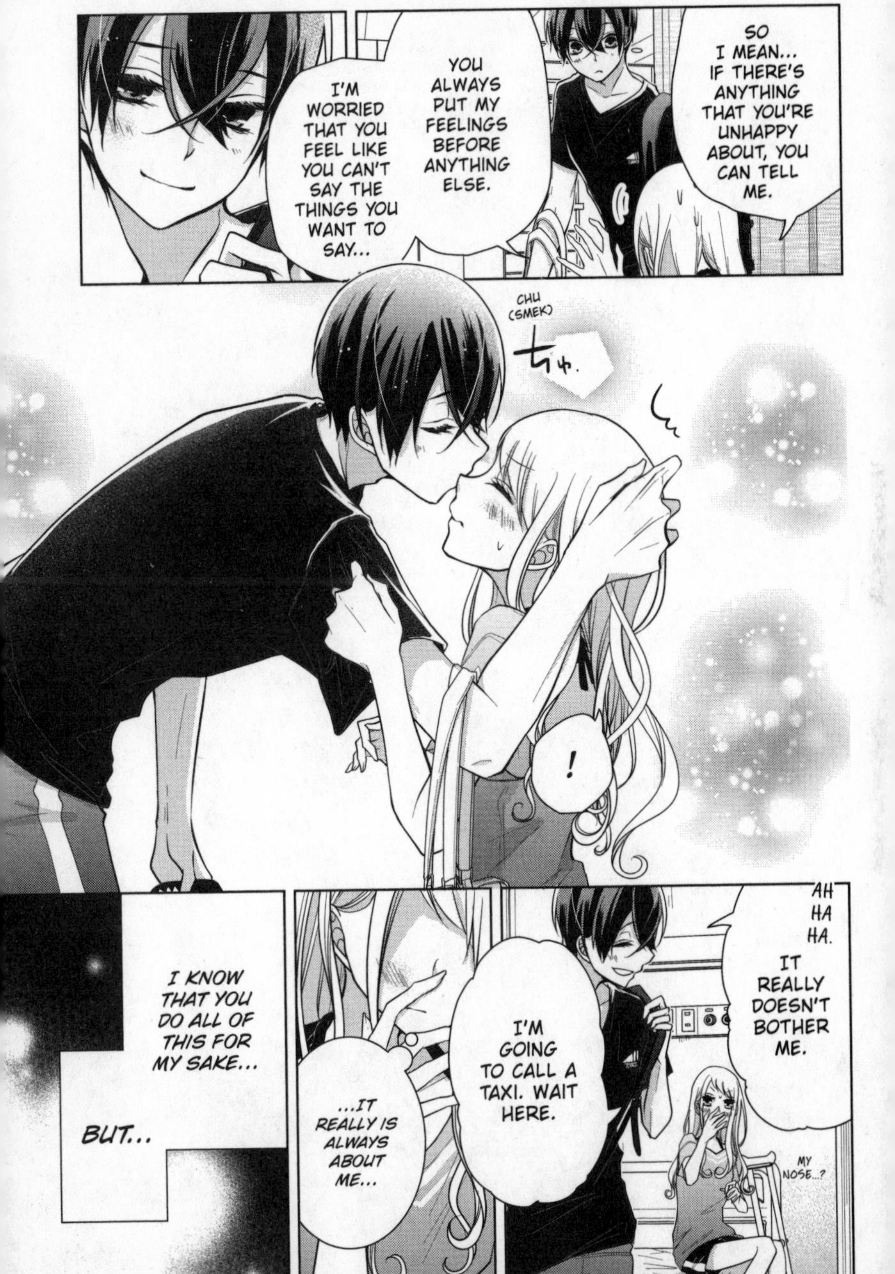
SO I MEAN... IF THERE'S ANYTHING THAT YOU'RE UNHAPPY ABOUT, YOU CAN TELL ME.
YOU ALWAYS PUT MY FEELINGS BEFORE ANYTHING ELSE.
I'M WORRIED THAT YOU FEEL LIKE YOU CAN'T SAY THE THINGS YOU WANT TO SAY...
CHU (SMEK)
!
AH HA HA.
IT REALLY DOESN'T BOTHER ME.
MY NOSE...?
I'M GOING TO CALL A TAXI. WAIT HERE.
...IT REALLY IS ALWAYS ABOUT ME...
I KNOW THAT YOU DO ALL OF THIS FOR MY SAKE...
BUT...

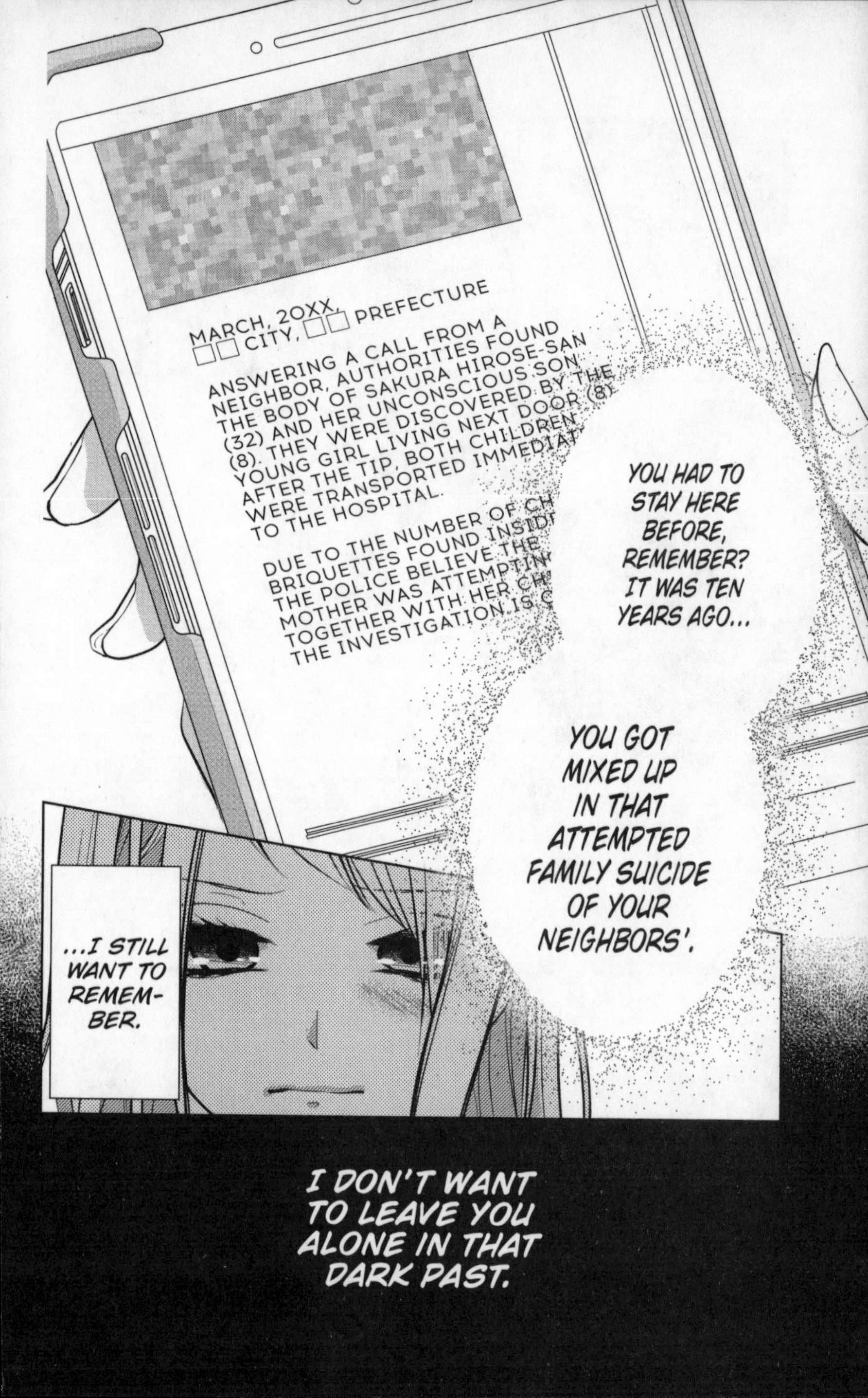

MARCH, 20XX,
□□ CITY, □□ PREFECTURE
ANSWERING A CALL FROM A
NEIGHBOR, AUTHORITIES FOUND
THE BODY OF SAKURA HIROSE-SAN
(32) AND HER UNCONSCIOUS SON
(8). THEY WERE DISCOVERED BY THE
YOUNG GIRL LIVING NEXT DOOR (8)
AFTER THE TIP. BOTH CHILDREN
WERE TRANSPORTED IMMEDIAT
TO THE HOSPITAL.
DUE TO THE NUMBER OF CH
BRIQUETTES FOUND INSID
THE POLICE BELIEVE THE
MOTHER WAS ATTEMPTIN
TOGETHER WITH HER CH
THE INVESTIGATION IS
YOU HAD TO STAY HERE BEFORE, REMEMBER? IT WAS TEN YEARS AGO...
YOU GOT MIXED UP IN THAT ATTEMPTED FAMILY SUICIDE OF YOUR NEIGHBORS'.
...I STILL WANT TO REMEMBER.
I DON'T WANT TO LEAVE YOU ALONE IN THAT DARK PAST.

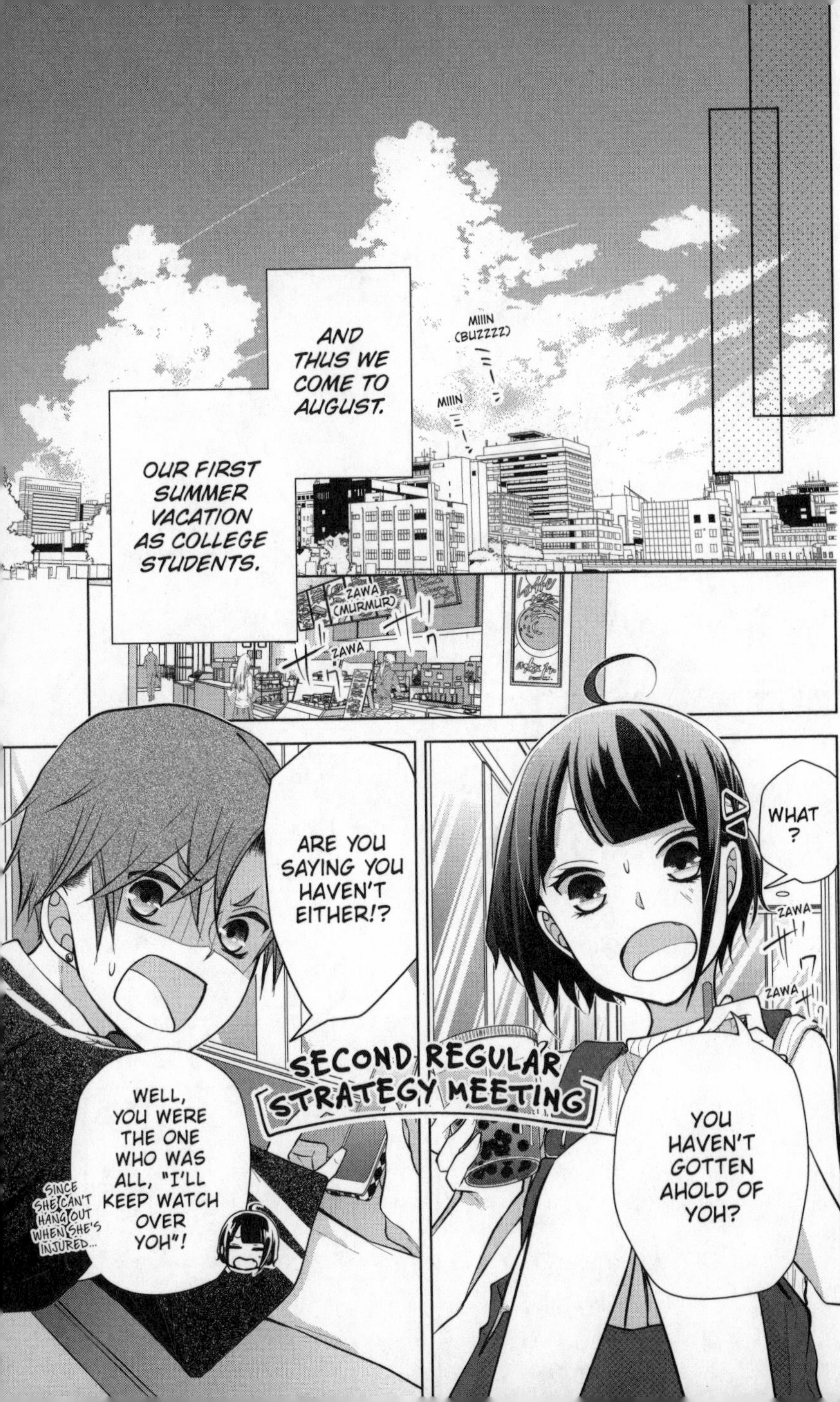
MIIN (BUZZZZ)
MIIN
AND THUS WE COME TO AUGUST.
OUR FIRST SUMMER VACATION AS COLLEGE STUDENTS.
ZAWA (MURMUR)
ZAWA
WHAT?
ZAWA
ZAWA
YOU HAVEN'T GOTTEN AHOLD OF YOH?
SECOND REGULAR STRATEGY MEETING
ARE YOU SAYING YOU HAVEN'T EITHER!?
WELL, YOU WERE THE ONE WHO WAS ALL, "I'LL KEEP WATCH OVER YOH"!
SINCE SHE CAN'T HANG OUT WHEN SHE'S INJURED...

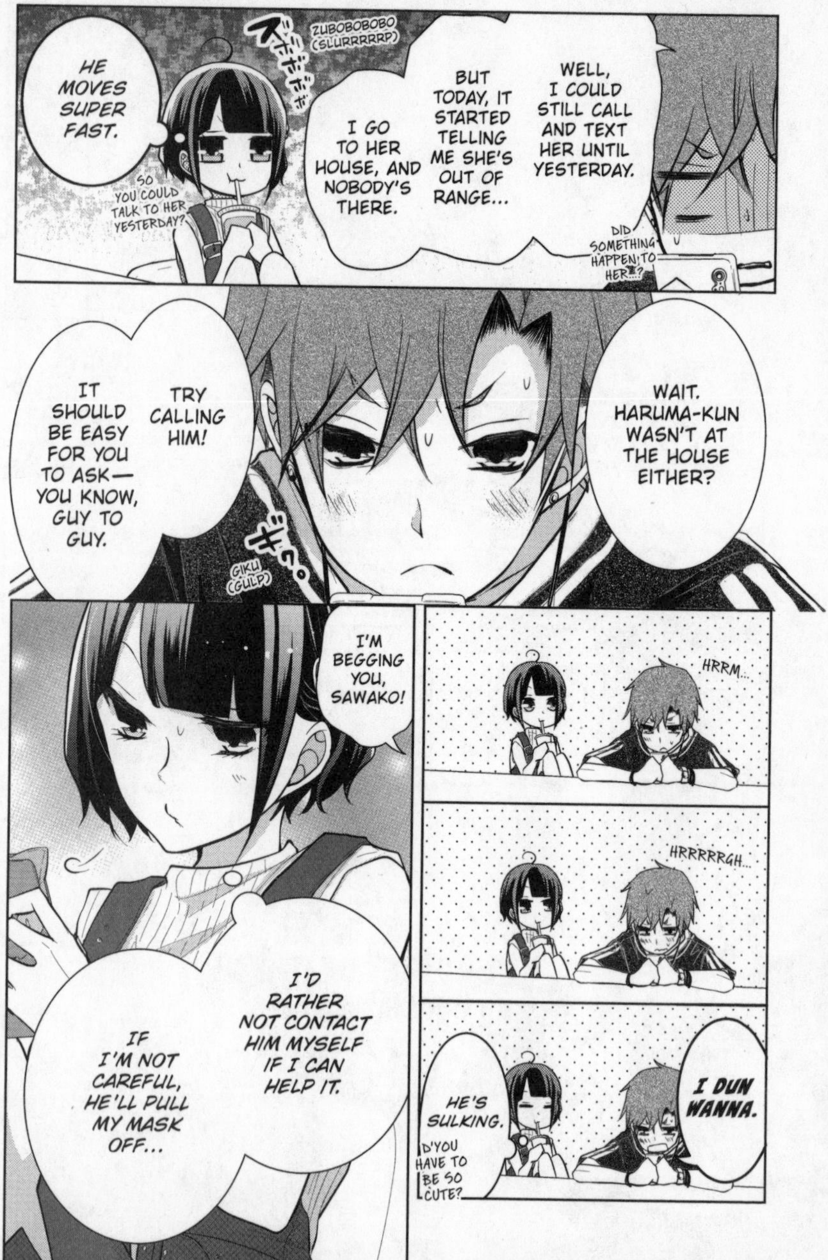
WELL, I COULD STILL CALL AND TEXT HER UNTIL YESTERDAY.
DID SOMETHING HAPPEN TO HER...?
BUT TODAY, IT STARTED TELLING ME SHE'S OUT OF RANGE...
I GO TO HER HOUSE, AND NOBODY'S THERE.
ZUBOBOBOBO (SLURRRRRP)
SO YOU COULD TALK TO HER YESTERDAY?
HE MOVES SUPER FAST.
WAIT. HARUMA-KUN WASN'T AT THE HOUSE EITHER?
GIKU (GULP)
TRY CALLING HIM!
IT SHOULD BE EASY FOR YOU TO ASK—YOU KNOW, GUY TO GUY.
HRRM...
HRRRRRGH...
I DUN WANNA.
HE'S SULKING.
D'YOU HAVE TO BE SO CUTE?
I'M BEGGING YOU, SAWAKO!
I'D RATHER NOT CONTACT HIM MYSELF IF I CAN HELP IT.
IF I'M NOT CAREFUL, HE'LL PULL MY MASK OFF...

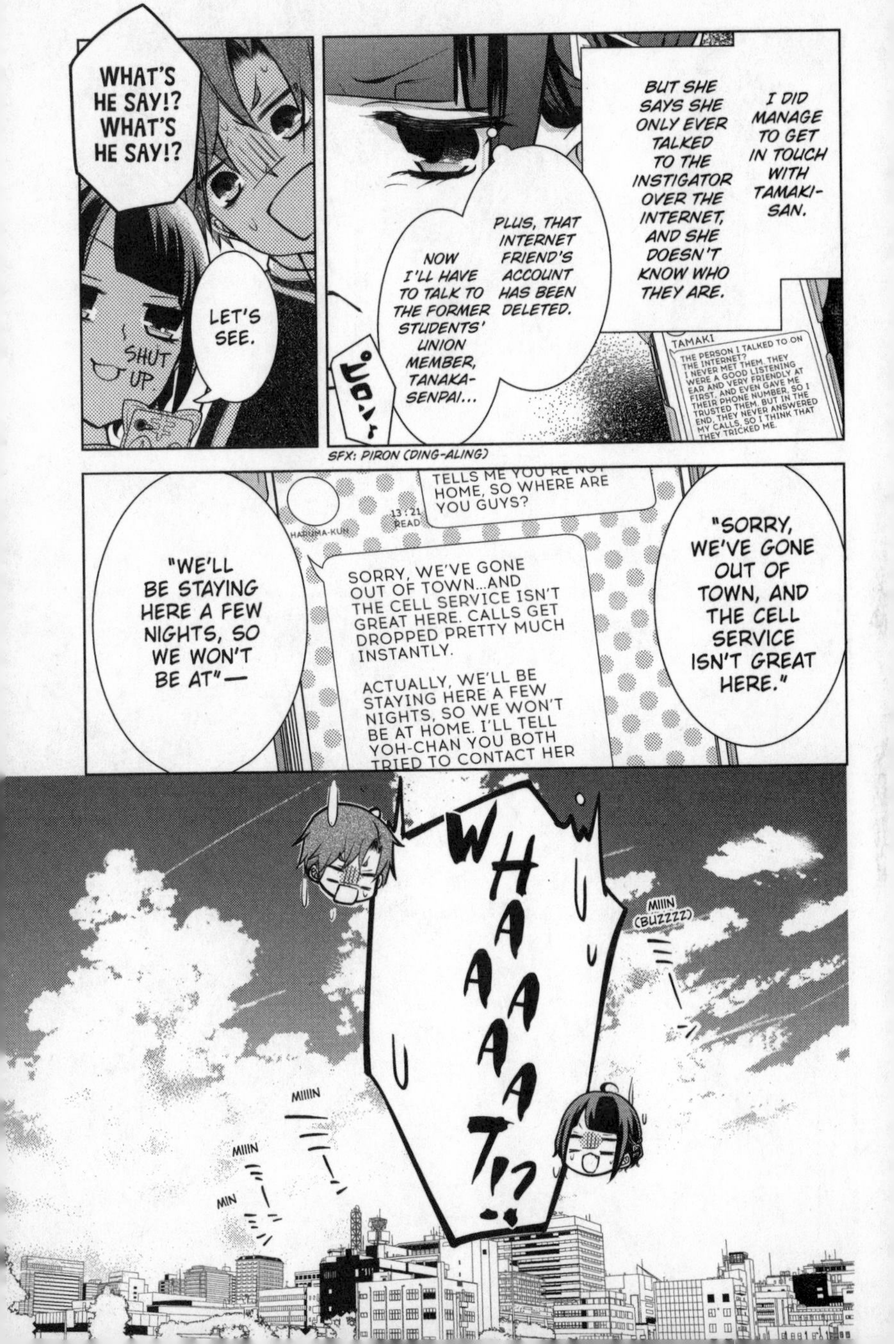
I DID MANAGE TO GET IN TOUCH WITH TAMAKI-SAN.
BUT SHE SAYS SHE ONLY EVER TALKED TO THE INSTIGATOR OVER THE INTERNET, AND SHE DOESN'T KNOW WHO THEY ARE.
TAMAKI
THE PERSON I TALKED TO ON THE INTERNET? I NEVER MET THEM. THEY WERE A GOOD LISTENING EAR AND VERY FRIENDLY AT FIRST, AND EVEN GAVE ME THEIR PHONE NUMBER, SO I TRUSTED THEM. BUT IN THE END, THEY NEVER ANSWERED MY CALLS, SO I THINK THAT THEY TRICKED ME.
PLUS, THAT INTERNET FRIEND'S ACCOUNT HAS BEEN DELETED.
NOW I'LL HAVE TO TALK TO THE FORMER STUDENTS' UNION MEMBER, TANAKA-SENPAI...
SFX: PIRON (DING-ALING)
WHAT'S HE SAY!? WHAT'S HE SAY!?
LET'S SEE.
SHUT UP.
"SORRY, WE'VE GONE OUT OF TOWN, AND THE CELL SERVICE ISN'T GREAT HERE."
TELLS ME YOU'RE NOT HOME, SO WHERE ARE YOU GUYS?
13:21 READ
HARUMA-KUN
SORRY, WE'VE GONE OUT OF TOWN...AND THE CELL SERVICE ISN'T GREAT HERE. CALLS GET DROPPED PRETTY MUCH INSTANTLY.
ACTUALLY, WE'LL BE STAYING HERE A FEW NIGHTS, SO WE WON'T BE AT HOME. I'LL TELL YOH-CHAN YOU BOTH TRIED TO CONTACT HER
"WE'LL BE STAYING HERE A FEW NIGHTS, SO WE WON'T BE AT"—
WHAAAAAAT!?
MIIIN (BUZZZZ)
MIIIN
MIIIN
MIN

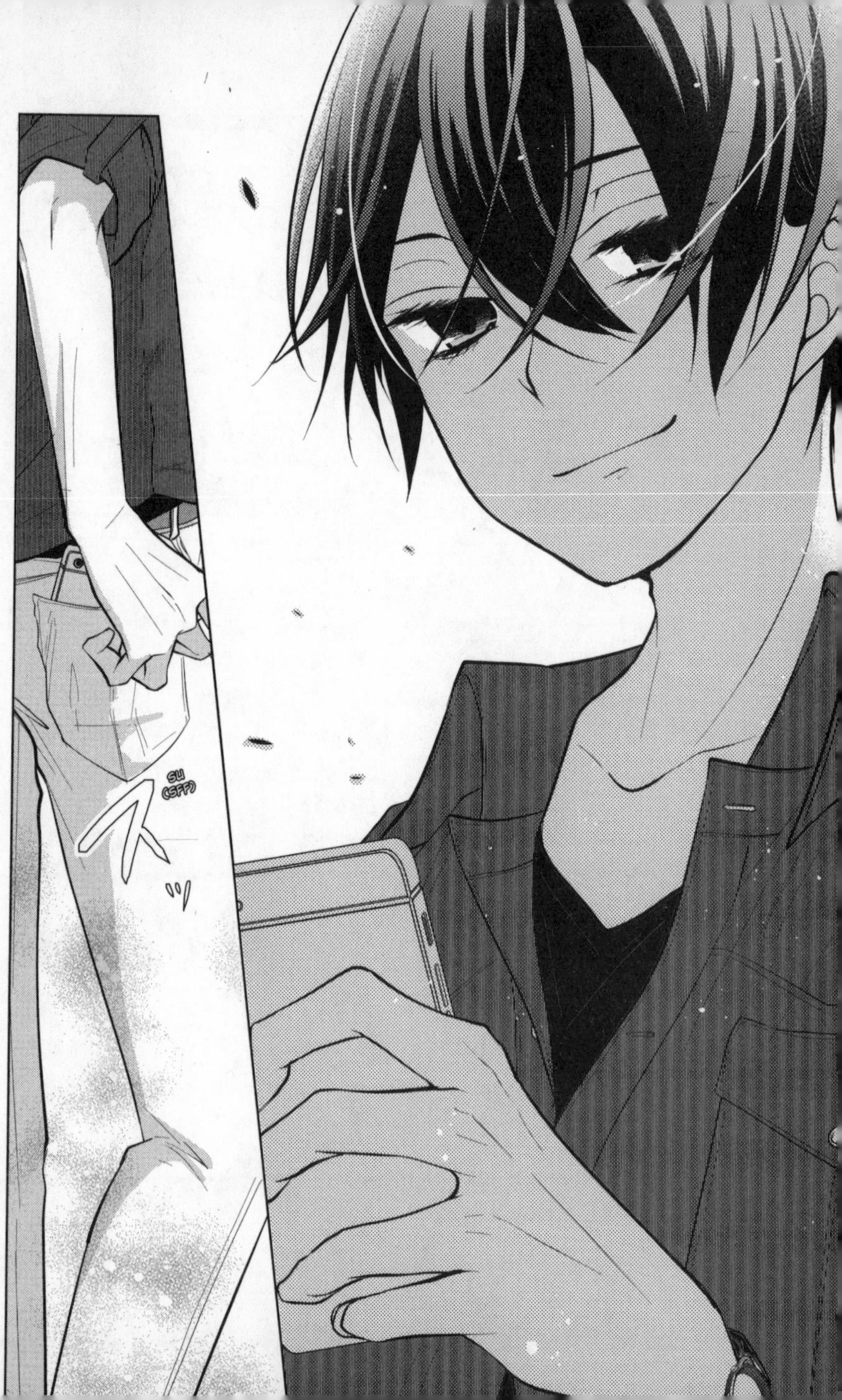
SU
(SFF)

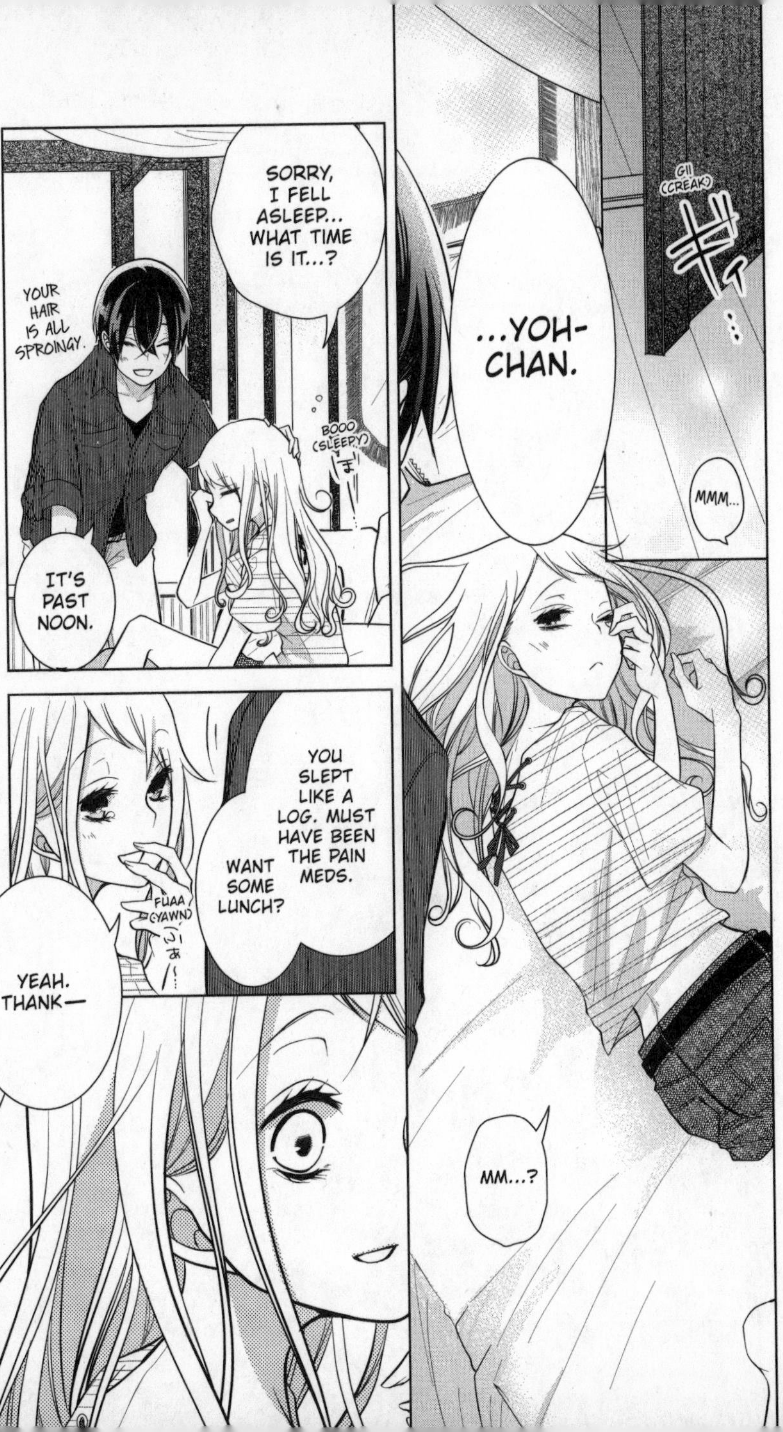
GII (CREAK)
...YOH-CHAN.
MMM...
MM...?
SORRY, I FELL ASLEEP... WHAT TIME IS IT...?
YOUR HAIR IS ALL SPROINGY.
BOOO (SLEEPY)
IT'S PAST NOON.
YOU SLEPT LIKE A LOG. MUST HAVE BEEN THE PAIN MEDS.
WANT SOME LUNCH?
FUAA (YAWN)
YEAH. THANK—

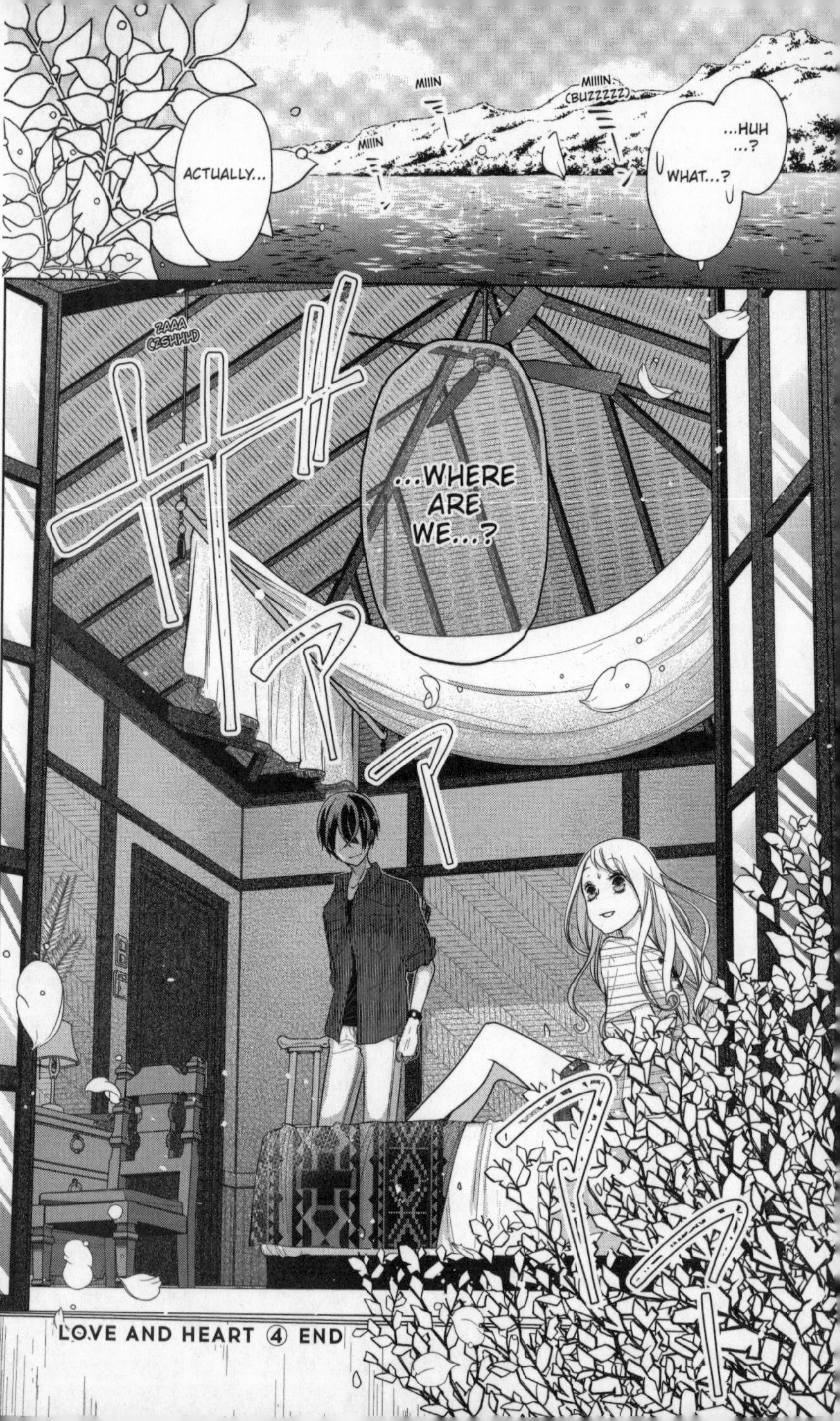
...HUH ...?
WHAT...?
MIIIIN (BUZZZZZ)
MIIIN
MIIIN
ACTUALLY...
ZAAA (ZSHHHH)
...WHERE ARE WE...?

LOVE AND HEART ④ END

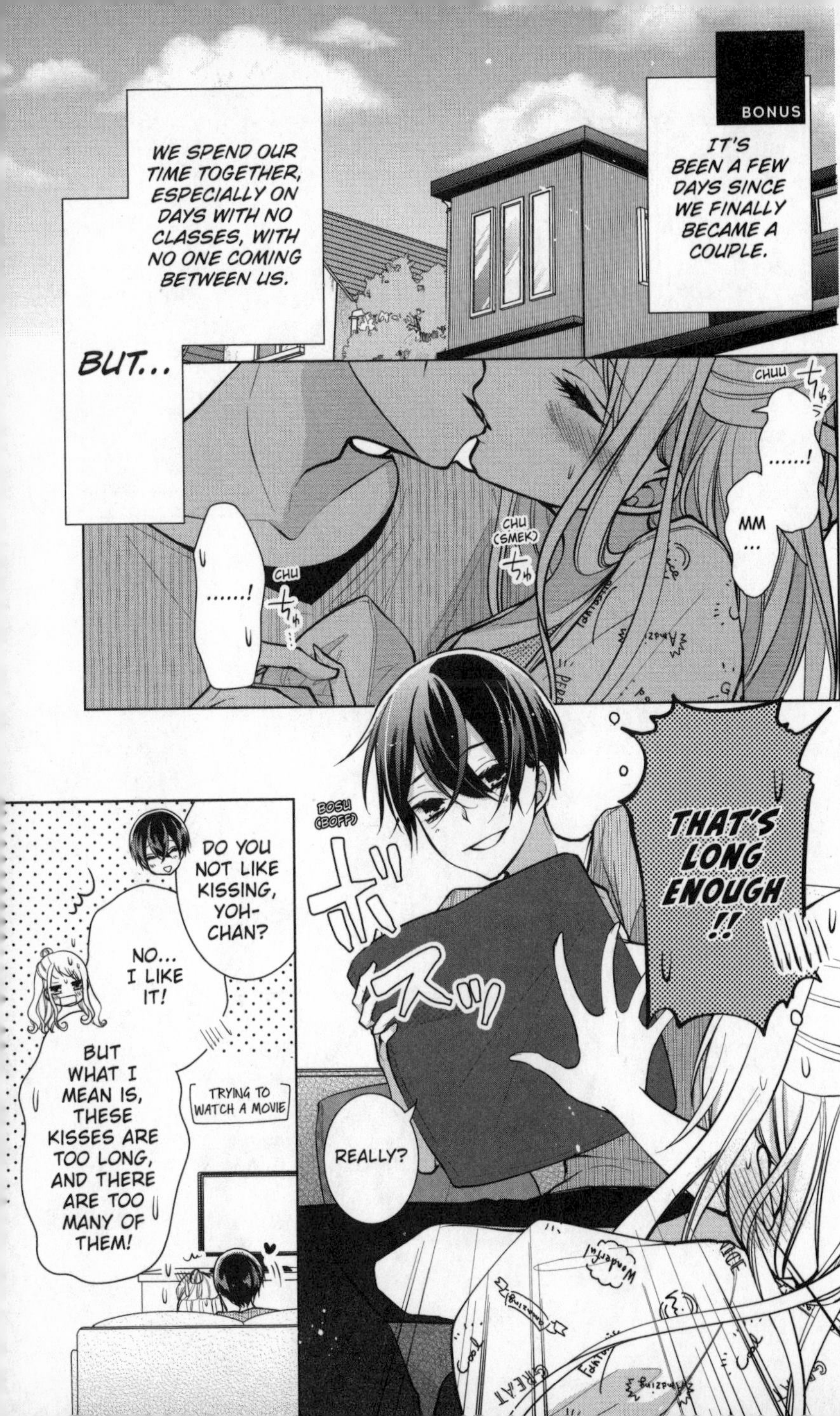
BONUS
IT'S BEEN A FEW DAYS SINCE WE FINALLY BECAME A COUPLE.
WE SPEND OUR TIME TOGETHER, ESPECIALLY ON DAYS WITH NO CLASSES, WITH NO ONE COMING BETWEEN US.
BUT...
CHUU
......!
MM...
CHU (SMEK)
CHU
......!
THAT'S LONG ENOUGH!!
BOSU (BOFF)
REALLY?
DO YOU NOT LIKE KISSING, YOH-CHAN?
NO... I LIKE IT!
BUT WHAT I MEAN IS, THESE KISSES ARE TOO LONG, AND THERE ARE TOO MANY OF THEM!
TRYING TO WATCH A MOVIE

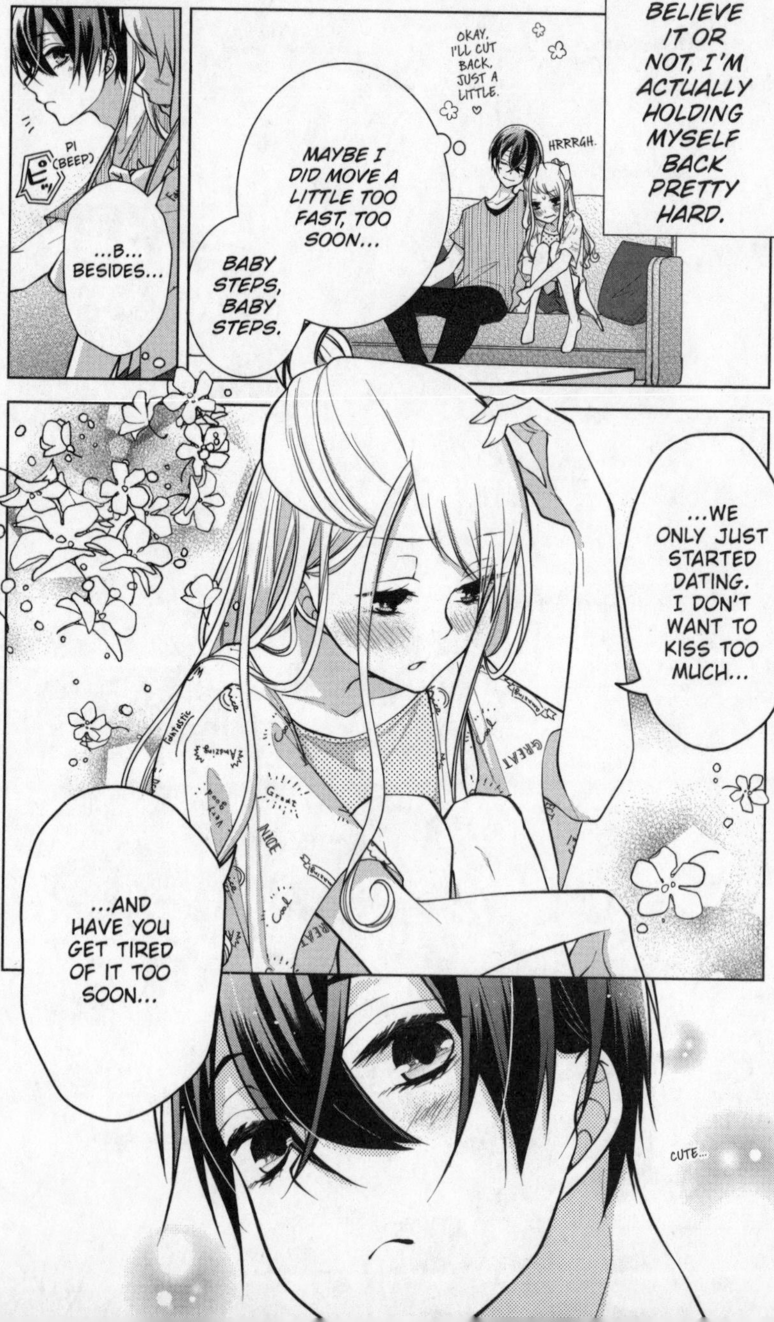
BELIEVE IT OR NOT, I'M ACTUALLY HOLDING MYSELF BACK PRETTY HARD.
OKAY, I'LL CUT BACK, JUST A LITTLE.
HRRRGH.
MAYBE I DID MOVE A LITTLE TOO FAST, TOO SOON...
BABY STEPS, BABY STEPS.
PI (BEEP)
...B... BESIDES...
...WE ONLY JUST STARTED DATING. I DON'T WANT TO KISS TOO MUCH...
...AND HAVE YOU GET TIRED OF IT TOO SOON...
CUTE...

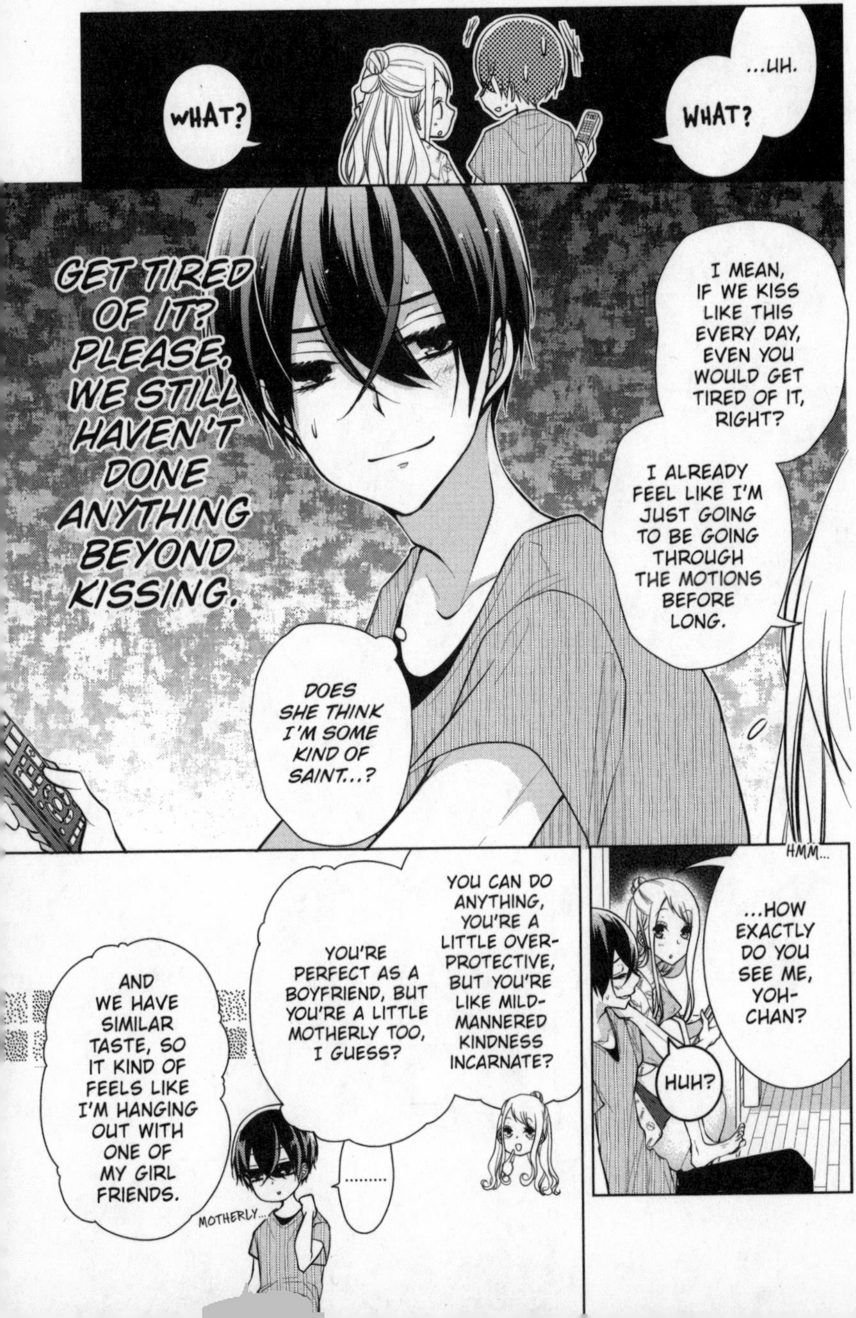
...UH.
WHAT?
WHAT?
I MEAN, IF WE KISS LIKE THIS EVERY DAY, EVEN YOU WOULD GET TIRED OF IT, RIGHT?
I ALREADY FEEL LIKE I'M JUST GOING TO BE GOING THROUGH THE MOTIONS BEFORE LONG.
GET TIRED OF IT? PLEASE. WE STILL HAVEN'T DONE ANYTHING BEYOND KISSING.
DOES SHE THINK I'M SOME KIND OF SAINT...?
HMM...
...HOW EXACTLY DO YOU SEE ME, YOH-CHAN?
HUH?
YOU CAN DO ANYTHING, YOU'RE A LITTLE OVER-PROTECTIVE, BUT YOU'RE LIKE MILD-MANNERED KINDNESS INCARNATE?
YOU'RE PERFECT AS A BOYFRIEND, BUT YOU'RE A LITTLE MOTHERLY TOO, I GUESS?
AND WE HAVE SIMILAR TASTE, SO IT KIND OF FEELS LIKE I'M HANGING OUT WITH ONE OF MY GIRL FRIENDS.
....
MOTHERLY...

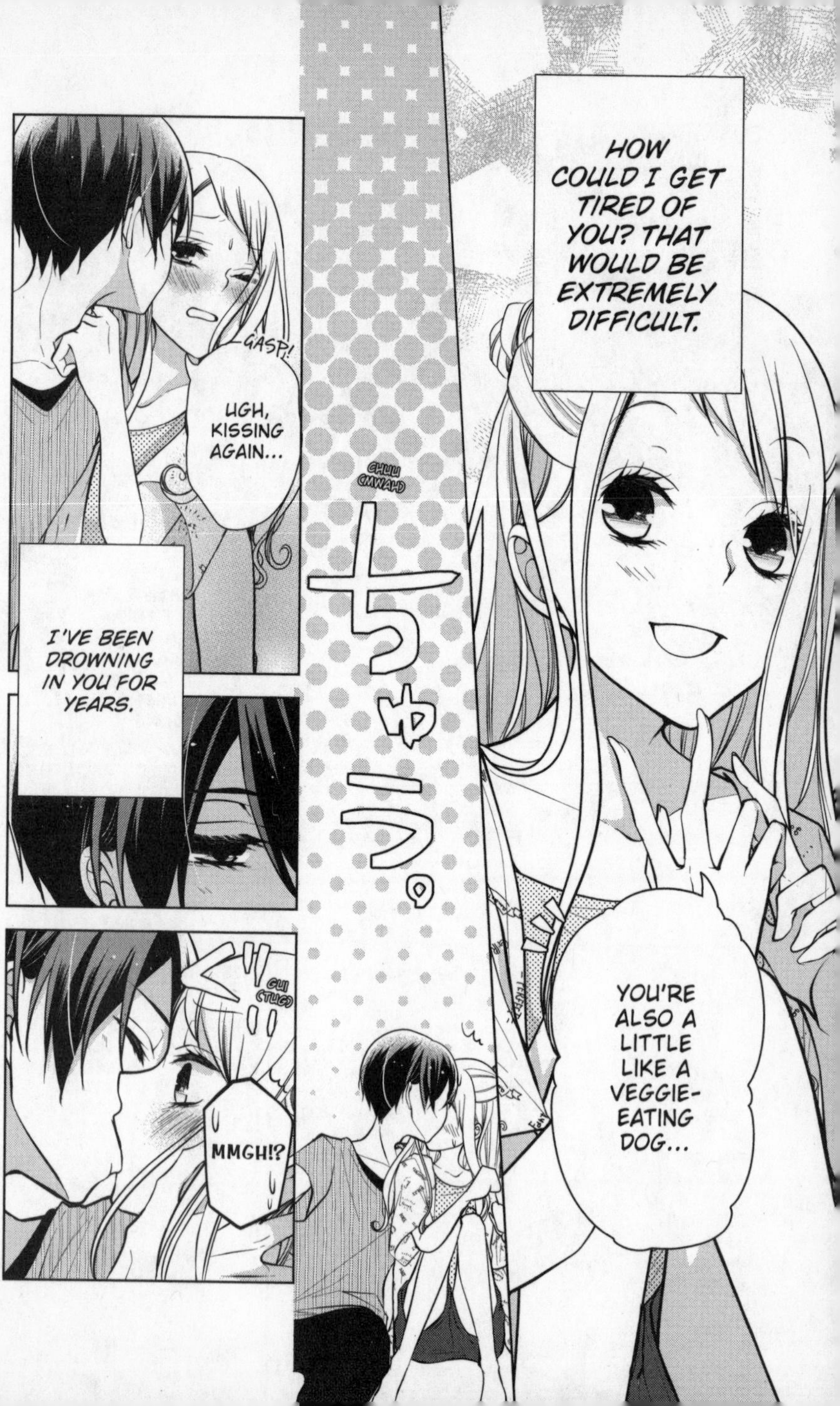
HOW COULD I GET TIRED OF YOU? THAT WOULD BE EXTREMELY DIFFICULT.
YOU'RE ALSO A LITTLE LIKE A VEGGIE-EATING DOG...
CHUU (MWAH)
ちゅう。
GASP!
UGH, KISSING AGAIN...
I'VE BEEN DROWNING IN YOU FOR YEARS.
GUI (TUG)
MMGH!?

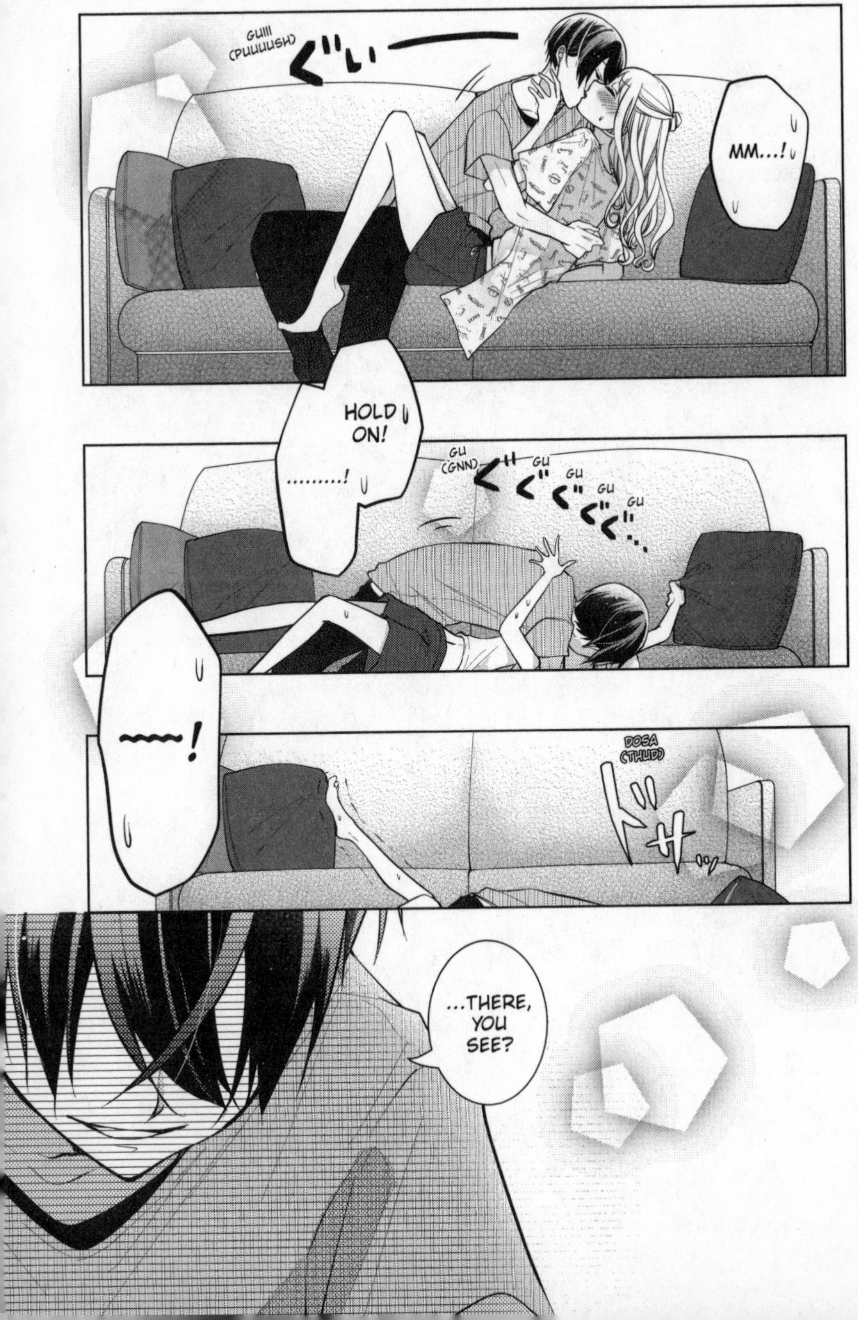
GUIII (PUUUUSH)
MM...!
HOLD ON!
.........!
GU (GNN) GU GU GU GU
~~~!
DOSA (THUD)
...THERE, YOU SEE?
~~~

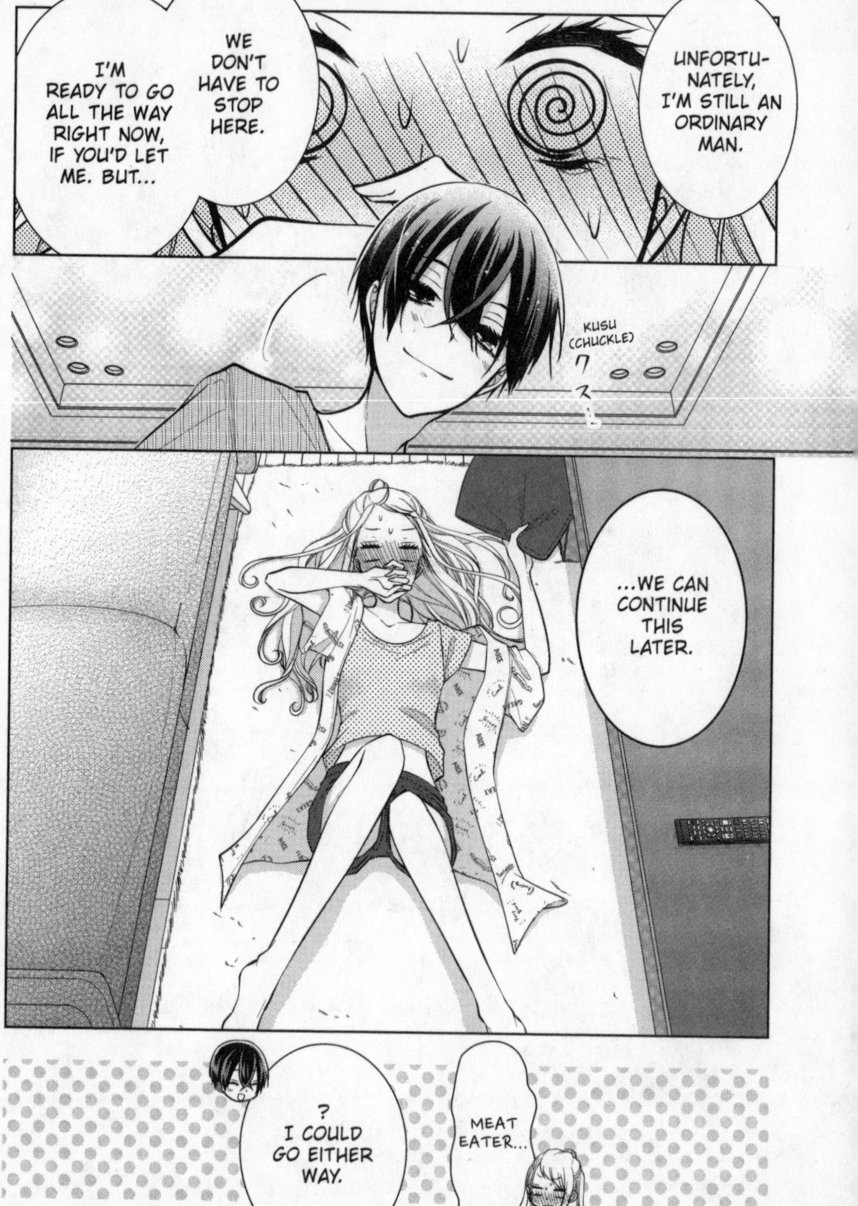
UNFORTUNATELY, I'M STILL AN ORDINARY MAN.
WE DON'T HAVE TO STOP HERE.
I'M READY TO GO ALL THE WAY RIGHT NOW, IF YOU'D LET ME. BUT...
KUSU (CHUCKLE)
...WE CAN CONTINUE THIS LATER.
MEAT EATER...
? I COULD GO EITHER WAY.

BONUS / END

TRANSLATION NOTES

Common Honorifics
no honorific: Indicates familiarity or closeness; if used without permission or reason, addressing someone in this manner would constitute an insult.
-*san*: The Japanese equivalent of Mr./Mrs./Miss. If a situation calls for politeness, this is the fail-safe honorific.
-*sama*: Conveys great respect; may also indicate that the social status of the speaker is lower than that of the addressee.
-*kun*: Used most often when referring to boys, this indicates affection or familiarity. Occasionally used by older men among their peers, but it may also be used by anyone referring to a person of lower standing.
-*chan*: An affectionate honorific indicating familiarity used mostly in reference to girls; also used in reference to cute persons or animals of either gender.
-*senpai*: A term commonly used to respectfully refer to upperclassmen in school or seniors at work. Its antonym, used for underclassmen, is *kouhai*.

Page 9
Grilled chicken (*yakitori*) and fried **meat skewers** (*kushikatsu*) are salty finger food designed to go with alcohol, making them popular fare at *izakaya* pubs throughout Japan. *Izakaya* are often frequented by groups of drunk, mostly male office workers, and so don't have the girliest of images.

Page 28
Nekomata are a type of mischievous cat monster that appears in Japanese and Chinese folklore. Said to be cats who lived so long that their tails forked into two, *nekomata* walk on two legs, assume human appearance, and cause various sorts of supernatural trouble.

Page 29
The *namazu* is a mythical giant catfish that lives underground, and whose thrashing is said to cause earthquakes.

Page 31
Light bulb soda is a fad drink, popular in trendy areas like Harajuku, that consists of a colorful beverage served in a decorated light-bulb-shaped container designed to stand out on social media sites such as Instagram.

Page 96
The Japanese phrase that has been applied to Wakana, Haruma, and Sawako in reference to the fact that they are only pretending to be nice is *neko wo kaburu*, which literally means "to wear a cat (on one's head)." So as Sawako's shirt warns us, always be careful when dealing with cats.

Page 156
In addition to referring to creatures that are herbivorous, the Japanese word *soushoku* refers to men or women who do not proactively pursue their mates, and is somewhat synonymous with the word "asexual." In contrast, a *nikushoku* (carnivore) is someone with a voracious sexual appetite.

LOVE and HEART

4

CHITOSE KAIDO

Translation: **ALETHEA AND ATHENA NIBLEY**

Lettering: **CHIHO CHRISTIE**

KOI TO SHINZO by Chitose Kaido
© Chitose Kaido 2020
All rights reserved.
First published in Japan in 2020 by HAKUSENSHA, INC., Tokyo.
English translation rights in U.S.A., Canada and U.K. arranged with HAKUSENSHA, INC., Tokyo through TUTTLE-MORI AGENCY, INC., Tokyo.

Yen Press
150 West 30th Street, 19th Floor
New York, NY 10001

Visit us at yenpress.com
facebook.com/yenpress † twitter.com/yenpress
yenpress.tumblr.com † instagram.com/yenpress

First Yen Press Edition: December 2021

Yen Press is an imprint of Yen Press, LLC.
The Yen Press name and logo are trademarks of Yen Press, LLC.

The publisher is not responsible for websites (or their content) that are not owned by the publisher.

Library of Congress Control Number: 2020950226

ISBNs: 978-1-9753-2048-5 (paperback)
978-1-9753-2049-2 (ebook)

10 9 8 7 6 5 4 3 2 1

WOR

Printed in the United States of America